Goddess Lost

ALSO BY RACHEL S. MCCOPPIN
AND FROM MCFARLAND

*The Hero's Quest and the Cycles of Nature: An Ecological Interpretation of World Mythology* (2016)

*The Lessons of Nature in Mythology* (2015)

# Goddess Lost

*How the Downfall
of Female Deities Degraded
Women's Status in World Cultures*

RACHEL S. McCOPPIN

McFarland & Company, Inc., Publishers
*Jefferson, North Carolina*

ISBN (print) 978-1-4766-9094-0
ISBN (ebook) 978-1-4766-4852-1

LIBRARY OF CONGRESS AND BRITISH LIBRARY
CATALOGUING DATA ARE AVAILABLE

Library of Congress Control Number 2022060912

© 2023 Rachel S. McCoppin. All rights reserved

*No part of this book may be reproduced or transmitted in any form or by any means, electronic or mechanical, including photocopying or recording, or by any information storage and retrieval system, without permission in writing from the publisher.*

Front cover image © 2022 Breakermaximus/Shutterstock

Printed in the United States of America

*McFarland & Company, Inc., Publishers
Box 611, Jefferson, North Carolina 28640
www.mcfarlandpub.com*

To Season and Landon

# Table of Contents

*Preface* 1

*Introduction* 3

**1**—Europe  9

**2**—The Middle East  57

**3**—The Mediterranean  89

**4**—India  120

**5**—Asia  148

**6**—Africa  185

**7**—The Americas and Oceania  212

*Conclusion* 248

*Bibliography* 253

*Index* 261

# Preface

In the recent #MeToo Movement, women are again on the forefront of change. The fight for women's rights has been a long, historical battle in many regions around the globe, and sadly there is more change that is needed as patriarchy still dominates much of the world. A step in eradicating patriarchy arguably comes through education of the past. Contemporary education curriculum often teaches primarily about patriarchal historical civilizations. This is a disservice to both our daughters and our sons. I would like my own children to know that belief systems existed all over the world that revered women as sacred, capable, and strong. Knowledge of the existence of civilizations that worshipped goddesses above gods, valued the authority of queens or priestesses over that of kings and priests, or viewed females as formidable warriors and leaders allows other possibilities outside of those of patriarchy to grow within the minds of the next generation. For this to happen, we all must become educated about our own collective history of the many divine and powerful women who once reigned.

Therefore, this book examines historical and mythic examples, as myths are the sacred religious narratives of a culture, from around the globe to argue that when women were revered as sacred in religious belief systems, they were more likely to be respected socially. Conversely, when religious reverence of goddesses and sacred women declined in many global mythological traditions, the social status of women also often declined around the world.

It is not the intent of this book to state that all world civilizations worshipped goddesses, or that the worship of goddesses was identical in all cultures. In addition, this book acknowledges that many of the details of the worship of goddesses worldwide have not withstood the test of time. Many myths have been lost, revised, or destroyed, and the intent behind the creation of such narratives often remains a mystery. Also, bias on the part of the storytellers often reshaped the intent of more traditional myths when they were captured in written form. In addition, bias from archeological interpretations occurred that diminished or misinterpreted the meaning(s) and/or importance of some discoveries regarding female divinities and/or leaders, as historically, anthropologists and archeologists "have tended to project the dominant patterns of gender relationships in their own culture onto societies that they observed. Their underlying assumptions regarding gender relationships have led them to undervalue the role and contribution of women" (Fishman 66). For example, myriad gravesites showing warriors, shamans, or leaders once perceived as male have been reanalyzed to reveal them as the graves of females who served in these roles. In addition, many Western archeologists throughout history analyzed discoveries through the lens of colonization, and therefore projected a false understanding of the significance of the find regarding the position of women. With an awareness of these biases in mind, the goal of this book is to trace the remnants of goddess reverence to show that often the worship of formidable female divinities helped allow women to serve in powerful religious and social positions precisely because their communities were quite used to envisioning power in the hands of a woman.

I would like to thank those who helped bring this book to fruition. First, I would like to thank Season and Landon for inspiring me on a daily basis to not only better myself, but to try and leave the world a little bit better for them. They have listened to countless stories that have inspired me, and hopefully these stories will remain with them and inspire them as they grow. I would also like to thank Joe, Mary, Tom, and Aaron for supporting me in the stages of researching and writing this book. Finally, I would like to thank the University of Minnesota Twin Cities and the University of Minnesota Crookston for supporting the travel and research necessary to write this book.

# Introduction

Throughout history, many civilizations revered goddesses, yet this reverence waned and was outright eradicated in many places around the globe. In many instances, at various historical moments, a tremendous amount of social effort went into diminishing the role of powerful goddesses and sacred women within myriad cultures' religious belief systems. Because such social and governmental effort was often systematically mandated to purposefully change existing religious beliefs, often by altering existing myths or creating new myths that perpetuated a revised patriarchal agenda, one should ask why this effort was initiated and maintained. One should also consider the level of social power these goddesses and sacred women held as to so threaten the patriarchal social and political systems that strove to gain dominance. Additionally, one should arguably look at what the effect of losing the worship of powerful goddesses had upon the community of women who worshipped them. This book will attempt to address these questions by looking at archeological sources as well as mythological narratives.

This book acknowledges that broad scholarly statements have historically been made that try to paint a romantic picture of universal goddesses and matriarchal communities being overthrown in myriad global communities by developing patriarchal systems. For instance, one of the most contested points within the study of goddesses is the existence of a primary female Mother Goddess or Great Mother who once reigned supreme in many civilizations. In the nineteenth and early twentieth centuries, scholars like Edward B. Tylor in *Primitive Culture* (1873) and Albrecht Dietrich in *Mutter Erde* (1905) argued that the concept of a Great Mother was universal (Reaves 5). Johann Jakob Bachofen proclaimed in the late nineteenth century that "there were three 'evolutionary' stages of human society: primitive promiscuity, followed by matriarchy, which was replaced by today's patriarchy" (qtd. in Adovasio, Soffer, & Page 250). Likewise, Fredrich Engels embraced the idea that civilizations had once been almost universally matriarchal. This idea flourished for decades, until it was embraced wholeheartedly by many cultures in the late twentieth century (Adovasio, Soffer, & Page 250). Scholars like E.O. James, Erich Neumann, Marija Gimbutas, Mircea Eliade, Gerda Lerner, and Riane Eisler perpetuated the concept that a Great Mother held a position of supremacy in many cultures around the world. However, this argument has been questioned in modern and contemporary times by many global critics who state that much of the above scholars' research made far-reaching and romanticized claims.

Despite the scholarly contention among many critics of Goddess studies, many respected archeologists and scholars of world mythology, like Joseph Campbell, Karen Armstrong, David Leeming, and Jake Page, decisively argue that though evidence may not exist to support a claim of a universal supreme Great Mother or widespread matriarchal communities, there certainly is ample evidence to show that many powerful, and sometimes supreme, goddesses were once readily worshipped in many global cultures. These same scholars agree that over centuries in many cultures throughout the world, myriad goddesses did become demoted because of a variety of reasons. Many goddesses lost their sacred significance within mythological narratives by purposeful religious, social, and political attempts to strip their power away from them in order to place it in the hands of a more powerful divine male(s).

Historically, the rise of patriarchy is often linked with the creation of organized civilizations. As agricultural communities became urban centers in places like China, Mesopotamia, Egypt, India, and Mesoamerica, key elements developed, such as "the emergence of property classes and hierarchies, ... the emergence and consolidation of military elites, kingship, the institutionalization of slavery, [and] a transition from kin dominance to patriarchal families as the chief mode of distributing goods and power" (Lerner 54). This period also produced widespread opportunities of trade and conquest among cultures, causing belief systems to alter with cultural diffusion. Many scholars contend that often during this process of urbanization and diffusion, beliefs in powerful goddesses, and subsequently respect regarding the social status of women, began to lessen. In Mesopotamia for instance, as well as many other global civilizations, processes to subordinate the position of women thus occurred; "female subordination within the family [became] institutionalized and codified in law.... With increasing specialization of work, women were gradually excluded from certain occupations and professions ... [and] women were excluded from equal access to education" (Lerner 54). This subordination of women in large part occurred because Mesopotamian "cosmogonies, which provide[d] the religious underpinning for the archaic state, subordinate[d] female deities to chief male gods, and feature[d] myths of origin which legitimate[d] male ascendancy" (Lerner 54). Leonard Shlain argues in *The Alphabet Versus the Goddess* (1999) that as many cultures began to develop the highly abstract skill of written language, their conceptions of religion moved from concrete notions of earth worship, in often the form of earth goddesses, to abstract notions of male gods, which set in motion the adoption of patriarchal governmental and social institutions. Whatever the reason, during the creation and propagation of patriarchal civilizations, many tactics were used to limit the power of goddesses, and thus restrict the social importance of women. Sometimes, cultures did not outright eliminate powerful goddesses within their mythological narratives, but instead shifted the power of these goddesses into divided and subordinate positions. This division and subordination can be seen in Greek mythology, for instance, when the dominant earth mother, Gaia, was replaced by a division of less powerful goddesses with myriad socially acceptable feminine roles, such as Aphrodite, the goddess of love, most often mythically portrayed as an object of male lust; Hera, the goddess of marriage and childbirth, most often portrayed as obsessed with jealously over the extramarital exploits of her husband; and the mostly silent goddess of the hearth, Hestia.

As patriarchal social, political, and religious structures continued to spread at different times throughout the globe, the belief in powerful goddesses often continued to lessen or become eliminated. For example, Semitic, Islamic, and Christian ideology further transformed existing belief systems in regard to goddess worship in the Middle East, the Mediterranean, and eventually throughout much of the world. As many cultures encountered Semitic, Islamic, and Christian beliefs that adamantly embraced one male divinity, the worship of primary and secondary goddesses was outright eliminated. Also, in times of European conquest and colonization, within places like Africa, the Americas, and Australia, similar patterns of replacing goddesses within sacred belief systems with European models of male divine dominance also appeared.

The religions and philosophies that historically demoted or eradicated many powerful goddesses still dominate the world today: Taoism, Confucianism, Buddhism, Hinduism, Judaism, Christianity, and Islam, were said to be "foundational to the ideology of women's inferiority in ... patriarchal systems" (Jeffreys 5). These organized religions and philosophical belief systems, especially the monotheistic faiths of Judaism, Christianity, and Islam, historically ostracized women by stripping them of representations of divinity in female form. Keller points to Taoism, Confucianism, Buddhism, Hinduism, Judaism, Christianity, and Islam as all being religions and philosophies that at one time commanded women "to be unconditionally obedient to father[s], husband[s], and/or sons. This male dominance ... [was] generally rationalized by the repeated insistence of the mental, moral, and spiritual superiority of men and the inferiority of women. This in turn ... [was] used to control women's labor, sexuality, and reproduction" (Keller 227). The feminist critique of patriarchal religions and philosophies that have come to dominate much of the world has long been a topic of focus; for example, Simone de Beauvoir argued in *The Second Sex* (1949) that patriarchal "Religion causes women to take, 'an attitude of respect and faith towards the masculine universe.' Religion founds men's authority over women and makes resistance difficult, because fear of divine punishment keeps women in their place" (qtd. in Jeffreys 17). Kate Millett in *Sexual Politics* (1972) likewise argued that the world's patriarchal religions and philosophies often became "the justification that men used for their rule over women, and ensured that male power was beyond criticism" (Jeffreys 18).

The connecting thread in most patriarchal world religions and philosophies, that again dominate the world today, is the perception that either divinity is envisioned as solely male, or divinity/spirituality is conceived of as most potent in male form. When a culture envisions divinity/spirituality as solely or supremely male, it often assigns males as being its most revered religious leaders, and often holds rules against women serving in these high-standing roles. When the realm of what is sacred and divine—often humanity's highest and most important conceptions about life—is envisioned as the domain of men, women miss the ability to fully nurture their own spiritual growth. Keller concurs, stating that the "most harmful aspect of patriarchal bias is the suppression or official denial of the Sacred Feminine" (Keller 227). Without examples of females in divine or sacred roles, women exist without sufficient role models for their spiritual and social potential: "There is little question that boys who are taught that god looks like them, but not like their mothers and sisters, grow up differently than girls who are taught the opposite" (Monaghan xi). Thus, this book examines the ramifications that occurred, especially regarding the rights of women, when many global cultures forfeited their reverence for religions that included a plethora of divine and sacred women in order to adopt new religious and philosophical ideologies that focused primarily on superior male divinity and/or sacrality.

Certainly, the process of demoting once revered goddesses appeared differently in each culture in which it happened; thus, this book is organized into chapters by global region (presentation of regions discussed are based only on goddess worship in such areas): Europe, the Middle East, the Mediterranean, India, Asia, Africa, and the Americas and Oceania. Some regional chapters, like Chapters 1, "Europe," and 5, "Asia," are longer than others such as Chapters 6, "Africa," and 7, "The Americas and Oceania" (which combines these two regions), only because the recording of written mythological narratives took place later in some regions as opposed to others. Thus, the preservation of mythic narratives that trace the transition of goddess worship in some regions can be more limited than others. For example, because of the progression of written language throughout Europe, due to the adoption of the Greek written language in about the fifth century BCE by the Romans, who created the Latin script, the myriad cultures of Europe, mostly in the Middle Ages (c. 500–1400 CE), were eventually able to preserve their mythic narratives. Because of this fairly early written preservation of European mythology, a good amount of material was retained from the oral tradition that initially held the sacred myths of pre-literate Europe. Additionally, the preservation of Asian mythology is fairly extensive due to the adoption of written language in China by at least 1200 BCE. Conversely, the written mythological record is less extensive in sub–Saharan Africa, the Americas, and Oceania, as most mythic narratives from these regions were not recorded until after colonization, and most in the nineteenth century. This is most certainly not to say that all global regions did not have vibrant and diverse mythic narratives, but sadly, many narratives, such as those from sub–Saharan Africa, the Americas, and Oceania, were only preserved through the oral tradition for centuries and have often been lost to history.

Patriarchy continues to exist in contemporary cultures, in part, because of the lack of knowledge women hold about their once powerful role within many global belief systems. Lerner states that "patriarchy can function only with the cooperation of women. This cooperation is secured by a variety of means," one of which is "educational deprivation; the denial to women of knowledge of their history" (Lerner 217). Looking at historical and mythological examples when goddesses were worshipped as supreme beings and when women served as social and religious leaders in their communities, can educate people about an alternative history, one different than what is often perpetuated by patriarchal principles. This book, therefore, strives to teach women about their long history of sacred importance as shamans, priestesses, warriors, administrators, regents, queens, pharaohs, and even goddesses.

## Chapter 1

# Europe

Many scholars acknowledge that in the Upper Paleolithic period, about 50,000–10,000 years ago, in the region of present-day Europe, a popular belief in the concept of a Great Mother as the earth itself existed. For example, many artistic representations of the Paleolithic Great Mother have been found throughout Europe. Lubell notes that the symbol of the vulva found in many Ice Age sites in Europe, such as "the thirty-thousand-year-old vulva stones of La Ferrassie, France," are representative of a belief in a Great Mother (Lubell 59). Upper Paleolithic cave art throughout Europe is also often connected to a belief in the concept of a Great Mother, as many cave paintings indicate what appears to be a representation of humans and animals going within the earth in order to be reborn. Adorning the interior of a cave with images of humans and animals suggests that the caves were conceived of as the womb of a female earth. For example, many Upper Paleolithic "paintings depict a kind of bear ceremonialism, apparently designed to ensure that the bear's spirit reunites with the larger cosmic spirit of the … [Great Mother] and returns to live another day" (Oelschlaeger 23). Thus, the Upper Paleolithic symbol of the bear is often referred to as one of the oldest symbols connected to humans (Baring & Cashford 70–1), and goddesses in later periods are often connected to such bear imagery, such as Artio, the Celtic bear goddess, and the Greek goddesses Callisto and Artemis. Female anthropomorphic bird-like artistic depictions are also quite prominent in the Upper Paleolithic period, as well as later in the Neolithic period, and many scholars suggest that these images also may represent the concept of a Great Mother. One of the most famous of these anthropomorphic bird-like representations is the Venus of Lespugue (c. 25,000–18,000 BCE) (Johnson 16). There are also numerous artistic representations of egg-carrying females, which are additionally believed to be possible depictions of a Great Mother from the Upper Paleolithic period (Johnson 22).

What the Upper Paleolithic period is most known for in regard to the study of goddesses is the appearance of many artistic statuettes of the female form, often identified as Venus figurines. More than 200 figurines have been found throughout Europe in such places as Germany, France, the Czech Republic, Siberia, etc. The majority of these figurines date from 25,000 to 23,000 years ago, but the oldest, found in the Hohle Fels Cave in Germany, dates from about 35,000 years ago (A. Dixson & B. Dixson). Most often the vast number of female figurines found are made from stone, bone, or ivory and depict the nude female form with a focus on exaggerated sexual and reproductive elements of the body; some figurines are also represented as pregnant (Burkert 11–2). The most famous of these Venus figurines include: the Venus of Willendorf, found in Austria; the Lespugue Venus, found in the Pyrenees Mountains between Spain and France; the Laussel Venus, found in France; the Dolní Věstonice Venus, found in the Czech Republic; the Savignano Venus, found in Italy; the Moravany Venus, found in Slovakia; and the mentioned Hohle Fels Venus, found in Germany (A. Dixson & B. Dixson).

There is contention among scholars as to what these Venus figurines represent. Competing theories abound stating that the statuettes "might be realistic depictions of actual women" or "ideal representations of female beauty" (A. Dixson & B. Dixson). However, the overabundance of these figurines, and the similarity between them in myriad civilizations, suggests to many scholars that they do not merely represent actual women, or an ideal of beauty for human women, but instead must represent concepts of "religious significance and be depictions of priestesses," goddesses, or ancestors (A. Dixson & B. Dixson). In addition, many archeologists historically classified these figurines as mere "fertility symbols" that do not portray conceptualizations of divinity or sacrality; however, a trait of many goddesses, captured in mythological narratives once writing was discovered, is certainly that of fertility, because fertility represented survival. For example, during the Neolithic period throughout much of Eastern Europe, including Hungary, Yugoslavia, Bulgaria, Romania, the Czech Republic, Slovakia, and Poland, as well as portions of Italy, Greece, and Turkey, which are discussed in the next two chapters, similar female figurines were commonplace, and it is highly accepted that these later Neolithic figurines represented *both* fertility and divinity. Thus, many contemporary scholars suggest that the sheer number of these similar female figurines from the Upper Paleolithic period provide evidence of a continuation of a similar belief involving the worship of goddesses, who could be identified as Great Mothers.

During the Neolithic period, the discovery that crops could be selected and harvested led to humankind adopting a sedentary lifestyle in many regions around the world. This sedentary existence led to the creation of the first civilizations, which in time developed political, social, and religious structures based on hierarchical belief systems to regulate the large populations. The first Neolithic communities originated in the Middle East's Fertile Crescent around 10,000 BCE; these are discussed in Chapter 2. Agricultural methods reached Greece in about 7000 BCE, and again this region is discussed further in Chapter 3, but in Europe this agricultural advancement did not reach areas such as Britain until about 4000 BCE, and Scandinavia later still.

Many scholars agree that goddesses dominated myriad Neolithic civilizations. The concept of a Neolithic Mother Goddess, a goddess who reigned over nature, agriculture, and fertility, appeared in many European civilizations. This conception of the Neolithic Mother Goddess was similar to the Upper Paleolithic belief that the earth itself was a Great Mother, because it was believed that the Neolithic Mother Goddess could produce all life from her continuous natural cycles. Armstrong concurs, stating that in Neolithic times, "the Mother Goddess fused with the Great Mother of the hunting societies" of the Upper Paleolithic period (Armstrong 46). This Neolithic Mother Goddess was therefore viewed as two-fold; the Mother Goddess nurtured all life that she birthed, but she also dominated over the destruction and demise of all natural elements in order to maintain the cycles of life, most predominantly displayed to Neolithic communities through the stages of the agricultural harvest. Thus, the Neolithic Mother Goddess in Europe, as the one who controlled the processes of life and death, held a clear position of authority and power for many Neolithic European cultures (Baring & Cashford 53).

However, over centuries, Proto-Indo-European and Indo-European invaders in the late Neolithic period and the Bronze Age (c. 3000–1000 BCE) modified the belief systems of many cultures throughout Europe, as well as the Near East, which is explored later in this book. From about 4500 to 2500 BCE, several distinctive cultures, broadly defined as Proto-Indo-European, expanded through the Pontic-Caspian steppes into Europe and Asia aided by horseback riding and wheeled wagons. For example, in about 3500 BCE, Proto-Indo-European Yamnaya tribes advanced into Romania and faced the existing Neolithic Cucuteni-Tripolye culture, which was a culture that likely practiced goddess worship, evidenced by myriad female figurines found at Cucuteni-Tripolye sites. It was largely these Cucuteni-Tripolye figurines, and others found at many other locations throughout Europe, that led famed, and controversial, archeologist Marija Gimbutas to assert her belief that the Cucuteni-Tripolye culture was matriarchal and worshipped a primary, universal Mother Goddess. Gimbutas, in her books *The Goddesses and Gods of Old Europe* (1974), *The Language of the Goddess* (1989), and *The Civilization of the Goddess* (1991), and authors like Riane Eisler in *The Chalice and the Blade* (1987), argued that in fact many Neolithic settlements of "Old Europe" worshipped a primary female deity, under a matriarchal rule and female-centered social structure. Gimbutas, Eisler, and others argued that these Neolithic communities of "Old Europe" were largely peaceful, as they did not have protective barriers surrounding their communities and did not display pride in weapons or warrior imagery in their artwork; therefore, they were easily overtaken by, as Gimbutas defines them, "Kurgan," better known as Proto-Indo-European, invaders who "created disastrous cultural upheavals" (Johnson 25). Gimbutas, Eisler, etc., proclaimed that the belief systems of the Proto-Indo-Europeans, and later Indo-Europeans, which favored male sky deities and the valor of warfare, eventually grew to dominate much of "Old Europe," resulting in female religious and societal authority shifting into predominantly male hands, thus birthing patriarchy.

However, many archeologists and scholars, such as J.M. Adovasio, Olga Soffer, Jake Page, Ruth Tringham, and Margaret Conkey, have felt that the work of Gimbutas, Eisler, and others who hold similar theories regarding the universal goddess matriarchies of "Old Europe," should be assessed with scrutiny (Adovasio, Soffer, & Page 255; Tringham & Conkley 37). Many contemporary archeologists and scholars feel that there is not enough evidence to prove widespread matriarchy or the universal worship of a supreme Mother Goddess collectively throughout most of the cultures of Neolithic Europe. Instead, many scholars believe, like David W. Anthony in his book *The Horse, the Wheel, and Language* (2010), that in place of the outright elimination of traditional goddess-oriented values at times of Proto-Indo European and Indo-European invasions, steppe cultures may have merged with existing European cultures, thus combining their belief systems.

The process of Proto-Indo-European cultures invading and often merging with existing populations throughout much of Europe continued into the second millennium BCE. For example, the Bell Beaker culture of about 2800–2300 BCE expanded into parts of Portugal and northern Africa, Great Britain, Ireland, and even Sicily. In 2500–2300 BCE, Proto-Indo-Europeans "expand[ed] from the Hungarian plain to Austria, Bohemia, Moravia, southern Poland, and southern Germany and start[ed] the most important Central European Bronze Age culture—Unetice" (Hay). The Unetice culture of about 2300–1600 BCE is "associated with the diffusion of Proto-Germanic and Proto-Celtic-Italic speakers" (Hay), which represented a break from the theorized Proto-Indo-European language into Indo-European language families, allowing the Proto-Indo-Europeans to become identified as Indo-Europeans.

The term "Indo-European" comes from a paper Sir William Jones wrote in 1786 regarding the similarity he found within the languages of Europe and other global regions (Campbell 60). Woodard states that "According to the most widely accepted model, the Indo-European language family contains ... [the following] principal branches": Anatolian, Indo-Iranian, Celtic, Hellenic, Italic, Germanic, Armenian, Tocharian, Balto-Slavic, and Albanian (Woodard 8). Anthony explains that the Indo-European languages most likely were passed down by elites in existing cultures aligning with Indo-European speaking migrants who brought superior weapons and luxury goods into existing communities (Anthony 6).

The Indo-European languages began to appear in written myths in the Bronze Age and Iron Age (c. 800 BCE–400 CE) (Woodard 29). There are many similar elements that appear in the mythology of the Indo-European cultures in Europe; in fact, Campbell states that Indo-European mythology was so connected among various cultures that it "was one mythology in different languages" (Campbell 60–1). For instance, many Indo-European myths highlighted a central male divinity, most often in the form of a sky god. In addition, Indo-European myths often included "an existing generation of gods that was preceded by two (and in some cases three) earlier generations of supernatural beings, each succeeding generation being presided over by a 'king in heaven' who ... usurped (or at least assumed) the power of his predecessor" (Woodard 142). Indo-European cultures also maintained patriarchal societal structures centering on kingship and sacred priests. War was also a way of life for Indo-European cultures, and success in warfare often defined a warrior's social role and legacy, which was of primary concern.

Many scholars, such as Joseph Campbell, Karen Armstrong, Anne Baring, Jules Cashford, and David Leeming, draw cautiously upon some of Gimbutas' assertions of goddess worship in "Old Europe." These scholars are unwilling to state that there is evidence that shows a Neolithic belief in a universal goddess throughout Europe and the Near East, or that these cultures were entirely matriarchal; however, they, like most contemporary scholars, do contend that there is a large amount of evidence to show that goddesses, oftentimes quite powerful goddesses, certainly were worshipped in many Neolithic cultures throughout Europe, and subsequently many Neolithic women, who were often envisioned as connected to these goddesses, did appear to hold high social and religious positions. The mythology that was finally written down in the Indo-European languages in the Bronze and Iron Ages supports the existence of these formidable Neolithic goddesses and high-positioned women. However, many of these Bronze and Iron Age myths present instances of strife between the traditional goddesses and the new Indo-European gods and male heroes. So, in part, Gimbutas and others were correct in looking towards Indo-European ideology as a factor for changing the Neolithic beliefs surrounding goddess worship, but instead of eradicating universal goddess worship and widespread matriarchal communities, the reality is that Indo-European beliefs systematically, over centuries, helped to not eradicate, but to transform, existing Neolithic conceptions of goddesses and powerful women into, most often, less powerful conceptions.

Many Indo-European ideologies partially embraced the goddesses of the cultures they encountered, incorporating them in some way into their own belief systems; for instance, "there is little doubt that a goddess representing the earth played an important role in the Indo-European religious tradition" (Reaves 10). Martin L. West concurs, stating that "among the Indo-Europeans, the earth-goddess is widely celebrated with the title of 'mother,' providing numerous examples from across the Indo-European spectrum" (qtd. in Reaves 11). In addition, Indo-European male deities often married traditional local goddesses to share their power. Over time, though, the goddesses that became wives of Indo-European gods were demoted to roles of subservience to their male counterparts (Noble 193–4). Rossi states that the "Indo-European style was to let their gods take over the local shrines, marry the resident goddesses, and ... [later] assume the names and roles of the deities formerly in charge" (Rossi xxv). In time, as patriarchal structures gained dominance, some mythological traditions began to showcase the demotion of a goddess by a male god or hero through violent means. And once the position of the goddesses had become demoted, the social rights of women soon followed.

The status of women in many existing European Neolithic cultures was increasingly demoted within patriarchal Indo-European communities. Many Neolithic communities were matricentric, meaning that women and men held equal status in the community, and women often served in powerful religious and social roles (Baring & Cashford 285). However, as civilizations grew, and positions of male authority developed further, many civilizations throughout Europe delineated clear roles for male leadership, as the rights of leadership in Indo-European cultures were often based on military prowess and violence. Baring and Cashford state that the Iron Age was dominated by a "mythology of war," where heroes were identified as such based on their might as a warrior, and kings became legendary if they were successful conquerors (Baring & Cashford 286). Therefore, like "the Paleolithic hunt, war brought men together in ... a shared heroic purpose whose intensity was such that no tilling of soil or herding of animals could emulate" (Baring & Cashford 286). Thus, Neolithic values faded away in favor of Iron Age ideology and technology, and the role of women became viewed as secondary to the might of the Iron Age male.

With the Iron Age value of male leadership, in the human and divine realm, women who once held high-standing religious and social roles saw their positions overtaken by male authority figures. For instance, many Neolithic European women once held the highly important social and religious position of priestess, as they possessed the image of the goddesses the people worshipped; however, the role of priestess faded as male priests rose in power to promote superior male deities. Thus, women systematically were no longer viewed as connected to divinity, and eventually they often became perceived as the property of men (Noble 193). For example, many Indo-European texts discuss how a bride could be purchased for an identified price, such as the exchange of cattle (Noble 193). Indo-European values proclaimed that male members of a household possessed ownership of a woman, which in turn secured their ownership of her womb and thus, the heirs she produced; any children a woman had would then be the property of her husband. This positioning of women to a lesser status in order to legitimize the male connection to his offspring is generally believed to have been a new social concept in many Indo-European societies (Noble 194).

It should be noted that often when one culture takes over another culture, many people still maintain their traditional beliefs while appearing to adopt the new faith. This is why it is vitally important to analyze the mythological sources of a culture, because myths often reveal conflict regarding new values intent on replacing well-loved traditional values. Thus, on a surface level, many myths show goddesses appearing to be dominated by male gods or heroes, befitting Indo-European ideologies, but when examined more closely, one can often identify mythic tenets that show the lasting, deep reverence the people held for their goddesses centuries after patriarchal ideologies dominated.

## Slavic and Baltic Regions

Slavic and Baltic regions offer an excellent display of the transitions that occurred from the Upper Paleolithic to the Neolithic period, and then to the expansion of Indo-European cultures in the Bronze and Iron Ages.

Many cultures that existed in present-day Slavic regions: Russia, Ukraine, Poland, Slovakia, Czech Republic, Bosnia, Serbia, etc., revered Paleolithic and Neolithic concepts of a Great Mother/Earth Mother, as "Most forces of nature and cosmological and landscape features were feminine in thought" (Hays-Gilpin 199). In Russia, for example, the land itself "was called Mother, and her physical features ... were also given maternal epithets" (Hubbs xiii). Phillips and Kerrigan explain that the "belief of a Mother Goddess has been central to Slavic spiritual beliefs for millennia" (Phillips & Kerrigan 56). Prehistoric goddess figurines were found throughout Slavic regions that suggest "that before the gods of war took their places at the head of tribal pantheons, the goddess was all powerful—for as the generator and nourisher of the Earth and its people, she was seen to hold sway over life itself. This belief can be traced through Slavic history right up to the present day" (Phillips & Kerrigan 56). The pre–Indo-European Earth Mother of Slavic regions was "Mati Syra Zemlya (Damp Mother Earth). Normally she was not given a specific form, but her spirit was said to be embodied in the fertile earth.... Even though she usually lacked a shape, she was seen as vibrantly alive and, therefore, helped everything in the soil to come to life" (Wilkinson 89).

When Indo-European ideologies merged with the pre-existing cultures that existed in Slavic regions, Indo-European Slavic mythological concepts were created. Though each Slavic region had important religious differences, there are still similarities throughout Slavic mythology that unite them. For example, the Indo-European Slavs worshipped a pantheon of primary male gods holding Indo-European roles, such as: Perun, the chief deity of the Eastern Slavs and the god of thunder; Veles, the shapeshifter god; Stribog, the god of wind; Dazhbog, the god of the sun; Belobog, the god of light; and Czernobog, the god of darkness (Vytkovshaya 102–3). It is believed that the Earth Mother, Mati Syra Zemlya, became Mokosh under Indo-European Slavic influence. Mokosh, as the Slavic Mother Goddess of fertility, was able to maintain a significant role in East Slavic belief, but her power had certainly lessened from pre–Indo-European conceptions, as she became envisioned as a myriad of separate gods and goddesses. Many less powerful Slavic female deities took over as representations of the once supreme Mati Syra Zemlya, such as: Lada, the goddess associated with spring and love; Kupala, the goddess of water; Dodola, the goddess of rain; and Marzanna, the goddess associated with winter and death (Vytkovshaya 103). These less powerful Slavic goddesses became mostly representations of nature, and certainly did not hold the power of the male Slavic gods, such as Perun. This denigration of once powerful goddesses into less powerful roles initiated the demotion of women's social and religious status, as many Slavic female shamans and priestesses lost their positions of sacred importance.

The people who inhabited ancient Baltic regions, the Neolithic pre–Aistians, like the Slavs, also worshipped a primary Earth Mother before encountering Indo-European groups. The marshy ground in which many of the pre–Aistians built their communities was believed to be the body of "their Great Goddess, the Mother Zhemyna or Mother Earth" (Vycinas 16). Again, archeological evidence supports the important place that the Earth Mother held within pre–Aistian conception: "Archeologists discovered not only ... statuettes of the Mother Goddess, but also drawings of her on the walls of early pre–Aistian huts, their temple-home-tombs" (Vycinas 23). The pre–Aistian Earth Mother was conceived of as a large serpent, a symbolic representation that was important in many cultures. Therefore, the pre–Aistians kept a holy water serpent within their homes, next to their hearth which held the holy fire, and the family's eldest mother was their "high priestess, who cared for the serpent and the fire, since they both meant the very presence of Mother Zhemyna in the home" (Vycinas 23–4). Thus, the status of women in pre–Aistian culture was quite high. Vycinas concurs, stating that pre–Aistian society was probably matriarchal, as "Women, especially mothers, in pre–Aistian society [were believed to stand] closer to Mother Zhemyna" (Vycinas 24).

Yet, as with Slavic communities, pre–Aistian "farming settlements, probably organized by matriclans, were destroyed by Indo-European nomadic herders" within Baltic regions (Hubbs 6). Thus, from "the third to the first millennium [BCE], a protracted struggle took place between the [pre–Aistian] farming cultures and the invading [Indo-European] herders" (Hubbs 6), and many pre–Aistian, and later Aistian, beliefs, such as the embrace of Mother Zhemyna and other matriarchal social aspects, became transformed. Where once Mother Zhemyna encapsulated all aspects of existence, now sky gods, such as Perkunas, the Indo-European Baltic god of thunder, were revered as superior. To demote the role of Mother Zhemyna, as was done in Slavic regions, many lesser goddesses, conceived of as the daughters of Mother Zhemyna, were created in order to modify the power of the once supreme Mother Zhemyna. Socially, changes were also reflected in the rights of women, as many women no longer held leadership roles in religious and social affairs. One example of this significant change can be seen in customs surrounding marriage. In Aistian culture, the bride would be the one who would carry water and fire from her mother's household, signaling her command of the spiritual well-being of the land; in this, and in other ways, the "newly wedded bride became the owner and the priestess of her new homestead" (Vycinas 48). This highstanding spiritual role for women changed when Indo-European concepts of patriarchy gained influence and dominated Aistian culture, allowing men to gain central command of spiritual affairs. The role of the priestess, that existed in pre–Aistian and Aistian societies, also declined, as "larger social units—tribes or nations—were formed ... [and became] commanded by an elder man, whose importance as the priest of the Sky" dominated (Vycinas 62).

Once the Slavs in the fifth and sixth centuries CE moved into Baltic regions, nations began to form, such as Prussia, Lithuania, and Latvia. With the arrival of the Slavs, patriarchal customs only continued to demote the religious reverence of goddesses and the social status of women in Baltic regions. Within the Baltic household, for instance, the status of women further declined as fathers, rather than mothers, "were the head and administrator of the family and homestead. The eldest son—rather than the youngest daughter—inherited the father's homestead and his name.... The other sons, when they married, took over the homesteads of their brides, bringing their father's names into their new homes. Consequently, daughters, when marrying, acquired the names of their husbands" (Vycinas 77).

A legend said to date back to the sixth century CE perhaps records the strife felt between the once matriarchal cultures of Slavic regions and the modification of these cultures due to increasingly Indo-European patriarchal systems. The legend takes places when the Slavic tribes, the Czechs, arrived in what is now the current Czech Republic, known then as Bohemia. According to the legend, the inhabitants of the area were a matriarchal society, ruled by Queen Libuse. When Queen Libuse died, the men attempted to take over control by declaring their prince, Přemysl, the new ruler. The women became "furious that the matriarchal system [was] coming to an end and a group of them declared war on men. This feud became bloody and lasted for hundreds of years" (Hodges 58). Legend states that a woman warrior, by the name of Divoká Šárka, emerged from the conflict. Divoká Šárka devised a plan to win the war against the male forces by killing their best male warrior, Ctirad. Divoká Šárka gained the trust of Ctirad and his forces by giving them large quantities of alcohol, of which they all quickly consumed. Once the men fell into an intoxicated slumber, Divoká Šárka and her band of women warriors, who were hiding close by, attacked the men, and killed them all, including Ctirad. Without their best fighter, the male forces struggled to gain dominancy, but in the end, it was the men who finally won the war, and the new "patriarchal ... system remained" (Hodges 58). Divoká Šárka refused to submit however, so she committed suicide by jumping off a cliff. There is no historical evidence to prove that any components of this legend actually took place; however, some historians "claim that this women's war could actually be a throwback to a much older historical fact, that early on, in prehistoric times, there could have been a matriarchal society ... [where] women had primacy ... [but] they were overthrown by men" (Carey). Hodges concurs, stating that this legend may have originated with the "folk memory of the pagan matriarchal society that was around thousands of years before Christianity" (Hodges 58). Therefore, it seems likely that this legend, at least in part, captures a resistant sentiment once held by the people of the region of the Czech Republic about the transition from a time when goddesses were worshipped and women were empowered, to an era of male dominance.

Around the ninth century CE, many Slavic people began to convert to Christianity. For example, in Russia, "at end of the tenth century," Prince Vladimir became Christian and abolished pagan practices throughout Russia (Vytkovshaya 102–3). In the region of the Czech Republic, Christianity also began to dominate around the tenth century. Slavs brought Christianity to Baltic regions in the tenth century, but Baltic regions did not fully convert until the fourteenth century. As happened in many other cultures, Christianity eliminated most elements connected to goddess reverence in Slavic and Baltic regions (Vycinas 93). However, as happened in many civilizations, the old beliefs of the people died hard, and in fact, many Christian concepts were merged with pagan beliefs. For example, the Slavic Mother Goddess Mokosh became associated with the "Christian Saint Paraskeva/Pyatnitsa" (Vytkovshaya 106). Many rites that once held deep connections with Mokosh were now held in honor of Saint Paraskeva/Pyatnitsa, as she represented "the mother/protector" of the people of Russia, holding dominion "over health, harvests and stock fertility" (Vytkovshaya 106). The reverence for the concept of Mother Earth remained strong in Slavic and Baltic regions and continues to this day. For instance, in "Volynia and Belorussia, people believed that each year Mother Earth became pregnant and anyone striking her before 25 March would bring terrible trouble on the family, putting at risk the Mother Earth's children—the crops that lay dormant in her belly" (Phillips & Kerrigan 54). In addition, in parts of Russia, "people performed a harvest-time ritual in Mother Earth's honor every August," where they would turn to each of the four directions of the earth and ask Mother Earth for favorable conditions (Phillips & Kerrigan 54). Even into contemporary times, the natural elements of the earth were thought to possess Mother Earth's power; "stones shaped like a woman's body ... [were] treated as sacred objects. People desperate for healing ... would travel for days to touch the stones and make offerings ... to them" (Phillips & Kerrigan 55). People who had converted to Christianity within Russia still believed that Mother Earth could "combat evil," "conquer illness," and forgive sins; "even in the twentieth century, the elderly asked Mother Earth for forgiveness of their sins if they feared death was close" (Phillips & Kerrigan 55). The veneration of Mother Earth was often merged with reverence for the Virgin Mary in Slavic and Baltic regions. For instance, Christian festivals for Mary often incorporated pagan concepts of Earth Mother worship, such as the restriction that no plowing was allowed on the Virgin Mary's Assumption Day (Phillips & Kerrigan 55). In addition, the pagan goddess Kostroma, the "personification of spring and fertility," was the focus of rites still practiced by Eastern Slavs into the nineteenth century (Larrington 108). Kostroma's rites were known as "spring's funeral," as her straw image was ritually burned, so that she could "rise again" to ensure fertility for the new season of spring (Larrington 108). Furthermore, Slavic and Baltic divine beings became the characters of folklore, such as: the Slavic vodyanye, malevolent water sprites; the vozdushnye, wind spirits; kikimory, female house spirits; and rusalki, female water spirits (Phillips & Kerrigan 60; Vytkovshaya 103). Slavic folklore also began to show sky maidens, who in summer rose "up out of the wells and ... [flew] to the clouds, carrying the water which ... [would] refresh the soil and help the harvests," as well as snow women who brought the first snow of winter (Vytkovshaya 107). These folkloric figures were clearly connected to traditional Slavic goddesses, showing that goddesses remained, and continue to remain, in the folk memory of the people. However, by delegating once powerful goddesses to the realm of folkloric characters, their power was stripped away from them as they came to be considered the stuff of fiction. Assigning once divine beings as folkloric figures was a popular tool used by patriarchal cultures, because the once divine figure appeared to still be within the culture, but was assigned a lesser role within folklore, so that over time, the divine being became viewed with suspicion and not reverence. For example, the rusalki are believed by many scholars to once have been Slavic water goddesses, but as folkloric rusalki, they are usually shown as young maidens who died too early and thus lure unsuspecting men to their deaths.

## Celtic Regions

Celtic mythology especially offers examples of the effect Indo-European concepts had on goddess-oriented mythology. The Celts are linked with the Indo-European Proto-Celtic Urnfield culture of Central Europe, which thrived around 1200 BCE. The Hallstatt culture was the fully Celtic descendant of the Urnfield culture that dominated much of Western and Central Europe from about the twelfth to the sixth century BCE in areas such as the British Isles, France, the Iberian Peninsula, and Italy. The La Tène Celts dominated from the fifth century BCE to the time of the Roman conquest in the first century BCE, taking over the Hallstatt culture without any noted cultural break. The La Tène culture dominated France, Belgium, Switzerland, Austria, Southern Germany, Hungary, the Netherlands, and parts of Romania. These Indo-European Celtic people consisted of tribal groups who spoke related Celtic languages and dialects and had similar, but varied, cultural beliefs and customs. As the Roman Empire expanded, the Celtic people moved into the areas of Wales, Ireland, and Scotland, where they are most associated today.

The Celts' societal structures were mostly patriarchal and hierarchical.

Communities were most often based upon the system of kingship, where the king or chieftain of each tribe was viewed as the tribal leader. Warfare was a way of life for the Celts, as their technological innovations and artistic representations portray; thus, the warrior was highly valued in Celtic society. Tribes were organized by kin groups, and land was generally passed down through the paternal line, so wives moved onto the land of their husbands. Wealthy men could have more than one wife, and it was the Celtic men who owned and inherited most of the property.

Despite the patriarchal societal structure of the Indo-European Celts, Celtic goddesses still held a prominent role in the Celtic pantheon. Many scholars believe that the high positioning of goddesses in Celtic mythology might come from the beliefs of the cultures that pre-date the arrival of Indo-European Celtic groups. However, even with the high positioning of Celtic goddesses within Celtic mythology, there is still conflict in the portrayal of Celtic goddesses and women within existing mythological narratives; therefore, this conflict might suggest strife between the beliefs of the invading Celts and the pre-existing beliefs of the people before their arrival. The position of Celtic goddesses was also affected by the influx of Roman beliefs that came with the many Roman invasions into Celtic regions, as Roman values led to components of Celtic culture being destroyed, such as Celtic goddesses being Romanized to fit Roman patriarchal standards. The social position of women subsequently declined during this time of Roman invasion, as many Celts were forced to adopt Roman conceptions of the proper role for women. Celtic beliefs surrounding goddess worship, and subsequently the role of high-standing women in religious and social affairs was most affected, though, by the arrival of Christianity to the last Celtic strongholds of Ireland, Scotland, and Wales. The most significant culprit for the conflicted presentation of goddesses and women within Celtic mythology comes from the Christian authors who recorded the myths with their own concepts regarding pagan goddesses and the role of women, as most Celtic mythology was recorded by Christian monks who transcribed the myths of the Irish and Welsh between the eighth and twelfth centuries CE.

There is archeological evidence, and also evidence within Celtic mythology, that in early times, the Celts worshipped a Mother Goddess figure who was an embodiment of the land. This Mother Goddess was the "most widely-known female deity" among the Celts (Wood 42). The name of this Mother Goddess appeared in many forms in various Celtic cultures, but the name Danu appears most often in Ireland. Evidence suggests that Danu was one of the most ancient Celtic goddesses, and that her name may have meant "wisdom or teacher" (Stone 48). Danu, as a Mother Goddess, was conceived of as the earth itself; in fact, two hills in a valley west of Killarney in Co. Kerry are still identified as "De Chich Anann (the 'Paps' [breasts] of Danu)" (Wood 46). Danu was also connected to fertility. Some scholars contend that the worship of Danu, and the other renditions of Celtic Mother Goddesses, may have come from pre–Indo-European cultures (Stone 25).

Archeological findings and myths show that the Celts often associated aspects of the natural world with goddesses; for instance, bodies of water were often connected to female divine figures such as Boann, the goddess of the River Boyne in Ireland, and Sequana, the goddess of the River Seine. In addition, a popular Celtic goddess, Epona, was worshipped as a fertility goddess and associated with horses. Epona "was often depicted riding on a mare, perhaps accompanied by a foal, dispensing the earth's bounty of bread, grain, or fruit" (Wood 135). The goddess Artio was the Celtic Bear Goddess from the region of Gaul. She was associated with rebirth, as the symbol of the bear conveys the regeneration of nature that occurs from winter to spring. Some scholars identify the symbolism of Artio to pre–Celtic times, even Paleolithic times, as evidence of bear worship has been documented throughout Paleolithic Europe, as was discussed early in this chapter.

In addition, there are many Celtic goddesses who are directly linked to the fertility of nature. Artistic renditions abound of Celtic fertility goddesses, such as the goddess Sheilah-Na-Gig, who in Celtic art is most often shown clearly displaying her vulva. Often, earth goddesses in many cultures are portrayed with images of sexuality precisely because their role was envisioned as replenishing the cycles of nature. In order for Celtic kings to receive their station, it was said that a fertility goddess, who held direct connections to the prosperity of the land, had to sanctify the coronation. This process, known as the Sacred Marriage, would require a sexual encounter with a priestess, serving in the role of the fertility goddess, and the new king, so that the newly appointed king could serve as the figurehead for the vitality of the land. Once the king aged, his vitality was viewed as lessening, so Celtic kings were sometimes sacrificed to the fertility goddess of the land in order for a new king to be introduced and revitalize the land with a renewed union with the earth goddess.

Also, mythic sources show goddesses in Celtic mythology as holding the ability to shapeshift into a variety of forms, appearing to humans as maidens, crones, animals, or other natural elements. In addition, hunting goddesses, whose depictions were often associated with warlike imagery, were abundant among the Celts (Green 186). Green states that the "most striking example of early Iron Age iconography depicting what might be interpreted as a hunter-goddess was found in a seventh century BCE warrior's cremation-grave at Strettweg in Austria" (Green 187). This warrior's tomb included a model wagon made of bronze that depicted a ritual stag hunt where a large statuette of an apparently divine woman is portrayed "supporting a great cauldron on her upstretched hands" (Green 187). In addition, "a bronze figure from the Ardennes Forest depicts a woman dressed in a short hunting tunic ... with a hunting knife in her hand, riding a huge, bristling boar. She has been identified as Arduinna, eponymous goddess of the Ardennes" (Green 188). Celtic hunting goddesses may have been so abundantly revered because the hunt was "associated not just with the chase and with killing but also with nourishment and renewal" (Green 188). Artistic imagery of Celtic goddesses supports this assertion, as many images of Celtic goddesses show them presiding over aspects of birth, death, and renewal. For example, the Iron Age Gundestrup cauldron shows many depictions of goddesses who are believed to be connected to aspects of death and regeneration (Green 191).

In addition, the Celts often envisioned their goddesses as taking on a tripartite aspect, which is apparent in both the archeological and mythic record. For instance, the belief in a triple Mother Goddess was "considered particularly powerful by the Celts" (Wilkinson 73). The triple Mothers represented "human fertility and the bounty of the earth, and ... [had] dominion over human life and well-being. They also seem[ed] to symbolize the span of human life"; thus, they would often "take the form of women of different ages" (Wilkinson 73). The Morrígan is an excellent example to show the tripartite and transformative aspects of the Celtic goddess, as she was said to represent all aspects of the life cycle, appearing as a maiden, mother, and crone, showing that perhaps at one time "the Holy Trinity was ... the Daughter, the Mother, and the Grandmother" (Stone 49). The Morrígan in this powerful position was credited with protecting the Tuatha de Danann, the divine pantheon within Celtic mythology, showing her to possess qualities in line with a Mother Goddess (Stone 49). Matthews supports this, explaining that the Morrígan's name "derives from the Celtic 'Great Queen,'" and that this conception of the Morrígan "stems from an early, pre–Celtic tradition," which places the Morrígan as "the genesis and nemesis of life" (Matthews 37). However, in Indo-European Celtic mythology, the Morrígan was demoted to being only a goddess of fertility, death, and war.

The Morrígan of Celtic mythology can appear as the goddess Macha. Macha appears in the Irish *Noinden Ulad*, where she is credited with clearing the land with her mighty axe to make way for agricultural pursuits (Stone 53), showing her to be closely aligned with nature and fertility. Macha was mythically said to have driven out two cruel rulers and ruled the land herself for seven years, until the five sons of one of the former rulers challenged her right to rule. Knowing that the sons of the former ruler camped in the forest near her kingdom, Macha disguised herself as a leper and went to meet them. Despite her apparent disease, each of the five sons, one by one, was overcome by a desire to sleep with her, and when each went away with Macha, she tied them to a tree, until all five brothers were at her mercy, and she could continue her rule (Stone 54). In addition, Macha appears in one of the myths tied to the most revered Celtic text, the *Táin Bo Cuailgne,* set in the first century CE of pre–Christian Ireland, but recorded in the twelfth century. In this myth, Macha appears as a mortal peasant woman who married a man from Ulster named Crunnchru. When she was heavily pregnant with their child, Crunnchru boasted that Macha could outrun the king's horses. Macha tried to resist, but she was forced by the king to make good on Crunnchru's boasting. Reluctantly, she took part in the race and beat the king's horses, but once she finished, she immediately gave birth to twins and then died. In a message intended for a burgeoning Celtic patriarchy, as the *Tain* records a time of great societal upheaval in Ireland that may reflect the transition of traditional beliefs to new patriarchal beliefs, Macha mythically gained revenge for her death by making her husband, the king of Ulster, as well as all the men of Ulster, undergo the pangs of childbirth for nine days every year. The embrace of this mythic scene that clearly shows both commiseration for Macha, as well as her formidable power, reveals the respect the Celtic people held for Macha. The fact that Macha is shown in this myth as holding the ability to teach the king of Ulster, and all his men, such an important lesson that is tied to the sole experience of women, also shows a clear respect for the rights of women within Celtic society.

The mythic *Tain* includes many examples of powerful goddesses and socially superior women. The plot of the myth is put into motion by Macha's curse, as the text begins with the kingdom of Ulster under attack by the kingdom of Connaught, which is led by the formidable queen Medb, who knows that the men of Ulster will be unable to take part in the fight because of the curse of their phantom birthing pangs. The *Tain* shows that one seventeen-year-old male, Cúchulainn, must single-handedly defend Ulster, because he is the only Ulsterman who does not carry their blood in his veins, and is thus exempt from Macha's curse. Thus, Cúchulainn successfully fights hundreds of men from Connaught, but a pivotal scene in the text shows him as transforming because of his encounter with the Morrígan.

The Morrígan first came to Cúchulainn in the form of a maiden who praised Cúchulainn's youthful vitality, but she was shunned by him, as he did not recognize her as divine. This scene could be reflective of the role of goddesses diminishing in the increasingly patriarchal culture of the Celts, where the might of a warrior was of highest regard; however, this seems not to be the case, as the Morrígan quickly takes over her power in the situation. The Morrígan came again to Cúchulainn in the middle of a primary battle, and she forced him to pay attention to her strength by shapeshifting into a variety of natural elements that displayed her as a formidable fertility goddess. She first appeared as an eel and battled with Cúchulainn in this natural form. Then the Morrígan appeared as a she-wolf and continued the fight, and finally she appeared as a "hornless red heifer" (*Tain* 136-7). Cúchulainn harmed each of these animals during the fight, again not knowing they were the renowned Celtic goddess in disguise. After these violent encounters, the Morrígan forced Cúchulainn to finally feel exhausted, and it was at this moment that she again appeared to him, this time in the form of an old woman. The myth shows that the Morrígan, as the old woman, possessed the very same injuries Cúchulainn gave to the animals he battled. The Morrígan, as the old, wounded woman, then offered milk to Cúchulainn, and in an intensely spiritual scene, she showed him that the milk she provided him psychologically healed him, but also healed the wounds he inflicted upon her.

As a goddess of death and fertility, the Morrígan's appearance to Cúchulainn serves to teach him the futility of fighting against what she represents. Up until the point that Cúchulainn met the Morrígan, he was able to defy all odds and overcome, single-handedly, all adversaries, which solidified him as a prime example of Celtic heroism. However, the Morrígan's interactions with Cúchulainn showed him a lesson regarding the cycles of life. The forms the Morrígan presented to Cúchulainn aligned with the stages of life; for example, while he felt young and strong, he saw her as a maiden; when he felt the fury of battle, he saw her in fierce animal forms, but when he felt a "great weariness" (*Tain* 137) after ceaseless fighting, Cúchulainn saw the Morrígan as an old woman. Thus, the Morrígan's symbolic lesson of the life cycle in these scenes enables Cúchulainn to accept the inevitability of his own death, which comes for him in a later myth when the Morrígan, in the form of a raven, lands on his shoulder during his last battle against the forces of Queen Medb. However, the Morrígan, as a fertility goddess, also teaches Cúchulainn that nature's cycles additionally assure the renewal of all living beings, just as she showed him when his drinking of her milk healed her from the wounds he had inflicted. The Morrígan thus holds the central authority within the myth, as her impact on Cúchulainn, the hero of the epic, is not matched by any male character within the text. Presenting goddesses, such as Macha and the Morrígan, in this powerful light, as the ones who impart wisdom to male heroes, is often a trait of Celtic mythology, thus showing the high regard the Celts often had for their goddesses, despite being of Indo-European descent.

Though Celtic society was patriarchal on many levels, as discussed, their social structure still often allowed women to hold a higher social position than many societies of the ancient world, and in large part, the fairly high social standing of women in Celtic societies was directly related to the lasting power associated to the goddesses of Celtic religion. One of the strongest indications of this again comes with the Sacred Marriage practices between king and priestess, as the ritual awarded priestesses high religious authority. In addition, the Celts of the first millennium BCE "gave women ownership and allowed them personal agency" (Noble 202). Wood states that in Irish and Welsh law, a woman could own property, and had "definite legal rights in matters which directly affected her position as mistress of the household and as mother, and this gave her some security within marriage" (Wood 132). Also, "Irish law granted women surprisingly generous grounds for divorce in comparison with other societies" (Wood 132).

Furthermore, Celtic women who served as governmental and martial leaders, as well as soldiers, are found in both mythic and historical records (Stone 47). For example, Plutarch stated that Celtic women "acted as ambassadors in battles ... and sat upon peace councils," and prophetesses, known as Banfathi "accompanied troops into battle, and were relied upon for advice and strategy" (Stone 47). There is also evidence of what appears to be females who were associated with warfare on Iron Age coins; for instance, a coin "minted in the first century BC[E] by the polity of the Redones (a Breton tribe whose main urban centre was at Rennes) [shows] ... a naked woman [who] sits astride a galloping horse, with what looks like a shield in her right hand and a sword in her left" (Green 182). In Brittany, there is also a "bronze figure of a [Celtic] female warrior ... dated to the first century BC[E] .... Her military identity is shown by the goose-crested helmet she wears ... [as] the goose is a well-documented La Téne symbol of aggression, and goose-bones have been found buried in Iron Age warrior-graves" (Green 184). In fact, Cross and Miles state that there were "many Celtic fighting women in pre–Christian Europe" (Cross & Miles 35). The Roman historian Ammianus Marcelinus stated that any who fought the Celts in Gaul "'would not be able to withstand one Celt in battle if he calls his wife to his aid. [She is] stronger than he by far ... especially when she swells her neck and gnashes her teeth and swinging her huge white arms, begins to rain down blows mixed with kicks, like the shot from a catapult'" (qtd. in Cross & Miles 35). The Celtic women warriors referred to by Marcelinus came from a long Celtic tradition that allowed women to train at "war colleges" (Cross & Miles 35). These war colleges are portrayed in the Celtic *Tain* when the old woman, Scáthach of Scotland, is the only person who can train Cúchulainn to become the fiercest warrior of the Ulstermen.

One of the most famous Celtic women warriors is Queen Boudica of the Iceni. Queen Boudica, who took over her husband's rule after his death in 61 CE, came from a long line of Celtic women who held high status and were revered as rulers. Jackson states that Celtic queens were quite common in Celtic history and legend (Jackson 7). It is believed that Boudica, and other Celtic queens like her, was directly connected in the minds of her people to conceptions of divinity. Boudica, as queen, was believed to be connected to the goddess Andraste, the Iceni goddess of war and victory; it was also through this connection that Boudica was able to serve, in addition to the role of queen, as high priestess to Andraste, giving Boudica semi-divine status. The high social standing of Queen Boudica directly aligns, then, with her people's acceptance of powerful goddesses, as when powerful goddesses are worshipped within a culture, then women are also able to maintain powerful social positions. However, Rome did not hold women in the same regard as the Celts. When the Romans sought to conquer Celtic lands, they brought with them their strict patriarchy that clashed with the Celtic view of women within religion and society. Romans believed that "women belonged to their male relations, who had the legal right to inflict punishment on them, including death" (Cross & Miles 32). The Romans felt that civilizations that allowed women to hold authoritative positions, especially military positions, were themselves weak; "If a man is subject to a queen—a *dux femina*—he is disgraced and the only way to erase this shame is to conquer her" (Crawford 25–6). Therefore, when Rome encountered Queen Boudica, they did not honor her right to rule. Instead, the Romans claimed her kingdom, pillaged its surplus, publicly flogged Boudica, and flogged and raped her two daughters as she was forced to watch. Cross and Miles state that "As co-heirs of their mother, the girls shared the divinity that was attached to her. Rape robbed them of their supernatural attributes and debarred them from claiming priestess status or inheriting her semi-divine role, breaking the 'mother right' or matrilineal descent" (Cross & Miles 32). Directly because Queen Boudica held tremendous power and influence, she was able to summon thousands of Celtic armies in the surrounding areas to seek revenge upon the Romans. Queen Boudica's armies sacked the cities of Camulodunum (modern Colchester), Londinium (London), and Verulanium (St Albans), which should have been an impossible task at the time. And though Boudica and her armies were finally defeated by Roman soldiers, causing her demise, she still lives on as a symbol of the strength that Celtic women were sometimes permitted within their communities, precisely because the Celts worshipped goddesses who held positions of authority. Cross and Miles concur; Boudica's success at rallying so many Celts to stand by her stemmed directly from her connection to divinity (Cross & Miles 34).

As shown with the high positioning of goddesses within Celtic belief systems, and the fairly high social position of many Celtic women, one can see that Indo-European values seem to have not entirely eradiated traditional concepts of reverence for women within the existing beliefs systems of the cultures they encountered. However, the view of goddesses and the social position of women would drastically change with the introduction of Christianity into Celtic lands. Inherent in Christianity is the belief that there is one sole God, and He is male. His primary position is that worshippers may revere no god or goddesses before Him, so the worship of all existing goddesses had to entirely be eradicated. Therefore, Christian officials often defined symbols connected to Celtic goddesses as dangerous and even evil. For example, the symbols of the goddesses' regenerative sexuality was stifled and replaced with Christian images that portrayed women as chaste and submissive. Lubell explains that "As deeply rooted ... Christian fear of the female came to prevail.... The patriarchy ... came to share an obsessive concern over woman's 'lust.' This prurient concern gave birth not only to a suppression of imagery but to an intolerance of female sexuality" (Lubell 129).

The lessening of the goddesses' power in Celtic Europe with the introduction of Christianity greatly affected the social positioning of women over time. Cross and Miles state that "Christianity's onward march in the British Isles involved wholesale suppression of rights and freedoms enjoyed by Celtic women from the earliest days" (Cross & Miles 35). For example, Christian values only allowed men to serve as priests, which mostly eliminated the religious role for many women in Celtic communities. Also, in 697 CE "a church law known as the *Cain Adamnan* prohibited women from fighting, bearing arms or taking any part in war. This law, which stripped women of the right to fight for their families or defend themselves, was presented as an act of kindness to women, relieving them of the obligation to train for war" (Cross & Miles 35).

Celtic mythology, again written down only after Christianity came to Celtic regions, shows a clear turmoil in the presentation of goddesses and powerful female characters. Often goddesses within Celtic mythology are presented as powerful, and in some cases superior, as shown with the portrayals of the goddess Macha and the Morrígan, but just as often, goddesses and other female mythic characters are presented with a complexity that shows them as being stripped of their power even within their own myths. A good example of this appears again in the *Tain* with the character of Queen Medb. The text introduces Medb in a scene that immediately shows her strength as a female character. As queen of Connaught, she is shown lying in bed next to her husband, King Áilill, but Medb is in no way portrayed as lesser than King Áilill, as would be the case in many other European texts showing a queen with her husband, the king. In fact, Queen Medb appears more powerful than her husband, as she proclaims to him that Connaught will go to war with Ulster because she desires to own the prized Brown Bull of Cooley. Queen Medb continues her primary role in the text as the central adversary against the protagonist Cúchulainn. It is Medb herself who serves to effectively direct the troops of Connaught; she also decides who enters the battle and when. Furthermore, she is portrayed as altering the landscape in order to assert her power. In addition, she is presented as overtly sexual, as Medb openly chooses for herself many sexual partners outside of her marriage. Dominguez states that Queen Medb "is a fully sexual being, one who often makes the first overtures, and is not 'punished' in the traditional manner of many female characters in medieval tales" (Dominguez 4). Dominguez further presents Medb as a Celtic warrior queen, similar to Boudica, and it is this portrayal of such a powerful woman within Celtic mythology that helps to shed light on what the true role of some Celtic women might have been. Caldecott concurs, stating that Queen Medb "is the queen most quoted to show the privileged position of Celtic women in the Iron Age. They were equal in every respect to men, and in some cases, they were superior. They could own property; they could, as kings did, 'divide gifts' and 'give counsel'; they could ride chariots, fight battles, dispose of lives" (Caldecott 167–8). However, there may have once been more to Medb's character than that of a formidable human queen. Green connects a sculpture from Gloucestershire of a Celtic warrior queen to Queen Medb. Green states that the sculpture depicts an image of a female from Lemington whose hair stands "out from her head in radiant lines and [who] wears a long robe.... On the base of the stone is a roughly incised inscription dedicating the stone to 'the goddess Riigina' (a version of the Latin 'Regina' meaning 'Queen')" (Green 185). This sculpture is quite important because the "inscription explicitly states that the female is a goddess" (Green 185–6). Green explains that the title of queen given to the goddess is highly important, as "she is addressed ... as both goddess and queen" (Green 186). This cross listing of queen and goddess might suggest a possible link with Queen Medb (Green 186). Many scholars believe that Medb's origin was probably a Celtic goddess of war, sovereignty, and fertility (Fleming & Husain 60). Green explains that Celtic fertility goddesses, like the character Medb herself, often combine "intense sexuality and fertility symbolism with concentrated aggression. She is the guardian of her land and fights to keep it safe; her sexual activity promotes the prosperity and fecundity of the land" (Green 186). Stone states that Medb is presented in some myths as "Owner of the Sovereignty of Ireland, the throne was Hers alone" (Stone 68). Scholars, like Green and Hodges, also connect Queen Medb to the goddesses Macha and the Morrígan in the *Tain,* as all the female characters in the epic serve a similar role to teach the men in the novel themes that are related to Celtic goddesses (Green 186; Hodges 92).

However, Queen Medb is not only portrayed in the *Tain* as powerful. Again, because the text was not recorded until after Christianity came to Ireland, the text reveals conflict between Celtic and Christian ideologies. Many scholars have pointed out that queen/goddess figures, like Medb and the Morrígan, were systematically demonized after the introduction of Christianity (Dooley 158). Though Medb is clearly one of the most powerful female characters of mythic literature, there still is ample evidence that she was demoted of her powerful role within the *Tain.* One of the best examples of this plays out at the end of the text when the Ulstermen stop experiencing labor pains and come to aid Cúchulainn in battle. The Ulstermen force the soldiers of Connaught to finally retreat. When Cúchulainn catches up to Queen Medb, the scene seems purposefully written to humiliate her. Cúchulainn finally finds Queen Medb when she is compromised by managing the effects of her menstruation; "Then Medb got her gush of blood" (*Tain* 250). Queen Medb tells a high official of her forces, Fergus, that she must go relieve herself, and Fergus scolds her, telling her that she has chosen a bad time as they are in the throng of battle. Medb states, "'I can't help it…. I'll die if I can't do it" (*Tain* 250). This is an odd moment in the text because it clearly presents Medb in a manner in which she has not yet been portrayed; the scene itself and the chastisement by the male character Fergus thus seems to be a later patriarchal textual inclusion. The text continues to show that while Medb was relieving herself, the effects "dug three great channels each big enough to take a household" (*Tain* 250). This scene again suggests that Medb might hold powers given to a goddess, as her blood and urine, which the text apparently connects in this scene, are able to alter the landscape. Dooley explains that similar mythic abilities are found in the Scandinavian *Poetic Edda* (c. 1270 CE) where divine women could alter landscapes by acts of urination or menstruation (Dooley 178). However, the humiliation of this final scene for Medb, as this scene marks her defeat when Cúchulainn spies her in this vulnerable state, seems intentional, and even out of place. Having Queen Medb lose the battle and be caught in a compromising position of humiliation by the text's male hero allows the narrative to fit better with the accepted heroic tradition of twelfth- to fifteenth-century European Christian narratives, when the *Tain* was recorded, so it is possible that this scene is merely a product of the Christian author(s) who wrote the story down centuries after its oral construction.

The first branch of the Welsh Mabinogi, written in the twelfth to thirteenth centuries CE, also shows a good example of a conflicted portrayal of a female queen with divine attributes. In this mythic text, again written after Christianity was brought to Wales but conceived centuries earlier, the character of Rhiannon is portrayed as a divine woman who appears to King Pwyll while riding a horse that he cannot overtake, though Rhiannon and the horse walk at what appears to be a slow pace. Finally, Pwyll catches up to Rhiannon, and the two eventually get married, making this otherworldly maiden a queen. The couple have a child, but it is what happens to their newborn baby that sheds light on Rhiannon in conflicted terms, similar to the portrayal of Queen Mebd in the *Tain*. Rhiannon and Pwyll's baby disappears in the dead of night. Afraid of being blamed, the child's nursemaids decide to kill a dog and spread its blood over the sleeping Rhiannon's face and hands, so that it will appear that she has killed and eaten her own infant son. The imagery invoked in this scene appears intentional, just as the odd scene of portraying Medb humiliated at the end of the *Tain*. Celtic goddesses were often portrayed as both givers and takers of life, as they often embodied both fertility and death, as discussed. When patriarchal structures, such as the Christian church in this case, attempted to lessen or eradicate the power of goddesses, they often focused most heavily on the seemingly vicious aspects of goddesses in order to vilify them. The symbolism of having Rhiannon first give birth to the next royal heir, and then reportedly eat her own child, certainly seems like an attempt to identify the aspects of fertility goddesses associated with death, like the Morrígan, as negative and sinister. When Rhiannon awakens in the text, she believes that she has done the worst deed imaginable. Rhiannon forces upon herself a punishment for her perceived crime, and again the punishment she chooses seems manipulated towards a patriarchal agenda. Rhiannon punishes herself by asking her subjects to sit on her back as she walks about the kingdom as if she was a horse.

Like Queen Medb's connection to divinity, much scholarship also recognizes that Rhiannon is believed to have come from the Welsh belief in the Goddess Rigantona, which translates "literally as Great Queen Goddess" (Stone 69). Rigantona was also thought to be connected to the Celtic Goddess Epona, who was the Mare Goddess, referred to as "Regina (Queen)" (Stone 69). There are other Welsh myths of Rhiannon that present her in the light of a goddess, as when a giant stole the eggs of her magic birds and was thus covered with feathers in punishment, or the myth of Cian that shows him saving a hare from a pack of hunting dogs, only to find the hare transformed into the beautiful Rhiannon in his arms (Stone 71). The myth of Cian also shows Rhiannon inviting Cian to live with her in her otherworld realm for many months, until Cian tries to have sex with her in a moment when she is enjoying her own solitude, and in revenge, she transforms into a giant mare and crushes Cian's thigh bone with her massive hoof (Stone 71). These myths show that Rhiannon was long considered divine among the Celts.

However, when Rhiannon acts like a horse to her people in the Mabinogi, the text mocks her instead of praises her once powerful divine connection to Rigantona or Epona. Envisioning a queen walking on all fours, while her subjects sit upon her back can be read as nothing but ridiculous, so it seems likely that the Christian author(s), who recorded the Mabinogi intentionally portrayed this once powerful female goddess in a clearly demoted format. The text continues by showing Rhiannon finally proven innocent when her son is found in the home of peasants who also have had their newborn colts abducted annually. The peasants thought the baby was given to them by a divine source in compensation for losing their colts each year, but when they realize the baby is the royal prince, they return him to his parents. There is much symbolism at work in these happenings; certainly, themes connected to the goddess are apparent, such as tenets related to life, death, and regeneration, as portrayed through the symbolic death and resurrection of the infant. Rhiannon's connection to the processes of death and renewal, though only hinted at, maintains a perhaps older intention in the myth preserved from its oral format. However, in its written form within the Mabinogi, the myth appears conflicted in regard to Rhiannon. When Rhiannon first meets Pwyll, her divine role is undeniable, but when she becomes queen, she merely is portrayed in human terms with sinister overtones, presumably meant to discredit her divine past. It is true that she is exonerated of guilt in the myth, but this is not her own doing at all. She is not portrayed as a Celtic goddess who holds the ability to regenerate life and alter nature at will; instead, she stands in the background being handed a fate that is out of her control. Rhiannon of the Mabinogi thus serves as but a remnant of a much more powerful goddess, showing again the purposeful demotion of the goddess within Celtic mythology when the myths were captured in written form by Christian authors.

However, in many areas throughout Celtic Ireland, Wales, and Scotland, a remarkable thing happened regarding goddess worship despite the arrival and spread of the Christian faith. The remote location of Celtic regions during its conversion to Christianity in the fifth century CE enabled these regions to create a faith that combined Christian and Celtic beliefs in a way that was quite different from other areas of Europe. Because of this merging of faiths, instead of the sheer wiping out of Celtic religious values, goddess reverence somewhat remained in Celtic regions, though often disguised. While goddess images were certainly regarded negatively by Christian officials, some images remained, such as the carved images of the goddess Sheilah-Na-Gig. Lubell contends that the many images of Sheilah-Na-Gig, carved in the twelfth to sixteenth centuries upon hundreds of churches in Ireland, Wales, and England, are connected to the same images found since pre-historic times and should be viewed as maintaining images of sexuality associated with the divine female (Lubell 139). Whereas Christian institutions were mostly successful at suppressing images of the sacred feminine, they were less successful in Ireland, Scotland, and Wales. In addition, though the Tuatha De Danann lost their divine status in a religious sense, they were, like the images of Sheilah-Na-Gig, also preserved in the folklore of Celtic regions, becoming fairies, sprites, pookas, etc. For example, it is generally believed that the sun god Lugh was demoted from his divine status but was still remembered in the form of the folkloric leprechaun. Again, as happened in Slavic and Baltic regions, diminishing the sacrality of once divine beings by making them folkloric figures allowed the people to still believe in them without worshipping them, and this compromise was tolerated by Christian officials. Therefore, once divine women became reimagined on the positive end as human saints, or on the negative end as witches, ghosts, etc. A good example of this manipulation of Celtic goddesses into acceptable Christian figures can be seen with the popular Celtic goddess Brigid, the goddess of fire, wisdom, protection, poetry, and healing. Stone states that Brigid's fire was protected by the "Daughters of the Flame," who were priestesses tasked with imparting Brigid's wisdom of "healing herbs" to the people (Stone 64). There are many myths that highlight the Celtic goddess Brigid healing the ill. However, in the process of Christianizing Celtic beliefs, the Goddess Brigid was transformed into the Christian Saint Brigid. Thus, "the fire at Brigid's shrine in Kildare, originally cared for by priestesses, was later cared for by Catholic sisters—until the decree of a Bishop declared it to be pagan, and ordered that the fire be extinguished in 1220 [CE]" (Stone 63). This process of maintaining once powerful goddesses in a transformed state allowed the people to more readily adopt the new Christian faith because the new faith appeared similar to what they were used to. Thus, myriad goddesses and their imagery remain alive and well in current Celtic regions throughout Europe, if one knows where to look.

## Germanic Regions

The origins of the Germanic speaking people are indistinct, though in the Bronze Age, they inhabited southern Scandinavia and northern Germany. The Indo-European Corded Ware culture likely arrived in southern Scandinavia by the early second millennium BCE (Reaves 27). Thus,

Proto-Germanic, "the last common ancestor of the Germanic branch of the Indo-European family of languages, most likely developed in southern Scandinavia" (Reaves 27–8). As Germanic tribes migrated, they often infringed upon the Celts. The Romans first encountered the Germanic people during the second century BCE, and they continued to encounter one another for centuries. The Germanic tribes during Roman times included the Franks, Langobardi (Lombards), Angli (Angles), Goths, Vandals, Burgundians, Saxons, etc. During approximately 300–700 CE, the Migration period, also referred to as the Barbarian Invasions of Germanic peoples, occurred throughout many areas of Europe. Through these migrations, the Germanic Franks, Huns, Goths, Vandals, Bulgars, and other Germanic and Slavic tribes ultimately gained control of "most areas of the former Western Roman Empire" (van der Crabben). The Visigoths sacked Rome and moved to rule over Iberia (Portugal and Spain); the Ostrogoths ruled within portions of Italy; the Franks ruled Gaul (France, Belgium, and northern Germany), creating what would become "the nucleus of the future states of France and Germany," and Britain was "invaded and settled" by the Angles and Saxons, who would become known as Anglo-Saxons (van der Crabben).

It is from Roman texts, primarily Tacitus's *Germania* (98 CE), that the written record reveals the beliefs of Germanic people, which certainly poses problems of accuracy, as the Romans sought to conquer the Germanic tribes. As seen with the Celts, the many Germanic tribes were diverse in their belief systems, but they still possessed a common language and "a common set of cultural practices, rituals, and a store of sacred knowledge, inherited from their forebears, which gave meaning to the world and their place in it. The common threads that connect distant Indo-European languages and mythologies with those of Northern Europe bear witness to this fact" (Reaves 28). The Germanic people were pastoralists and warriors. Like the Celts, their societies were mostly patriarchal, with chieftains chosen to serve as communal leaders. Familial ties did not always secure the role of chieftains, as an integral part of Germanic societies was that the chieftain had to earn the role of leader from his skills in primarily warfare. Judicial roles were also given to leading men of the community. However, again similar to the Celts, women still could hold important social positions. Germanic women "provided a network of kinship ties," worked at farm labor, and also went to battle on occasion (Wemple 6). Germanic women were also believed to hold spiritual powers that could advance their social positioning; the Roman Tacitus stated that Germanic women were believed to hold "a certain uncanny and prophetic sense," so that the men of the Germanic communities "neither scorn to consult them nor slight their answers"

## Chapter 1—Europe   35

(Tacitus 143). Tacitus also declared that the Germanic people revered many female ancestors (Tacitus 143).

Many Germanic beliefs held ties with other Indo-European religious concepts; Reaves explains that early Germanic religion, like its Indo-European counterparts, "is often described as solar in nature, and religious symbols reflected in artifacts of the period appear to be concerned with the motion of the sun and cycles of birth, death and rebirth" (Reaves 27). In addition, the "ancient belief that it is possible to influence the fertility of the land through ritual sexual intercourse is well-documented" in Germanic cultures (Reaves 29). Another common Indo-European belief among Germanic people was the worship of a principal male deity, who for the Germanic people was Woden, Odin in Norse religion. Again, like the Celts, despite being Indo-European in origin, the Germanic people also worshipped a variety of prominent goddesses, which, again like the Celts, accounted for the ability of women to hold high social and religious roles in Germanic societies.

There are "over 1,100 dedication stones" found throughout Germanic regions that venerate an Earth Mother figure (Egeler 31). Reaves states that "the Germanic people widely venerated a goddess personifying the Earth under a variety of names, such as Nerthus, Ertha, Freya, Frija, Frigg, etc. A closer examination of these scattered accounts unveils many common threads which demonstrate the continuity of her character for over a millennium, indicating that these sources speak of one figure known by many different destinations" (Reaves 3). This concept of the earth as a unified Mother Goddess may have survived from the Neolithic cultures that encountered the Germanic tribes (Reaves 12), as it seems to have done with the Celts. Reaves contends that "In Germanic sources, Mother Earth holds a prominent position…. The evidence is … overwhelming. She is present from the beginning of the record," as recorded by Tacitus, who states that the Germanic tribes in common "worshipped Nerthus, who is *Terra Mater*, Mother Earth" (Reaves 298). The scale of the worship of an Earth Mother among the Germanic people was quite widespread, as Reaves states, "with one cult spread across at least seven northern European nations, the scale of *Terra Mater*'s worship in the first century [CE] must have been massive" (Reaves 89).

The Earth Mother of the Angles and the Lombards was Nerthus (Reaves 298). It is believed that an annual procession would take place in honor of her that involved sacrifice within a lake, which has been archeologically confirmed by the discovery of many "ceremonial objects recovered from bogs and wetlands" (Reaves 70). Tacitus also discussed in his *Germania* that the Nerthus processional contained "several ceremonial wagons," some of which have indeed been excavated (Reaves 72). Tacitus also discusses the ceremonial drowning of slaves in honor of Nerthus (Tacitus 135). Johnston Staver confirms that "Human sacrifices were almost certainly a feature of earth worship. The bodies recovered from Danish bogs, having been ritually killed by strangulation, could have been offered to the Earth Mother in a place where they knew the earth would draw the body down and out of sight, as it sank in the bog and 'Nerthus' took her offering" (Johnston Staver 151).

In addition, archeological evidence from primarily the Netherlands presents myriad images from the second and third centuries CE of a "German goddess named Nehalennia" (Reaves 69). In some of her images, "she is shown with two other goddesses, associating her with the threefold Matronae of Central Europe" (Reaves 69), making her conception similar to the triple goddesses of Celtic religion. The Germanic Anglo-Saxons also worshipped an Earth Mother. They enacted a ritual known as Æcerbót, which was intended to replenish the fertility of the land by the union of a sky god with the Earth Mother. Reaves explains that the ritual included "a pagan communal procession honoring the earth goddess, which is supported by both literary and archeological evidence across the Germanic-speaking regions" (Reaves 81).

However, as with the Celts, when the Germanic people encountered the Romans, their religion and social structures began to change. Reaves states that as "the Iron Age progressed, the core of the Roman army came to be recruited from free Germania, and after their service ended, these young men returned home filled with knowledge of Roman culture" (Reaves 20). Because of this introduction to a different social model, archeologists have noted that religious practices also began to change during the end of the Roman Iron Age and into the Migration and Vendel (550–793 CE) periods. Thus, ritual locations moved "away from natural sites such as wetlands and open-air spaces, which formerly had been the focus of sacrality, to the residences of the newly-established ruling elite" (Reaves 20). This shift in places of worship was "reflected in the cosmology and social norms expressed in Germanic myths and rituals during the literary period, which place less emphasis on the natural cycles and more on social hierarchies and their interactions" (Reaves 20–1). This transformation in religious values away from nature marked a lessening of the worship of nature goddesses as well, as their prominence became demoted in place of patriarchal values. And, just as with the Celts, it was ultimately the introduction of Christianity to the Germanic people that finally solidified the almost full annihilation of the religious belief in Germanic goddesses. The Vandals, Burgundians, Ostrogoths, and the Franks were among the first to convert to Christianity in the fifth and sixth centuries; while the Saxons late in the eighth century and the Scandinavians in the tenth century were among the last of the Germanic people to convert to Christianity.

As discussed earlier, the Celts merged many of their religious beliefs, practices, and conceptions of divine beings into either acceptable Christian concepts, or into folkloric beliefs. The same is true for the Anglo-Saxons and other Germanic peoples. For instance, the Angles replaced conceptions of their old Germanic sky god, Woden, with the Christian God, and their Earth Mother with the Virgin Mary (Reaves 298). In addition, traditional Germanic perceptions of the Earth Mother continued across Europe in the Middle Ages within folklore, where "a matronly figure ... [made] the snow and rain fall. She dwell[ed] in ponds and wells from which babies ... [were] born.... Closely associated with agriculture, spinning and domestic affairs, she visit[ed] homes at Yule along with her husband Woden, richly bestowing blessings on the industrious and punishing the lazy. She is Mother Nature herself, the old heathen Earth Mother" (Reaves 299). In addition, as mentioned, the ritual in honor of the Earth Mother, Æcerbót, though it had pagan Germanic roots, was allowed to remain in Anglo-Saxon communities because it was restructured as a Christian practice. As discussed earlier, Æcerbót was originally addressed to the Earth Mother "who caused grain to sprout and grow, with a call to the sky god to send the necessary rain" (Ellis Davidson 62). In Christian times, the prayers in Æcerbót were reimagined and presented to now "the Christian God [who took] the place of the old Indo-European sky god ... [and] impregnated the earth," while "statues of the Virgin Mary ... were carried around to bless the fields" in place of the Earth Mother (Reaves 77). Also, European festivals to honor the Harvest Queen, which were permitted by the Christian church, were "almost certainly festivals based on the old Germanic festivals of Earth Mother worship" (Johnston Staver 151).

The Anglo-Saxon role of women remained somewhat elevated, even after they had converted to Christianity. Anglo-Saxon "women could hold, devise, inherit, and sell land in Anglo-Saxon England" (Clark 211). Anglo-Saxon women "had a high level of self-determination. A significant indicator of this was land ownership. Women, in many cases, exercised land ownership to the same extent as men. That women had this ability is a significant indicator of their status in society" (Clark 222). Furthermore, Anglo-Saxon women possessed "the power, to some extent, to determine their own destinies. They may have been able to choose to marry and have children. Moreover, upon divorce or widowhood, they were presumptively the custodians of their children" (Clark 222). In addition, Anglo-Saxon women were able to hold "various occupations ... that could be pursued in lieu of, or in conjunction with, marriage. One of those occupations was the life of the convent," where both men and women could receive an education (Clark 217).

It is likely that Anglo-Saxon women were able to maintain some of their social rights within the community even after converting to Christianity because their Germanic female ancestors held prominent social roles prior to converting to Christianity. For example, Anglo-Saxon women often "contribute[d] to the defense of the tribe" by fulfilling the role of warrior (Clark 234). Anglo-Saxon women were viewed as capable of being warriors because their Germanic ancestors allowed women to serve in the role of warrior, which was largely due to the fact that the Germanic people had divine models of warrior goddesses, such as: Baduhenna, a western Frisii goddess of warfare; Sandraudiga, a goddess whose name means "she who dyes the sand red"; and the Idis goddesses who were also tied to battle. In addition, some Anglo-Saxon women were initially allowed high-standing positions in the Christian church, and some were even canonized as saints early on, such as Æthelthryth, known as Saint Audrey, and Saint Hilda of Whitby. In the early periods following their conversion to Christianity, Anglo-Saxons identified women as deserving of high religious recognition because again, their Germanic beliefs prior to their conversion revered women in high-standing religious roles because of their connections to powerful goddesses.

However, as the Anglo-Saxons adopted more and more patriarchal social and religious structures, gradually forming the kingdom of England, the social roles for Anglo-Saxon women began to lessen. Women were no longer viewed as necessary in battle and gradually lost "their power and influence in the church" (Clark 229). For example, as Lina Eckenstein states, "'Most of the [Anglo-Saxon] women who were honoured as saints in England belong to the first hundred years after the acceptance of Christianity'" (qtd. in Clark 229). After this period, the religious and social role of Anglo-Saxon women only continued to decline as Christian values dominated, and women became identified as inferior. Clark concurs, stating that "The church's teachings stressing the inferiority and subordination of women undoubtedly had an effect on how women were perceived in [Anglo-Saxon] society" (Clark 234).

The Anglo-Saxon poem *Beowulf* is a good source to explore the role of goddesses and the subsequent lessening of the social status of women within Anglo-Saxon culture. *Beowulf* was written down between the seventh and eighth centuries CE by an anonymous author after its Germanic origin in the oral tradition. Because this text, like many Celtic myths, records a pagan story within a Christian era, there are again many conflicted scenes.

Though the protagonist, Beowulf, is certainly the focus of the text, there are important female characters within this religiously complex myth. Wealhtheow, queen of Denmark, and Hygd, queen of Geatland, have small roles within the text, but the tasks they perform carry meaning about the role of women within Germanic culture. The queens serve as hostesses within the text, as "they carry the cup of mead around the hall and offer it to the warriors" (Porter). Porter points out that when Wealhtheow first presents the cup to the hall, she gives it to King Hrothgar, then the other Danish warriors, and finally Beowulf, but the second time she presents the cup, she gives it to King Hrothgar first, and then skips the warriors and presents it directly to Beowulf (Porter). Porter explains that the order the hostess offers the cup assigns rank to the men within the hall, so it can be interpreted that it is the queen in this scene who elevates Beowulf's rank, as he has promised to kill the Danes' menace, Grendel. Queen Hygd also is portrayed as holding this important role of cupbearer in the text. McCoy further finds meaning in Queen Wealhtheow serving as cupbearer. McCoy states that during the Germanic Migration period, "One of the core societal institutions of the period was the war band, a tightly organized military society presided over by a chieftain and his wife. The wife of the war band's leader, according to the Roman historian Tacitus, held the title of veleda, and her role in the war band was to foretell the outcome of a suggested plan of action by means of divination" (McCoy). The veleda thus was viewed as holding a sacred significance for the Germanic people, as she could use mystical forces to influence the outcome of the battle (McCoy). The veleda also served warriors "a special cup of liquor that was a powerful symbol of both temporal and spiritual power in the war band's periodic ritual feasts" (McCoy). McCoy argues that Queen Wealhtheow "is almost certainly the Old English equivalent of the Proto-Germanic title [of] ... 'veleda.' Wealhtheow's 'domestic' actions in the poem—which are ... enactments of the liquor ritual described above—are indispensable for the upkeep of the unity of the war band and its power structures" (McCoy). Therefore, the epic, "despite its Christian veneer, 'hint[s] at the queen's oracular powers" (McCoy). Queen Wealhtheow shows that she indeed does possess traits in common with Germanic veledas, as she is shown consulting with her husband, King Hrothgar, on political matters. For instance, Wealhtheow advises Hrothgar not to make Beowulf the heir to the Danish kingdom after he has successfully killed Grendel, but to hold the throne for her own sons. She also speaks to Beowulf of this same desire. Queen Wealhtheow's political interventions "illustrate her self-confidence," and the poet of the text "gives no reason for us to believe that her demands will go unheeded" (Porter), showing the high position of women in Germanic society.

Additionally, the character of Queen Hygd "also held at least some political power, and this is shown most clearly when she attempts to deliver the kingdom of the Geats to Beowulf following Hygelac's death on the battlefield, in effect passing over her own son, Heardred" (Porter). Hygd's oversight of her son may be explained by anthropological evidence that "concludes that the social arrangement in Beowulf, though patrilineal, dimly reflects the matrilineal ... and matrilocal ... organization of early Germanic society" (Porter). According to a matrilineal and matrilocal system of organization, "lineage is traced through the women" (Porter). Therefore, this totemic system states that if a father "bequeathed his ... wealth and status upon his son, this patrimony would pass out of his own natal clan and into the matriclan of his affines. To avoid passing his ... wealth into another family, then, the father must choose another male relation related to his own mother through another female relation. The closest relation in this case would be the son of a sister ... and Beowulf is ... the son of Hygelac's sister" (Porter). Therefore, when Queen Hygd passes over her own son, perhaps she "wishes to keep the kingdom in her husband's family, not because she or her deceased husband doubts the abilities of Heardred, but because the totemic system prescribes that it should be so" (Porter). Again, this type of detail within the Old English text of *Beowulf* presents remnants of the religious, social, and political importance of women within pre–Christian Germanic societies.

In addition, there is some indication that Wealhtheow, like Queen Medb in the *Tain,* may be connected as queen to earlier Germanic conceptions of divinity. McCoy states that the "Hrothgar/Wealhtheow association as presented in the poem may be an echo of an earlier ... conception of ... [the Germanic] Frija and Woðanaz [Woden].... Woðanaz is the war band's chieftain, and Frija is its veleda" (McCoy). Therefore, Wealhtheow may hold associations with the Germanic goddess Frija, as she possesses a piece of jewelry that holds the same name as the goddess, a sacred fiery necklace referred to as the Brosinga mene (Old English); thus, it seems plausible that "both figures refer to the same ancient archetype" (McCoy). Like the presentation of Queen Medb in the *Tain,* transforming a divine being into a mortal queen within an epic seems to be a decisive attempt to demote the power of the goddess, as a mortal queen is more easily overlooked in the recesses of a larger tale, as certainly happens with Wealhtheow in *Beowulf.* Given the history of Anglo-Saxon England, it is likely that the demotion of the divine figure that Wealhtheow may have once been happened long before the recording of *Beowulf,* but the fact that the text has captured the complexity of characters like Wealhtheow, showing her to be perhaps a remnant of divinity, and certainly a holder of significant societal power for women from Germanic times, is significant.

Though there are female characters, like Wealhtheow and Hygd, who are presented in high-standing positions within *Beowulf,* their presentation is only fleeting, as they are by no means primary characters within the epic. The only principal character who is female within *Beowulf* is Grendel's mother; it is the text's treatment of her that shows the true demotion of reverence for women by the time the text was written down in Anglo-Saxon times. Grendel's mother is portrayed as more powerful than her feared son, Grendel. After Beowulf kills Grendel by ripping his arm off, Grendel's blood soaks into the ground and awakens his mother, who resides within the earth in an underwater lair. The symbols apparent in the introduction of Grendel's mother recall concepts associated with Germanic goddesses. The blood soaking into the earth and awakening Grendel's mother is reminiscent of the necessity of blood sacrifice once believed to be owed to Germanic Earth Mothers. In addition, Grendel's mother's title within the epic might also reveal a more distant identity for her, as only identifying her as "mother" instantly ties her to a representation of a Germanic Earth Mother, such as Nerthus. Additionally, Grendel's mother's home, that is literary within the earth, also connects her to Germanic Earth Mothers, as the interior of the earth was believed to be the domain, even womb, of such goddesses. Furthermore, because Grendel's mother is able to live where no mortal can survive, as her abode is deep underwater, so deep that "no man alive is so wise to know the nature of its depths" (*Beowulf* 86), and because massive mystical sea creatures protect her lake, her connection as a former Earth Mother additionally seems likely. Also, Grendel's mother is presented as a formidable opponent to any warrior within the text, as she is greatly feared by the Danes, even to a greater degree than her son, which again shows her connection to Germanic conceptions of divinity.

Despite the high possibility that Grendel's mother may be connected to a former Germanic Earth Mother, she is portrayed within the text as monstrous, and this presentation is certainly intentional. Similar to the presentations meant to demote Queen Medb in the *Tain* and Rhiannon in the Mabinogi, the presentation of Grendel's mother is meant to cast her, and any former divine associations of her, as evil. Grendel and his mother are portrayed as being shunned from the community and forced to live as outcasts within the wilderness, because as the text declares, they are descendants of the biblical Cain. This association of evil with characters who have close connections with pagan concepts is common in texts copied during Christian times. Grendel's mother is purposely defined as evil within the text, so that she can be properly dealt with by the hero portrayed as Beowulf. This portrayal, though, presents a complex problem, as the Germanic people would not have labeled their own goddesses as evil. Beowulf's killing of Grendel's mother is portrayed by the Christian author of the text in terms of a Christianized hero defeating old pagan adversaries, which again was a common device for Christian texts of the period. Many earth goddesses throughout history were portrayed mythically as evil, so that Christian heroes could override their power, allowing Christianity to become the dominant religious belief system. Christianity often used symbols of water or serpent-like creatures as representations of pagan beliefs needing to be eradicated, so that Christianity might thrive; some examples include Saint George defeating the dragon, Saint Columba scaring away the Loch Ness monster, or Saint Patrick driving the snakes out of Ireland. However, this epic poem is complex because Beowulf is not a Christian hero. The tale occurs before the coming of Christianity, so Beowulf is a Germanic warrior who should hold beliefs associated with his Germanic people, such as revering Earth Mothers. Therefore, the death of Grendel's mother does not solidify heroism for Beowulf in Germanic terms, because, though the author identifies Grendel's mother as evil, she does not appear all that evil when audiences see her in action within the poem, especially when considering her as a Germanic Earth Mother. She simply lives in the recesses of nature outside of the community, a place identified by Christians, but certainly not Germanic people, as pagan. Beowulf also seeks out Grendel's mother, even though it was he who was responsible for brutally killing her son, as she does not come for him or the Danes in the text. Also, Grendel's mother possesses the only object that can kill her—an ancient sword in her lair, so Beowulf, seemingly too easily, proceeds to murder her with it. Because of the nebulous circumstances resulting in Grendel's mother's death, Beowulf's heroism is questionable in Germanic terms. Additionally, because Beowulf, at the end of the epic, is merely killed by another mystical, and therefore pagan, creature—this time a dragon, and because his kingship did little to protect his people from a future filled with hardship, the overall meaning of the poem, and Beowulf's role within it, remains muddled between Germanic and Christian values.

As time progressed in Anglo-Saxon England, it was the invasion of the Normans in 1066 with William the Conqueror that further decreased the social positioning of Anglo-Saxon women. Though the Normans had Germanic connections as well, as William the Conqueror was the great-great-grandson of the Viking Rollo, the first ruler of Normandy, the Normans had long "adopted French customs and laws" (Clark 224), which positioned women as inferior. Thus, "the world of the Anglo-Norman[s] ... was very much a man's world" (Clark 226), as the Normans embraced "a culture steeped in chivalry; men were knights and women were to be protected" (Clark 234). In time, Norman law dominated, which squelched "any rights Anglo-Saxon women held. Anglo-Norman women thus lost the right to own land, as well as the other rights connected to landholding" (Clark 226). Also, "customs regarding marriage and the selection of a husband changed dramatically for [Anglo-Saxon] women after the Norman Conquest. [Anglo-Norman] women generally had little choice in the selection of a husband" (Clark 227). In addition, the "Normans were Christians without a heritage of female saints; women had never played a substantial role in their religious culture. Thus, it is likely that the coming of the Normans merely aggravated the growing [Anglo-Saxon] tendency within the church to vilify women" (Clark 234).

## Norse Regions

The Norse were also a Germanic group of people from Scandinavia. From the eighth to the eleventh century CE, Vikings expanded to many parts of Europe and left an important impact on the Early Medieval period. Norse communal structures were similar to the social structures of other Germanic peoples. As with Anglo-Saxon communities, Norse social structures were mostly patriarchal. Men in Norse society held most of the dominant positions as chieftains, kings, noblemen, government officials, hunters, traders, and seafarers; "only men could hold political and legal offices, and only men could speak at legal assemblies and testify as witnesses before a court" (McCoy). If Norse women were caught committing adultery, Norse men could legally kill them (McCoy). But, like Anglo-Saxon communities, Norse women did hold certain rights that held them above many other societies of the time. For example, Norse women could own property and obtain a divorce (Davis-Kimball, *Warrior*, 218). Also, Ibn Fadlan in his *Risala* (tenth century CE) recorded that Norse men and women were regarded as equal in "strength and physical fitness.... For recreation, women competed as equals with men in the sport of *glima*, a type of wrestling that is still popular today in Iceland" (Davis-Kimball, *Warrior*, 218). Most importantly, women could also hold prominent roles as seeresses, warriors, and queens within Norse society.

Norse religious beliefs were based off Germanic religious beliefs; Germanic mythology "is built upon that same foundation as that of the Scandinavians, and the principal deities are the same. Woden ... is the Odin of the North. Donar [is] the Scandinavian Thor.... Fro seems to have answered to Freyr" (Reaves 256). The Norse pantheon consists of the Aesir and the Vanir. The Aesir, with Odin as its primary leader, dominated the Norse pantheon, but some scholars believe that the Vanir represent an older pantheon of nature-based fertility deities, that perhaps may have been worshipped prior to Indo-European invasions. This seems fitting as the Earth Mother "Nerthus is most often identified as one of the Vanir" in Norse mythology (Reaves 62), as are the Norse deities associated with nature and fertility, Freyr and Freyja. Reaves also states that Frigg, Odin's wife, should be identified as one of the Vanir, as she is the mother of Freyr and Freyja (Reaves 278–9). Ellis Davidson notes that in fact all of the wives of the Aesir gods may have originally been goddesses of the Vanir (Ellis Davidson 125).

Norse mythology notes that a war between the Aesir and the Vanir led to the domination of the Aesir over the Vanir, but that the Aesir took members of the Vanir into their own pantheon to maintain some elements of their worship. Reaves explains that the Vanir represented "powerful natural forces: earth and sea, as well as the fertility and fecundity of the land and the loin. The Aesir could not hope to defeat such powers" (Reaves 282), so they opted to merge with the Vanir rather than try to annihilate them. Mythology often offers a story to explain the maintenance of older divine beings within a transformed ideology; thus, Norse mythology includes a narrative that explains the male-dominated Aesir pantheon taking over power from the earth goddesses of the Vanir. Still, as is often the case, despite the effort to introduce a more patriarchal religion, with Odin as all-father, maintenance of the reverence for powerful goddesses continued in Norse religion. Ellis Davidson explains that the "religion of the Vanir was bound to ... the turning of the earth ... whose blessing would help to bring the harvest.... There seems to have been many who worshipped them with fervor and devotion, finding their cult nearer, more rewarding and comforting than that of the sky god and the willful god of war" (Ellis Davidson 126).

The Norse goddess Frigg was the wife of Odin, and the Queen Mother of the Aesir. Though Frigg was married to Odin, she often was said to live separately from him in Fensalir, "surrounded by other goddesses or divine women," such as: Eira, who possessed the "knowledge of ... healing herbs"; Hlin, who "protected those in danger"; Syn, who defended the innocent; Sjofn and Lofn, who dealt with issues of love; Var, who "watched over vows and contracts," and Gefjon, "who cared for all women who chose to live ... without a husband" (Stone 350–1). Frigg, in Norse mythology, was also a goddess associated with the earth, which suggests her traditional role may have been that of an Earth Mother; Reaves supports this, stating that "Old Norse sources certainly do not lack evidence that Frigg is the Earth Mother" (Reaves 212). Frigg's role in the myth "The Death of Baldur" explicitly shows her in the role of Earth Mother.

In the myth, Baldur is presented as the son of Odin and Frigg. He is portrayed as a fertility god, and as such, he is associated with light and renewal, and all the elements of nature are said to love him. Part of this love that all environmental elements felt for Baldur might come from the fact that his death would unleash Ragnarök, which would cause all living things to perish, including the Norse divinities. Frigg, who was said to know all things, is shown within the myth as acting to try and stop her son's inevitable death by a course of action that only an Earth Mother could take. She appeals to every living creature upon the earth to make a promise not to ever harm her son, and thus avoid Baldur's death. Frigg's ability to converse with every organism and get all natural elements to follow her will shows her as a powerful Earth Mother, even when she is a demoted member of the Aesir. However, in the myth, Loki, the Norse trickster, finds the one element Frigg forgot to implore—mistletoe. Loki takes mistletoe back to Hodur, a blind god of the Aesir, and urges him to throw it at Baldur during a contest where all the gods take turns throwing items at Baldur, with the assumed knowledge that nothing can harm him. The mistletoe, though, kills Baldur instantly.

The myth continues to show another powerful earth goddess—the Norse goddess of the underworld—Hel. Hel in Norse mythology ruled the underworld realm of Nifhelheim, the land of the dead. She was mythically portrayed with half of her body being healthy and vibrant, while the other half was a rotting corpse. Stone states that Hel, or Hella, may be connected to the Germanic Goddess of the hearth Holla (Stone 355). The name Holla "is not only cognate with the term hell, but also with holy, heal … [and] whole…. It seems somewhat ironic that Holla, initially the Goddess of the hearth fire of each home, was later associated with the burning fires of Hell" (Stone 355), as Christians later assumed the name to identify their version of the afterlife for the sinful. The Norse goddess Hel in the myth of Baldur certainly holds tenets in line with the presentation of earth goddesses, as she aides the Earth Mother representative Frigg in trying to release Baldur from death. Hel is asked by Frigg to free Baldur from her domain, and Hel, like Frigg did, states that she can only do this if again all of the elements of nature are in support of this action. To show their support, all environmental elements must weep for Baldur. Often earth goddesses were portrayed as reigning over both fertility/renewal and death, since death is necessary for the continuation of life. Often both aspects of renewal and death were presented in one traditional goddess, such as the Celtic Morrígan, Greek Demeter, Egyptian Isis, etc. Though Frigg and Hel are presented as separate goddesses in Norse mythology, their united effort in this myth of death and renewal suggests that they may have once been combined under one conception of an Earth Mother. As shown in Slavic and Baltic mythology, goddesses who once held supreme roles often were divided into less powerful goddesses in an effort to contain the authority of the once supreme goddess; this division of power is necessary to allow the head of patriarchal pantheons, in this case Odin, to become the supreme divine being.

Loki, in playing the role of the trickster, who must initiate change into a stagnant world, disguises himself in this myth as a giantess and refuses to weep for Baldur, thus unleashing Ragnarök. It does not appear that Loki acts in a way to maintain patriarchal structure in this myth, as Loki does not supersede the power of the two earth goddesses Frigg and Hel; instead, Loki acts as an agent of their agenda, as he unleashes a natural path that is assuredly in line with myths involving Earth Mothers. Instead of viewing Frigg and Hel as failures in this myth for not being able to save or resurrect Baldur, their mythic message teaches audiences the lessons many myths of Earth Mothers convey—that the natural world needs death to be reborn. Reaves concurs, stating that "Baldur's death is likened to the spring thaw" (Reaves 228). Like spring following the dormancy of winter, Ragnarök revitalizes the earth precisely because it destroys the earth, as after the destruction of Ragnarök, a new earth is born, with Baldur resurrected. Myths of a male god resurrecting because of the help of earth goddesses are quite abundant within many global cultures, and it is most often the case that the revitalizing act can only be accomplished because of the supreme power of the earth goddesses.

The Vanir goddess, Freyja, is also an ancient goddess with Germanic roots. Before the Migration period, she is believed to have been connected to Frigg as the same Germanic Earth Mother. The golden boar of the Norse Freyja, and her Germanic counterpart, was identified by Tacitus "as the major emblem of the Mother of All Deities" (Stone 341). McCoy also states that Frigg and Freyja were ultimately the same Germanic goddess, pointing to the similarities of their name structures and mythic personalities (McCoy). However, in Norse mythology, Frigg became presented as Odin's dutiful wife, and Freyja was often portrayed as little more than a sex object, much like the Greek Aphrodite. Again, this separation of Frigg and Freyja from what was at one time likely a united Earth Mother served to assign them less powerful, patriarchally acceptable roles. It should also be noted that a large part of Norse mythology was recorded by a single Christian author, Snorri Sturluson, in the thirteenth century CE, well after the Norse had converted to Christianity, so mythic portrayals of Frigg and Freyja further project Christian concepts of the proper roles for women. Therefore, like many myths discussed so far in this chapter, myths of Frigg and Freyja, as well as most Norse myths, appear complex as they combine Germanic, Norse, and Christian elements.

As stated, the Norse goddess Freyja is often connected in Norse mythology to sex, lust, and fertility. She is often identified in fickle terms, as the mistress of Odin, and the goddess who has many other amorous affairs, including one with her brother Freyr. However, if one looks more deeply into the content of many Norse myths, and into the widespread reverence the people held for Freyja, one can see that Freyja possesses elements of her character that present her as quite powerful, as well as quite ancient, showing her connection to traditional Germanic concepts. Again, Freyja is a member of the Vanir, which immediately suggests that her worship precedes that of the Aesir. Also, like other fertility goddesses, Freyja is associated with death. Freyja serves in a role similar to Odin's, who selects the most valiant warriors to join him in Valhalla after their deaths, as she too rides the battlefields to choose among the fallen who will reside with her at her own domain, Folkvanger, which like Frigg's domain of Fensalir, is separate from that of Odin's. This power that matches Odin's also suggests Freyja's heightened role as more than a sex object. Freyja is also said to be the goddess of magic and prophecy. Her magical abilities are best represented in her necklace, the magic Brisingamen, which was able to produce bountiful gifts, making her a beloved provider of her people. She also possessed a falcon-feathered cloak that enabled her to metamorphose into a falcon and fly. Freyja also held the ability to prophesize the future, a gift she bestowed to the völvas, female seeresses in Norse religion. In this way, Freyja has been connected to shamanism. Her famous chariot pulled by cats speaks towards this, as cats were considered capable of leading völvas upon their spirit journeys, and Freyja was the preeminent example of how to partake on such journeys (Ellis Davidson 121).

Another important Norse goddess was Idun, who possessed the golden apples of immortality, which kept the deities in an eternally spring-like state of youth. Idun's most famous myth involves Loki stealing her and her golden apples, which resulted in the aging of the gods. This myth presents Idun as another earth goddess, in some ways similar to Frigg and Freyja, as Idun was only able to return to the Aesir after being transformed into a seed, showing her connection to the fertility of nature. Likewise, Sif was an earth goddess associated with the harvest and autumn, and Skaði was the goddess of winter. The Norns and the Disir are additional divine female figures in Norse mythology who carry great importance. The Norns are "fate figures" who are presented as spinning the fate of mortals. Some sources state that the Norns "are present at a child's birth, assisting the mother in labour and prophesying the child's fate" (Larrington 155). In addition, the Disir are "female fertility spirits, or female ancestors, to whom sacrifices were made. As spirits of the dead, they were associated both with Hel and with Freyja" (Larrington 155). Also, Valkyries, like Freyja, are Norse mythological women who choose from among half of the best of the fallen warriors to take to Odin's Valhalla to await Ragnarök. Young states that "Valkyries are brave, wise, and extraordinarily beautiful celestial women warriors.... They confer immortality on and are the reward of heroic warriors in the afterlife.... [Thus,] they are intermediaries between humans and gods, guides for the dead, and the means to rebirth" (Young 53). Some accounts state that the Valkyries will also fight at Ragnarök (Larrington 156).

The allowance for some high positions for women within Norse communities again arguably stems from the reverence for many powerful goddesses within Norse religion. For instance, the reverence for the divine Valkyries, and for such battle goddesses as Freyja, who in addition to being a fertility goddess was also depicted as a war goddess, allowed the Norse people to readily accept women serving as warriors/shield-maidens, as they had done in Germanic communities. Archeology supports the existence of shield-maidens, as Davis-Kimball states that a good number of what appears to be the graves of Norse women warriors have been uncovered throughout Scandinavia (Davis-Kimball, *Warrior*, 218). Many grave goods of females show that "they were entombed with an array of weapons," instead of the more typical household tools and jewelry associated with female graves, suggesting their warrior status (Davis-Kimball, *Warrior*, 218). In addition, völvas, who just like the goddess Freyja held prophetic and mystical abilities, thus excelling in seiðr/seid, were also highly revered within Norse communities. The existence of Norse völvas has been confirmed by archaeological finds. Many female graves have been unearthed "containing unusual and strange items not typically found in Viking graves. These include special sticks or wands, intoxicants and unusual collections of small objects, such as owl pellets" ("Seeresses"). The *Saga of Erik the Red* also confirms the role of the völva; the text describes a völva who practiced seiðr/seid on behalf of the whole settlement; she was "accompanied by an entourage of young girls—the spirit helpers" who helped awaken the spirits "the seeress need[ed] to make contact with" ("Seeresses"). It was believed that völvas "possessed such strong powers that even the leader of the gods [Odin] benefit[ed] from their help and advice" ("Seeresses"), as was shown in the "Völuspá" from the *Poetic Edda* (c. 1270 CE) when Odin found out from a völva about the coming destruction of the world in Ragnarök ("Seeresses"). It should not go unnoticed that this mythic portrayal of a völva shows a woman instructing the leader of the Norse pantheon about religious matters, as this is a rare occurrence for many mythological narratives worldwide. Many Norse women also held both royal and sacral duties that were often combined. For example, it seems likely that the only remains within the grandiose Oseberg ship burial, of two females, showed that one or perhaps both women were of royal standing and may have also served in shamanic roles, given the sacred objects that accompanied their burial, such as ornate staffs, cannabis seeds, luxurious attire, and numerous animal sacrifices (Gräslund 93). Similar burial remains of Norse females found at Valsgärde also included grave goods that perhaps indicate the royal and religious status of the interred women (Gräslund 93). For example, in "a tenth century woman's grave, a richly decorated animal's head carved from walrus ivory with eyes of carnelian was found, a unique object interpreted as the upper part of an animal-headed staff" (Graslund 93). Such an object indicates very high status, as well as "a magic/religious function" for the buried woman (Gräslund 93). Thus, again it is evident that Norse culture allowed women to hold prominent social positions directly because of the people's widespread respect for formidable Norse goddesses.

However, once Christianity was legalized in Scandinavia, as elsewhere, the reverence for Norse goddesses almost entirely disappeared. The worship of Freyja, in particular, bothered the Christian church, as Freyja had a large following. With the eradication of Norse goddesses, the societal role of women declined as well; though in Norse culture, this took time, as the Christian church initially had to compromise its position regarding the rights of Norse women (Mundal 238). In time though, Norse women could no longer divorce their husbands, as divorce was against Christian law (Mundal 238). In pre–Christian Norse society, if a wife was abused by her husband, it considerably injured the honor of her husband, and she could divorce, but this right disappeared under Christian law. In addition, when Christianity arrived into Scandinavia, the acceptance of women as warriors drastically declined, as the place of the woman was thought to be best suited within the household. Prestigious religious roles held by women, such as that of the völva, also disappeared. Mundal states that the female roles of "the völva, the soothsayer, and to a certain extent, that of doctor, or healer" were eradicated under Christian rule; in fact, "In Christian times, women who practiced these roles were criminalized" (Mundal 244). As was often the case with prominent religious positions for women in many cultures, the introduction of Christianity ostracized Norse women who served prominent religious roles as demonic; for example, "in the Middle Ages the Danish word for seeress ... meant witch" ("Seeresses"). Thus, the rituals of the völvas and other female religious officials began to be "connected with dangerous and harmful magic.... Laws were issued in the Middle Ages ... to suppress pagan rituals. Seid and all other magic was [thus] forbidden" ("Seeresses"). Mundal states that this "criminalization of traditional women's roles may ... have strengthened the new ideas that women were, by nature, more sinful than men" (Mundal 244). Mundal explains that in Christian times, "supposed differences in character, abilities, and intellectual competence between women and men were unequivocally tied to biological difference. The male represented the perfect human, the female was inferior to the male ... [because] in patriarchal Christianity, she was less 'Godlike' than the man" (Mundal 249).

Therefore, Norse, and other European, women began to be viewed as having a "weaker character" than men and were believed to be naturally sinful, so they were not permitted to serve in high religious roles within the new Christian faith (Mundal 249). These new Christian views of women greatly contrasted with traditional Norse conceptions of women. Mundal points to the creation myths of both cultures as evidence of the different views of women; in Christian culture, Eve was made from Adam's rib for merely his "pleasure and comfort"; whereas in the Norse creation myth, the first woman, Embla, was created simultaneously with the first man, Ask, and both first humans received "exactly the same characteristics from the gods" (Mundal 249). These patriarchal Christian concepts about women would transform the rights of Scandinavian women, and most women throughout Europe, for generations to come.

## Europe in the Middle Ages, Renaissance, and Beyond

As seen with Slavic, Baltic, Celtic, Germanic, and Norse cultures, it was Christianity that eventually eradicated the worship of pagan goddesses throughout Europe. This elimination of envisioning the sacred as feminine led to a sharp decline in the religious and social standing of women throughout much of Europe in the Middle Ages. Jeffreys explains that Christianity in Middle Age Europe gave "authority to traditional, patriarchal beliefs about the essentially subordinate nature of women and their naturally separate roles" (Jeffreys 5). During this period, a woman's place was "to be confined to the private world of the home and family" (Jeffreys 5); in addition, it was believed that "women should be obedient to their husbands [and] that women's sexuality should be modest and under the control of their menfolk" (Jeffreys 6). It was also believed, through the spread of Christian authority, "that women should not use contraception or abortion to limit their childbearing" (Jeffreys 6).

However, despite church efforts to eliminate pagan beliefs and practices in medieval Europe, many people still practiced rites that maintained at least a remnant of traditional goddess-oriented reverence. For example, pagan fertility rites, such as European spring festivals that honored the folkloric May Queen, showed a continued reverence for traditional fertility goddesses. In such spring festivals, the May Queen arrived in a cart or chariot drawn by oxen, and her partner or "consort" was the Green Man; in some regions of Europe, "the couple was 'married.' So May Day celebrated the Sacred Marriage and the ritual of the regeneration of life," as it had done in pagan times (Baring & Cashford 411). As with medieval

European springtime celebrations, in many cases, the people were permitted to maintain other pagan festivals through a new Christian lens. For instance, the Christian holiday of Easter reassigned springtime pagan fertility festivities, such as those associated to the goddess Eōstre, the Germanic goddess of spring, to the day that Christ was said to resurrect. The connection in themes, Christ resurrecting from the dead during the precise time of year in which European pagans venerated the regeneration of nature through the aid of earth goddesses, was thus not overlooked by the Christian church in choosing this time to celebrate Christ's resurrection. Similarly, pagan celebrations of winter solstice, such as Mothers' Night and Yule, were absorbed by the church into Christmas celebrations honoring the birth of Christ. MacLeod explains that the "Germanic ritual year began on the 25th of December ... [on] *Modranect* ('Mothers' Night') ... a pagan festival that ... acknowledged the Earth Mother in order to ensure the abundance in the upcoming spring season"; it, like pagan Yule festivities, "was absorbed into the celebrations associated with Christmas" (MacLeod 173). Likewise, the popularity of the Celtic Samhain, the day when it was believed that this world and the otherworld intersected, influenced the Christian church to allow the people to celebrate the festival as All Hallows' Eve with the church's corresponding holiday of All Saints' Day the following day. In addition, many Europeans celebrated Christian saints on days that were once attributed to pagan divine beings, such as Saint Brigid's feast day each February 1, which marked the start of the Celtic Imbolc.

Many European pagan goddesses, however, were not cast as saints. Instead, to best suit Christian ideology, myriad pagan goddesses became defined as evil within festival practices. For example, German and Scandinavian Christmastime celebrations still revered the mythic Wild Hunt but recast former goddesses in sinister roles. Before Christmas became a Christian holiday, pagan Yule celebrations had darker components, as fear accompanied the shortest days of the year during the winter solstice. The Wild Hunt featured either Woden/Odin, or the goddesses Frigg or Freyja, as leading a furious nighttime hunt, which assaulted any living creature who was unfortunate enough to be in their path. In pagan times, the hunt was viewed as a necessary means of sacrifice in winter to replenish the earth for springtime growth, as sacrifice to an earth goddess to ensure the revival of nature after winter was common. In Christian times, the celebrations associated with the Wild Hunt were continued, but the Christian church reassigned the meaning of the hunt as a night where those who have sinned would be driven from the earth by frightful characters who were reminiscent of former pagan gods and goddesses, such as a female huntress named Berchta, Perchta, etc. (Reaves 189). Characters like

Perchta/Berchta, who were almost certainly descended from Germanic earth goddesses, were most often demonized in medieval folklore. For example, on Perchten nacht in Bavaria and Austria, Frau Perchta/Bertcha often appeared in monstrous form, as the "Christmas belly-slitter," who punished the lazy by disemboweling them.

In addition, folklore and fairy tales provided an outlet to preserve, as well as further demote, the once powerful status of Europe's many traditional goddesses. Myriad European goddesses became portrayed as the characters of folktales and fairy tales because these stories were viewed by the Christian church as an acceptable outlet to place old pagan religious concepts precisely because they were clearly defined as fictional. For instance, Jacob Grimm, of the Brothers Grimm, recognized that the women found in many of the German folktales he recorded were a "remnant memory of a pre-Christian goddess" (Reaves 90). In fact, many female characters of folktales and fairy tales found all throughout Europe resemble traditional European goddesses, as they are capable of initiating mystical acts that only mythic goddesses could accomplish, such as "causing sudden and otherwise inexplicable illnesses in humans or animals, [controlling] changes in weather..., or affecting the fertility of fields and livestock" (Zipes 58). Sometimes these mystical folkloric women are cast in benevolent terms, such as the German folkloric figure of Mother Holle/Frau Holda, who causes snow to fall to earth, and is thus believed by many scholars to be a remnant of the Germanic Earth Mother (Reaves 89). In addition, Arthurian legends also portrayed characters who were representations of former pagan divine females, such as the Lady of the Lake and Morgan le Fay. Written by Christian authors hundreds of years after the events discussed in the texts, Arthurian legends attempted to capture accounts of Celtic beliefs during Christian conversion, though these accounts, as products of their time and culture, mostly offered a heavily inaccurate representation of Celtic beliefs. Despite this, some Arthurian women still held attributes that acknowledge a time when goddesses and priestesses were adored by the people. For example, in the Arthurian legend "Sir Gawain and the Green Knight," Morgan le Fay, who some scholars believe is a remnant of the Celtic goddess the Morrígan, controls all events of the tale and thus influences Arthur's court in a significant way.

However, most often the mystical attributes of many folktale and fairy tale women that connected them to traditional goddesses, like shape-shifting, concocting magical potions, and summoning changes in the environment, were the precise elements that defined them as evil. Folklore and fairy tale women, such as Snow White's mother in Grimm's first edition of "Snow White," the Slavic Baba Yaga, or the twelve witches of the Irish folktale the "Horned Women," were portrayed as evil precisely because they possessed mystical abilities that were used for sinister purposes. Thus, in the Middle Ages, and beyond, the portrayal of women in folktales and fairy tales as evil allowed audiences of the stories to view both former divine goddesses and current human women in a similar sinister light.

The presentation of women in folktales and fairy tales achieved the same result that mythology accomplished in its presentation of powerful goddesses—both served as examples for the social roles permitted to women. Powerful goddesses of mythology helped women achieve high social standing because they served as sacred figures in the religion of the people. Conversely, the powerful, but now defined as evil, women of folklore and fairy tale helped European society shape its expectations of women in negative ways. Thus, knowledgeable, independent, or otherwise deemed socially different European medieval women were often watched closely by communal authorities for their potential use of evil means. In this way, the atrocities of the witchcraft hunts and trials of Europe in the Middle Ages and the Renaissance (c. 1300–1699 CE) were condoned both by the Christian church and the people of many European communities. For instance, in 1487, two Dominican friars, Jakob Sprenger and Heinrich Kramer, wrote the *Malleus Maleifcarum* (*The Hammer of Witches*), which was a "Church-commissioned guide for eradicating witches" (Shlain 366). In large part, this text helped fuel the witchcraft frenzy that dominated Europe during this period, leading to approximately sixty thousand people, the vast majority of whom were women, being executed as witches (Shlain 365). There is no doubt that the European witch hunts intentionally targeted women; in fact, "witch hunting was *woman* hunting. A chronicler in 1600 wrote, 'Demons take no account of males ... and among a hundred witches, there's scarcely a man to be seen'" (Shlain 364). Women were accused of witchcraft for myriad reasons, such as marks on their bodies, being old or deemed a social outcast, or for being a healer/midwife. Particularly women who possessed knowledge of the healing arts, such as herbal remedies, were identified as possessing dark wisdom, though the practice of women serving as healers and midwives extended back to pagan times and was once viewed as essential. Using torture techniques, women were forced to admit to witchcraft, and then often murdered in horrendous fashion, which most often occurred by being burned alive, "since inquisitors believed this form of execution left a deeper impression on the public" (Shlain 368). Shlain states that "The tornado of gender terror and sadism that indiscriminately sucked women up into its vortex during the European witch craze has no parallel in human history" (Shlain 368), as many global civilizations believed in witches in this period, but Europeans were the only people to "persecute, torture, and burn them alive in large numbers" (Shlain 365).

Despite the drastic decline of the status of women in the European Middle Ages and Renaissance, some women were still able to achieve relatively high social standing. Jackson states that during the Middle Ages, some women were able to achieve a sense of power as "duchesses and rulers of their own smaller domains, such as Matilda of Tuscany, who sanctioned most papal acts" (Jackson 8). Also, in the Middle Ages, women were making some advancement in the arts, as evidenced in the emergence of such artists as En of Tavara, Hildegard of Bingen, Marie de France, and Christine de Pisan, as well as female patrons such as Eleanor of Aquitaine and Marie de Champagne (Allan, Bishop, & Phillips 65). In the Renaissance in Europe, women gained further seats of power, as "it was women who ruled Europe when their men marched off on the Crusades..., and it was women who ruled when their men did not return. They fought wars of conquest as well as of defense; they negotiated treaties, murdered enemies, arranged mergers, instituted reforms, squandered fortunes, inspired their countrymen—and had babies" (Jackson 8).

Like many pagan queens, some of the women who were able to elevate their power during the European Middle Ages and Renaissance did so because of a proclaimed connection to a goddess of antiquity. For example, some believed that prominent European figures such as Jacquetta of Luxembourg, and her daughter, Queen Elizabeth Woodville, and granddaughter, Queen Elizabeth of York, were descended from the water goddess Melusine, as the counts of Luxembourg were believed to have claimed descent to Melusine through their ancestor Siegfried of Luxembourg. One legend of the water goddess Melusine states that a count spotted a beautiful woman while he was in the wilderness hunting (Allan, Bishop, & Phillips 70). The count felt at once that he was in love with the woman, which fit Melusine's mystical skillset because she was said to be able to immediately make any man fall in love with her. The legend tells that Melusine agreed to marry the count only if he promised never to see her on the Sabbath day. The count agreed, so they were married; however, when they had children, all of the children were "disfigured in some way" (Allan, Bishop, & Phillips 70). As time progressed, the count questioned why his wife could not be seen on the Sabbath, so he sought her out on this day and was horrified to see that half of his wife's body had transformed into that of a serpent, or some renditions of the legend say a fish. Distraught, the count began to deeply distrust his wife, but he stayed with her despite this, until one day, their youngest son burned down the local monastery, killing over one hundred monks. The count could no longer contain his feelings that his wife was evil, so he approached her and accused her of this; she in turn left him forever.

It is significant that some medieval queens may have proclaimed a connection to pagan goddesses, as it supports the idea that women could attain some form of social power if the people remembered their reverence of traditional goddesses. However, in the European Middle Ages, with the church's hunt for witchcraft, proclaiming such a connection to a pagan divinity was highly risky. For example, Jacquetta of Luxembourg was put on trial for witchcraft, which eradicated much of her wealth and social standing and could have ended her life, though in 1470 she was exonerated of the charges (Hollman 280). Her daughter, Queen Elizabeth Woodville, was also accused of witchcraft in 1484 when the English parliament declared Richard III as king, instead of her own children with King Edward IV. Among the reasons listed for declaring Queen Elizabeth Woodville a witch was the belief "that Edward and Elizabeth's marriage only came about 'by Sorcerie [sic] and Wichecrafte [sic], committed by the said Elizabeth, and her Moder [sic] Jaquett [sic]'" (qtd. in Hollman, 280). Popular belief of the time, which led to her being accused of witchcraft, expressed concern that Edward IV was tricked into falling in love with Elizabeth Woodville because of the mystical skills she obtained from the goddess Melusine. In addition, many people believed that Elizabeth Woodville possessed the sinister ability to politically alter the events of her time as queen, as well as the events that followed the fall of the House of York to the House of Tudor. Had Jacquetta of Luxembourg or Elizabeth Woodville lived during the height of the witchcraft trials in 1560–1630, their perceived mystical power might have afforded them a more tragic end.

Also, to some extent, the power of Queen Elizabeth I in the Renaissance/Elizabethan period (1558–1603) was also gained and maintained due to her alignment with goddess imagery, as well as calculated connections with feminine religious symbols within Christianity. For instance, the imagery used in portraits of Elizabeth I were intentionally connected to images of classical divine virgins, such as the Greek Artemis, Astraea, and Athena ("Symbolism in Portraits"). Period poets, such as Sir Walter Raleigh, a favorite of the queen, "helped to promote the cult of Elizabeth as a moon goddess with a long poem he wrote during the late 1580s, 'The Ocean's Love to Cynthia' [otherwise known as Artemis], in which he compared Elizabeth to the Moon" Goddess ("Symbolism in Portraits"). The unusual circumstances that led to Queen Elizabeth I in obtaining her position of power during her reign was also strengthened by her calculated connection to the Christian Virgin Mary, as this association allowed subjects to view her not as an ordinary royal woman of her era, but as divinely ordained by a Christian symbol of female sacrality. As McClure and Wells explain, "An examination of literature, drama, and the visual arts reveals substantial use of imagery traditionally used to describe [Queen Elizabeth

I] as connected to the Virgin Mary.... This association ... provided Elizabethan propagandists and their audience with compelling ways to express, enhance, and justify the queen's authority" (McClure & Wells 38). The concept of the Virgin Mary allowed Christianity a means to embrace femininity as connected to divinity, as many scholars believe that the Virgin Mary holds connections with traditional goddesses, as she is believed to be the virgin mother of Christ, and was present at his birth, death, and rebirth—all tenets commonly associated with myriad pagan goddesses. Though, with the Virgin Mary, the distinction within Christian ideology that she is mortal and not divine qualifies her sacrality as being given to her only by means of the solely powerful God. Thus, the Virgin Mary, like the virgin Queen Elizabeth I, were both revered but were still mostly under the control of powerful patriarchal restrictrions.

In contemporary times, European women are still largely deemed unequal and are often discriminated against in social, political, and religious settings because of their sex. A good example still lies in the fact that women continue to be denied the right to serve as priests within the Catholic and Eastern Orthodox faiths. In addition, European women today also earn fifteen to twenty percent less than their male counterparts in the workforce; women continue to be underrepresented in politics and public life throughout Europe, and forty three percent of women in Europe "have experienced some form of ... abusive and/or controlling behaviour when in a relationship" (*EU External Action*). Therefore, though much has been done in contemporary times to secure equality for women throughout European countries, much more still needs to be done to elevate the status of women within Europe, so that they may increasingly serve as social, political, and religious leaders of their communities, just as they did in ancient times. Reimaging the sacred as feminine will arguably help this process.

## Chapter 2

# The Middle East

As discussed in Chapter 1, there is contention regarding the specific role of goddesses within European cultures, as much of this information only came about after written language was introduced in Europe, placing Christian influence into the myriad mythological texts of Europe. However, there is little doubt about the massive role that goddesses, even a central Mother Goddess, played in the regions within the Middle East. Lerner concurs, stating that "The strongest argument in favor of the religious significance of the ... [goddess] is the historical evidence ... derived from myths, rituals, and creation stories" found throughout the Middle East (Lerner 148). Therefore, ancient Anatolia, Mesopotamia, the Levant, and Persia serve as some of the best places in the world to see the significance, and subsequent demotion, of goddess-oriented beliefs.

## Anatolia

Ancient Anatolia, modern day Turkey, has produced evidence of goddess reverence that lasted in the region for over seven thousand years, "from the Neolithic sites of Hacilar and Çatal Hüyük to the time of St. Paul's confrontation with Goddess worship in the city of Ephesus" (Stone 183).

The early Neolithic site of Çatal Hüyük (7500–6500 BCE) in Anatolia is often central to the discussion of the role of goddesses within the Neolithic period. Burkert argues that "the most intriguing, most impressive and most unambiguous discoveries" in regard to goddesses are those from Çatal Hüyük (Burkert 12). Çatal Hüyük produced striking wall reliefs of what appears to be a "Great Goddess with uplifted arms and straddled legs"; Burkert interpreted this imagery as a "Great Goddess" who was the "birth-giving mother of the animals and of life itself" (Burkert 12). Çatal Hüyük also produced murals of women, possibly priestesses, partaking in what appears to be ceremonial activity while "wearing vulture masks and wings," indicating their high status (Stone 183). In addition, archeological excavations at Çatal Hüyük have unearthed myriad goddess figurines, such as were previously discussed in Chapter 1. One such figurine shows what appears to be a Mother Goddess or Great Goddess "enthroned, giving birth, flanked and supported by lions" (Campbell xviii). Another figurine shows a goddess "back-to-back with herself, in one aspect embracing an adult male and in the other, holding a child" (Campbell xviii). Many archeologists and scholars, such as Burkert and Campbell, believe that these images provide proof that the citizens of Çatal Hüyük worshipped a goddess as the head of their pantheon, and furthermore, that similar religious beliefs were maintained throughout Anatolia and other locations in the Middle East, as well as in places like Egypt, Crete, Greece, etc. In fact, Burkert argues that the evidence of supreme goddess reverence provides "overwhelmingly clear proof of religious continuity of more than five millennia" in these regions (Burkert 13).

Also, in Anatolia during the middle of the third millennium BCE, there are numerous goddess images from such sites as: Alaca Hüyük, Boghazköy, Beycesultan, Kültepe, Gavurkale, as well as from one of the most famous sites in connection to goddess worship—Ephesus (Stone 184). Records from this period indicate that the Anatolian goddess Hanna was the "Divine Ancestress" of the people, whereas the Goddess Kamrusepa "presided over magic and healing," and the divine sisters Istustaya and Papaya "spun the threads of the future" (Stone 195). Also, not far from Ephesus was an ancient shrine to the Goddess Beycesultan; this shrine held "double altars adorned with sacred horns," which was a Neolithic symbol popularly used for goddess worship even as far as the Greek island of Crete (Stone 204).

However, as occurred throughout Europe, descendants of Proto-Indo-European speakers began to move into Anatolia as early as 3000 BCE, and again their presence revised the existing beliefs of the residing Hattian populations in the region in regard to goddess worship. By 2300–1700 BCE, more Indo-European tribes, the "most powerful" of which were the Hittites, also entered Anatolia in a "devastating series of invasions," conquering Anatolia in about 1740 BCE (Baring & Cashford 397). The Hittites "established themselves as the ruling caste" and left "a trail of devastation" in the region; "in Anatolia alone some 300 cities were sacked and burned, among them Troy (c. 2300 BC[E])" (Baring & Cashford 156). With the arrival of the new Hittite ideology, the existing Hattian beliefs of female divinities were altered. For example, the existing Hattian inhabitants of Anatolia "worshipped a sun-goddess, Estan" (Lerner 157). The Hittites synthesized "elements of both cultures, worship[ing] a sun-god, Istanu, who was a revised version of the sun-goddess Estan, now changed to a male. This male god was, in the New Hittite Empire, worshipped as 'father' and 'king'" (Lerner 157). The traditional Hattian goddess shrines were in time taken over by Hittite male clergy (Stone 185). In addition, Hattian beliefs originally embraced matrilineal customs, but a "transition from matrilineal kinship and royal succession to patrilineal kinship and succession" occurred with the Hittites attaining leadership over the Hattians (Lerner 154). Thus, Hattian customs were slowly eradicated over a period of about three hundred years (Lerner 157).

The Hittite myth of Telepinu displays an example of seemingly new Indo-European concepts of male divinity along with what appears to be older concepts of powerful female divinities. In this myth, the Hittite fertility god, Telepinu, is portrayed as shutting himself up in a cave, which causes the earth to enter into a severe drought. This drought threatens the lives of all the beings of earth, even the gods. The supreme storm god, Taru, tries to lure Telepinu out of his cave, but Taru is unsuccessful. Taru needs the help of the goddess, Nintu, the mother of the gods, to get Telepinu out of the cave, so he can restore fertility to the environment. Nintu knows that the only way to lure Telepinu from his cave is to have a bee sting him. Nintu's understanding that a bee can reinstate fertility shows her in the role of a possible Mother Goddess. The fact that Taru needs Nintu to return the earth to a fertile state places the goddess Nintu in a distinguished role and suggests that she once served a more prominent role within preexisting belief systems in Anatolia. Within the myth, Taru and all of the other male gods are helpless with the state of affairs, which of course spells out life or death for all living beings. However, the goddess Nintu tells Telepinu, "'Let what has been deprived be restored'" (Rosenberg 180)! Due to the efforts of Nintu, Telepinu's anger disappears, and fertility is restored. Thus, it is Nintu, in the role of what appears to be a Mother Goddess, who is the only one capable of restoring natural order after a season of dormancy. This myth, which was prized by the Hittites, as it was enacted annually in Anatolia, shows that Nintu still held a position of prominence in Hittite culture, suggesting that her traditional role, which might have once been elevated as a supreme Mother Goddess, was not eradicated solely because of Indo-European influence at this early period.

In the twelfth century BCE, the Hittite Empire fell, allowing groups of other Indo-Europeans, referred to as the "Sea People" to invade Anatolia. Groups coming from Thrace, in present day Bulgaria, entered Phrygia, and in time became known as the Phrygians. Though Phrygia was overrun by Indo-Europeans, it was one of the most important locations of goddess worship within the ancient world, especially because of its worship of Cybele, the Mother Goddess, and her son-lover Attis (Baring &

Cashford 399). It appears that the worship of Cybele as a Mother Goddess had very ancient origins within Anatolia, extending back to the goddesses depicted at Çatal Höyük, as Cybele was often referenced in a similar fashion to those supreme goddesses. In fact, in Phrygia the worship of Cybele "hardly changed throughout [an] ... immense period of time," from Neolithic times to the Iron Age (Baring & Cashford 393). Again, this maintenance of Mother Goddess worship among Indo-European groups reminds one not to assume that Indo-Europeans strictly eradicated the worship of prominent goddesses.

The reverence of the Phrygian Mother Goddess, Cybele, is extremely well known because of her widespread and lasting worship, as both the Greeks and Romans later adopted her into their own pantheons referring to her as the "Mother of the gods." In fact, Baring and Cashford state that statues of Cybele have been discovered as "far away as Ukraine, the Crimea, Romania and Bulgaria" (Baring & Cashford 399). Cybele was the "Lady of Ida" or the "Goddess of the Mountain"; she was also the "guardian of the dead and goddess of fertility and wild life" (Baring & Cashford 393). Cybele was often depicted seated on a throne between two lions, showing her to be a supremely powerful Mother Goddess.

A mythic narrative from Greece provides perhaps a remnant of Cybele's role in Anatolia as a Mother Goddess. It is said in some versions of this Greek myth that a man named Attis was born from a union between his mother and an almond tree. Upon seeing Attis, the goddess Cybele was said to fall in love with him, though she was his grandmother, or mother in some versions of the myth. As Attis grew, he did not return the affection of Cybele, so Cybele drove him insane, which caused him to castrate himself and later die, metamorphosing upon death into a flower. This myth discusses what is referred to in Mythic Studies as the "male consort" within Neolithic Mother Goddess mythology. Attis's castration and subsequent death illustrates the necessity of death for all mortals, as this is what the male consort is meant to represent in the myths where they appear with a Mother Goddess. The agricultural imagery of Attis's castration, which he did with a harvesting sickle, showed Neolithic audiences that, just as with the harvest, Attis's severed member, which represents fertility, and his actual body upon death, served as symbolic seeds and fertilizer for the continuation of life. Thus, myths of the male consort show that all mortals must make similar sacrifices. Cybele's role within this myth is to oversee and assure the continual processes of life, which is the same role that most Mother Goddesses within Neolithic myths of the male consort must perform.

In time, Greek colonists replaced the worship of Cybele at the shrine of Ephesus with their own goddess Artemis, the goddess of the wilderness and the hunt. However, in Ephesus, Artemis appeared, like Cybele, as a Mother Goddess, and in fact, Artemis may have at one time in Greek religion been conceived of as a Mother Goddess, which is discussed in the next chapter. Artemis's shrine at Ephesus became one of the most important sites of goddess worship in the ancient world; in fact, in ancient times it was one of the Seven Wonders of the World. Later, the Romans also held the shrine of Ephesus in extremely high regard. The Romans also worshipped Cybele as the "Mother of the gods." In addition, the Christian Virgin Mary also chose Ephesus to spend her remaining years after the death of Jesus.

## Mesopotamia

Ancient Mesopotamia included present-day Iraq and parts of Turkey, Syria, and Iran. It housed such civilizations as the Sumerians (c. 2900–2350 BCE and 2112–2004 BCE), Babylonians (c. 1900–539 BCE), and Assyrians (c. 1900–612 BCE). Like Anatolia, Mesopotamia also offers a rich discussion of the progression of goddess reverence.

Mesopotamia is often referred to as the cradle of civilization because the Neolithic Revolution is said to have occurred at this favorable location between the Euphrates River and the Tigris River as far back as 10,000 BCE. Archeological evidence has been found from this region's Neolithic period that shows again female figurines that were produced by the Halaf and Samarra cultures, suggesting that goddesses were a substantial part of the religious beliefs of this region.

The Sumerians were a nomadic people who settled in the region of Mesopotamia because of its bountiful resources. The Sumerians were thought to have been influenced by the cultures of the existing populations in the area. After thousands of years of goddess worship among cultures in the region, such as with the Halaf and Samarra cultures, the Sumerians also maintained many similar views (Stone 234). The Sumerians established firm rule throughout Mesopotamia by the fourth millennium BCE and continued to rule through the third millennium BCE, developing extensive city-states, such as Uruk, Lagash, and Eridu, and producing the writing system of cuneiform in about 3200 BCE, allowing the sacred myths portraying goddesses to finally emerge.

Reverence for goddess worship in greater Sumer is clearly evidenced; Shlain concurs, stating that in the Sumerian pantheon, "goddesses possessed considerable power" (Shlain 47). Even the concept of a supreme goddess is evident among the Sumerians, "as Creator of heaven and earth" (Stone 232). The Sumerians venerated the Great Goddess Nammu, who represented the primordial element of water (Shlain 47). Stone states that the goddess Nammu is possibly "the earliest recorded name of a universe-creating deity so far discovered anywhere on earth" (Stone 236). Nammu is described on extremely ancient fragments as the "Mother of all Deities"; she was said to have also initiated the creation of the first human beings by designating the task to her divine daughter Ninmah (Stone 236). The goddess Ninmah became known as Ninhursag and was also revered as a Mother Goddess among the Sumerians. Ninhursag is often depicted as the goddess who resides over the birth of animals and humans alike. The goddess Nina/Nana also is portrayed as a very ancient Mother Goddess in Sumer; she is often presented as a "serpent-tailed or fish-tailed" goddess who resides in the primordial sea (Stone 237). In addition, Ninlil was the goddesses of grain, and as such, she was highly revered for maintaining the survival of the people. The goddess Nidaba was attributed as "the tutelary deity of writing, preceding any male deities to whom this important cultural contribution was later credited" (Stone 240). Nidaba was also described as a serpent or a woman with the tail of a serpent.

Inanna was the most well-known goddess among the Sumerians; in fact, her worship endured for over four thousand years (Baring & Cashford 192). Inanna was the goddess of fertility, love, war, and political authority. Her title was Queen of Heaven and Earth, showing her supreme importance (Baring & Cashford 192), as Inanna maintained "full power of judgement" over the "law of heaven and earth" (Stone 242). Early on, Inanna, like the preceding Nina/Nana, was symbolized with serpent imagery, as her name was often "accompanied by a serpent coiling about a staff" (Stone 241), though this imagery would later change.

Myths of the goddess Inanna present her as a prime example of a Neolithic earth goddess. Mythically, Inanna was said to marry the mortal Dumuzi. Though first resistant to marry a mortal, as she was divine, Inanna is portrayed as needing to unite with Dumuzi to attain continued fertility of the land. Therefore, their sexual union is explicitly described in such a way that makes it clear that their act solidifies the success of the agricultural harvest because Inanna's body is described as the earth itself: "Inanna spoke: 'Who will plow my vulva?/ Who will plow my high field?/ Who will plow my wet ground?.'...Dumuzi replied: 'Great Lady.... I, Dumuzi the King, will plow your vulva'" (qtd. in Wolkstein & Kramer). This myth shows the importance of the ritual of the Sacred Marriage, as was discussed within Celtic culture in Chapter 1, as Inanna's and Dumuzi's sexual union solidifies the continued propagation of the harvest, thus securing the survival of all. The ritualized enactment of the Sacred Marriage between Inanna, played by a priestess of Inanna, and Dumuzi, played by the current Sumerian king, took place annually during the spring equinox to assure a successful agricultural season (Shlain 49). Sumerian kings "spoke of themselves as Dumuzi" to show that they had been honored by Inanna (Stone 245). Frankel states that according to the principle of the Sacred Marriage "the king could only rule as the accepted spouse of the goddess," and in so doing, the king pledged himself to the land (Frankel 110). This process, such as was discussed within Celtic culture, made it "rare for kings to hold office for life, as they were replaced each time the land (the goddess), needed to be revitalized, which was often thought of as an annual process" (Frankel 110). Again, bestowing the power to authorize a king's rulership to a goddess is an important point of consideration, as it shows the extremely high value of Inanna, and thus her priestesses, within Sumerian culture.

The myth of Inanna and Dumuzi outlines again the role of the earth goddess's male consort. As seen with the Phrygian Attis, the male consort after sexual union with the earth goddess succumbs to death, as all mortals eventually do. It is thus Dumuzi's role, as it is the duty of other representations of mythic male consorts, even kings, to fertilize the earth through sexual activity with an earth goddess, as well as through their deaths. The Sumerian myth "Inanna's Descent into the Underworld," which later is recounted as an Akkadian and Babylonian myth, shows Inanna, and later her Akkadian/Babylonian variant Ishtar, aiding in the death of Dumuzi, who will later become Tammuz in Akkadian and Babylonian ideology. In this myth, Inanna/Ishtar journeys into the land of death to test if her authority as a goddess of fertility and life will outweigh the supremacy of her sister Ereshkigal, as ruler of the underworld. Inanna/Ishtar knocks on the gate of the underworld demanding entrance. At this early stage of the myth, her tone suggests that she believes she is superior to Ereshkigal; "If thou openest not the gate to let me enter,/ I will break the door, I will wrench the lock,/ I will bring up the dead to eat the living'" (qtd. in Jastrow). The myth shows that Inanna/Ishtar is allowed into the underworld, but her egotism is immediately thwarted when she is systematically stripped of everything that connects her to her divine status. Finally, after Inanna/Ishtar has witnessed the horrors of the underworld, she is forced to stand before her sister totally demeaned. Ereshkigal then shows her authority over the underworld by giving Inanna/Ishtar every disease mortals must suffer with, and then hanging Inanna's/Ishtar's depleted body from a meat hook, as she talks to her about the mortal experience of death. The myth makes it clear that Inanna/Ishtar is powerful in her role as a fertility goddess, but it shows that her sister, Ereshkigal, is just as strong in her role as a goddess of death. The pairing of Inanna/Ishtar and Ereshkigal together encapsulates the traditional role of many earth goddesses, as was seen with the Norse pairing of Frigg and Hel, as they are often identified as both the givers of life and the ones responsible for taking life away. The myth concludes with Inanna/Ishtar giving her lover, the mortal Dumuzi/Tammuz, up for sacrifice, causing him to die and stay in Ereshkigal's realm, so that Inanna/Ishtar can go back to the land of the living and repair it to its former fecundity, as everything on earth stopped reproducing without her presence. Therefore, the myth makes it clear that Dumuzi's/Tammuz's sexual virility, which fertilized Inanna as an earth goddess, as well as his physical death helped to produce a successful harvest for the people, ensuring their survival.

Again, this myth, and other myths of Mother Goddesses/earth goddesses and male consorts, articulates for audiences the necessity of death for all living beings, which can make such myths appear harsh. Armstrong explains that:

> Neolithic myths continued to force people to face up to the reality of death. They were not pastoral idylls, and the Mother Goddess was not a gentle, consoling deity, because agriculture was not experienced as a peaceful, contemplative occupation. It was a constant battle, a desperate struggle, against sterility, drought, famine and the violent forces of nature.... Food is produced only by a constant warfare against the sacred forces of death and destruction. The seed has to go down into the earth and die in order to bring forth its fruit, and its death is painful and traumatic [Armstrong 46–7].

However, these myths of a male consort and a Mother Goddess/earth goddess provide audiences the assurance that within nature, life does not end with death, as these myths often show that the mortal male consort is reincarnated or resurrected. This is certainly true in this myth, as Inanna/Ishtar shows that Dumuzi/Tammuz went into the earth, described as the underworld, to renew the cycle of life, as mythically he was said to resurrect each year with the coming of spring, though it was not Dumuzi/Tammuz personally, but another male consort chosen to represent him in annual enactments of the myth. This symbolism of natural reincarnation or resurrection thus gives audiences a message that their respective Mother Goddess/earth goddess will similarly conduct this process for them as well.

Because of the deep reverence the Sumerians held for Nammu, Nina/Nana, Inanna/Ishtar, Ereshkigal, and other goddesses, the social role for women in the early periods of Sumerian culture was high. Sumerian women were able to own property and take part in business endeavors with their spouses. Archeological evidence discovered in royal tombs in Ur shows that "ruling queens shared in the status, power, wealth, and ascription to divinity with kings. They tell us of the wealth and high status of some women at the Sumerian courts, of their varied craft skills, [and] their obvious economic privilege" (Lerner 61). Sumerian women could also hold important social and religious roles in the community by serving in such positions as physicians and priestesses. For instance, the eldest daughter of wealthy families would often become a high priestess (Nemet-Nejat 99). This revered position of high priestess maintained the Sacred Marriage rites discussed earlier, and so carried tremendous power in both religious and political affairs.

For centuries, the Sumerians lived south of the Semitic-speaking people of Akkad, Babylon, etc., who initially accepted the supremacy of their neighbors, but in time, "a long struggle for power" developed (Baring & Cashford 180). The Akkadians defeated the Sumerians with Sargon the Great and maintained power throughout the twenty-fourth to twenty-second centuries BCE. The Akkadians connected their Semitic beliefs with the practices of the Sumerians, which caused many representations of goddesses, especially of the concept of a supreme goddess to be demoted. Haarmann states that the "power of the Sumerian female divinities was crippled in the transition process to Akkadian civilization" (Haarmann 171). The Sumerian Mother Goddess, for example, was "replaced from the head of the pantheon of gods," giving "way to a male god, usually the god of wind and air or the god of thunder, who more and more, as time [progressed, came] to resemble an earthly king" (Lerner 152). Likewise, former Sumerian earth goddesses began to "appear as daughters and wives of ... gods" (Lerner 152), just as occurred within many European cultures. Thus, the god Enki, god of wisdom, fertility, and fresh water, replaced the power of Ninhursag, who, as stated, was formerly a Sumerian Mother Goddess and one of the most important and oldest goddesses of the region, by marrying her, so that in later myths, she appeared merely as the diminished consort of Enki (Nemet-Nejat 102–3). In addition, mythic narratives of the period also show the god of wind and air, Enlil, raping Ninlil, the goddess of grain, before marrying her in order to secure some of her power, as there is evidence to suggest that Ninlil's power might have "preceded the importance of Enlil in Nippur" (Stone 234). Scenes of a male god raping a goddess are common in mythology, such as when the Greek Zeus raped Hera in order to strip her of her power. This type of graphic imagery in mythology was likely created by patriarchal ruling systems to send a message to audiences that the male god, in overpowering the goddess, has secured the right to rule over her. This violent mythology was also used to justify harmful abuse towards women as socially inferior beings, as within Mesopotamia, and Greece for that matter, the rights of women drastically decreased once this type of patriarchal mythology began to appear.

Into Akkadian rule, women continued to maintain high social roles for a time. Nemet-Nejat states that under Akkadian rule, "the earliest known ... [high] priestess was Enkheduanna, the daughter of the Semitic

King Sargon (c. 2300 BCE)," and in fact, to "ensure religious legitimacy for his rule, Sargon was the first high king in a long line of monarchs to appoint his daughter as high priestess of the moon god, Nanna, at Ur" (Nemet-Nejat 99–100). Lerner states that "Since Enkheduanna was also a lifelong cultic devotee of the Sumerian goddess Inanna, her appointment symbolized the fusion of Inanna with the Akkadian goddess Ishtar" (Lerner 67). However, this fusion of respect for Sumer's goddesses, and in turn the rights of women, eventually came to an end as the Akkadians continued to revise Sumerian beliefs regarding goddess worship throughout the centuries. Nemet-Nejat elaborates, "In the third millennium BCE many female goddesses held important positions, reflecting the high position of women in the Sumerian city. [But] by the second millennium BCE the gods reflected a society in which men were prominent" (Nemet-Nejat 112). Thus, "the position of goddesses in relation to gods and of women in relation to men [was] downgraded" under Akkadian rule (Baring & Cashford 182). Baring and Cashford explain that after 2300 BCE, the "status of women in Sumerian society deteriorated" (Baring & Cashford 159). In Lagash, in about 2350 BCE, because of social pressure brought about by the Akkadians, who were soon to conquer Lagash, documents by Lagash's ruler, King Urukagina, identify some of the first legal rights for citizens that demonstrate the once positive role for women, and then the decline of this role; "'Women of former times each married two men, but women of today have been made to give up this crime.' The edict continues to state that women committing this 'crime' in Urakagina's time were stoned with stones inscribed with the evil intent. Elsewhere, the edict states that 'if a woman speaks ... disrespect-fully [sic] to a man, that woman's mouth is crushed with a fired brick'" (Lerner 62–3).

By 1900 BCE, the Semitic-speaking Amorites took control of much of Mesopotamia, and it was during this time that the Amorite King Hammurabi created the Babylonian Empire. The culture and myths from this period show a further devaluation of both the portrayal of goddesses and the overall social rights of women. For example, the influx of Semitic patriarchy under Akkadian and Babylonian rule demoted the power of the goddess Inanna. When Inanna merged with the Akkadian and later Babylonian goddess Ishtar, she became primarily associated with death and destruction, and mostly lost her life-affirming aspects of the former Inanna, as an earth goddess of life and fertility. The Sumerian classic text, the *Epic of Gilgamesh* (2150–1400 BCE), later recorded and revised by the Akkadians and Babylonians, displays the shifting role of Inanna into Ishtar. Campbell states that the *Epic of Gilgamesh* certainly presents Ishtar in a negative light (Campbell xxiii). In the text, Gilgamesh, a Sumerian king of Uruk, is depicted as needing to undergo a revision, as he is deemed to be an unjust king by his people. Gilgamesh is sent an animalistic companion, named Enkidu, by the Mother Goddess Ninhursag, to teach him what matters most in life. The epic shows Gilgamesh and Enkidu partaking on a quest into Ishtar's sacred Cedar Forest. Gilgamesh and Enkidu proceed to annihilate the trees of Ishtar's Cedar Forest, which draws the attention of the guardian of the forest—the giant Humbaba. Together, Gilgamesh and Enkidu kill Humbaba, which summons Ishtar. Upon seeing Gilgamesh, Ishtar makes it clear to Gilgamesh that she would like to marry him. However, Gilgamesh wants nothing to do with what is supposed to be the most revered of Sumerian goddesses because, as Gilgamesh states, all of Ishtar's mortal husbands, like Tammuz (Sumerian Dumuzi), can only expect death after such a union. The fact that Gilgamesh utterly refuses Ishtar signals a demotion in her value from previous ideology. In retaliation for destroying her Cedar Forest, killing her guardian Humbaba, and shunning her romantic advances, Ishtar sends the Bull of Heaven to wreak havoc upon Gilgamesh's city of Uruk. Gilgamesh and Enkidu fight and eventually kill the Bull of Heaven, ripping it limb from limb. Further insulting Ishtar within the myth, Enkidu throws part of the Bull of Heaven's corpse at her, utterly disregarding her authority. The masculine imagery of a desecrated bull being thrust at a once supremely powerful goddess in a purposefully violent manner attests to the fact that Akkadian and Babylonian cultural shifts were certainly in place regarding the role of Inanna/Ishtar, as often the symbol of the bull represented the male consorts' relationship with a Mother Goddess/earth goddess.

Cauvin states that in this period of intercultural contact among the Sumerians, Akkadians, and Babylonians, "a virile male figure whose principle significance ... explicitly concerned war" (Cauvin 126) began to appear in the mythology of the region. This strong male figure represented a "deep concern with virility which prefigures what will be the promotion into mythology of gods and heroes in combat" (Cauvin 126). Thus, the role of males within the mythology of this region began to shift. Instead of serving only as a personification of a necessary sacrifice to a Mother Goddess/earth goddess, as Dumuzi/Tammuz and other male consorts did, mythic male characters began to be displayed in myths as active and exceedingly capable, especially in feats associated with warfare (Cauvin 125). The cultural beliefs that resulted from mythic males finding autonomy and adventure, instead of merely sacrifice, began to send a message to audiences that stressed the importance of an individual human life, as opposed to a never-ending system of birth, death, and rebirth that was central to traditional belief systems involving Mother Goddesses and earth goddesses. Thus, an ideological shift occurred in cultural values that ultimately demoted the role of Mother Goddesses and earth goddesses in order to elevate the role of male divinities and mythic male heroes, such as is evident in the *Epic of Gilgamesh*. However, without the promise of ever-lasting life through nature's cycles, that was inherent in goddess ideology, a fear of death began to emerge in this era; "A new attitude to death appeared about 2500 BC[E]: death came to be regarded as the absolute end and opposite of life.... Death became something final, terrifying, remorseless and without the promise of rebirth" (Baring & Cashford 159).

In addition, during this period when the importance of a singular human life became more valued than the messages of goddesses who served as representatives of nature, the environment began to be viewed in large part as something that could be altered or tamed by human beings, again primarily men. Therefore, the mythology of Mesopotamia shifted to present tales where the sacrifice of the mythic male consort, for example, was no longer necessary for the continuation of nature's cycles. And, Mother Goddesses and earth goddesses, who required the death of male consorts, began to be cast in a light that showed them as monstrous for their appetite for sacrifice. The result was the creation of myriad myths that explained this transition of humankind's perceived self-importance and superiority over nature with the presentation of mythic males who conquered formidable, even monstrous, female opponents who served as mythical characterizations of once revered earth goddesses. Leeming and Page explain that "female power was no longer seen primarily as a nurturing force but as an aberration from the frightening depths, one that must be conquered or destroyed" (Leeming & Page, *God*, 123). This is why Gilgamesh in *The Epic of Gilgamesh* refuses to marry Ishtar; this myth, captured in a time of transition within Mesopotamia, sends a new message that Ishtar's requirement, as an earth goddess, for the sacrifice of male consorts is an abhorrent demand that only a monstrous goddess would require, so the new mythic male, Gilgamesh, defeats the old goddess-oriented traditions when he shuns Ishtar.

The role of goddesses within Mesopotamia would only become further denigrated under continued Babylonian rule. As discussed, mythology presented a prime avenue for religious authorities to present ideological changes they deemed beneficial to their purpose; "For millennia one of the most important ... instruments of socialization was the 'spiritual education' carried out by the ancient priesthoods.... Their most powerful weapons were the 'sacred' stories, rituals, and priestly edicts through which they systematically inculcated in peoples' minds the fear of terrible, remote, and 'inscrutable' deities" (Eisler 84). Thus, with enough organized indoctrination on the part of political and religious authorities in Mesopotamia, the people adopted new beliefs that eventually fully contrasted with the beliefs of their ancestors regarding the worship of goddesses.

In about 1100 BCE, the "relationship of societal change and changes in theogony become even more explicit" within Mesopotamia (Lerner 153). The Babylonian myth, the *Enuma Elish*, serves as an ideal example of the extent to which demoting once powerful goddesses had become a priority in this period. The *Enuma Elish* stands as one of the best mythic examples of a powerful male god stealing the authority of a traditional Mother Goddess. The myth displays the Mother Goddess Tiamet, a massive serpent-like goddess who resided in the primordial sea, as being killed off by her son/grandson Marduk in a decisively brutal manner, so that Marduk could declare his own patriarchal supremacy. The *Enuma Elish* presents Apsu, the ocean, and Tiamat, primordial water, as creating the earth. In time, their offspring, the lesser divine beings of the pantheon, eventually wanted to take over their parents' supremacy. The lesser divinities easily killed their father Apsu, but they found that they did not have what it took to kill their mother Tiamet. Marduk, alone, showed his siblings that he could slay Tiamet when he threw a net over her enormous body; he then caused the wind to enter into her, which made her body explode. Marduk then "cut her womb" and "straddle[d] the carcass" (Sproul 101). In seeing this display, the lesser gods unanimously gave the superior seat of power within their reorganized pantheon to Marduk.

Baring and Cashford state that the Mesopotamian Iron Age, which began about 1250 BCE, witnessed "the completion of the process begun in the Bronze Age, in which numinosity was transferred from the Mother Goddess to the Father God," as outlined in the *Enuma Elish*, which became the first recorded myth to show the replacement of a Mother Goddess who generated "creation as part of herself by a god who 'makes' creation as something separate from himself" (Baring & Cashford 273). This type of myth, where a male god, usually younger and initially inferior, brutally dominates a once formidable goddess, becomes a common device in many regions of the world during the Iron Age to instruct people about changes in religious and political ideology. The legacy of the *Enuma Elish* in Mesopotamia was long lasting, as it paved the way for similar myths to serve as a springboard for casting traditional goddesses aside by the violent efforts of younger males. Baring and Cashford explain that the many myths from the Iron Age that showcase "a sky or sun god, or male hero, conquer[ing] a great serpent or dragon can be traced to this Babylonian epic, in which humanity was created from the blood of a sacrificed god and no longer from the womb or a primordial goddess. Its influence can be followed through Hittite, Persian, Canaanite, Hebrew, Greek and Roman mythology" (Baring & Cashford 274). The *Enuma Elish* also solidified a message of mankind's control over the natural environment that would dominate mythology in many regions for centuries to come. Perhaps the most lasting legacy was how myths like the *Enuma Elish,* which delivered superior power to a sole male god, paved the way for the dominance of monotheism; as Baring and Cashford state, it is "Marduk's desire for his word alone to prevail [that] would find its historical legacy in Yahweh's words: 'I am the first and I am the last; and beside me there is no God' (Isa. 44:6)" (Baring & Cashford 283).

The patriarchal belief systems of the Babylonians further transformed existing cultural views on women in the region (Lerner 66). Under Babylonian rule, the Code of Hammurabi made the demoted social role of women quite evident: male kin held "the right of disposal over their female relatives," so a "man's wife and children [were considered] part of his property to be disposed of as such" (Lerner 90). The codes of law that have been preserved from Mesopotamia: the Codex Hammurabi, the Middle Assyrian Laws, the Hittite Laws, as well as later biblical law, made clear the decreasing role of women within the region (Lerner 103). These codes of law, among others, placed "a great deal of attention ... on the legal regulation of sexual behavior" for women (Lerner 103–4). In these codes of law, the "father's authority over his ... [daughter] was unlimited.... The main value to a family in having daughters was their potential as brides" (Lerner 106). The right of the husband over his wife was also clearly stated, as a "man could divorce his wife or reduce her to the status of a slave and marry a second wife, if she 'persists in behaving herself foolishly wasting her house and belittling her husband'" (Lerner 113–4). In addition, "the wife owed absolute fidelity to her husband," with the penalty for adultery often resulting in death (Lerner 115). Lerner states that even "the accusation of adultery could prove fatal"; if the community accused a woman of adultery, she would have "to 'leap into the river for her husband.' The river-god would then decide on her guilt or innocence" (Lerner 115). Furthermore, "The various laws against rape all incorporated the principle that the injured party was the husband or the father of the raped woman. The victim was under an obligation to prove that she had resisted the rape by struggling or shouting" (Lerner 116).

The Assyrians became an independent Semitic state within Mesopotamia in the fourteenth century BCE, and in the centuries to follow the Assyrian Empire became a major power throughout the region. The Semitic Assyrians furthered the low social positioning of women within society. Middle Assyrian Laws stated that husbands held the right to have their wives physically chastised, such as having their breasts torn off, or nose or ears cut off (Lerner 117). The Middle Assyrian Laws also specified the obligation of "domestic women, [defined as] sexually serving one man and under his protection ... and designated as 'respectable,'" to wear a veil to distinguish themselves from "women not under one man's protection and sexual control ... designated as 'public women'" who remained unveiled (Lerner 135). This aspect of veiling women as a signal of man's dominance over them would become a tenet of the three dominant monotheistic religions to come from this region—Judaism, Christianity, and Islam. In time, "the institutionalization of patriarchy" within Mesopotamian societies, "created sharply defined boundaries between women.... The lifelong dependency of women on fathers and husbands became so firmly established in law and custom as to be considered 'natural' and god-given" (Lerner 141).

With the monotheism of Judaism, Christianity, and Islam, that would come to dominate this region, the reverence for all goddesses was eliminated, causing even greater decline in the social rights of women.

## The Levant

In addition to Mesopotamia, there is evidence of goddess worship among the Semitic people of the Levant, which includes the area directly east of the Mediterranean: present day Israel, Jordan, Lebanon, Palestine, and Syria. During this region's Late Bronze Age (1550–1200 BCE), the Levant had ties with Mesopotamia and other surrounding regions like Egypt, and because of this, there was a transferal of many cultural beliefs among various regions. During this period, the Akkadians ruled much of the Levant, followed by the Semitic Amorites, and then the Semitic Canaanites.

The Ancient Semitic people of the Levant initially worshipped many gods and goddesses; "Features of the cosmos, such as the sun, moon, and rain, and aspects of human civilizations, such as writing or war, were seen as the reflections of the divine personalities, both male and female, who were the sponsors of these cosmic and cultural realities" (Gruber 120). Canaanite goddesses have been recorded in tablets from Ugarit and Emar as divine beings of central importance in the region's Late Bronze Age. In addition, archeologists have discovered numerous female figurines from Israel, suggesting "the deep entrenchment of feminine values in Israelite culture" (Shlain 115).

One of the first principal goddesses in the Levant was Asherah/Athirat; she was conceived of as the "original, all-powerful *Magna Mater* of archaic Canaan" (Stuckey 115), and sometimes identified as the Queen of Heaven. Stuckey states that "an image of Asherah stood in the Solomonic temple for close to 236 years, that is, at least two-thirds of the temple's existence" (Stuckey 39). While Asherah/Athirat continued to maintain a prominent place in Canaanite religion, "El, her male consort, gradually appropriated her power until by the start of the third millennium BC[E], he became Canaan's chief deity" (Shlain 115). Another primary goddess was Ashtart/Astarte, daughter of Asherah/Athirat and El. Like Ishtar, and Asherah, the goddess Ashtart/Astarte was sometimes worshipped as the Queen of Heaven in the Levant. Ashtart/Astarte and Ishtar hold many similarities, and may be the same goddess, as their names and myths suggest (Stone 113). The worship of the goddess Ashtart/Astarte existed for thousands of years, until about 300 CE when her most sacred shrine in Aphaca was closed by the Byzantine Emperor Constantine, who also closed other temples attributed to goddess worship in Syria, Lebanon, and Israel (Stone 113). There were many portrayals of Ashtart/Astarte as the "Mother of Semitic peoples" at places like Beth Shan, Beth Shemesh, Beit Mersim, Gezer, and Byblos, where her image was portrayed with a serpent entwined around her, or with "heifer horns, that held the disc of the sun" (Stone 115). Stone states that the worship of Ashtart/Astarte, or the other names associated with her, such as Atargatis, Asherah, Anat, and Shapash (Stone 100) lasted into "biblical times, as Hebrew [scriptural] passages reveal (Sam. 7:3,4; Judges 2:13, 3:7; I Kings 11:5 and Jer. 44:15–19)" (Stone 113).

Another principal Canaanite goddess was Anat, the goddess of fertility and war, who was both sister and wife of Baal, the storm god. In about 1000 BCE, Baal was elevated to the head of the Canaanite pantheon, but Anat's most famous myth shows her as quite a formidable goddess in her connection, like Inanna/Ishtar, to the agricultural cycle, suggesting that Anat may have at one time held a superior position over Baal. In this myth, Baal seemingly full of self-conceit, confronts Mot, the god of death and drought, about his consistent threat to throw the earth into sterility. Mot, like Ereshkigal in the Sumerian/Babylonian myth discussed previously, teaches the necessity of death to Baal by swallowing him, so that he ends up experiencing the underworld. Without Baal's ability to produce rain, the world falls into a state of drought, so that all life is threatened. Anat, with Shapash, the goddess of the sun, rescues Baal in the underworld after El, the Canaanite high god, is unable to do so. After saving Baal, Anat kills Mot; "At these words the enraged Anat took hold of Mot. She cut him with a blade, winnowed him with a winnowing fan, parched him with fire, ground him with a millstone and finally scattered him in the fields for the birds to eat" (Kerrigan, Lothian, & Vitebsky 105). Because the goddess Anat is the only one capable of saving the male god Baal, responsible for providing rain, and killing the male god of death, Mot, Anat's role as a central Mother Goddess seems to predate the myth. Anat's portrayal as a superior Mother Goddess is further illustrated in the myth with her treatment of Mot's corpse, as she treats the corpse "in exactly the same way as a farmer treats his grain," showing her control of the agricultural cycle (Armstrong 49–50). Anat, in the myth, then returns to Baal, and again showing her superior abilities, resurrects him, further signaling Anat as a Mother Goddess, as this ability to control the cycles of life, death, and rebirth is common for Mother Goddesses. Like the Mesopotamian ritualistic enactments of the Inanna/Ishtar and Dumuzi/Tammuz myths, the Canaanites also reenacted this myth in a belief that it was essential to maintain a successful harvest.

Another myth of Anat involves, Kothar, the Canaanite god of crafts, making her a divine bow. On Kothar's way to deliver the bow to Anat, Aqhat, the son of a ruler of the time, stole Anat's bow. Anat offered Aqhat immortality if he would give the bow back to her, but he responded, "'A bow is for warriors. Are women, indeed, taking up hunting?'" (Gruber 122). Anat retaliated by having Aqhat killed by one of her warriors, Yatpan. Aqhat's older sister, Pughat, avenged Aqhat's death by killing Yatpan; in this way, Pughat oddly "proves that wielding weapons of death is indeed women's work" (Gruber 122). Gruber explains that "the attribution of both natural forces and cultural arts of civilization to goddesses enhanced the role of women seen to have such positive divine qualities" (Gruber 121); therefore, this myth sent a strong message that Canaanite women were capable of holding similar tenets to the goddesses worshipped in the region, such as serving as warriors. Furthermore, the myth shows that any man who disagreed, deserved to be "punished by death" (Gruber 122). If this myth accurately reflects even a semblance of Canaanite belief, then it creates an argument that Canaanite women were, for a time, treated respectively because of the reverence the people held for their goddesses. However, the rights of women drastically declined in this region with the embrace of the Hebrew concept of monotheism (Gruber 121).

In about 1250 BCE, transitioning from the Bronze Age into the Iron Age, the Hebrew Israelite tribes settled in Canaan and introduced their concept of monotheism, which was decidedly different than the Canaanites' polytheistic beliefs. As Canaanite power lost influence, the Israelites dominated the region, and transformed the beliefs of the people. The Hebrew belief in the god Yahweh, as the sole God, eventually eradicated the beliefs in goddesses throughout the Middle East. Mythically, Yahweh was able to gain primary authority because he was the god who defeated other divinities. Yahweh was said to take part in "a life-and-death battle against Marduk ... of Babylon," and winning this battle, Yahweh proved his ability to protect the people (Gerstenberger 85). It is significant that Yahweh must battle Marduk to gain the seat of power within the Canaanite pantheon, as Marduk is the same god who mythically had to battle his monstrous mother Tiamet in order to secure his leadership over the

Babylonian pantheon centuries earlier. This transferal of divine power through violence projects a clear message that male brutality is central to eradicating traditional beliefs once tied to central female deities. Again, similar to the portrayal of the Babylonian myth of Marduk and Tiamet, the Canaanite goddesses were often purposefully vilified in order to sway the beliefs of the people against former religious conceptions. In fact, Campbell states that the Hebrew Israelites "were considerably more ruthless than the Indo-Europeans in putting down local goddesses" (Campbell xxii), as according to the Israelites' belief in one God, all goddesses would have to be eliminated, and this they did with a fervor yet witnessed.

Rossi explains that the Hebrews "turned their backs ... resolutely on the goddess," as they proclaimed that the goddess of the Canaanites was an "'Abomination' (2 Kings 23:13)" (Rossi xxiv). For the Hebrew Israelites, a monotheistic stance was paramount, and Yahweh alone reigned supreme, causing local goddesses to be spurned and finally eradicated. Shlain states that "The new Israelite religion introduced the first examples of *religious* intolerance in human history.... Yahweh despised the worship of images, and by making faith in monotheism the paramount criterion of human worth, the Israelites took the stance that they were superior to those people who continue to worship idols" (Shlain 80). It is important to note that the "Israelites' sectarian prejudice" was contrary to the other religions of the period, as "everyone except the Israelites" believed in large polytheistic pantheons; thus, it was common for cultures to incorporate foreign religious beliefs into their own beliefs (Shlain 80). But fully contrasting this, the First Commandment in the Hebrew Old Testament, "'I am the Lord thy God. Thou shalt have no other gods before me'" (Exod. 20:2–3), made it clear that the worship of the monotheistic God demanded "the disappearance of the Goddess" (Shlain 82). Shlain explains that the First Commandment in the Hebrew Old Testament states that "Yahweh will not tolerate mention of a Goddess. Given that the Hebrews ... emerged from Egypt, the most goddess-worshipping culture in the ancient world, the First Commandment represented a sharp rupture with the past. And given that all people acknowledge that life is a conjoining of masculine and feminine principles, the exclusion of any female presence from the First Commandment makes it the most radical sentence ever written" (Shlain 82). Therefore, in this period the "balance between the female and male divine images is lost. Now a father god establishes a position of supremacy ... and he is gradually transformed into the consortless god of the three patriarchal religions known today: Judaism, Christianity, and Islam" (Baring & Cashford 274). Thus, this shift in religious belief would have a profound and lasting influence upon the world regarding feminine sacrality.

The monotheistic conception of a sole God, placed God as separate from the earth; whereas, the goddess was the earth (Baring & Cashford 274). Thus, Hebrew beliefs contributed towards a "desacralization of nature and human life, which starkly contrasted with the.... Neolithic agriculturalist's vision" that viewed death as part of a cyclical and natural process, one that was deeply connected with concepts of goddesses. As civilizations advanced in the Levant, the loss of a close relationship with the environment caused many spiritual views to become modified. For example, Oelschlaeger looks towards the Hebrew belief in Yahwism (c. 1400–1050 BCE) as an "evolution in ... ecological transition" (Oelschlaeger 42), as "the Hebrews rejected not only nature gods and mythology but also natural place as having any basic importance," as God (Yahweh) was "entirely outside nature" (Oelschlaeger 42). Therefore, the Hebrews were among "the first people to conceive themselves as living a life whose meaning was defined apart from nature. And Yahwism is clearly the most abstract of ancient belief systems, for Yahweh was not a nature god but a god above nature who had designed the world expressly for his chosen people" (Oelschlaeger 42–3). Once this shift occurred away from a value of nature as divine, then the mythic messages of the regenerative value of nature, messages most often associated with goddesses, became altered or largely omitted from mythic and religious scriptures. Campbell reiterates that within Semitic belief systems:

> we have for the first time a separation of the individual from the divine.... We are separated from God, God is separated from his world, man is turned against nature, nature is turned against man. You do not have this separation in the mythologies of the Great Mother.... All other mythologies that I know of have as their primary divinities those representing nature, which are within us as well as out there.... The whole history of the Old Testament is Yahweh against the nature cults. The Goddess is called the Abomination, and she and her divinities are called demons and they are not given the credit of being divine. And along with that comes the feeling that the divine life is not *within* us; divinity is out there.... After this change, how do you get to the divine? By means of the particularly endowed social group: the tribe, the caste, the church.... And so we have the most radical split here in the history of civilizations and mythologies anywhere between the masculine principle, which is given all power, and the female principle, which is deprived of it, and her world of nature and its beauty is impugned [Campbell 86–7].

As with many of the cultures already discussed, conflict certainly existed between "the new patriarchs and the old religion" (Jeffreys 22), as efforts to try to eradicate former goddess worship often did not entirely wipe out longstanding traditions. In fact, it is believed that among some Israelites, a belief in a consort to Yahweh once existed. In Jeremiah (7:17–18), women and children are referenced as venerating the Queen of

Heaven, though this goddess's name is not referenced in the Bible (van der Toorn 83). Gerstenberger states that there is also biblical evidence that "the worship of the Queen of Heaven was practiced in Jerusalem, [as well as] among other places, and involved the entire family. Children gathered wood, fathers kindled the fire, and women baked sacrificial cakes (Jer 7:18). The women's contribution to this ... form of worship seems to be regarded as the most important" (Gerstenberger 15). To honor this traditional goddess, women would bake "a simple breadlike cake.... Forms of baking such cakes both in female shapes and as star-shaped symbols have been found in.... Syria. In the palace at Mari on the Euphrates River alone, forty such forms were discovered" (Gerstenberger 15–6). Gerstenberger thus states that the discovery of these cakes "means the critique of the national Yahweh faith in Jeremiah 44" came from many members of the community (Gerstenberger 16). In addition, multiple figures of nude goddesses "have been found in Israelite cities" from this period, "primarily in excavated private homes" (Gerstenberger 16). These instances of the lasting worship of goddesses show evidence of how long-standing beliefs, such as those regarding the Queen of Heaven, took time to be eradicated among the common people.

Scholars question what goddess could be "hiding behind this honorific title" of the Queen of Heaven in the Bible (van der Toorn 85). Gerstenberger believes it is Ishtar (Gerstenberger 16), but Karel van der Toorn attempts to address this question by looking into Aramaic texts "written by Jews mainly from Elephantine" (van der Toorn 85). For example, "One of the Elephantine papyri recorded an oath in the name of Anat-Yahu. This name is most likely interpreted as a genitival construction, meaning 'Anat of Yahu,' Anat being the name of a goddess, and Yahu a variation of Yahweh," making it likely that "the Jews of Elephantine worshipped Anat as the consort of Yahu (Yahweh)" (van der Toorn 85). Around 1300–1200 BCE, Anat's worship spread south, as "a temple built by Ramses III found at Beth Shan in modern Israel, calls her 'Queen of Heaven, Mistress of All the Gods'" (van der Toorn 87). By the time the Jews discuss the Queen of Heaven in Jeremiah 7:18 and 44:15–19, it appears that the goddess Anat had "become a divine protectoress of common people" (van der Toorn 88). Many scholars point to the Jews of Elephantine and argue that their beliefs were not a representation of the "Israelite religion in the homeland; however, the widespread confidence that the 'real' Israelite religion ... was without a goddess received a blow when archeologists discovered several Hebrew inscriptions containing a reference to 'Yahweh and his Asherah'" (van der Toorn 88). Asherah, as discussed earlier in this chapter, was once conceived of as a Mother Goddess of the Levant, so she also served as a prime possibility "to be considered ... as the consort of Yahweh" (van der

Toorn 88). Karel van der Toorn additionally looks towards the "frequency of the formula of blessing 'by Yahweh … and by his Asherah'" to conclude that "in certain circles at least, Yahweh was conventionally associated with Asherah" (van der Toorn 89). Shlain concurs by stating that Asherah's importance to the people must have remained high, as the Old Testament portrays Yahweh and His prophets as repeatedly rallying against the goddess Asherah, in order to sway the people's opinion of her, as there are "forty entries in the Old Testament condemning the worship of Asherah" (Shlain 115). In addition, many Israelite female figurines, known as Astarte figurines (Ashtart/Astarte was Asherah's mythic daughter), or "'Mother-Goddess' figurines within the scholarly literature," were found all over "Palestinian soil," and are viewed "as evidence of a flourishing [goddess] cult in the popular religion of Israel, from 1200 until about 550 BC[E]" (van der Toorn 91). Despite the existence of lasting goddess worship in the Levant, it is clear that no goddess held an equal role to that of Yahweh; "Neither Asherah, [Astarte, Ishtar,] nor Anat ever fulfilled a role in Israelite and Judean religion comparable to that of the national god Yahweh. They were never more than his consort.… The priority of the male is evident" (van der Toorn 91). However, in time, the last vestiges of goddess worship in the Levant would become viewed as fully against Israelite and Judean religion, and would no longer be tolerated.

The Old Testament's presentation of Jezebel shows a prime example of the purposeful vilification of women who still venerated goddesses in the Levant. In the ninth century BCE, Jezebel was a Phoenician princess in modern-day Lebanon, and as Phoenicia was at the time Canaanite territory, she worshipped the polytheistic Canaanite pantheon of Baal, Anat, and Asherah. Jezebel married King Ahab of Israel and moved to his kingdom. Though Israel worshipped Yahweh, it is said that Jezebel took four hundred and fifty prophets of Baal and four hundred prophets of Asherah with her to Israel (Hodges 81). Jezebel's Canaanite faith was tolerated by King Ahab, who built her an altar for her Canaanite deities (Hodges 82). However, in the Book of Kings (I Kings 18:13 and II Kings 9:7), Jezebel is said to have ordered the death of some of the prophets of Yahweh in an act of intolerance of her part. Infuriated by this, the prophet Elijah challenged Jezebel's prophets to a test of spiritual might to see who could set fire to a sacrificed bull. The prophets of Baal "started to dance and cut themselves," but Elijah "called on God and, instantly, the beast burst into flames" (Hodges 82). At this, Elijah, in "shockingly cold retribution, … slaughtered all of Jezebel's men" (Hodges 82). Queen Jezebel was "furious, and in a dramatic, bold move, [she] established herself as her enemy's equal, by saying: 'If you are Elijah, so I am Jezebel.' She threatened Elijah: 'Thus and more may the gods do if by this time tomorrow I have not made you like one of them'" (Hodges 82). Elijah was filled with terror at the proclamation of Queen Jezebel, so he fled to Mount Sinai. According to the Book of Kings, Jezebel, and her husband King Ahab, continued to rule in blasphemous fashion. In time, Ahab died in battle with the Syrians, and Jezebel's son, Joram, or Jehoram, became king. Elijah's successor, Elisha, started a civil war to oust Joram, replacing the seat of power with Jehu, who killed Joram. Jehu then publicly insulted Queen Jezebel, "calling her a whore and a witch"; however, Jehu knew that to officially assume the throne, he would have to kill Jezebel, which stands as "a testament to Jezebel's true power" (Hodges 82). Jezebel is said to have known that her demise was eminent. She chose then to sit at her dressing table and prepare herself for death by putting on make-up and doing her hair, so that she may appear as a queen should in her time of death. Once Jehu arrived, Jezebel leaned out of her window and called insults to him, whereupon he ordered her servants to push her out of the window. After falling to her death, a group of dogs tore her body to pieces.

Jezebel throughout this biblical tale is clearly portrayed with malicious intent. She is portrayed as irrational and unjust for killing the prophets of Yahweh, though her husband, the king, could have intervened; she is also defined as a figure of "wantonness" (Hodges 83) for putting on make-up before her death, and finally she is verbally accused of being a "whore and a witch" (Hodges 83). However, it is the final treatment of Jezebel, having dogs tear her to pieces, that reveals the extent to which new ideologies strove to eradicate any worshippers of another faith, especially if those worshippers were powerful women who revered traditional goddesses. It is clear that Jezebel's extremely negative portrayal in the Old Testament is almost entirely due to the fact that she worships a faith that differs from that of the Israelites, one that openly worships goddesses, and likely allowed her to assume the position of power she is portrayed as holding in the tale. Hodges concurs, stating that "For Christian revisionist writers, Jezebel not only represented women having power, a voice, an opinion, but she embodied the old religion. To secure the worship of the newer god, Yahweh, Jezebel not only had to be killed, but her reputation besmirched, her name dragged through the dust just as her body had been by the pack of dogs" (Hodges 83).

With the final elimination of goddesses in the Levant, there is evidence that the status of women profoundly dropped as well. Most of the literature that accounts for the positioning of women in the Levant's Bronze Age and Iron Age (1200–539 BCE) comes from the Hebrew Bible. The Old Testament would come to serve as an anchor for the Abrahamic religions of Islam, Judaism, and Christianity. These three religions would carry their influence throughout the world, until they became dominant global religions, as they still are today. The patriarchal ideology regarding women that is outlined in their shared sacred text, the Old Testament, that disregards any female as divine, would also dominate much of the world's perception and treatment of women, as was seen with the Old Testament's tale of Jezebel.

At one time, women in the ancient Levant performed many religious roles, such as priestesses, "prophetesses, sages, and diviners who mediated between gods and humans" (Gruber 126), though as time progressed, most of these roles would be eradicated. Judith Plaskow states that "'In polytheism ... many positions of influence were open to women, whereas the new religion barred women from leadership and consolidated a new all male priesthood of Yahweh'" (qtd. in Jeffreys 23). Because the Hebrew God was viewed as male, and because he held attributes that Israelite society deemed masculine, men became the leading religious authorities; "Accompanying this almost total masculinization of the divine realm is the depiction in the Hebrew Bible of an almost exclusively male clergy" (Gruber 149). Stuckey declares that "After 1000 BCE, 'public, male-dominated institutions,' along with monarchy and priesthood, took over from the domestic world as the centre of 'organized community life,' and bureaucracies developed to support them. The result was that women became almost invisible in public religious life" (Stuckey 30). Lerner remarks that "the Old Testament male priesthood represented a radical break with millennia of tradition and with the practices of neighboring peoples. This new order under the all-powerful God proclaimed to Hebrews and to all those who took the Bible as their moral and religious guide that women cannot speak to God" (Lerner 177-8). This "emphasis in Judaism, Christianity, and Islam on a single male deity bolstered a belief [for centuries to come] in all three of these ... [religions] that only males may serve as clergy" (Gruber 121). Women, therefore, lost the high social standing they once held as religious leaders, but this was not all they lost. Gruber states that "In the long run the near elimination of the female from the religious realm, both as divinities and as clergy, contributed to the devaluation and disempowerment of women, which has characterized most Jewish and Christian cultures until recently" (Gruber 150).

As has been discussed, many cultures historically used mythic tales to create a new religious agenda to win converts. The Old Testament is no different. The Book of Genesis makes it clear to audiences that the Hebrew God did not require any female help to create the earth and its inhabitants. Lerner states that the "creation story in Genesis departs significantly from the creation stories of other peoples in the region. It is Yahweh who is the sole creator of the universe and all that exists in it. Unlike the chief gods of neighboring peoples, Yahweh is not allied with any female goddess nor does he have familial ties. There is no longer any maternal source for the creation of the universe and for life on earth" (Lerner 180). This calculated exclusion of the female in creation thus solidifies for audiences an explanation that instead of needing to supersede or eradicate a traditional goddess's power, this new ideology makes it evident that it does not require the worship of a goddess at all, as Yahweh can perform all tasks associated with the male and the female.

In addition, the story of Adam and Eve in Genesis calculatingly presents the character of Eve in an especially negative light in order to revise more traditional ideologies in which women played more substantial and respected roles. Shlain concurs, stating that Eve seems precisely "designed to convert those members of the Israelite nation who still held the Goddess in high regard" (Shlain 115). Baring and Cashford explain that the tale of "Eve is in part the story of the displacing of the Mother Goddess by the father god" (Baring & Cashford 492). In Genesis, Eve is portrayed as the human embodiment of the former, more powerful, Mother Goddess (Baring & Cashford 492). Creation stories from myriad cultures, certainly the cultures of the Middle East, most often featured female divinities as playing a central role in creation. Presenting Eve in Genesis as merely human, instead of divine, immediately strips the first, and one of the only, major female representatives in the Old Testament from holding any power whatsoever. In the traditional mythological narratives of the region, "the Mother Goddess who brought death was also the Mother Goddess who gave birth to all creatures first, so that the two phases of existence could be unified in one goddess who cares for both, the Great Mother. Here, the former unity has been split and the two roles polarized, so that the father god takes over the role of creation while the human woman is responsible for destruction" (Baring and Cashford 494). Furthermore, the symbols of the goddess inherent in Mesopotamian religious belief are intentionally within Genesis, such as: "the tree of knowledge, the forbidden fruit, [and] the snake, with its association with the fertility goddess and female sexuality" (Lerner 194). Baring and Cashford explain that the "Tree of Life was one of the primary images of the goddess herself" (Baring & Cashford 496); "All over the Near East, Egypt, Crete and Greece the tree was planted in the temples of the goddess, particularly the fig, palm, cypress, apple, sycamore and olive.... In northern Babylon the goddess of the Tree of Life was called the 'divine Lady of Eden' or Edin" (Baring & Cashford 486–8). In various mythological traditions, the Tree of Life connected the sky to the earth and underworld. The serpent was often a staple image to reside within the Tree of Life, as it was the guardian of the fruit the Tree of Life held. In fact, the Tree of Life had been associated with the "serpent or dragon (winged serpent) for over 1,000 years before Genesis was written" (Baring & Cashford 496). For instance, in 2025 BCE, a cup from the Sumerian King Gudea of Lagash reveals "two winged dragons" along with "uniting snakes" meant to represent "the incarnation of the god Ningizzida, one of the names of the consort given to the Mother Goddess, to whom the cup is inscribed: 'Lord of the Tree of Truth'" (Baring & Cashford 496). Shlain concurs, stating that "In every earlier culture [of the region], the snake was one of the Goddess's most potent power symbols" (Shlain 113). Therefore, it is made clear that "Yahweh's first disciplinary act was to sever this ancient connection" with the female portrayed in creation, Eve, and the snake, making the snake a clear representation of evil (Shlain 113). Eve is shown "to be severed from the snake, and she is to be ruled by her husband. If we understand the snake to be the symbol of the old fertility-goddess, this condition is essential to the establishment of monotheism. It will be echoed and reaffirmed in the covenant: there shall only be one God, and the fertility-goddess shall be cast out as evil and become the very symbol of sin" (Lerner 197). Thus, Eve is portrayed as weak and drawn to sin, ultimately being held as the one responsible for bringing sin and death to all mankind, as well as the pain of childbirth to women. The declaration that Eve was created from the rib of Adam also intentionally marks Eve, and thus all women, as inferior to men. Eve is finally taught in the story to accept a submissive role to her human husband, and through him to God, which the story makes clear is to be the role for all women to come.

In addition to the portrayal of Eve within the Old Testament, the figure of Lilith in Hebrew conception should also be examined. Lilith originated in Mesopotamia around 2000 BCE and was said to be "endowed with the wings, legs, and talons of a powerful bird"; "Scholars speculate that she may have been associated with the moon and primal female sexuality, and was regarded as a protectoress of pregnant women, mothers, and children" (Kimball-Davis, *Warrior,* 93). However, about 1600 BCE, when Semitic groups from the Levant came into Babylon, Lilith underwent a demotion; "Both texts and artwork reveal that her overt sexuality was now seen as threatening; she became known as a 'Bringer of Death,' a winged monster with the face of a beautiful woman who preyed on newborns and stole the nocturnal emissions of men to breed a race of demons" (Kimball-Davis, *Warrior,* 94). Within the Old Testament, the only mention of Lilith states "'Wildcats shall meet with hyenas, goat-demons shall call to each other; there too shall Lilith repose, and find a place to rest' (Isaiah 34:14–15, New Revised Standard Version)" (qtd. in Kimball-Davis, *Warrior,* 94). With this ambiguous mention of Lilith in the Old Testament, "biblical scholars are divided over exactly how to interpret this description," except to point out that "it confirms Lilith's traditional [divine] association with owls (symbols of night and death) and fertility," while placing her and her former power as belonging to "the company of goat-demons and other unsavory types" (Kimball-Davis, *Warrior*, 94).

Kimball-Davis explains that Lilith became a prominent figure in Judaic folklore, and it is her role here that may reflect the significance of Lilith's former divine role. In Talmudic folklore, Lilith was shown to refuse the supine position during sex with Adam; "In a rabbinical commentary known as *The Alphabet of Ben Sira*, Adam and Lilith's quarrel is described thus: She said, 'I will not lie below you.' He said, 'I will not lie below you, but above you.' She responded, 'We are both equal because we both come from the earth.' Neither listened to the other.... [At this, Lilith] pronounced the Ineffable Name of GOD and flew into the air" (Kimball-Davis, *Warrior*, 94). Adam begged God to retrieve Lilith, so three angels were sent to get her; when she refused, she was threatened with having one hundred of her children die each day. Still, Lilith refused to come back to Adam, so in revenge of her punishment, she stated that she would likewise kill the children of Adam who did not wear a protective amulet with the three angels upon it (Kimball-Davis, *Warrior*, 94). Lilith's insistence of equality with Adam and the reference of her ability to have hundreds of children, as well as her ability to threaten death to so many, strongly suggests her former role of divinity. Thus, these portrayals of Lilith look similar to the presentations of other mythic goddesses around the globe whose conceptualizations were intentionally revised to better fit patriarchal agendas.

The Old Testament further offers insight into how the social role of women deteriorated with the creation of monotheism. Lerner states that regions throughout the Middle East, such as Mesopotamia, practiced matrilocal marriage rites, so that the wife was permitted to remain "in her parents' house" after marriage (Lerner 167). This matrilocal arrangement gave women "greater autonomy and gave [them] the right to divorce"; however, it is clearly "the patriarchal family structure [that] dominates biblical narrative" (Lerner 168). The "stories of the patriarchs in Genesis" specify the "transition from matrilocal and matrilineal to patrilocal and patrilineal family organization" (Lerner 167). In addition, in the Bible, the wife was expected to call "her husband 'ba'al' or 'master,'" and in "the Decalogue, the wife is listed among a man's possessions, along with his servants, his ox, and his ass (Ex. 20:17)" (Lerner 168). Also, according to biblical law, women were expected to be virgins at the time of marriage, and they had to be faithful to their husbands upon penalty of death; for example, Deuteronomy 22:20–21 states that "the customary punishment for a bride discovered not to be a virgin on her marriage night was that: 'They shall bring out the damsel to the door of her father's house and the men of her city shall stone her with stones that she die'" (qtd. in Keller 231). It was also customary that all Israelite women "were expected to marry and thus pass ... from the control of their fathers (and brothers) to that of husbands and fathers-in-law. When the husband died before the wife, his brother or another male relative assumed control over her and married her" (Lerner 168–9). Hebrew men, however, "enjoyed complete sexual freedom within and outside of marriage" (Lerner 170). Men in the ancient Levant were permitted to have multiple wives and a harem; "Polygamy was widespread among the patriarchs" (Lerner 170), but married women could be condemned to death for any sexual encounter with a man other than her husband. Keller states that in "the Bible, one finds explicit images of violence against women and children.... For example, we are told that when the Israelites attacked the Midianite peoples and destroyed their cities ... they were commanded to 'kill every male among the little ones, and kill every woman that hath known a man by lying with him. But all the women children, that have not known a man by lying with him, keep alive for yourselves'... (Numbers 31: 17–18, 35)" (qtd. in Keller 230). Arguably, because of the lack of divine or sacred women within the Bible, and because of the way women were subsequently treated within the Bible, Israelite "men succeeded in exerting their power over and suppressing women in the home, in the state, and in the religious sphere" (Gruber 149).

Judaism, which was created from the ancient Israelite religion, is the oldest surviving monotheistic religion in the world. Taking much of its foundation from the Hebrew Bible, Judaism also eradicated all conceptions of divine women within its ideology, and thus promoted patriarchal views against women. Some women, who were honored in the Bible as matriarchs and prophetesses, such as Rebecca, Rachel, and Miriam, were revered within early Judaism, and this allowed some Jewish women to be respected members of their communities for their religious adherence. However, women within Judaism were mostly second-class citizens, who were under the full authority of their male relatives and husbands. Armstrong states that in "Jewish law, women ... [were] marginal creatures, excluded from mainstream social and religious life, like children and slaves" (Armstrong viii). Judaism maintained restrictions against women, pertaining to the "importance of virginity, chastity and honour " in an effort to control the rights of women (Jeffreys 28). These "rules included dire punishments for women who were seen to have escaped the control of their male heads" (Jeffreys 28). Jeffreys explains that within Judaism, as well as later within Christianity and Islam, "Women's bodies were the possessions of their fathers and husbands to do with as they willed" (Jeffreys 29). Thus, many women were "given and taken in marriage" (Jeffreys 29). Judaism, and again later Christianity and Islam, also emphasized "the importance of virginity on the wedding night" (Jeffreys 28). Furthermore, "a husband could divorce his wife for any cause which made her disagreeable or unpleasant to him, and there were hardly any checks on the arbitrary and sometimes even capricious use of this prerogative of the husband (Exodus xxi. 2; Deuteronomy xxi. 14, xxiv. 1)" (Kidwai 16). Most women, on the other hand, were not able to obtain a divorce (Kidwai 16). In addition, women were not permitted to make a vow that held any significance, as the vows of women "were not binding on her unless allowed by her father or husband.... Even if she vowed a vow unto the Lord, and bound herself by a sacred bond, it was of 'none effect' (Numbers xxx. 3–7)" (Kidwai 13). In both Judaism and later Christianity, the sex of women was often identified as inherently impure; for example, following the birth of a child, a woman was viewed as unclean; however, "the birth of a boy create[d] fewer cleanliness problems than the birth of a girl child" (Jeffreys 30). Judaism, as well as Christianity and Islam, also identified menstruating women as impure.

In the rabbinic and medieval periods, Judaism became even more "effectively controlled by rabbis and their Talmud," which began to define the place for women as only "inside marriage and that a woman in transition, not yet married or, for whatever reason, exiting a marriage, is dangerous" (Stuckey 43). Rabbinic sources required "women to be covered. According to these later sources, a husband could charge his wife with misconduct if she bared her hip, leg, shoulder, arm, or chest in public, and display of hair was considered an act of immodesty" (Jeffreys 28). In addition, at this time, there existed "strict laws of chaperonage, which firmly forbade private meetings between a man and a woman. These measures were all aimed at protecting men from the temptations that women embodied" (Jeffreys 28). It was in these periods that heavier strictures against women were carried out; for instance, the "separation of the sexes in the synagogue was enforced because it was understood to protect the 'sanctity of worship' from the 'intrusion of sexuality'" (Jeffreys 30). Finally, without the worship of goddesses in Judaism, women were not envisioned as being connected with divinity; therefore, women were not permitted to hold central religious roles within Judaism, such as serving as rabbis; this restriction is still upheld in Orthodox communities.

## Persia

The Persian Empire, which was centered in modern day Iran, began in the sixth century BCE, and was founded by Cyrus the Great. Cyrus the Great united the separate tribes throughout the region, and defeated important kingdoms, such as that of Babylon. Under the rule of Darius the Great, the Persian Empire reached as far as Europe and the Indus Valley.

The Persians were descended from the Indo-Iranians, who were an Indo-European subgroup. Persians worshipped gods such as: Ahura Mazda, the king of the gods; Mithra, the god of the sun; Azar, the god of fire; Zorvan, the god of time and destiny, and Vayu, the god of wind. Like other Indo-European inspired belief systems, Persian gods held positions of superiority of goddesses, but some goddesses still maintained a degree of reverence in ancient Persia, such as the goddess Al-Lat, who was believed to be a triple goddess with the goddesses Manat, the goddess of fate and death, and Al-Uzza, the goddess of love and war (Wilkinson 110). Shlain explains that Al-Lat was also referred to as al-Rabba, the Sovereign; her position was so revered in Persia that even after the spread of Islam, "the priests who attended the shrine at the Kaaba were known as 'the sons of the Old Woman'" (Shlain 279). Also, Anahita was worshipped as the goddess of water, fertility, and warfare. It was said that "All the life in the universe began and ended with Anahita, for she was the goddess of water.... She was the source of all the streams that coursed down Mount Alburz to the cosmic ocean; she was the fount of all the fertility these waters released on Earth. No more benign or nurturing goddess than Anahita could be imagined—and yet this formidable figure was anything but motherly in her aspect" (Allan, Phillips, & Kerrigan 32). Anahita could be vengeful, as she was often depicted in a chariot drawn by four massive steeds, named Rain, Wind, Cloud, and Sleet (Allan, Phillips, & Kerrigan 32). Anahita was also viewed as a warrior goddess, who could be invoked by those at war, and by those who fell in battle. With this high regard for powerful Persian goddesses, women in ancient Persia were mostly "considered the equals of males. Women could own land, conduct business, receive equal pay, could travel freely on their own, and in the case of royal women, hold their own council meetings on policy" (Mark).

In the fifth century BCE, the king of the gods, Ahura Mazda, rose to become the principal divinity within the monotheistic religion of Zoroastrianism. Zoroastrianism, a faith still in existence today, practiced concepts that centered on free will against the forces of good and evil. Proclaiming a new monotheistic ideology, lesser Persian divinities, like the former goddesses who were once revered as powerful deities, were shed in the worship of Ahura Mazda.

It is believed that women mostly lost social status in many pre-Islamic societies after the introduction of the patriarchal religion of Zoroastrianism with Ahura Mazda serving as the only example of divine representation. After the wide acceptance of Zoroastrianism, women become expected to adopt domestic duties as their central concern, which cost them the loss of some powerful social and religious positions. For instance, Zoroastrianism did not allow women to serve in religious roles, as again when a male God is envisioned as the sole example of divinity, the allowance for women to serve in prominent religious positions diminishes. Women also became largely viewed as needing the guardianship of their fathers, husbands, sons, or other male relatives under the adoption of Zoroastrianism. In addition, women held no legal status; they were largely viewed as property and "sold for a price set by their male guardians. A woman, after the death of her husband, was treated just like another property" (Kidwai 8). Despite this, some pre–Islamic tribes did allow women to hold important social positions. For instance, Hatoon al-Fassi states that in the ancient Arabian kingdom of Nabataea, some women still could hold ... [considerable] legal rights (al-Fassi 129).

It was largely the concepts of Zoroastrianism, as well as Hebrew beliefs, that shaped the birth of the new faith of Islam. The Prophet Muhammed (569–632 CE) spurred the creation of the Islamic faith, which was largely based off of the Hebrew Old Testament as well as the teaching of the Prophet Mohammed and the Qur'an. Islam adopted a monotheistic belief in Allah as the all-powerful God. Merely decades after the death of the Prophet Muhammad (632 CE), "Islam was in control of the eastern part of the southern Mediterranean coast," and within two centuries after the Prophet Muhammad's death, Islam spread "to the Atlantic (Spain and France) and to India," and only continued to spread from there as by the tenth century, "Muslim lands boasted the most extensive cities in the Western hemisphere" (Stuckey 136–7). Between the eleventh and fifteenth centuries, a "number of ... Muslim dynasties and empires" developed, as Islam spread "south and east in Africa and further into north India and the rest of Asia" (Stuckey 137). After Islam became the established religion of many of these regions, most traces of the earlier belief systems surrounding goddess worship were eradicated, because at the heart of the Prophet Muhammed's message was that adherents "must abandon iconic ... polytheism for the revelation of an imageless, monotheistic God" (Shlain 281).

Stuckey states that women initially played prominent roles in the rise of Islam (Stuckey 134). For instance, Muhammad's wife, Khadija, was influential in helping to spread the Islamic faith (Stuckey 134). In addition, women within Muhammad's family were viewed as equals; in fact, another of his wives, Aisha, was known to have been consulted by the Prophet Muhammad on religious matters, and even led forces against those who opposed the Prophet Muhammad (Stuckey 134). Armstrong states that "Women were among the first converts to Islam, and the Qur'an gave women rights of inheritance and divorce that Western women would not receive until the nineteenth century" (Armstrong, x). The Prophet Muhammed was said to improve property rights to women; in addition, women were also now able to sometimes be educated, and under certain instances, women could take part in economic and even political affairs. Female infanticide was also abolished. Additionally, during the lifetime of the Prophet Mohammed men and women prayed together in mosques (Shlain 287). And women under the new Islam were sometimes permitted on the "battlefield with men" (Stuckey 135). Also, revered women were common in Islamic mysticism, as "Islam boasts many female saints" (Stuckey 155). In addition, Keller states that the Qur'an included "women-honoring and—protecting passages," such as the "sura on women where men are specifically forbidden from incest with any female relatives of the extended family" (Keller 233). Women were also allowed to separate from an abusive husband, and "adult men were to care for widows and orphans and not steal their wealth" (Keller 233).

Though the position of women did somewhat improve under the introduction of the new faith of Islam, in many ways it did not improve. Leaders of the Islamic religion eventually reduced women again "to second-class citizens," as presiding "jurists habitually interpreted Qur'anic injunctions with a patriarchal bias that proved damaging to women" (Armstrong x). Stuckey points out that the Qur'an "more directly than other monotheistic sacred texts, concerns itself with women," as it makes clear the roles that men and women should perform (Stuckey 128). The Qur'an proclaims that men and women were created by Allah from "one soul"; therefore, women are considered spiritually equal (Stuckey 128). However, the Qur'an (*Sura* 4: 34) also states that "men are superior to women because of the 'qualities with which God [has] gifted [men] above [women]'.... The passage continues: 'Virtuous women are obedient' and chaste. If women are disobedient, then men should 'remove them into beds apart, and scourge them'" (qtd. in Stuckey 129). In addition, the Qur'an discusses "how husbands should exercise their headship over women, stating that, 'Virtuous women are obedient and careful during their husband's absence.... But [husbands should] scold those [wives] who [they] fear may be rebellious; leave them alone in their beds and beat them'" (qtd. in Jeffreys 27). The Qur'an does allow women to inherit, "but men inherit the equivalent of two women's portions (*Sura* 4: 12)" (Stuckey 129). Thus, Stuckey states that "interpretations of the Qur'an increasingly resulted in the seclusion of women in the home and the exclusion of women from public life, though in varying degrees depending on place and time" (Stuckey 141).

As the centuries progressed, Muslim women were further restricted in social, political, and religious affairs. For example, "a consensus developed that in Islam, women should be barred from politics" (Jackson 4). Also, it became required that during religious worship, women should be "segregated from their men by a screen and regulated to the back of the mosque" (Shlain 287). As time went on, women were only allowed to pray within mosques when men were absent, and some Islamic sects prevented women from entering mosques altogether; thus, women, "whose spirituality had been beyond dispute for untold millennia, were deprived of the basic right to conduct, participate in, or even to attend services" (Shlain 287). Additionally, it was generally during the ninth and tenth centuries that Islamic law required upper-class women to wear veils and to be largely secluded from society (Stuckey 137).

Many of these mandates against women are still in practice today by some supporters of Islam. In fact, Keller states that "Practices of male supremacy continue to be violently enforced by patriarchal clerics and politicians in some regions of Islam" (Keller 234). For example, "when Khomeini took power in Iran in 1979, [forming the Islamic Republic of Iran,] feminists were among the first executed" (Keller 234). Keller states that since "this time, many of the improvements in the human rights of women in Iran, won through decades of struggle—such as access to education (won in 1910), abolition of the veil (1936), the vote (1962), a curb on the absolute male right of divorce (1973), free abortion on demand (1974), and a ban on polygamy and the right to maintenance after divorce (1976)" were lost due to strict religious standards that continue to mandate extremely inferior roles for women in contemporary Iran (Keller 234) and throughout much of the Middle East today.

## Chapter 3

# The Mediterranean

The debt owed to the religious beliefs coming out of the Middle East to the Mediterranean, and then most of the Western world, is tremendous. As Kerrigan, Lothian, and Vitebsky state:

> It is scarcely an exaggeration to claim that almost every myth and legend found around the Mediterranean world has some kind of Akkadian or Sumerian parallel.... Religious ideas ... diffused across the area from the original Sumerian source. Individual gods and goddesses appear to undergo a gentle transformation as they move across from one culture to the next. Thus Inanna ... clearly shares similar characteristics with Ashtart and Anat, who in turn are associated with the Greek Pallas Athene [sic] [Kerrigan, Lothian, & Vitebsky, 136–7].

Thus, the similar portrayal of highly respected goddesses as found in the Middle East, such as the concept of a superior Mother Goddess, can also be found throughout the Mediterranean, specifically in the areas of Greece and Italy. The tremendous amount of archeological and mythical evidence of goddess worship in the Mediterranean makes it a region that deserves its own chapter in this book.

## Greece

One of the earliest civilizations in Greece was the Cycladic civilization, which thrived from approximately 3000–1100 BCE. Similar to the female figurines found throughout Europe, as discussed in Chapter 1, numerous female figurines were also found throughout the Cycladic islands; the Cyclades have "yielded thousands of distinctive marble figurines ranging from a few inches to several feet in height.... Because of their frequent placement in graves, it is likely that female figures had some importance in spiritual belief and ritual. Since females held important roles as goddesses or as priestesses in Greece and in the surrounding cultures, it is likely that Cycladic women held significant ritual roles as well" (Vivante 221–2).

It is also well documented that the worship of goddesses was quite prevalent in the Neolithic Minoan civilizations of Greece (c. 2700–1400 BCE), which were located on the island of Crete and other outlying islands surrounding the Greek mainland. Baring and Cashford state that the legacy of goddess worship has been remarkably preserved through the artistic representations found in Minoan civilizations (Baring & Cashford 54). In fact, Minoan civilization is often viewed as the quintessential Neolithic example to support evidence of a belief system centralized on the principle of a supreme Mother Goddess who was connected to, or was a representation of, nature. Though there are multiple representations of goddesses in Minoan culture, it is believed that all representations of these goddesses were conceived of as being connected together in a unified conception of a supreme Mother Goddess.

Again, the vast number of predominantly female figurines found on Crete suggest a widespread belief in a Mother Goddess, and other dominant earth goddesses. The Minoan site of Koumasa on Crete, for example, revealed female figurines that were found wearing bell-shaped skirts, with "one of them apparently pregnant," alongside depictions of animals (Goodison & Morris 117). Peter Warren states that these Koumasa female figurines are potentially depictions of a Mother Goddess identified as a "'Mistress of Animals and Nature'" (qtd. in Goodison & Morris 117). There were also three famous female figurines found from the palace of Knossos on Crete that are often interpreted as representatives of earth goddesses or priestesses who are portrayed as holding snakes while their breasts are exposed (Goodison & Morris 125).

There is also much artistic evidence for the reverence of goddesses who hold positions of superiority within Minoan religion. For example, in Phaistos on Crete, a circular pedestal table was unearthed that shows "three female dancing figures with bell skirts.... The all-female cast suggests a special dance performed by a particular group.... The gesture of the central figure, with two arms raised, is one which in later images usually indicates a goddess" of superior position (Goodison & Morris 123). In addition, a fresco from Akrotiri on the island of Thera, modern day Santorini, shows images of a significant goddess surrounded by "five women, who are involved in the collection and offering of the stamens of the saffron crocus" (Goodison & Morris 126). The goddess figure from Akrotiri is seated, and her divinity is "clearly signaled," as "she sits on a tripartite platform and is flanked by a griffin and by a monkey, who offer her the stamens. The exotic and supernatural creatures mark her off from the human participants" and portray the goddess as possessing tremendous power in connection with mysticism and the environment (Goodison & Morris 126). Many Minoan gold signet rings have also been uncovered, which reveal engravings of "finely-detailed ritual scenes during the fifteenth century BC[E]. They can be broadly grouped into scenes of processions, epiphany, and rituals involving tree-shaking and baetyl [sacred stone]-hugging" (Goodison & Morris 128). Goodison and Morris state that "worshippers on many rings approach a seated goddess," like the fresco from Akrotiri, and on other rings, worshippers seem to be in a state of "ecstatic vision," as they appear to be dancing with "distinctive gestures" (Goodison & Morris 128). Another ring from Archanes shows a male shaking a tree and embracing a baetyl; a superior goddess figure also seems to be supervising the actions of the male (Goodison & Morris 128).

Again, as has been repeatedly discussed, there appears a direct connection between the reverence of these female goddesses and the rights of women socially in Minoan society. Many Minoan archeological sites have revealed artistic representations of women "performing ritual activities, including making ritual offerings and performing liquid or animal sacrifices," and Vivante states that these "many visual representations of women seem to portray their high social or political status" within Minoan culture (Vivante 222–3). In addition, many pieces of Minoan artwork, such as the famous depiction of women leaping over bulls in contest with male partners, suggests that women held at least equal status to males within Minoan culture. Grammatikakis states that "According to all existing descriptions from ancient Greek historians and philosophers like Plato, Thucydides, Strabo, but also from all the archaeological findings, [Minoan] men and women lived freely and peacefully and participated equally in all daily activities, sports, and games" (Grammatikakis). Therefore, the "Minoan civilization represents a paradigm of a ... society in which the woman played a dominant role. She was the 'mother' but also the 'active woman,' who participated in all city activities" (Grammatikakis).

However, in about 1425–1050 BCE, "greater regional diversity and striking changes in religious expression" were found in Minoan culture, and this was directly tied to the dominance of the Mycenaeans (sometimes referred to as Achaeans) during this period. The Mycenaeans were an Indo-European people who entered Greece in about 1900 BCE and gained dominance over the Minoans in the years to come. Like other Indo-European cultures already discussed, they were largely "a militaristic, warlike culture intent on conquest [and] raiding" (Vivante 2223). As has been discussed in the two previous chapters of this book, Indo-European concepts vastly transformed many of the existing beliefs of the Minoans, including their reverence of primary goddesses. The Mycenaeans revered "patriarchal stories of sky gods ... analogous to those of other Indo-European cultures" (Vivante 224). And as was seen with other cultures that experienced an influx of Indo-Europeans, the new Mycenaean groups altered the existing Minoan beliefs of primary goddesses to suit their own mostly patriarchal pantheons. For instance, there is evidence that the Mycenaeans chose to worship at existing Minoan sacred sites reserved for the reverence of goddesses, but they transformed the reverence at the sites away from traditional goddesses to new male deities; "after their conquest, temples to male Mycenaean gods, such as Zeus and Apollo, were established over the sanctuaries of the female deities worshipped there before conquest. At the sites, the earlier predominance of female images was increasingly replaced by male images, and later Greek stories tell of these ... takeovers" (Vivante 224). These "takeovers" of goddesses by male gods appear often in Greek mythology, and are repeatedly portrayed in violent terms, as was the case in some myths from Mesopotamia, such as the Babylonian myth of Marduk's violent takeover of the goddess Tiamet.

As also evidenced in the Middle East, a shift in the conception of time seems to have occurred when Minoan culture merged with that of the Mycenaeans. This transformation can be understood through looking at the change in death practices between the two cultures. Jacquetta Hawkes states that "'Before they came under Achaean [Mycenaean] influence the Cretans [Minoans] characteristically did not make much of death and funerary rites,'" but after Achaean expansion, there is evidence of great "wealth and labor" being displayed to honor the dead, showing that the Achaeans/Myceneans "'brought with them a social and ideological organization oriented more toward death than life'" (qtd. in Eisler 54). As was discussed in Mesopotamia, death became conceived of as an end, not another beginning as it would have been conceived of under the worship of earth goddesses with their representations of nature's ceaseless cycles. According to this new Mycenaean linear conception of time, individuals began to be viewed as fighting against a timeframe that would ultimately run out. The singular lives of human beings and the pursuit of an identity-driven legacy would become matters of paramount focus for the Mycenaeans. Thus, portrayals of heroes in Greek mythology began to emerge as examples of how to evade the finality of death, which was done by living an exemplary, singular life that produced a lasting legacy (McCoppin, *Hero's Quest*, 7). For example, Homer's *Iliad* repeatedly discusses the Achaean value of a singular identity and legacy.

However, as also discussed in the last two chapters of this book, instead of the outright eradiation of goddess reverence, there is evidence to show that the Mycenaeans incorporated Minoan concepts about goddesses into their own belief systems. Many of the religious beliefs of the Minoans, "especially the worship of female divinities—and the apparently important positions of women..., seemed to have continued alongside the imposition of patriarchal belief systems" from the Mycenaeans (Vivante 224). For example, images, such as "birds, horns-of-consecration, double axes, snakes, plants," important to Minoan concepts of female divinity, were "adopted by the invading Mycenaeans" (Goodison & Morris 131).

As time continued under Mycenaean rule, a conception of a unified Mother Goddess was divided into separate, and thus less powerful, representations of goddesses. Some of the first representations of separated divinities were often related to traditional conceptions of Minoan Mother Goddesses or earth goddesses. For example, "In the Argolis, the most powerful region of Mycenaean Bronze Age culture, the cult of Hera is pre-eminent. Her functions here seem to involve agriculture, pastoral fecundity, marriage, adolescent transitions, and war, as well as the annual renewal of her virginity" (Voyaztis 145). In this early portrayal of Hera, she closely resembles Minoan conceptions of a Mother Goddess/earth goddess. Reaves concurs, stating that "Hera was [once conceived of as] a cyclical earth-goddess" (Reaves 293). Further attesting to this is the fact that Hera once shared with the god of the Ocean, Oceanus, "the epithet 'origin of all things'" (Reaves 294). However, this portrayal of Hera would in time become more and more demoted, until she appeared in Classical and Hellenistic Greek mythology as merely the scorned and jealous wife of Zeus.

As discussed previously in this book, the process of separating concepts of a unified Mother Goddess/earth goddess into less powerful, separate goddesses, who each possess feminine traits viewed as permissible according to the new culture's view of women, is a trend seen in many cultures after Indo-European invasion and/or the perpetuation of patriarchal social structures. This process of demoting once powerful goddesses continued throughout Mycenaean rule, and into the later rule of the Indo-European Ionians and Dorians, and is well documented in the mythology of the Archaic (750–479 BCE), Classical (479–323 BCE), and Hellenistic (323–30 BCE) periods. For instance, as Greek civilization advanced, the goddess Aphrodite, who like Hera was once conceived of as a supremely powerful earth goddess, became little more than a sex object within Archaic, Classical, and Hellenistic Greek mythology. And, male deities, who were once worshipped as minor gods, became elevated in status in order to better fit the patriarchal social and political structures that gained dominance. For example, the head of the new pantheon, Zeus, was once only a minor Minoan deity before he became repositioned as the primary male sky god under Mycenaean rule. With the elevation of superior male gods, the social role of women drastically dropped in Greek society.

Once authors like Homer and Hesiod began recording myths during the Greek Archaic period, the conflicting feelings in regard to the shift in belief systems from primary goddess worship to principal male deities can be witnessed. Vivante states that "intensely misogynistic voices emerge[d]" in the Archaic period, such as Hesiod, whose *Theogony* showcases the "shift of power from female to male deities that culminates in the reign of Zeus as an exceptionally powerful, male god" (Vivante 226). Yet, Barnes explains that also in this period, many communities still practiced belief systems similar to the Neolithic Minoans of Crete (Barnes 103). Therefore, many recorded myths present a conflict in matters associated with Greek divinities, such as was seen in the myths of Europe and the Middle East. Often Archaic myths conceded that "officially Zeus was the supreme deity," but they sometimes showed goddesses as "more powerful than gods" (Eisler 113). This documentation of the conflicted feelings regarding Greek goddesses is only heightened in the Greek myths from the Classical and Hellenistic periods.

Within the written Greek mythological tradition, a conception endures that there still was a Mother Earth Goddess, who mostly appeared in creation stories. Most often this Mother Earth Goddess was referred to as Gaia. For example, this concept of a unified Mother Earth Goddess still appeared in the fourth century BCE, as shown on the Derveni Papyrus, housed at the Archeological Museum of Thessaloniki, which states that "Ge, Meter, Rhea, and Hera are the same one. She was called Ge (Earth) by convention—Ge and Gaia according to each one's dialect, and Meter (Mother) because all things are born from her." In addition, Hesiod's creation myth also shows a unified conception of a Mother Earth Goddess in his portrayal of Gaia. However, Hesiod also mythically explains how rule was transferred to male deities from Gaia. In this myth, Gaia emerges out of nothingness and then gives birth to a son, Uranus. Her son then becomes her husband, making him the ruler of the newly created divine pantheon that he and Gaia produced by their sexual unions. This mythic detail immediately thwarts the importance of Gaia as a Mother Earth Goddess by giving rulership to her son/male consort. Mythically, Uranus then orders Gaia to withhold their offspring within her womb, so that Uranus cannot be overthrown by them. Uranus's assertion of his dominance in this explicitly brutal manner suggests uneasy feelings about the take-over of a Mother Earth Goddess by a male divine being. Uranus's irrational demand is portrayed even mythically as overly brutal in its control over women and their own bodies. Gaia appeals to her son Cronus, who still resides within her womb, to save her by emasculating his father with a sickle while Uranus and Gaia are having sex. This request on the part of Gaia is odd, as it asks audiences to assume that Gaia as Mother Earth cannot help herself. Additionally, Gaia's request of her son Cronus to emasculate his own father, the current ruler, seems directly connected to Neolithic religious rites of male consorts and Mother Goddesses/earth goddesses coming from the Middle East, as discussed in the previous chapter. Instead of "priestesses of the Great Goddess or Mother Goddess in the female-oriented religion dismember[ing] the sacred king ... to fertilize the soil so that it would produce an abundance of crops" (Rosenburg 4), this scene of Greek creation places all action within male hands and revises the sacred act of sacrifice for a goddess to now justify the young god Cronus overtaking power. As was seen with other European and Middle Eastern myths, this myth lessens the power of the central Mother Earth Goddess by introducing a plot structure that shows young, virile males, in the forms of Uranus and Cronus, who possess warrior abilities, certainly all Indo-European concepts, as being the only ones fit to rule in place of their own mother. Rosenburg states that Hesiod's creation myth thus provides written evidence of the transition from an older female-centered belief system to a new patriarchal religion, stating that when "Cronus becomes ruler of the world, the divine family is in transition from the mother-dominated society to the father-dominated society that will follow under the rule of Zeus" (Rosenburg 4). Lerner explains that "Hesiod did not invent this myth of transformation, [as] ... Hesiod's *Theogony* [merely] reflects a change in religious and gender concepts, which had already taken place in Greek society" (Lerner 204) with myriad Indo-European invasions.

Hesiod's mythic version of creation continues to show that after castration, Uranus's semen fell into the sea, and initiated the birth of the goddess Aphrodite. The fact that Aphrodite is shown in this myth to be born before any member of the Olympic pantheon, including its head Zeus, might suggest that Hesiod, and/or the culture that created the myth through the oral tradition for centuries before it was written down, was trying to come up with a way to maintain the power of Aphrodite, a goddess who was revered as an immensely powerful deity before she was reimagined as the sexual plaything of the gods. Many revered Aphrodite as the "First Mother"; in fact, she was identified as "Oldest of the Fates" at her shrine at Athens (Stone 379). Aphrodite, as a traditional Mother Goddess/earth goddess, was also conceived of as being connected to the cycles of life. At Delphi, Aphrodite was known as "She of the Tombs," and she was "Originally the deity of rebirth" (Johnson 80). However, as happened with many goddesses throughout the long history that shaped classic Greek mythology, the "conception of Aphrodite was altered by the northern invaders of Greece ... to suit the new religion. The Great Goddess was split into separate deities, each fragment representing one of her diverse aspects" (Johnson 80). Aphrodite was thus left with only the "realm of physical love, her larger relation to life and death suppressed.

The other Olympian gods condescended her, and she was generally held in low esteem among them" (Johnson 80).

Hesiod's creation myth continues on to show that after Cronus emasculated his father, he became the new head of the pantheon, and then, like his father, he attempted to keep his own offspring from taking his power. Cronus asserts his dominance by ordering his sister and wife Rhea, also identified in Greek mythology as a Mother Earth Goddess like her mother Gaia, to hand over all of their children to him, so that he may eat them. Again, the myth presents this act as an injustice, as it reverses the birthing process. It shows a male attempting to take children within his body as a woman would while pregnant, but it clearly demonstrates the barbarity of this act, as with the male, it shows only a process of destruction. Audiences can't help but feel bad for Rhea, and thus side with her against Cronus, which is an odd device to use if the myth is entirely supposed to advocate the justification of male rule. Zeus, last of the babies to be born of Rhea and Cronus, escapes being swallowed by his father, because Rhea, seeking the advice of her mother Gaia, comes up with a plan to whisk the infant Zeus away to the island of Crete, and instead gives a rock swaddled in cloth to Cronus to swallow in place of the baby. It is of course significant that Zeus is reared on Crete, the Minoan stronghold of Mother Goddess/earth goddess worship, as this mythic detail hints at the origin of Zeus. In the myth, once Zeus is fully grown, he leaves Crete and seeks out his father, Cronus, in order to force him to purge his other five divine siblings. Being successful, Zeus then leads his siblings, with the help of the mythic Hundred-handers and Cyclopes, in waging war against Cronus and his Titan pantheon. Zeus, along with his siblings, who become the Olympians, gains the right to rule the head of the pantheon because of his youth, virility, warrior prowess, and command of the sky, showing Zeus as displaying quintessential Indo-European concepts. Zeus then repeats the process of his grandfather and father by marrying his sister, Hera, in order to seize her power, again just like Indo-European gods often did to traditionally more powerful goddesses.

As stated, Hesiod's myths, recorded after centuries of Indo-European influence with the Mycenaeans, Dorians, etc., contain "political connotations" meant to sway popular opinion towards "the cult of Zeus with its patriarchal norms" (Barnes 103). However, more traditional, goddess-oriented beliefs also certainly "lay in the background of the poet Hesiod when he wrote how the new powers came to control his world" (Barnes 105). Barnes specifically looks toward another of Hesiod's myths, which displays Zeus defeating the enormous female serpent-like creature Echidna, identified as the Mother of Monsters, as well as her mate, Typhon, in order to declare his dominance. According to Hesiod, when

Zeus finally defeated Typhon, "'great Earth groaned'"; Barnes states that the reference to "'Great Earth'" is "Mother Earth, patroness of the old order in which women had been central and the cycles of the seasons paramount" (Barnes 106). Eisler concurs that Hesiod's *Theogony* reveals remnants of conflicted feelings of cultural shifts between old and new beliefs, as he states that Hesiod's text is replete with examples of earlier ideology; "For example ... it is the Goddess of old [who] gives birth to Heaven and ... alone—bears the sea. Hesiod's world is already male dominated, warlike, and hierarchic. But it is still a world in which the old partnership ... [and] values are not completely forgotten" (Eisler 107–8). This is seen in the conflicted nature presented in some of the mythic scenes of creation, such as Hesiod's commiseration for the plights of both Gaia and Rhea at the cruel hands of their husbands.

There also exists alternative accounts of creation in Greek mythology that present a more powerful role for the early female players, showing perhaps the conflict the people felt in changing their belief systems from goddess worship to that of a leading male pantheon. Another myth of creation shows that out of chaos, the goddess Eurynome emerged. Eurynome transformed into a dove that laid an enormous egg. Ophion, a massive serpent, encircled the egg to protect it. As discussed in the first two chapters of this book, the imagery of a bird, egg, and serpent would have been well-known images associated with earth goddesses. When the egg in this myth hatched, all the elements of nature were born: "Uranus, the sky; Ourea, the mountains; Pontus, the sea; and all the stars and planets. Gaia, the Earth, and her mountains and rivers emerged at the same time" (Wilkenson 14). After all of nature emerged from the egg, the myth shows both Eurynome and Ophion going to Mount Olympus, the Greek home of the deities, to rule. However, Ophion started to brag that he, instead of Eurynome, was responsible for creation, which enraged Eurynome, so she thrust Ophion down into the underworld forever. This Greek version of creation assuredly gives central authority to the superior power of the goddess Eurynome (McCoppin, *Lessons*, 70).

Looking at the relationships of Zeus with his female counterparts also helps to identify how Greeks resolved transitioning beliefs from female to male divine dominance. There are references to earlier wives of Zeus before Hera, the Titanesses of wisdom Metis and Themis for instance, and it is these references that might indicate the transition that occurred once the Myceneans dominated the people of Greece (Stone 372). The union of Metis and Themis to Zeus as his early wives, as they were worshipped well before he was, suggests that at early stages of transitioning belief systems in Greece, worshippers needed to identify with a male divine leader who received divine counsel from wise female divine beings. Similarly, once Zeus married Hera, her early role in myth was one of counsel, as she was the direct granddaughter of the revered Mother Earth Goddess, Gaia. Classic Greek mythology specifically shows the connection of Hera to Gaia by identifying Hera as direct heir to Gaia's golden apples that were guarded by the serpent Ladon in the Garden of the Hesperides.

The continued relationship between Zeus and Hera is wrought with clues of the struggle between the old female-oriented belief systems and the new dominant male-centered religion. As stated earlier, many scholars contend that the worship of Hera as a Mother Earth Goddess existed before that of Zeus (Reaves 294), as many of the most beloved temples in Greece, before the worship of primary male divinities, were dedicated to Hera at places like Crete, Samos, and Perachora. At Olympia, Hera's sacred temple stood as dominant before "Zeus had even a tiny altar in the town" (Stone 376). The myths of Hera and Zeus perfectly articulate the very real struggle for the people's adoption of male superiority over more traditional female divine authority; "One of the best known versions of the dysfunctional marriage is the whole Zeus-Hera cycle, in which an archaic Earth Goddess, whose temples were said to have been the largest in pre-patriarchal Crete and Greece, is demoted to the status of a nagging wife constantly punishing her philandering husband" (Leeming & Page, *Goddess*, 98). As the years progressed into the Classical period of ancient Greece, the myths of Hera reveal her clear degradation. One such myth presents Hera as so overcome with rage at Zeus, that she drugged him, making him fall asleep, whereupon she tied him up and threatened to overpower his rule. However, once Zeus regained control, he thrust Hera's son Hephaistos down to earth from Mount Olympus, because he had helped her contain Zeus, which caused Hephaistos to forever walk with a limp. Still infuriated with Hera, Zeus tied her wrists to heaven and hung heavy anvils around her ankles, so "thoughts of further revolution were crushed beneath the weight of torture" (Stone 376). It was myths such as these, that demoted Hera in the minds of the Greeks as merely the goddess of marriage.

Leeming and Page point to another shocking mythic account of Zeus taking power away from Hera. The myth starts by admitting that Hera "inherited the mantle of the Great Mother of all" from her mother Rhea and grandmother Gaia (Leeming and Page, *Goddess*, 99). Thus, with her tremendous power, Hera helped Zeus defeat the Titans, securing power for the Olympic pantheon; after this, the myth shows Hera retreating to Crete. However, Zeus followed her there in order to seduce her, and thus take her power for himself. Mythically, Hera refused Zeus's advances, so he disguised himself as an injured bird. With her guard down, Hera lifted up the bird to help it, befitting a Mother Earth Goddess, but the bird transformed back into Zeus, whereupon he was said to have thrown Hera "down and spent his passions on her, leaving her exhausted and humiliated on the ground. So ashamed was Hera that she agreed to take the unusual step not only of marrying her brother, but of promising to stay only with him" (Leeming and Page, *Goddess*, 99).

In addition, Leeming and Page convey another myth where Zeus rapes his own mother Rhea. In this myth, Rhea tried to temper the growing power of Zeus's position by attempting to prevent his marriage to Hera. If Hera married Zeus, it would transfer her power to the will of her husband. Marriage for a Greek goddess was rarely beneficial, as the most powerful Greek goddesses in the Classical period were the ones who remained virgins, like Artemis and Athena. In this myth, however, Zeus told Rhea that she could not stop him from marrying Hera, and to prove his might, he told her that he would rape her, his own mother. In retaliation, Rhea changed her form into a massive serpent. Zeus, in retaliation, also metamorphosed into a serpent; "Not to be outdone or thwarted in his revenge, Zeus too turned into a serpent and coiled about his mother with such muscular power that she could no longer move. When she was finally still, he fulfilled his threat, raping her and leaving her with none of her former powers" (Leeming and Page, *Goddess*, 99–100).

As with other Neolithic cultures, the serpent was a dominant symbol used in connection to the goddesses in Minoan culture, and this imagery certainly carried over into many Greek goddesses of the Classical and Hellenistic periods, such as Athena, who wears the gorgon Medusa's skin. Many Greek goddesses possess serpent guardians, such as Ladon who guarded Hera's golden apples and Gaia's serpent of Delphi. Many scholars have discussed the reason why so many serpents appear in Greek mythology in connection to earth goddesses, as well as the goddesses of many other cultures around the world, such as was discussed in the Middle East in the creation story of Adam and Eve. Frankel points to both serpents, and their dragon counterparts, as often being connected to earth goddesses in Greece, India, the Middle East, Mesoamerica, etc. (Frankel 68) because the "snake reflected the Great Goddess, changing from young to old and then cycling back to young as the world renewed in the spring. It … shed its skin, like a woman birthing a new organism from itself. Depicted coiled in several successive rings, the serpent mimics cyclical evolution and reincarnation" (Frankel 70). In addition, serpents are often conceived of as connected with both the upper and lower world—life and death—as they are associated with dens and caves, which were often considered to be the realm of the underworld. Venomous species of serpents also possess the ability to cause almost instantaneous death, thus adding to their imagined mystical qualities. Earth goddesses and serpents thus possess similar abilities. So, when Rhea transformed herself into the quintessential image of a serpent within her myth to evade Zeus, she thus sent a message to the audience of the myth about her powerful role as a Mother Earth Goddess. However, when Zeus also shows the same ability to transform into the shape most often associated with earth goddesses, then audiences would recognize that Zeus was capable of superseding the power of the old earth goddesses, just as audiences saw in Mesopotamia when Marduk overtook Tiamet, and in the Levant when Eve was punished for her connection to the Old Testament's serpent.

The many mythic episodes where Zeus seduces other women also provide evidence of a contrived attempt at reducing the power of once more primary female deities. As stated, in order to supersede the power of traditional goddesses, many new Indo-European gods married existing local goddesses. To achieve this same benefit, Zeus was portrayed as seducing, and in many cases raping, many traditional goddesses throughout Greece, such as: Alkmene, Aegina, Hesione, Demeter, Dione, Leda, Lato, Semele, Eurynome, Europa, Persephone, Io, etc. (Stone 376). Just as an Achaean warrior proves his dominance over an enemy by force in tales such as the *Iliad*, Zeus proves his dominance over traditional goddesses by his ability to seduce them. For instance, the Greek myth of Semele, the mortal mother of the god Dionysus, is a prime example of Zeus's seduction. In this myth, after being seduced by Zeus, Semele asks to see his full divine form, but when he complies, Semele is burnt to ashes by his brilliance. Some scholars contend that Semele may have come to Greece as a more ancient Phrygian earth goddess, so when she appears in this myth, it is with the intent of portraying Semele, the once powerful goddess, as now a weak and foolish woman when compared with the splendor of Zeus.

Also, in looking at the myth of the Titan Prometheus and his hand in creation, one sees evidence of a patriarchal attempt to portray human women as inferior, just as the majority of Greek myths strove to portray their goddesses as inferior to their gods. In the myth of Prometheus, he makes male human beings out of clay and gives them fire, so that they may prosper. However, Zeus punishes Prometheus for giving fire to humankind by condemning him to have his liver devoured daily by an eagle in Tartarus. Zeus then assigns men the punishment of having women sent to them, in the form of the first woman, Pandora. Zeus gives Pandora a box full of the elements that humans must suffer against and orders her not to open it, knowing that because she is a woman, as the myth states, she will be unable to resist opening the box and will thus unleash all of the earth's ills onto mankind. This mythic explanation of women as weak, conniving, and the cause of worldly suffering is certainly a result of centuries of religious indoctrination meant to demote the power of goddesses as deserving of subservience, which directly promotes a message that women are thus deserving of the same inferiority. Again, some scholars state that Pandora may have at one time been a more powerful goddess, whose clear demotion is made evident in this revised Greek creation myth. For example, Kate Millett "identifies the Pandora myth as bearing traces of an older Mediterranean fertility goddess, because, in Hesiod's version, 'she wears a wreath of flowers and a sculpted diadem in which are carved all the creatures of land and sea'" (qtd. in Jeffreys 25). By mythically recasting Pandora as a weak, mortal woman, she is not only stripped of her divine role, she becomes an everlasting symbol within the patriarchal system embracing the revised myth of why women should be treated with degradation. Pandora, like Eve, thus becomes a scapegoat to explain why existing patriarchies oppress women.

The Greek goddess Demeter, goddess of the harvest and one of the original six Olympians, also reveals ample evidence of the mythic transfer of power from primary goddess-oriented beliefs to patriarchal values. Demeter, like Aphrodite and Hera, was believed to be worshipped in a more principal form as a Mother Earth Goddess before her power became degraded as the centuries progressed. Though Demeter lost some of her traditional symbolism, worshippers still maintained their reverence for this ancient goddess in her traditional role as an earth goddess, as Demeter was revered as the Greek goddess of the harvest.

The most popular myth involving Demeter, that displays the abduction of her daughter Persephone, portrays both elements of Demeter's traditional role as a Mother Earth Goddess and elements that show her in a degraded form under the will of Zeus. In this myth, the god of the underworld, Hades, abducts Persephone and forces her to live with him in Hades. Demeter in her anger and sorrow at losing her daughter is viewed as so powerful of a goddess that she jeopardizes life on earth because she causes the fertility of the harvest to be halted. Even Zeus in the myth is forced to respond to Demeter's anger by declaring a deal between Demeter and Hades that allows Persephone to return to her mother during the seasons of growth and live with Hades during the seasons of dormancy. It is significant that both Zeus and Hades must bow to the will of Demeter in this myth. However, this myth, that is undoubtedly very old as it references Neolithic plot structures as found in similar myths from the Middle East, adds the male influence of Zeus to its narrative in an apparent attempt to interject the power of Zeus, as Zeus is clearly indicated in the myth as the father of Persephone, and the one who allowed Hades to abduct her in the first place. Also, Zeus's authority is seemingly intentionally showcased in the myth when he comes up with his compromise, which does not fully grant Demeter what she desires by returning everything to how it was before Zeus allowed Hades to abduct his daughter Persephone. Therefore, though Demeter is able to sway some of Zeus's power by way of her lasting authority, she still must bend to his patriarchal rule and accept his compromise.

There is another character in the myth of Demeter and Persephone who connects the myth to the maintenance of traditional goddess-oriented belief systems. In the myth, the character of Baubo is said to come to Demeter while she is mourning Persephone's abduction, and in order to aid Demeter in returning to her duties as goddess of the harvest, Baubo raises her skirts, showing her genitalia, which convinces Demeter to smile despite her pain, thus causing the reinstatement of the cycles of nature. Baubo then offers "Demeter the reviving ritual cup of *kykeon* (a potion of meal, mint, and water)" (Lubell 20). Therefore, Baubo "not only gave solace and thus shared in the sorrows of the Great Mother but also reenergized the goddess to be the nurturer of earth's fecundity" (Lubell 20). Lubell argues that Baubo's inclusion in the myth may signal that she at one time "played a more significant part in sacred fertility rituals associated with Demeter" (Lubell xv–xvi). Baubo was likely connected to very old agricultural rituals where "specifically appointed women squatted over the newly plowed fields and gave ... their menstrual fluid ... back to the earth.... In the fiercely misogynist climate of later patriarchal cultures, these old, old female rituals that had been closely connected with the earth and its cycles faded away or were effectively obliterated.... [Thus,] gradually, Baubo was transformed into an obscure creature of long-forgotten rituals" (Lubell 5).

The myth surrounding Demeter, Persephone, and Baubo was a central aspect of religious ritual, known as the Eleusinian Mysteries, throughout Greece into the Hellenistic period, and even extending into Roman times. The Eleusinian Mysteries were viewed as highly sacred. It is believed that initiates would make pilgrimages to the site of Eleusis, where mythically Persephone was said to be reunited with her mother after her time in Hades, signaling her, and the land's, rebirth each spring. Once at Eleusis, initiates would take part in highly secretive rites that were said to grant them a favorable afterlife, seemingly because taking part in the ritual gave them newfound understanding of the promise of rebirth after death, as found in nature's ceaseless cycles. Accounts of what occurred during the rites of the Eleusinian Mysteries discuss initiates making their way through long passageways within dark caves to commemorate Persephone's ordeal in Hades (Stone 371). Once the initiates had made it through the ritual and emerged from the caves, they were greeted by fertile fields and "wondrous sunshine" (Stone 371). This maintenance of the cultic following of Demeter into the Classical and Hellenistic periods shows that the traditional beliefs of a dominant Mother Earth Goddess was never fully eradicated for the common people, despite ample patriarchal attempts.

The virginal goddess of the wilderness and of the hunt, Artemis, is also an exemplary candidate to see how older goddess-centered beliefs manifested themselves in later time periods of patriarchal rule in Greece. Artemis was a later addition to the Olympic pantheon, but there is much evidence to link her to older belief systems within Greece, just as was seen with Hera and Demeter. Armstrong states that Artemis may even "be a Paleolithic figure" (Armstrong, 38). In addition, because of her connection to the wilderness, Artemis is often identified as the Minoan Mistress of Animals (Stone 381). As discussed in Chapter 2, Artemis's role as a Mother Goddess at her sacred shrine at Ephesus in Anatolia also points to her having an older origin than how she is presented in Classical and Hellenistic Greek mythology. Pausanias said of Artemis at Ephesus that "'All cities worship Artemis of Ephesus, and individuals hold Her in honour above all deities'" (qtd. in Stone 381). It is clear, though, that the central worship at Ephesus for Artemis as a primary Mother Goddess was purposefully demoted once she appeared in Hellenistic Greece.

Though Artemis is not portrayed as a powerful Mother Goddess in Greek mythology, she still is often depicted as a goddess who maintained a high degree of reverence. Unlike Hera and Aphrodite, who often were portrayed as stereotypical, and even at times comical, Artemis was portrayed with power even within Hellenistic Greece because she mythically chose to not marry a man and to remain a virgin. It is this aspect of remaining untouched by a man that allowed Artemis to be portrayed as an independent goddess who maintained her own authority. Most myths of Artemis show her as content living far removed from the Olympians in the deep recesses of the wilderness. She is often portrayed as alone or as being accompanied by only women followers. Thus, Artemis appears autonomous in her myths, standing alone as the goddess who seldom must bow down to the will of Zeus because she seems to have little to do with his affairs. These strong portrayals of Artemis again show the continued reverence that Greek worshippers felt for their traditional religious beliefs.

One popular myth of Artemis, involving the character of the mortal man Actaeon, shows her powerful and autonomous nature, but it also, in some ways, maintains a negative portrayal of Artemis under a patriarchal lens. The myth presents Actaeon, a hunter, spying on Artemis while she is bathing in the wilderness. Artemis sees him, and as a punishment for what she considers to be an assault, she turns Actaeon into a stag. Actaeon's hunting dogs see the stag, and not recognizing it as their master, tear Actaeon to pieces. This myth shows Artemis as certainly formidable, reflecting perhaps the fear audiences might have still held for the goddesses their ancestors revered in more elevated roles, but it also simultaneously casts Artemis as a villain. Many Classical and Hellenistic myths show remnants of Neolithic earth goddesses abusing male consort symbols, identifying them as bloodthirsty and dangerous to the men they encounter, similar to how Gilgamesh defined Ishtar when she wished to marry him. Identifying the actions of goddesses as overtly harsh meets a patriarchal agenda of showing them not as aiding the processes of nature, that are both destructive and regenerative, but as only destructive, and thus monstrous and cruel.

The goddess Athena also presents a formidable figure in Greek mythology, but unlike Artemis, whose respectability comes from her fierce independence and seclusion within wild environments, Athena is very much a goddess who was modified and nurtured within Classic and Hellenistic mythological depictions to display patriarchal religious and social agendas. Athena, like Artemis, mythically demands to remain a virgin, and thus, like Artemis, she is allowed within Greek mythic narratives to remain powerful and seemingly autonomous. But unlike Artemis, Athena rarely is portrayed as entirely independent, as Athena is most often mythically linked with the wishes of Zeus, her creator. On the surface, the admiration for Athena makes it seem that the ancient Greeks revered formidable women, but when her role is examined more closely, it is not hard to see that her mythic contributions are often portrayed as female divine authority that is safely contained under male leadership.

The myth of Athena's birth displays a transfer of power from her formidable Titaness mother, Metis, to Zeus. In yet another sexual escapade of Zeus, he takes over the power of Metis when he learns that their encounter produced two offspring—Athena, and a son who would one day overthrow his power, just as he had done to his own father, Cronus. Again, in a mythic scene used to justify Zeus's superior position over a once powerful goddess, Zeus swallows Metis, performing the same act he despised in his own father. However, Zeus soon finds that he comes down with an overwhelming headache. Hephaestus, in trying to alleviate Zeus's headache, hits him upon the head, and a fully-grown, fully armored, Athena appears. This portrayal of Athena's birth marks her as a goddess who was born directly from the overthrow of her mother by the male leader of the Olympic pantheon. Being birthed from a male, the body of Zeus, and not from the female body of a goddess, secures ultimate power into the hands of Zeus, as he mythically is portrayed here as even capable of the one act associated with only women—birth. The ever-present mythic reminder of Athena shows worshippers that Zeus, like the Hebrew Yahweh, possesses the right to reign because he is superior to all goddesses who came before him, as he can overpower them and even secure the abilities that were once only theirs.

Athena became in Classical and Hellenistic times the goddess of wisdom and strategic warfare. She was portrayed as looking formidable, as she was most often depicted in full armor, but truly Athena often appears as little more than a spokesperson for Zeus's patriarchy in many Greek myths. A perfect example of the created role of Athena to serve a patriarchal agenda appears in Aeschylus's play *Eumenides* (458 BCE). *Eumenides* succinctly provides evidence of the conflict regarding the shift in perception of matriarchal to patriarchal power structures in Greece. Lerner contends that the "force and importance of [the] symbolic downgrading of the mother is ... elaborated in Aeschylus's *The Furies* [*Eumenides*]," as this play "has been interpreted by a number of critics as signifying the last defense of Mother-Goddess power against patriarchy" (Lerner 205). The play shows that after Orestes murders his mother, Clytemnestra, in vengeance for her having killed his father, Agamemnon, Orestes is then pursued by the Erinyes, also known as the Furies. The Erinyes were thought to be chthonic goddesses, more ancient than the Olympians, and as such, they represented within the play traditional, goddess-oriented belief systems. It is especially significant to the play that the Erinyes relentlessly pursue Orestes for the murder of his mother, as they contend that the murder of one's mother is the worst crime one can commit. The Erinyes' central argument in the play is that Orestes's crime of killing his own mother is the most heinous of crimes based on the belief that the mother's bloodline defines kinship. However, the play's aim is to show that this belief is an outdated remnant of matriarchal power; thus, the play's dialogue places kinship only through the father's line, which serves to lessen Orestes's crime, since he killed his mother to avenge his father.

The play begins with Orestes being utterly tormented by the Erinyes at the Oracle of Delphi, which is quite significant for its portrayal of the degradation of more traditional goddesses. Apollo was attributed as the god who reigned over the Oracle at Delphi; however, this male rule was not always in place. The Oracle at Delphi belonged initially to the Mother Earth Goddess Gaia. The Homeric Hymn to Apollo is another myth that displays a justification for eradicating older female-oriented belief systems, when Apollo, as the son of Zeus, kills Gaia's python guardian of the sacred oracle, so that he may secure rule over the oracle. In Apollo killing the python, he shows audiences that he is now the dominant male god at the site. Starting the *Eumenides* at the contested site where Gaia lost her power to the young Apollo is a fitting choice, as the play will attempt to make a similar assault against the power of all traditional goddess worship by its completion.

In the *Eumenides*, Orestes leaves Delphi, because apparently the power of the old goddesses was too strong there, portrayed in the play through the

Erinyes holding the ability to ceaselessly torment him there and the ability of the ghost of his mother, Clytemnestra, to repeatedly voice her outrage to him while at Delphi. Orestes instead makes his way to Athens, so that he will be protected by Athena, who will hold a council among the gods to decide Orestes's fate, which really is presented in the play as a debate regarding matrilineal or patrilineal kinship ties, or more succinctly matriarchy versus patriarchy. Apollo is one of the gods present at the council, and he, not surprisingly, argues that one should no longer assume that kinship is passed matrilineally; instead, he contends that patrilineal kinship should now be viewed as superior:

> "Not the true parent is the woman's womb
> That bears the child; she doth but nurse the seed
> New-sown: the male is parent; she for him,
> As stranger for a stranger, hoards the germ
> Of life, unless the god its promise blight.
> And proof hereof before you will I set.
> Birth may from fathers, without mothers, be:
> See at your side a witness of the same,
> Athena, daughter of Olympian Zeus,
> Never within the darkness of the womb." [Aeschylus]

Athena, then, is pointed out here by Apollo as being the perfect spokesperson to argue against matrilineal descent because she herself was birthed directly from the male Zeus. Thus, the play concludes with Athena holding the final vote that will ultimately declare that kinship should move away from matrilineal identification to only patrilineal lines, making the murder of a mother, Clytemnestra, by her son, Orestes, allowed, and thus, fully eradicating the power of the old religion of dominant goddesses. Athena states:

> "Mine is the right to add the final vote,
> And I award it to Orestes's cause.
> For me no mother bore within her womb....
> I vouch myself the champion of the man,
> Not of the woman, yea, with all my soul,—
> In heart, as birth, a father's child alone.
> Thus will I not too heinously regard
> A woman's death who did her husband slay,
> The guardian of her home" [Aeschylus].

In having the goddess Athena proclaim that the true parent of a child is in actuality the father as opposed to the mother, the arguments made by the chthonic Erinyes, representatives of more traditional, matriarchal belief systems, are presented as false, outdated, and even dangerous. Lerner states that "It is Athena's deciding vote, which frees Orestes and banishes the Furies and with them the claims of the Mother-Goddess" (Lerner 205).

All of the members of the council applaud Athena's wisdom, but the Erinyes voice their rage at such a conclusion. To squelch the rage of the ancient Erinyes, again the goddess Athena steps in, because she is the only one who is able to voice what should be offensive arguments about eradicating the importance of the mother and her line, as she looks to audiences to be a nurturing goddess who will protect them, and who also is renowned for her wisdom, but in reality she is a goddess who was purposefully modified in Classical and Hellenistic mythology to perpetuate patriarchal power structures. When audiences hear the wise Athena making proclamations against goddesses and women in general, it is easier for them to accept such arguments because she is of course a woman and a goddess. Therefore, in the play, Athena tempers the rage of the Erinyes by promising them that they will still be worshipped by the people, but only if they allow themselves to be transformed away from their more ancient, and thus troublesome, traditional identification into amenable pawns without power. Again, not surprisingly, given the goal of the play, the Erinyes readily agree and transform into the benevolent Eumenides.

Many famous Greek myths also recount male heroes who clearly serve a patriarchal agenda by the hero's degradation or defeat of powerful mythic goddesses. For example, Homer's famous epic, the *Odyssey*, written in the eighth century BCE, is full of powerful female characters, both divine and human, who are degraded by Odysseus, as he is guided to complete his quest by the spokesperson for patriarchy—Athena. For instance, the character Circe is portrayed in the *Odyssey* as a witch, though she clearly depicts tenets in line with portrayals of traditional earth goddesses. Circe is able to transform men into animals, as she does with Odysseus's men by transforming them into swine. Circe also lives alone on her own secluded island that is full of tamed beasts, aligning her with more ancient earth goddesses who held their power within natural environments, such as the Minoan Mistress of Animals. Circe also shows that she possesses connections with the underworld, which again is common for traditional earth goddesses, as she is the one who instructs Odysseus how to make his necessary journey to Hades. When Odysseus meets Circe, their interaction certainly suggests an element of conflict between traditional and new belief systems in Greece. Odysseus is told by the messenger god Hermes that he must have sex with Circe upon meeting her, which points to a long history of the male hero receiving affirmation by sexual union from a goddess, as discussed in the Sacred Marriage rituals. However, in showing the patriarchal agenda of the text, Hermes also instructs Odysseus to be wary of Circe's witchlike trickery, as audiences would have known the "danger a mortal man risks in sleeping with a goddess: death or emasculation" (Van Nortwick 55), as was highlighted with Gilgamesh and Ishtar.

To ward off Circe's magic, Hermes tells Odysseus to overpower her in bed by holding his sword to her throat. This explicitly violent act asserts Odysseus's male dominance over Circe, showing, like many other Greek mythic males, that his might overpowers her authority. This type of mythic scene reinforces to audiences the idea that the new patriarchal religion is more powerful than the old religion. Another important female character in the *Odyssey* is the goddess Calypso, who also lives alone in a wild environment that she controls, showing, like Circe, her earth goddess status. As an earth goddess, Calypso offers Odysseus immortality, which was the symbolic promise to Neolithic male consorts, as they would symbolically live forever through the natural cycle, but like many Greek mythic male heroes representing a rising patriarchal system, Odysseus denies the reward of the earth goddess, just as he did with Circe, and asserts his own desires, which for him, is to return to his home of Ithaca and resume his rule as king. Finally, Odysseus's wife Penelope also plays an important role in the text. Penelope is portrayed as maintaining the kingdom of Ithaca independently for twenty years in Odysseus's absence, but her rule abruptly ends when Odysseus returns home, with the help of Athena. Once home, Odysseus proclaims his ultimate authority by murdering Penelope's suitors and ambiguously hanging twelve of her maids, who were loyal to Penelope, but had affairs with her suitors. Odysseus then cleanses his home with fire, eliminating the years of Penelope's rule.

Another famous Greek hero is Theseus. Theseus earned his title as hero in his defeat of the Minotaur from Crete. This myth presents a political agenda meant to degrade the remaining reverence for the powerful Minoan goddesses of Crete. The myth shows Theseus, the prince of Athens, as volunteering to go to Crete to destroy the Minotaur, because Crete is shown to hold more power than Athens, and to assert their power, they required Athens to send fourteen youths to be sacrificed to the Minotaur. When Theseus arrives at Crete, he gets vital help from the princess of Crete, Ariadne, who immediately falls in love with him. It is Ariadne's help that allows Theseus to easily kill the Minotaur and thus strip Crete of its power. Theseus is deemed a Greek hero with this single violent act, he flees Crete with Ariadne, has sex with her, and then abandons her on the island of Naxos, so that he may return to Athens and try to become king.

Bulls were a well-known symbol throughout Crete; for example, the Minoan Palace of Knossos is surrounded by myriad representations of bulls, so it would have been clear to audiences of Theseus's myth that the Minotaur—half man, half bull—was a symbol that was connected to the goddesses of the Minoans. As Neolithic symbols connected to Minoan earth goddesses, the bulls of Crete may be a representation of male consorts, and like other myths of male consorts, their sacrifice may have been required to replenish the cycles of nature. Therefore, in portraying Theseus as brutally killing the Minotaur, he is presented by a patriarchal agenda as eradicating the power of the old goddesses. Conway supports this in stating that the Minotaur was created as a mythic device to demonize "Minoan political authority. The defeat of the Minotaur, who could be viewed as the prince of Minos ... signals a reversal of power with the fall of the Minoans and the rise of the Mycenaean Greeks" (Conway).

There are many other elements within this myth that serve a patriarchal agenda against Minoan traditional beliefs. Barnes states that "for millennia" the myth of Theseus and the Minotaur was meant to represent "all that was bad in Crete and that the Athenians and the Greeks were meant to replace" (Barnes 101). For example, Europa, the mother of King Minos of Crete, was said to have come from Phoenicia, and some scholars state that Europa, like many other mortal women within Greek mythology, may have also once been a more powerful goddess. However, Europa in this myth appears as merely another of Zeus's conquests, as Zeus was said to appear to Europa in the form of a white bull who seduced or raped her, depending on the version of the myth, and then carried her away to Crete to give birth to the son he left her with—King Minos. Showing Europa as a mortal woman who gets seduced or raped by Zeus in the form of a bull sends a patriarchal message that any association with the bulls of Crete and Europa, who again might have once been a goddess, is now controlled by Zeus. The myth continues to show King Minos growing up and marrying Pasiphae, another mythic mortal woman who may have once been revered as a goddess on Crete. The myth itself hints at Pasiphae's divine status, as she is said to come from Colchis as the daughter of the sun god Helios. However, Pasiphae's role within this myth of the Minotaur also shows her as degraded, as she was said to have sex with an actual bull while dressing up as a cow, which causes her to become pregnant with the Minotaur. Mythically presenting Pasiphae as a mortal woman who lusts after an animal is certainly a mythic device meant to strip Pasiphae of any power she might have once held on Crete, so that she becomes remembered by audiences as merely a joke.

Another famous myth involving a young male hero who violently kills a representation of a traditional goddess can be perhaps best seen in the Greek myth of Perseus and the gorgon Medusa. Like other Greek heroes, Perseus slays Medusa in a vicious manner by cutting her head off. This violent act is aided by the patriarchal Olympic pantheon, as the gods Hades and Hermes, as well as the goddess Athena, all give Perseus mystical items that will help him achieve his mission, of which he accomplishes with ease. However, there is more to Medusa than simply a snake-ridden monster. Once again, the symbol of the serpent was used to support the patriarchal agenda of conquering the power of the old goddesses. By literally covering Medusa in serpents, she mythically appears not as sacred by as horrific; this intentional mythic portrayal degrades any divine status Medusa may have once held, as well as denigrates the traditional goddess-oriented symbol of the serpent. Frothingham states that Medusa, like many female mythic characters who are portrayed as monsters in Greek mythology, was indeed once revered as a goddess. A depiction at Corfu portrays the gorgon Medusa standing among many animals, showing her to be an earth goddess, who "is conceived here as the Great Mother ... as both a serpent goddess and a mistress of beasts" (Frothingham, 357). Medusa, and the other gorgons of Greek mythology, was originally "not an evil demon ... but primarily a nature goddess ... an embodiment of the productive and destructive forces of [nature]. After dominating in pre–Hellenistic times, she was given in later times a subordinate part in the Olympian system" (Frothingham, 349). Campbell also agrees, stating that "the legend of Perseus beheading Medusa means, specifically, that the Hellenes overran the earth goddesses' chief shrines and stripped their priestesses of their Gorgon masks, the ... apotropaic faces worn to frighten away the profane. That is to say, there occurred in the early thirteenth century BC[E] an actual historic rupture, a sort of sociological trauma, which has been registered in this myth" (Campbell 152–3).

As has been seen in the other cultures discussed in this book, the degradation of goddesses and female characters within Greek mythology reflected the treatment of women within Greek culture during the Classical and Hellenistic periods. As stated, women were once highly regarded within Minoan societies, as myriad artistic representations of Minoan women portray them as queens, priestesses, athletes, etc. However, after Mycenaean and other Indo-European groups began to dominate Greece, causing patriarchy to form and spread, the social status of Greek women mimicked what was being reflected within Greek mythology regarding goddesses and female mythic characters. Some women were able to hold important roles within Greek religion, primarily serving as priestesses, such as the famed Pythia from Delphi, though these positions were uncommon, and increasingly became the right of priests. However, for the majority of women in Greece, their role became shockingly subservient. The family structure in the Classical and Hellenistic periods in Greece was severely patriarchal. Women were controlled by their fathers, other male relatives, or their husbands. Lerner explains that "Women in Athens were ... lifelong minors under the guardianship of a male" (Lerner 203). Vivante states, "Athenian women were not considered legal persons in their own right, but as legal minors they were required to have a male guardian ... their fathers as daughters, their husbands upon marriage, and return to their fathers, sons, or other male relative if widowed or divorced" (Vivante 241). Therefore, Athenian women were "treated only as a property that was marketable and could be transferred from one to the other" (Kidwai 6). Women were ceremoniously taken from their father's household to their husband's household in marriage ceremonies, and it was there that women remained throughout the majority of their lives. Athenian women were confined to the home and were primarily restricted from taking part in communal affairs (Vivante 240). Women of the household were kept hidden in a remote part of the house, where no contact by males could occur, unless they were close relatives. In addition, married women were also required to be veiled, just like in ancient Mesopotamia. This tradition of forcing women to wear an explicit signal, a veil, to show the public a man's ownership of a woman would also become a practice that was adopted by Christianity in Greece.

Many Greek philosophers, such as Aristotle, "institutionalize[d] and rationalize[d] the exclusion of women from political citizenship as the very foundation of the democratic polity" (Lerner 211). Likewise, the Greek philosopher Plato "classes women together with children and servants, and states generally that in all the pursuits of mankind the female sex is inferior to the male" (Kidwai 6). Thus, this ancient Greek view of women would be used by Western civilization "for centuries in its science, its philosophy, and its gender doctrine" (Lerner 211). Lerner also contends that because of the development of patriarchy in Greece, as well as the introduction and adoption of Christianity in Greece, much of Western civilization would go on to incorporate "the assumption of female insubordination and inferiority ... so completely ... that it appeared 'natural' both to men and women" (Lerner 211). This assumption of women as socially, politically, and spiritually inferior largely remains intact today, as women in contemporary Greece still struggle to obtain equality in political and social affairs, in the workplace, and in the home. Women also are still banned from serving in the roles of priest, bishop, etc., within the Greek Orthodox Church.

## Italy and the Roman Empire

The Italic people, who were descended from Indo-European speakers, migrated to Italy during the region's late Bronze Age (1800–900 BCE). Just as with Greece, there are elements of Latin and Roman culture that display Indo-European elements, such as the belief in a supreme sky god, who was in the case of the Romans, the god Jupiter. Also, the Romans in large part adopted the religion of the Greeks, so many Roman deities maintained the roles they held in Greek religion. However, some goddesses appeared to hold more prominent roles in the Roman pantheon than they did in the Greek pantheon, such as Juno (Hera) and Minerva (Athena). Juno and Minerva were revered as two members of the top triad of Roman divinities, alongside Jupiter (Zeus). So, instead of the divine triad directly following the Greek triad of Zeus, Poseidon, and Hades, the Romans revered Jupiter, Juno, and Minerva as their top three deities. Allowing two goddesses and one god to reign at the top position of the hierarchy of divinities is certainly unusual in a religion that was shaped by Indo-European influence; however, many scholars believe that this arrangement probably derived from the Etruscans, the pre–Indo-European people of Italy. The Etruscans, like many other pre–Indo-European cultures, held goddesses in high regard, so many scholars attribute the Etruscan worship of the triad of two goddesses, Uni and Menrva, with the god Tinia, as influencing the Romans to maintain reverence for two goddesses in the highest positions of their pantheon. The Romans also incorporated other deities from the Etruscans into their religion, such as the goddess Vesta, goddess of the hearth. However, just because Juno and Minerva held these high positions in Roman religion, the two were still most often portrayed in similar fashion to how they appeared in Greek mythology. Thus, it was clear that Jupiter was the true head of the Roman pantheon.

Also, somewhat contrary to Classical and Hellenistic Greek religion, Roman religion maintained a strong reverence for the concept of the Great Mother, known to them as the "Mater Magna." Apuleius in the *Golden Ass*, published in the late second century CE, discusses this belief in a unified Great Mother that was widely held throughout the Roman Empire:

"I am Nature, the universal Mother, mistress of all elements, primordial child of time, sovereign of all things spiritual, queen of the dead, queen also of the immortals, the single manifestation of all gods and goddesses that are.... Though I am worshipped in many aspects, known by countless names ... yet the whole round earth venerates me. The primeval Phrygians call me Pessinuntica, Mother of the gods; the Athenians ... call me Artemis, for the islanders of Cyprus I am Aphrodite; for the archers of Crete, I am Dictynna; for the Sicilians, Persephone; and for the Eleusinians their ancient Mother of Corn ... the Egyptians who excel in ancient learning worship me with ceremonies proper to my godhead, call me by my true name, namely Queen Isis" [Apuleius 197–8].

Romans adopted the concept of the Great Mother from Anatolia with the worship of the goddess Cybele, as discussed in Chapter 2 of this book. Cybele's worship in Rome became so widespread that in 204 BCE, the Romans journeyed to Anatolia to retrieve a sacred black meteorite representing the goddess Cybele and brought it back to Palatine Hill to seek Cybele's favor for Rome. However, it appears that the Romans largely adopted the worship of the Great Mother to gain political advantage. Munn contends that adopting the concept of a Great Mother allowed Romans to legitimize the rulership of male deities, as was seen in the Sacred Marriage rituals in Anatolia, Greece, and elsewhere (Munn 12).

Still the somewhat increased reverence that Roman goddesses, like Juno, Minerva, and the Magna Mater, held within Roman society played a role in elevating the rights of women within Roman society to a better position than the role of women in Greece. For instance, some women were allowed to hold high religious positions in ancient Rome. The famous Vestal Virgins held high honor in Roman society; they "played symbolic roles in public religious ceremonies of major political import to the state. Their principal function was to preserve and perpetuate Rome's sacred rites and the fire of the city" (Vivante 267). In addition, there existed "a number of rites that provided an opportunity for women of different ages—and at times, different social classes—to come together and to forge closer ties with one another" (Vivante 267). Also, Roman women often held more communal positions than the women of ancient Greece; "it is clear that [Roman] women engaged in a wide variety of activities, including several paid occupations" (Hallett 261). Roman women were also allowed to venture into public. Furthermore, some Roman women possessed the ability to hold "power in their individual households and extended family groups, romantic relationships, religious associations, and (at times) political decision making at the highest levels of Roman governance" (Hallett 261). Though, it should be said, that most of these women who held such elevated social and political positions belonged to the minority of elite Roman women. These high-standing women were also permitted "to inherit land and other possessions in their own right" (Vivante 287).

Despite these allowances, most Roman women were strictly stifled under the patriarchal values of the Roman Empire. Patriarchal lineage was a key element of Roman rule. According to Roman law, a woman was considered entirely dependent; "As an unmarried girl she was under the perpetual tutelage of her father during his life, and after his death of her agnates by blood or adoption. When married, she and her whole property passed into the power and possession of her husband. In fact, she herself was treated as a property by her husband … [with] no more right than a purchased slave. At certain stages of Roman law a husband was given the right to kill his wife" (Kidwai 3-4). The marriage age for a typical Roman girl was about twelve years old. After marriage, a Roman woman was treated like a child "by her husband and master, who was invested with the plentitude of paternal power over her just as over her daughter" (Kidwai

4). Married Roman women were also required to be veiled, just as their Middle Eastern and Greek counterparts were. In addition, Roman women also could not hold civil or public office (Kidwai 4). Again, in large part, these stipulations upon the rights of Roman women were connected to the worship of mostly stereotypical, patriarchal goddesses carried over from Greece and other regions.

Many mystery religions became popular in ancient Rome; "Mystery traditions focused on initiation of devotees, who sought preferential treatment in the underworld, as well as happiness and prosperity in this world" (Stuckey 85). These mystery religions were part of Greek culture for centuries, such as the Eleusinian Mysteries in Greece, and they were carried all throughout the Greco-Roman world. These mystery religions most often associated themselves with deities who had died and resurrected within mythological narratives, like the Greek Persephone, Dionysus, and Orpheus, as well as the Egyptian Osiris and Phrygian Attis. Stuckey states that "one of the titles of such [resurrected] deities was 'Saviour'" (Stuckey 86). In addition, "The dominant deity in almost all the Mysteries was ... a [Mother] Goddess—[Egyptian] Isis, [Phrygian] Cybele, [Greek] Demeter, for instance—to whom the saviour deity, usually Her child, was subordinate" (Stuckey 86). Cults associated with the goddess Cybele were found all throughout the Roman Empire. Cybele's cults would enact the famous myth of Cybele and Attis, discussed in Chapter 2, which would result in some of the followers of Cybele, the galli, castrating themselves to honor her, just as Attis was castrated within the myth. In his myth, Attis died as a result of his castration, but as a deity associated with fertility, like other Greek, Mesopotamian, and Egyptian fertility deities, Attis was believed to resurrect annually in association with nature's cycles by the decree of the Mother Goddess Cybele.

In Rome, Christianity, which was based off of Judaism and began to be practiced as its own religion in the first century CE, appeared as only another of these mystery religions that existed within the vast Roman Empire. Many of the concepts from the other mystery religions in the Roman Empire influenced the burgeoning new faith of Christianity and helped shape its doctrine in the Roman Empire. For instance, the Christian figure of Christ took over the familiar role of the resurrected deity just discussed. Additionally, the Virgin Mary, though demoted to mortal status, adopted the role of the once primary Mother Goddess of the old mystery religions. Borgeaud connects the popular Roman mystery religion of Cybele and Attis with the development of Christian concepts, stating that the story of the shepherd Attis deeply resembled the story of Christ, and Cybele, the Great Mother/ Magna Mater, became the "Mother of God, on a throne strikingly similar to the one used by the Mother of the gods [Cybele]" (Borgeaud 124).

In fact, the Christian apostle Paul is credited as helping to make Christianity more accessible to the people by combining elements from the mythology of Greece, and other cultures, with Jewish religious beliefs. Shlain discusses how Paul, formerly Saul of Tarsus, was a "thoroughly Hellenized Greek Jew," and because of this, he was exposed to the beliefs of the mystery religions in the area (Shlain 229). After rejecting his Jewish upbringing, because he believed Christ revealed the true path to him, Paul traveled throughout Asia Minor where the cult of Cybele and Attis was prominent. Shlain states that the popular imagery for the cult of Cybele and Attis, which often showed Attis being "tied to a tree with his arms outstretched," until he died, and "returned to life through the agency of his mother" three days later, may have been incorporated into Paul's Epistles (c. 40–50 CE), which were the earliest documents of Christianity that would go on to "influence everyone who subsequently wrote about Jesus," including the authors of the Four Gospels written around 60–110 CE, many years after the life of Jesus (Shlain 231). Because Paul was able to make Christianity recognizable, by using familiar mythic elements that people were already accustomed to, he went on to become the most effective "proselytizer before the new sect than any other disciple" (Shlain 231). For instance, Paul "was indispensable to the new religion" because Paul managed to sell a monotheistic God to polytheists by providing God "with a family," by revealing that Yahweh beget a son from a human Mary (Shlain 235), just as the Greek Semele, Dionysus's mother, "had been inseminated by the chief deity [Zeus], and she was but one of many mortal/divine matings in Greco-Roman mythology" (Shlain 235). The fact that Mary is presented as human, and not divine, within Christian doctrine is certainly intentional, as it is clear that Paul utterly rejected the existence of any goddesses within Christianity, as Judaism had done. At the sacred shrine to Artemis (Roman Diana) at Ephesus, Paul declared: "'The sanctuary of the great goddess Diana/ will cease to command respect/ and then it will not be long/ before she who is worshipped by all Asia/ and the civilized world/ will be brought down/ from her divine pre-eminence (Acts 19:27)'" (qtd. in Stone 206).

Not surprisingly, with Paul's rejection of goddesses, came a clear positioning of women in an inferior role:

> Paul insisted that the church's hierarchal pyramid be exclusively male. Jesus stood at the apex. Below, on the next tier, were eleven of the original twelve apostles plus Paul, who had not been a member of Jesus's inner circle. This arrangement excluded Mary Magdalene, who had been a member. Each apostle had appointed a bishop.... The bishop of Rome, or pope, functioned as Christ's vicar on earth. The pope steadily consolidated his authority over Western bishops who wielded absolute authority over religious matters....

Women's spirituality, which had been undisputed for thousands of years, became suspect in this new wing of the religion.... By the year 200 [CE], the Orthodox had formally relegated women to the back of the church and had eliminated all imagery or references related to the Goddess from the New Testament [Shlain 239].

Early envisioning of Christian concepts had to further contend with how to best present the Virgin Mary. In focusing on the miraculous pregnancy of Mary, and her ability, though a virgin, to birth the son of God, Borgeaud states that early Christian councils had to seek a means to define Mary as human and not divine, just as Paul did (Borgeaud 129). The images and stories surrounding the Virgin Mary allows her to assume the role of the goddesses who came before her, such as: "Cybele, Aphrodite, Astarte, Isis, Hathor, Inanna and Ishtar. Like them, she is both virgin and mother, and, like many of them, she gives birth to a half-human, half-divine child, who dies and is reborn. Jesus, like Attis, Adonis, Persephone, Osiris, Tammuz and Dumuzi before him, descends into the underworld of hell, where regeneration has always taken place, and his ascent and resurrection, like theirs, is understood to redeem all incarnate beings from the limitation of mortality and time" (Baring & Cashford 548). For almost five hundred years, the images of Mary were of a concern to religious officials, as the artistic representations often emulated previous representations of Mother Goddesses. For example, "Portraits at the end of the fourth century and beginning of the fifth show Mary seated in the same position as [the Egyptian goddess] Isis with Horus, wearing the mural crown of Cybele or Diana, and with the gorgon of Athena painted on her breast.... In fact, it looks as if the imagery of the older goddesses had passed directly on to the figure of Mary" (Baring & Cashford 551). Additionally, places held in worship of earlier goddesses became centers of worship for the Virgin Mary; for example, the Temple of Isis in Soissons, France and the Temple to Athena, the Parthenon, both became dedicated to Mary (Baring & Cashford 551). Even the most popular of sites to honor the Great Mother since the Bronze Age—Artemis's shrine at Ephesus, became Mary's shrine (Borgeaud 129). As stated in Chapter 2, Mary also was said to spend her last days at Ephesus (Borgeaud 129).

Given the trouble that people still conceived of the Virgin Mary as the traditional Great Mother, the Roman Emperor Constantine, who in 312 CE denounced the Roman deities as pagan and converted to Christianity, making Christianity a privileged religion in the Roman Empire, felt that he had to make a statement about the conflict between the Great Mother goddess, and Mary, the Mother of God. Constantine was said to have taken a statue of the Great Mother from Kyzikan and brought it back to Byzantium where he "mutilated" it by removing the sacred lions that stood at the Goddess's side and repositioned her hands to not hold back lions, but to show a stance of piousness and protection for his city (Borgeaud 131). The continued adoration of Mary in ways that resembled goddess worship also caused church officials in 431 CE to form a council in Ephesus that proclaimed that Mary should be "honored" but not "adored" (Baring & Cashford 550). As was seen in Celtic cultures that transferred Celtic deities into Christian saints, Mary was officially decreed a human saint. Borgeaud states that "Solidifying Mary as a human saint made the reverence attributed to Mary as firmly the human mother of Christ, so that worship for the Mother of the gods became reversed from former conceptions, to the son, Christ, being worshipped before his mother" (Borgeaud 129).

However, as discussed in other cultures thus far, even though the Christian church made it clear that Mary held no divinity, many people, even to this day, still revere the Virgin Mary in terms that appear similar to the traditional worship of the Great Mother. When the Julian calendar was adopted, the festival of Cybele's and Attis's Hilaria became moved to May 1, so May became the month sacred to the Great Mother Cybele. Once Christianity dominated, May became identified with Mary; thus, on May 1, "the statue of Mary was, and still is, crowned and garlanded with flowers, and drawn through the streets. The magnificent floats holding the Virgin Mother and her Son … may be the last vestiges of those effigies that were once borne through the streets of Rome, Alexandria, and Babylon" for the Great Mother (Baring & Cashford 410).

Again, Christianity's eradication of conceptualizing divinity as feminine would cause the social role of women to further decline throughout the Roman Empire, including in Constantinople in the Eastern Roman Empire, and would stretch throughout the rest of the Western world, so that in time, it would define women as the inferior sex, a definition that would hold for centuries, even into contemporary times. Stuckey explains that "Like most of the Mysteries, early Christianity was egalitarian, and so it attracted converts from all walks of life, large numbers of whom were women. The New Testament makes no secret of the fact that female converts were deeply involved in the spread and development of the new spirituality" (Stuckey 90). As discussed, some women in ancient Rome could hold prominent religious positions, and the same was true for early Christianity, as some women were able to "function as prophets, apostles, evangelists, deacons, priests, and even bishops" (Stuckey 91). Some Christian women were also able to hold leadership positions because it was believed, early on, that women sometimes held prophetic abilities (Stuckey 91), such as was seen with the sybils in pagan Rome. In fact, many contend that Jesus valued the spirituality of males and females alike. For instance, Jesus "included women in his innermost circle of disciples," such as Mary Magdalene, to whom he appeared first after resurrecting (Keller 231). However, this allowance for women to hold powerful religious roles would soon come to an end, as "women's leadership became a contentious issue quite early in Christianity's development" (Stuckey 91). For example, "the gospel attributed to Mary Magdalene was not included in the canon of New Testament writings selected by the early church fathers, [likewise] women's spiritual leadership in the early Christian church was suppressed" (Keller 231).

From the second to the fifth centuries CE, and into the Middle Ages, "the Christian church became increasingly patriarchal" (Stuckey 88). In this period, the "Fathers of the Church," the "bishop-theologians who were all men ... preached and wrote on the numerous controversies of the developing Christian church" (Stuckey 88). It was during this period that "opponents of women's leadership gained ascendency, and eventually the church declared most branches of early Christianity in which women were prominent to be heretical" (Stuckey 92). By the third century CE, "early church Fathers such as Tertullian, Chrysostom, and Augustine of Hippo had started to elaborate a Christian tradition of misogyny and hostility toward ... women" (Stuckey 88). In the fourth century CE, Augustine created several "extra-scriptural doctrines based on his interpretation of Christianity's canonized texts," that repeatedly touted an agenda that proclaimed women as "morally weaker than men and justified their subjugation because they, like Eve, were temptresses" (Shlain 250). Keller believes that the "myth of Eve's culpability for humanity's expulsion from the Garden has been used through the centuries as a model for scapegoating women for the social ills of patriarchal societies" (Keller 232). Augustine also supported the idea that Christian women should remain veiled, stating that "the problem for women was the 'sex of their body,' which prevented them from being in the image of God and this meant that they were, 'bidden to be veiled'" (qtd. in Jeffreys 28). Revered Christians saints, such as "St. Bernard, St. Anthony, St. Bonaventure, St. Jerome, St. Gregory the Great, and St. Cyprian, all cursed women, and showered such abuses upon the sex as 'the organ of the devil,' 'the foundation of the arms of the devil, 'a scorpion ever ready to sting,' 'the gate of the devil and the road of iniquity,' 'the poison of an asp, the malice of a dragon,' and 'the instrument which the devil uses to gain possession of our souls'" (qtd. in Kidwai 29).

Kidwai states that "even the Reformation did not do much to relieve women" of extreme patriarchal prejudice (Kidwai 23). Armstrong states that despite Martin Luther's own marriage, he "had little time for women, who were to be punished for Eve's sin by exclusion from public life. A woman, he decreed, was to remain in the home 'like a nail driven into the wall'" (Armstrong ix). As stated in the first chapter of this book, these heinous views against women "erupted most visibly during the Middle Ages and early modern age with the torture and burnings by the Catholic and Protestant church hierarchies of many thousands, perhaps millions, of women accused of being witches in Europe and in the Americas—a holocaust against women rationalized (in part) by citing scripture (Exodus 22:18)" (Keller 232).

Esposito states that as Christianity spread and dominated the West, it promoted the "ontological necessity of God's being male and that men were God's redemptive ministers, leaders of the church and interpreters of scripture and tradition. Women were either seen as the source of evil, irrational or immoral, or idealized as mothers but unfit by their nature to teach and minister" (Esposito 6). Thus, "God was imaged in male terms, in terms of power and hierarchal relationships, while women were the corresponding objects of subjugation and domination, exploitation, and injustice" (Esposito 6). Therefore, with Christianity's demand that divinity should not be imagined as female, the social definition and rights of women reached despicable lows that carried forward from Rome into the greater Western world for centuries to come. In many ways, this legacy still holds firm today.

## Chapter 4

# India

As with the Mediterranean, the long history of goddess worship, and the overwhelming archeological and mythic record showcasing this history, makes it important to discuss India as a region of special focus within this chapter.

In the fourth and third millennia BCE, it is believed that goddesses held a prominent position in the Neolithic Dravidian cultures of the Indus Valley. Shlain explains that archeological evidence reveals that throughout the subcontinent of India, "there once flourished relatively egalitarian, Goddess-worshipping cultures" (Shlain 160). Most significantly, the two sites of Mohenjo-Daro in the south and Harappa in the north, show archeological evidence of significant goddess worship (Lang 35). Many female figurines and artistic images suggesting the reverence of goddesses have been found at these, and other, sites throughout India. Shlain states that the "large majority" of these artifacts recovered from the Indus Valley appear to represent the veneration of a "Mother Goddess" (Shlain 160). This depiction of a Mother Goddess shows her as being connected to "vegetation and fertility"; for instance, one seal discovered in the Indus Valley "depicts a tree emerging from the womb of a nude woman…. Another seal shows a naked woman emerging from the bush, and a row of kneeling figures pictured beneath her who appear to be worshipping her" (Lang 27). In addition, representations of "animal-and bird-faced goddesses" have also been found in the Indus Valley and speak towards a "common religious" belief that connected these Mother Goddesses with nature, as well as with "procreation and fertility" (Gupto 39). Thus, many scholars believe that "The Indus Valley people had their major deity in the forms of mother goddesses" who were conceptions of the land itself (Gupto 39).

Aligned with the reverence for Mother Goddesses in Neolithic India, there appears to have been high social positions for women within the Indus Valley. Srivastava states that "in pre-historic India, gender discrimination was non-existent" (Srivastava). In addition, "Polyandry was common in matriarchal communities" (Srivastava). It is also believed that these Neolithic communities were matriarchal and matrilineal, and that they afforded women high-standing social and religious positions, which again supports the assertion that when powerful goddesses are revered by a community, the rights of women in the community are strengthened.

However, when the Indo-Aryans, a subgroup of Indo-European speakers, started to migrate into northwestern India around 1800–1500 BCE, elements surrounding the worship of Neolithic goddesses became transformed in the Indus Valley. Like other global regions, the Indo-Aryans slowly merged with the existing cultures of India, bringing with them their patriarchal and patrilineal concepts. During the Vedic period of about 1500–500 BCE, the fully established Indo-Aryans introduced their Vedic religion, outlined in the Rig Veda.

The religious beliefs of the Indo-Aryans held similarities with other Indo-European groups. For example, the superior male sky gods that came with Indo-European groups into Celtic and Germanic regions, the Middle East, and the Mediterranean, also appeared in Vedic India. Like other Indo-European inspired sky gods—the Slavic Perun, Greek Zeus, and Norse Thor—the sky gods of the Indo-Aryans, such as the early Vedic trinity of Indra, Mitra, and Varuna, also donned weapons associated with the sky, such as "fire, wind and storm, the lightning bolt and the thunder's roar" (Baring & Cashford 297). In the Vedas, many goddesses appear as secondary deities who do not hold equal power to that of the male gods.

However, like other Indo-European cultures, there appears some reverence for powerful goddesses in the Vedas, especially in connection to nature. For example, the goddess Aditi is portrayed as birthing the earth (Lang 39). In addition, the earth itself in the Vedas is portrayed as feminine; "supplicants ask the goddess Earth to provide them with nourishment just as a nursing mother feeds her child … [and] a funeral hymn requests that the dead man go to the lap of the Earth, his mother" (Lang 39). Also, a reference to the goddess Devi, as conceived as the feminine earth, appears in hymn 125 of the Rig Veda, stating:

> "I am the Queen, the gatherer-up of treasures, most thoughtful, first of those who merit worship/.... Through me alone all eat the food that feeds them, each man who sees, breathes, hears the word outspoken/.... I make the man I love exceedingly mighty, make him a sage, a Rsi, and a Brahman/.... On the world's summit I bring forth the Father: my home is in the waters, in the ocean./ Thence I extend o'er all existing creatures, and touch even yonder heaven with my forehead./ I breathe a strong breath like the wind and tempest, the while I hold together all existence./ Beyond this wide earth and beyond the heavens I have become so mighty in my grandeur" [Rig Veda, Book 10, Hymn CXXV].

Furthermore, the Vedas portray the dawn and night in the form of goddesses as well. Because of the presence of some significant goddesses in connection with the natural world, as was often the case with the diffusion of Indo-European speaking groups into existing populations, the Indo-Aryans appear to have merged their beliefs with at least some of the religious concepts of the early populations in India.

Perhaps because some goddesses retained positions of relative importance in the Early Vedic period (1500–1000 BCE), Indian women still maintained some important social roles that may have been similar to the positions they held before contact with the Indo-Aryans' patriarchal concepts. For instance, Indian women were able, for a time, to maintain some "spiritual authority" by participating "equally in some rituals" (Keller 228). Early Vedic society also allowed women to still hold religious offices; the Vedas mention "several women seers and sages, of which Sulabhā Maitreyī, Gārgī Vāchaknavī, Lopāmudra, Ghōṣa, Visvavārā, Vadavā Prāchiteyī, and Sikatā Nivāvarī represented renowned female authors of the Vedic mantras" (Pal). Women could also take part in religious ceremonies and rituals by accompanying their husbands to offer sacrifices, as a man was viewed as only able to "become a spiritual whole [when] he was accompanied by his wife [to ritualistic sacrifice], as the gods were thought not to accept the materials offered by a bachelor" (Srivastava). Some women could also receive an education in early Vedic society. In addition, early on, women were allowed to select their own husbands, and remarry if their spouses died, though women were not permitted to obtain a divorce in this period. However, these rights for women would only fall as Indo-Aryan ideology became more widespread.

The Indo-Aryans in the Later Vedic period (1000–600 BCE) developed increasing social and political organizational systems as small kingdoms began to form; this led to increased social stratification identified in the Indo-Aryan caste system of India. The caste system placed Brahmins, priests and scholars, at the top tier of society, exclusively granting sacred religious roles to elite men, thus stripping women of the high-standing religious positions they once held in pre–Aryan and even Early Vedic societies. As time went on, Brahmin priests worked to lessen the reverence the people held for their traditional goddesses. For instance, Brahmin priests purposefully suppressed the role of pre–Aryan goddesses in the Vedas, as there are numerous accounts where the feminine of the original Sanskrit was purposely translated as masculine (Stone 211). In addition, some temples that were once devoted to goddesses were intentionally replaced by images of Indo-Aryan gods. As discussed in other cultures, this purposeful revision of traditional religion to suit new ideologies was common following the arrival of Indo-European groups that sought to perpetuate patriarchy. The next tier of society according to the Indo-Aryan caste system belonged to the rulers and warriors of India, "who monopolized political and military power and who were the primary patrons of the priestly rites and ceremonies" of the Brahmins, which resulted in connecting religious affairs to political pursuits (Lang 37). The designation of only elite men to oversee the top two tiers of society utterly alienated women from serving in almost all religious, social, and political matters within their communities. In addition to losing social and religious positions, women increasingly lost basic rights that had once been viewed as naturally theirs. For instance, women began to be considered the property of their husbands (Keller 228), and matrilineal inheritance structures shifted to patrilineal inheritance restrictions (Pal), though unmarried daughters still had some rights of inheritance upon their father's property (Srivastava). Sons also became prized over the birth of daughters, as sons continued the family linage when patrilineal succession overtook matrilineal succession (Srivastava). As the Vedic period continued and moved into the Classical and early medieval periods in India, patriarchal structures became even more strengthened, which further lessened the social positioning of women in India.

From about 800 BCE to around 300 CE, the Hindu synthesis began to form from pre–Indo-Aryan concepts, Vedic Indo-Aryan concepts, as well as additional elements introduced into its ideology. Because of centuries of indoctrination regarding Indo-Aryan patriarchal values, many Hindu goddesses were portrayed in mythic narratives as subdued, meek, and docile, fitting stereotypical definitions of acceptable behavior for women. However, just as was seen in Greece and other cultures already discussed in this book, many people embraced the new ideology slowly, remaining resistant to shed long-held beliefs regarding traditional goddesses. Thus, the presentation of goddesses in Hinduism often incorporated aspects of goddess worship that seemed to come from the existing populations of India before Indo-Aryan contact. For example, many Hindu goddesses, such as Durga and Kali, exude tremendous power and authority, leading some scholars to believe that these goddesses, in particular, may be remnants of pre–Aryan Mother Goddesses (Gupto 38). Thus, the conflicted history shaping Hindu mythic narratives often presents great complexity in the presentation of Hindu goddesses.

One of the earliest and most revered Hindu goddesses is Durga. As stated, many scholars point to Durga's reverence as possibly coming from, or being similar to, the Mother Goddesses of the Neolithic Indus Valley civilizations. Durga appears in her earliest form as a goddess of the mountains, who possesses protective aspects of her personality. Seals found in the Indus Valley depicting a Mother Goddess reigning over tigers are often attributed as early forms of the goddess Durga. Durga is also often identified as synonymous with Devi, the personification of the feminine earth, as found in the Rig Veda. Durga's mythic portrayal later evolved into primarily a war goddess, who is often depicted riding a lion while carrying weapons in each of her many hands. In this warrior role, Durga's primary role is to battle demons who threaten the universe, as she does in one of her most famous myths when she takes on the power of the male gods to save them from the powerful buffalo demon—Mahisasura. The most common version of this myth states that Mahisasura obtained power that made him invincible to any male, so "he subsequently defeated the gods in battle and usurped their positions" (Kinsley 96). Outraged by this, the Hindu gods emitted anger from their bodies, which created the goddess Durga. Durga then sought out the demon Mahisasura and easily defeated him, "demonstrating both superior martial ability and superior power" (Kinsley 97).

Though the goddess Durga appears quite formidable, it is important to note that she is still a product of a patriarchal culture; "Durga is an instrument for the gods and is therefore not as independent as she may appear" (Hedman). Durga, as the myth of Mahisasura shows, obtains her power from the male gods to become formidable and accomplish deeds that they deem necessary. Even Durga's creation is mythically attributed as being a result of a male symbolic birth, as it is the rage of the male gods that causes Durga to be created. This is an important distinction—Durga appears as a powerful goddess, one who looks on the outside to be a wonderful example to audiences of female strength and vitality, but when she is examined more closely, one finds a goddess who is powerful only to further a patriarchal agenda, much like the way the Greek Athena was portrayed. Therefore, like Athena, Durga is often mythically portrayed as an instrument the gods use to protect their hierarchy of power, thus protecting patriarchal social and political structures.

The reverence of the goddess Kali is also thought to be quite ancient, as she, like Durga, is often thought to be connected to the Mother Goddesses of the Neolithic Indus Valley civilizations. In Hinduism, Kali is said to have been birthed directly from Durga, instead of from the male gods, which might mythically be an element that maintains Kali's ancient origin as a Mother Goddess. In Hindu religion, Kali is associated with death and destruction; she is:

> almost always described as having a terrible and frightening appearance. She is always black or dark, is usually naked, and has long, disheveled hair. She is adorned with severed arms as a girdle, freshly cut heads as a necklace, children's corpses as earrings, and serpents as bracelets. She has long, sharp fangs, is often depicted as having claw like hands with long nails, and is often said to have blood smeared on her lips. Her favorite haunts heighten her fearsome nature. She is usually shown on the battlefield, where she is a furious combatant who gets drunk on the hot blood of her victims, or in a cremation ground, where she sits on a corpse surrounded by jackals and goblins [Kinsley 116].

Kinsley states that although other "'mother goddesses ... give life, Kali takes life, insatiably.... If mother goddesses are described as ever fecund, Kali is described as ever hungry. Her lolling tongue, grotesquely long and oversized, her sunken stomach, emaciated appearance, and sharp fangs convey a presence that is the opposite of a fertile, protective mother goddess" (Kinsley 126). Therefore, unlike Durga, Kali does not often serve in the role of protector within her myths, as when Kali begins to do battle, she often gets so frenzied, by drinking the blood of her victims, that she "begins to destroy the world that she was supposed to protect" (Kinsley 120).

One of the most famous myths of Kali shows her battling the demon Raktabija. Durga is said to summon Kali to help her defeat Raktabija, because Durga found that when she fought the demon, the blood from any injury she produced caused the demon to multiply, until the whole battlefield was full of demons. Thus, Kali appeared from the forehead of Durga, and with her fearsome countenance and her unfettered wrath, she proceeded to devour every last demon, and then danced on their corpses.

Another myth that displays Kali's unfettered wrath introduces her as a young, beautiful goddess who is desired by all the gods (Leonard & McClure, 158–60). Kali, though, is said to thwart the advances of the male gods, so they take revenge upon her by murdering her. The gods behead Kali and place her head on the body of a prostitute. As portrayed in many cultures thus far, this extreme case of violence to a goddess by male gods is a common mythic occurrence; it resembles Marduk's violent overtake of Tiamet, Zeus's rape of myriad goddesses, and Apollo's massacre of Gaia's sacred serpent. However, this myth of Kali is unique in that it shows Kali's furious response to the injustice done to her.

Kali responds to the gods' act with insatiable violence. She takes it upon herself to resurrect herself by merging her decapitated head with the body of the prostitute. In this form, Kali goes on to live among humankind, having sex with any willing man she can find, only to murder him after the act of copulation. She kills the young and old, the rich and poor, the virtuous and unjust, and she does not try to contain her wrath. The myth of Kali states that she:

> had been overcome by a hatred of all living things, and at the same time by a desire ... to annihilate all creatures as she fed on them. She could be seen crouching at the edge of graveyards; her jaws cracked bones like the maw of a lioness. She killed like the female insect devouring the male; she crushed the beings she brought to life like a wild sow turning on her young. Those she killed, she finished off by dancing on their bodies. Her lips stained with blood exuded a dull smell of butcher shops [Leonard and McClure 160].

It is clear that Kali's portrayal in this myth shows her as dangerous. Mistreated by the gods, she unleashes unfair treatment to mortals, not to gods;

therefore, the myth projects Kali as untrustworthy. Again, many myths from other cultures purposefully showcase representations of traditional Mother Goddesses in an overtly harsh fashion to try and teach audiences that the ways of the Mother Goddess are uncivilized and unnecessarily harsh, instead of portraying tales of the Mother Goddess who must occasionally use violence as a display of the requirements of nature to continue its cycles. Gupto concurs, stating that Kali's overtly harsh portrayal in myths might be "determined by the Indo-Aryan patriarchal ideology" that strove to define Kali as dangerous instead of as how Mother Goddesses initially were portrayed—as both givers and takes of life (Gupto 71). Gupto explains that the civilizations of the late Neolithic period once worshipped a "kind of proto-Kali, a mother goddess who was possibly incorporated into the Vedic culture.... And the Aryan priesthood, threatened by the feminine element, projected the goddess with demonization along with sexual images and symbols. They found [Kali] useful for justifying plunder and bloodshed and yet did not want the female image to be popular among the patriarchal mindsets of the time" (Gupto 71-2).

Therefore, Kali, and other goddesses like her, are often considered dangerous in Hindu ideology, unless they can be subdued by the control of male forces. In an attempt to quell the ferocity of Kali, she is portrayed in Hinduism as one aspect of the goddess Parvati, who is the consort of the god Shiva. Therefore, in Hindu narratives, when Shiva's consort appears as a humble domestic partner, she is Parvati, and when she is incensed, she is Kali. Parvati and Kali are thus both identities of the same central goddess. Sometimes Durga and other goddesses, like Sati, are also considered consorts of Shiva and are, thus, also connected as the same central goddess as Parvati and Kali.

The concept of pairing goddesses to male gods is thought to have occurred soon after the Vedic period. The top trinity of divine beings in Hinduism are all male: Brahma is the creator; Vishnu is the preserver; and Shiva is the destroyer, and each of these top male gods are paired with female consorts: Saraswati with Brahma; Lakshmi with Vishnu; and Parvati/Kali with Shiva. In connecting these Hindu goddesses to male deities, the male deities gain strength in the pairing, just as was seen when Zeus married Hera. However, the goddesses often lose power when they are paired with a male god. Thus, this pairing of goddesses with gods was often a patriarchal tool used to harness the power that traditional goddesses, such as Kali, once held.

Thus, Kali appears to lose strength by being paired with Shiva. In myths that display Kali and Shiva, Kali's anger needs to be quelled by Shiva. Mythically, the Hindu gods are often identified at a loss over how to pacify Kali's anger after she enters a fit of impassioned fury and goes on a killing spree. Shiva often steps in, as a father would to a toddler throwing a tantrum, and calms Kali down. For example, a myth from southern India portrays Shiva in a dominant role to an unruly Kali (Kinsley 119–20). The myth states that Kali takes up residence in the deep wilderness and is terrorizing the community with her acts of extreme violence (Kinsley 119). Kali's behavior causes one of the devotees of Shiva to beg Shiva to get rid of Kali. When Shiva arrives, "Kali threatens him, claiming the area as her own" (Kinsley 119). But, Shiva calms Kali down by challenging her to a "dance contest" in which Shiva ends up utterly defeating Kali, so that she is forced to retreat into docility (Kinsley 119). Myths like this one, that identify a once powerful goddess needing to be controlled by a male god, sends a message to audiences that women similarly require the intervention of men to temper their unharnessed emotions.

Sometimes, the myths between Shiva and Kali do not so easily convey a message that Kali's emotionally charged behavior needs to be subdued by Shiva. Instead, sometimes Kali appears to be the one who supersedes the power of Shiva. For example, there are many iconographic images that portray Kali as dominant to Shiva. Often it is Kali who is portrayed as "standing or dancing on Shiva's prone body, and when the two are depicted in sexual intercourse, she is shown above him" (Kinsley 120). These representations suggest that Kali "was never fully subdued by [Shiva] and is ... represented as a being who is uncontrollable and more apt to provoke Shiva ... than to be controlled by him" (Kinsley 120). In addition, often Kali mythically takes on the role of scapegoat for some of Shiva's apparent erratic behavior. For instance, Kali is often blamed for inciting Shiva "to take part in dangerous, destructive behavior that threatens the stability of the cosmos" (Kinsley 117). Instead of Shiva just embodying the natural necessity of destruction, as a traditional Mother Goddess would have been identified, Kali is often blamed for some of Shiva's acts that seem overtly harsh. Blaming a goddess for what appears to be overly harsh or random acts of violence is another way for patriarchal structures to define goddesses, and subsequently women, as untrustworthy, unfair, and prone to uncontrollable emotion. Therefore, the myths of Kali end up being complex, which again is quite common when a culture experiences the revision of traditional conceptions of their goddesses, as discussed with myriad cultures thus far.

The Hindu goddess Saraswati, and others like her, represents another type of Hindu goddess from that of Durga and Kali, as Saraswati, unlike Durga and Kali, does not seem to be a goddess who developed from pre–Aryan concepts of a powerful Mother Goddess. Saraswati does appear in the Rig Veda, but only as a minor river goddess, as most rivers in the Rig Veda were attributed as being goddesses. In the formation of the religion of Hinduism, Saraswati grew in identity and importance, but in many ways, she became a goddess determined by Vedic patriarchal terms. Thus, Saraswati's role in Hinduism is defined as the consort of the god Brahma, the male creator of the universe. In the role of Brahma's consort, Saraswati often conveys stereotypical attributes of ideal femininity, as defined by patriarchal agencies. She is often portrayed as the docile goddess of knowledge and the arts. In some myths, Saraswati is born directly out of the mouth or forehead of Brahma, again showing a mythic account that supersedes the mother in birth, sending a patriarchal message that is similar to Eve being born from Adam's rib or Athena being born from Zeus's head.

When Saraswati was mythically born from the forehead of Brahma, Brahma was said to immediately feel great lust for her. Saraswati, however, did not return his affection, so she tried to flee from his sight. Brahma, though, made sure that Saraswati could not flee his divine gaze, as he grew five heads making it possible for him to spy on Saraswati from any direction. In time, Shiva intervened and corrected the situation, helping Brahma calm down enough to realize that he must perform a sacred cleansing ritual to purify himself. However, during this period, wives were needed to perform such rites, so it was decided, by the male gods, that Saraswati must marry Brahma, so that he could be purified once more.

Another myth of Saraswati and Brahma explains that after the two were married, Brahma while awaiting the delayed arrival of Saraswati became frustrated, so he asked the gods for their advice on how to handle the situation. The gods responded by creating Brahma a new wife, Gayatri. When Saraswati saw Gayatri, she became upset and cursed Brahma, declaring that she, instead of Brahma, would be more worshipped by the people in sacred temples, which is a mythic account that is supposed to explain why Brahma, the creator god, indeed does have fewer temples than Saraswati.

Both of these myths appear similar to myths from other cultures already discussed that strive to present representations of goddesses within patriarchal parameters. In both of these myths of Saraswati, she is portrayed within the confines of a strict patriarchal pantheon. In the first myth discussed, Saraswati tries to attain her own independence from Brahma, but she ultimately fails. Her mythic birth shows her to be under the rigidity of a system where the creator god is her father and also her husband, thus sending a message to audiences that she is not, and will never be, fully independent, a message that likely was intended for Hindu women. When Saraswati was mythically married, she was also clearly portrayed as under a patriarchal system, as she was easily replaced by another wife as a gift the gods bestowed upon Brahma. Saraswati's anger at being merely replaced by Gayatri causes her to seek some revenge, in that she will be worshipped more openly by the people than her husband, as Saraswati is certainly a goddess still revered in contemporary India. However, the myth does not attribute her reverence to her own qualities, but to a curse she laid upon Brahma, which ultimately sends a message to audiences that she, like all women, possess qualities that should be held suspect. This patriarchal identification of the goddess Saraswati would then go on in the years to come to identify women in increasingly low terms throughout India.

Likewise, the goddess Lakshmi often is portrayed as another goddess who was created and preserved to serve patriarchal agendas in India. Lakshmi is the highly revered Hindu goddess of wealth, good fortune, and prosperity. She is believed to have been created in the Later Vedic period, and the patriarchal identification of this period remains a large part of her early portrayal in Hindu ideology. Instead of being portrayed as a powerful and independent goddess in her own right, Lakshmi is often an embodiment of traits viewed as acceptable for women by patriarchal standards, which are most amplified by her interactions with her consort Vishnu. In the most common mythic version of one of Lakshmi's rebirths, she was said to rise from the gods' efforts to churn the ocean of milk, which again places her birth in the hands of male gods. Lakshmi was then said to be attracted to Vishnu's authority in churning the ocean of milk, so they became consorts. Lakshmi's consistent loyalty and subservience to Vishnu are traits that are often highlighted in her myths to serve as a guide for how Hindu women should function in their relationships with men. For example, Lakshmi is most often presented as an ideal wife to Vishnu, as she is ever loyal and obedient. She is said to have taken on different forms in each of her lifetimes just to be with Vishnu in each of his incarnations, becoming Padma, Sita, etc. Lakshmi is also sometimes viewed as an intermediary between humans and Vishnu, as she helps the sometimes strict Vishnu feel compassion for the well-being of humanity.

The creation or reimagining of goddesses like Saraswati and Lakshmi, who mostly embody preferred characteristics for women within a patriarchal society, presents the trend found in many cultures to demote a central goddess into many representations of less powerful goddesses who can serve as representations of male definitions of acceptable behavior. Though Hera and Aphrodite were revered in Greek culture, they became, as patriarchal structures dominated, male representations of femininity, which stripped them of any real power and sent audiences a message that women were jealous but unable to control their husbands, like Hera, or full of lust and little intellect, like Aphrodite. Many Hindu myths similarly display myriad goddesses who portray male social messages of proper behavior for women. Hedman states that many of the "protective" or "creative" goddesses in Hindu mythology possess "qualities that are controlled by male gods" (Hedman). Goddesses like Lakshmi and Saraswati, and many others portrayed in Hindu religion, "respect and pay attention to their husbands" above all else, and in doing so, they send a social message that the qualities the goddesses hold in their myths are positive, and they should therefore instruct women on how to behave in a similar fashion (Hedman). Again, this presentation of goddesses in largely subservient positions would go on in Indian society to further denigrate the social positing of women.

As stated, the god Shiva is often connected not only to the formidable Kali, but also to the goddesses Parvati and Sati. The goddess Sati is identified in Hindu ideology as Shiva's first wife. Mythically, before Sati and Shiva were married, Sati was already fully devoted to Shiva; to win his favor, she proved her devotion by displaying acts of extreme asceticism. And indeed, her steadfast ascetic practices gained Shiva's attention, as he decided to marry Sati. This display of extreme loyalty, at the expense of one's physical well-being, is often required of the consorts of Shiva, as Parvati, his next consort, also gains Shiva's favor by similar behavior. Sati's loyalty, because she is a revered goddess, sends a message to women that they should behave in a similar fashion with their own husbands, sacrificing their own well-being to benefit the needs of their spouse. Shiva and Sati are mythically shown to live happily for some time, until Sati learned that her father had been mistreating Shiva, because Shiva maintained the appearance of an unkempt ascetic. To protest her father's prejudice towards Shiva, and to show her devotion to her husband, Sati committed suicide by burning herself alive. Sati believed that in doing so, she would be reborn again as Shiva's wife outside of the influence of her father, which indeed happened later, when she was reborn as Parvati. Sati's sacrificial act shows the ultimate devotion of a wife to her husband, which, as discussed, was the societal demand placed upon wives in early Hinduism. Hidman states that Hindu goddesses, like Sati, sent messages to audiences that declared that ideal wives were to be devoted to their husbands by continually demonstrating "unselfish sacrifice" for them, and "Goddesses like Sati ... that fulfil this ideal, became important role models for Hindu women" (Hedman). Thus, this mythological episode became a dark practice in Indian culture where women periodically sacrificed themselves by throwing themselves upon their husbands' funeral pyres to show their devotion in an act that became known as "sati," in commemoration of the goddess. Initially, the act of sati was viewed as voluntary, and signaled the ultimate fidelity of a wife to her husband, but as time went on, there are cases that identify that the practice was not always voluntary, as widows were sometimes pressured into committing the act if they had no children to care for them.

The goddess Parvati, who again is the reincarnated Sati, is often portrayed as the docile consort of Shiva, as she is quite the opposite of Kali. Parvati in Hinduism is displayed as the goddess of fertility, love, and marriage. Like Saraswati and Lakshmi, Parvati also appears to have been conceived in the patriarchal culture of the Later Vedic period. Therefore, many of Parvati's attributes are similar to those of Saraswati and Lakshmi, as Parvati is shown most often in her myths to be a pillar of loyalty to Shiva and an example of proper behavior for women according to patriarchal demands.

One of Parvati's most famous myths presents her, like Sati, as striving to attain the attention of Shiva through her own acts of extreme asceticism. Parvati was said to perform "all the traditional mortifications, such as sitting in the midst of four fires in the middle of summer, remaining exposed to the elements during the rainy season and during the winter, living on leaves or air only, standing on one leg for years, and so on. Eventually she accumulates so much heat that the gods are made uncomfortable and persuade Shiva to grant Parvati's wish, so that she will cease her efforts" (Kumar). Again, Parvati, like Sati, goes out of her way to perform ascetic acts, apparently not for her own spiritual benefit, but to win the love of Shiva, which she successfully does, as the two become married. Shiva and Parvati eventually have children and live together happily. In the myths that portray Parvati and Shiva, Parvati often serves to temporarily avert Shiva from his role as the god of destruction, so that creation can occur. It appears that the united Shiva and Parvati represent the regenerative aspects once portrayed in traditional Mother Goddesses who harbored the power to create, destroy, and recreate in one form. Kumar concurs, stating that without his "female half, or female nature, the godhead of Shiva is incomplete" (Kumar). However, it is significant that Parvati, as a goddess, often only quells Shiva's desire to destroy; she often does not destroy or create much of anything herself. Shiva, on the other hand, can hold power with or without Parvati. Therefore, Parvati "can be seen as [another] symbol of the patriarchal description of the goddess. She is an instrument for the male side, and she is in no way challenging the male power position" (Hedman).

India's epic literature of the Later Vedic period likewise portrays female characters who serve as models of proper behavior for women within a patriarchal society, thus revealing how far the rights of Indian women had fallen since pre–Aryan times. However, there also appears in the epics of Indian literature some female characters who display traces of strength and power, perhaps revealing a glimpse of the former roles goddesses and women once held in pre–Aryan India.

The *Ramayana*, written approximately in the fifth to fourth century

BCE, presents the character Rama as an avatar of the god Vishnu, along with the three sons of his father King Dasharatha. Rama is supposed to be the successor to his father's throne, but this becomes thwarted when King Dasharatha gets tricked by his youngest wife, Kaikeyi, to have her own son, Bharata, become the next king. To make matters worse, Kaikeyi, who is clearly portrayed in a negative light, sending a message that women should be watched carefully, demands that her husband, the king, banish Rama into a wilderness exile for fourteen years. It is in Rama's forced exile that audiences see a clear oppositional female character to the conniving Kaikeyi in the form of Rama's wife Sita.

Like Rama, Sita is also an avatar of a divine being, as she is the goddess Lakshmi in human form. Sita is also described as the daughter of the Mother Earth goddess Bhūmi, who is sometimes conceived of or connected to Devi, the representation of the earth discussed in the Rig Veda. In fact, even though Sita appears as a mortal in the text, she is birthed directly from the soil, which is her mother. The connection that Sita holds to the Mother Earth goddess Bhūmi presents Sita in a respected position in the text, as she is identified as an avatar of a goddess, but also as connected to traditional beliefs that identify Bhūmi as the earth itself in the form of a Mother Goddess. In identifying Sita as mortal but also holding divine qualities, she becomes a good example to see how mythic goddesses can influence the expectations for human women within a society. Sita has long been identified as the exemplar for women in Hindu society. Hedman states that for centuries in Indian society, "the perfect woman live[d] for her husband," and Sita served as the "ideal" of this concept; thus, young girls in India were "often told to behave like Sita" (Hedman). Sita is certainly loyal to Rama; for instance, when he is exiled, Sita chooses to follow Rama into the wilderness. Once there, Sita displays behavior that connects her to her divine role while they endure Rama's exile, as Sita is portrayed within the epic as repeatedly connected to the natural environment from which she was birthed. For instance, Sita consistently reminds Rama to pay homage to the goddess of each particular river they cross.

However, because this is a text written after Indo-Aryan invasion and years of patriarchal indoctrination, Sita also displays behavior that marks her as a creation to perpetuate a patriarchal agenda. During Rama's forest exile, for example, Sita easily falls for a plot set forth by the demon king Ravana to abduct her. On a side note, Ravana was said to learn of Sita's whereabouts after his sister tried to seduce Rama, but instead was assaulted by him when he mutilated her face. The events leading to Sita's abduction present her in a negative fashion, as the mythic scene shows Sita acting in a way that defines her, by the patriarchal culture of the time, as inferior because of her sex. For example, Sita is told by Rama and his brother Lakshmana, who also chose to accompany Rama into exile, not to trust her environment. This is a problem because Sita is supposed to be connected deeply to the environment, in her own divine role and her connection to her mother, the earth itself, but instead Sita is portrayed as needing to listen to Rama in order to be protected. Rama and Lakshmana draw a protective circle on the ground around Sita and tell her, before they leave her alone to go hunting, not to trust anything and not to leave the protection of their circle. Again, if Sita was an earth goddess in full force, she certainly could go anywhere she pleased in the natural environment that birthed her. The fact that Sita needs such close protection by her husband and his brother defines her, and women within Hindu culture at the time, as in need of the protection of men. And in fact, according to the text, Sita does need the protection of Rama because she leaves his protective circle soon after being left alone and approaches one of Ravana's demons, who is disguised as a golden deer that was said to hold the sparkle of gems. Again, given Sita's connection to the natural environment and the elements within it, it is questionable why she would so easily fall prey to such a trick, especially because the deer is false and adorned with the materialistic beauty of gold and gems. It seems an earth goddess would recognize such a scam, but again the intent of the text, in part, is to serve a patriarchal agenda and send a message that women are fickle and naïve creatures, a message that would only become strengthened in the centuries to come in India.

Sita is duped, and thus is abducted and taken to Ravana's compound. The text states that Sita avoids being raped by Ravana; however, when Rama is able to rescue Sita, he is primarily concerned with Sita's "purity," as Rama, and the text, defines Sita's "purity" as remaining free from Ravana's sexual assault. To dispel Rama's concern, Sita, though offended, voluntarily walks through flames unharmed to prove that she is still "pure." This act, that is similar to Sati's sacrificial death for Shiva, signals Sita's connection to divinity, as she, in proof of her "purity," is able to do what humans are unable to do—walk through flames unharmed. But again, the act loses its power when it is viewed in the context of this epic, as Sita is all but forced to perform the sacred act because of the insult her husband makes against her. Also, in a contemporary interpretation, it is upsetting that the text explains Sita as the one to blame if she was raped or not, as well as the text's assertion that Sita would be impure if she was raped. Even in the context of the era in which the epic was written, Sita reacts as offended when she is made to prove herself to Rama. To make matters worse, the text shows that Sita is forced to again prove her "purity" when Rama returns to his own land and becomes king. Once Rama becomes king, the people now demand that Sita prove her "purity" again by walking through fire one more time, and though Sita feels she doesn't need to prove this again, and Rama agrees with her, Rama, as king, feels obligated to bend to the will of his people. However, Sita, now a queen and pregnant with Rama's twin sons, chooses to not succumb to the will of her kingly husband or his people. Instead, she leaves the kingdom and returns to the seclusion of nature, where she gives birth to her sons. Later, Rama seeks Sita out and asks her to return home, pleading for her to walk through fire one more time, but Sita refuses Rama and instead performs a task that seems contrary to her submissive portrayal throughout the majority of the epic.

Instead of succumbing to the will of Rama and the people of his kingdom, Sita refuses to prove herself a second time. Sita states that she has tired of life and decides to leave her earthly existence by returning to her Earth Mother. After this declaration, the text shows that the earth itself opens up and receives Sita in the same way in which she was birthed. This scene shows Sita in a powerful light that clearly connects her to traditional Mother Goddess imagery. As has been repeatedly discussed, cultures that reassigned roles for their goddesses often produced complex myths regarding how myriad goddesses were portrayed, and this is certainly true in this epic. Sita, in being presented as both human and divine, is showcased as being both inferior and superior. As a mortal wife, she often submits to the will of Rama and frequently appears weak and in need of his protection. However, Sita's final act of resistance allows audiences to reconsider the character of Sita in divine terms. It is hard to not view her final act as powerful, as it clearly asserts her independence and mystical ability. Thus, as Luthra states, Sita's final act marks her as a character who refuses to compromise to patriarchal systems (Luthra 141). Even Mahatma Gandhi reflected upon Sita's final act of resistance, stating that "'Sita was the incarnate *satyagrahi* ... the essence of *satyagraha* is that one does not fight back with the same weapons as the oppressor. It takes much greater strength to offer dignified non-violent resistance to oppression and injustice than to retaliate with violence'" (qtd. in Luthra 154). However, like Sati, the first wife of Shiva, it should also be noted that Sita's only way of reacting against the patriarchy that exists in her husband's kingdom is to sacrifice her life. Thus, her act is one of defiance as well as retreat.

The epic *Mahabharata,* written between the third century BCE and the third century CE, relates an earlier time, from about the ninth to eighth century BCE. The *Mahabharata* also presents female characters who at times display great strength and at times represent acceptable behavior for women within the patriarchal culture of the time in which the epic was recorded. In the tale, the king of Hastinapur, Pandu, cannot father children due to a curse placed upon him. This curse causes Pandu to give the throne of Hastinapur to his blind brother Dhritarashtra. It is these events that reveal an important female character in the epic—Pandu's wife, Kunti. Kunti asks the gods to father her children in Pandu's name. As a result, Kunti has sex with a series of gods: first Yama, the god of death, who fathers Yudhishthira; then Vayu, the god of wind, who fathers Bhima; and finally Indra, the god of storms, who fathers Arjuna. Pandu's second wife Madri also sleeps with the divine Ashvins, and they father Nakula and Sahadeva. The fact that the epic allows these mortal women to birth the children of gods connects the women to divinity themselves, though the later glory the sons achieve in the epic is attributed as coming from their divine fathers rather than their human mothers.

Through the character of Draupadi, the text reveals what might be a remnant pertaining to the rights of women in the historical time period the text portrayed rather than when it was written down. The text shows that it is Draupadi's father who will choose the man Draupadi will marry based on who wins a competition he has prepared. In the *Mahabharata*, Arjuna and his brothers compete for Draupadi, along with many other young men. Whoever can lift a bow of impossible weight, strike an arrow through a fish's eye that is fixed to a rotating plate on a roof, by looking at its reflection in water, can win the princess. This seemingly impossible act is indeed accomplished by the text's primary hero Arjuna, who is thus able to win Draupadi's hand in marriage.

Revealing a suitable marriage partner through competition in which many males vie for the hand of a royal maiden is a common mythic event. A competitive act to find the best suitor for a woman seems to present women as objects who are owned, and thus may be given away as a prize by their fathers. Or, conversely, such mythical competitions to win the hand of a prized maiden may display what might be historical references to women who held certain rights of power. If a maiden was so prized that men had to compete to win her hand in marriage, then it suggests a time in which women were valued as worthy of male competition; perhaps even referencing male consorts needing to win favor of goddesses or goddess representatives. Thus, the difficulty in obtaining Draupadi's hand in marriage may hint at Draupadi serving as a traditional goddess representative. Furthermore, the text intimates that indeed Draupadi may have connections to divinity, as like Sita, she is said to be born from a supernatural birth, as "Draupadi is born fully formed from … sacrificial fire" (Mukhoty 9).

The text continues to show Arjuna and Draupadi returning home to Arjuna's mother, Kunti, to tell her the good news of their impending marriage. Arjuna tells Kunti that he and his brothers were blessed with "substantial alms" in the competition. Kunti, portrayed as misunderstanding what Arjuna meant, as she thought her sons were all awarded many gifts, tells all of her sons that they have to share what they won. The text states that because the brothers had always obeyed their mother, they agree to all share Draupadi as their wife. Draupadi then marries all five Pandava brothers. Scholars, such as Srivastava, state that this scene might point to a pre–Aryan or early Vedic practice where women indeed married multiple husbands (Srivastava). Also, in the *Mahabharata* itself, the character of Kunti, who again also had multiple divine males fathering her children, states "'In days of yore women went about freely doing as they pleased. There was no obligation to be faithful to their husbands'" (qtd. in Pattanaik 176). Thus, Pattanaik states that the attention drawn out in the *Mahabharata* surrounding Draupadi's multiple husbands signals a "shift from matriarchy to patriarchal traditions" (Pattanaik 176). This shift is also evident in the Vedic period text, the *Upanishads*, that introduces a storyline where a king named Shvetaketu is presented as a seeker of sacred knowledge. In the text, Shvetaketu sees his mother with another man, and when he tells this to his father, he is shocked to hear that his father only says "'All women are free to do as they wish'" (Pattanaik 175). Believing that under social acceptances such as this, no man would ever be able to know who his paternal father was, Shvetakeu in the *Upanishads* decrees "that henceforth a woman could have sexual relations only with her husband or with whomever he selected" (Pattanaik 175).

The trial scene in the *Mahabharata* also shows Draupadi taking on a role that might reveal a historical time when women held higher social status. This scene might relate back to the strife felt when Indian culture shifted their religious views from primarily goddess worship and possible matriarchy to a patriarchal pantheon and social structure. The epic shows that the Kauravas, the one hundred sons of King Dhritarashtra, and cousins to the five Pandava brothers, are jealous of the Pandavas, so the Kauravas, led by Duryodhana, the eldest brother, challenged Yudhishthira, the Pandava eldest brother, to a rigged game of dice. Though Yudhishthira knew the dice game was set up, he felt that he had to take part in the dice game, or it would lead to war for his people, so he agreed to play. Since the game was a trick, Yudhishthira indeed gambled everything away, including himself, his kingdom, and his wife Draupadi. However, the text clearly shows that Draupadi does not stand for this offense. Instead, when Draupadi was told she must give herself away as a slave to Duryodhana, she refused to go to the court and instead recited an argument based solely on logic. Draupadi asked Yudhishthira who he gambled away first—himself or her? Since he gambled himself away before gambling her away, she argued that she was still queen; therefore, Yudhishthira had no right to give her away, as he was no longer king when he made his decision.

Duryodhana, wielding his patriarchal power, ignored Draupadi's arguments and ordered one of his brothers to forcibly bring her to the court. Draupadi was then dragged before the court by her hair. In this scene, she repeatedly questioned "the all-male assembly about the legality and morality of the assembly" (Mukhoty 5), and of the right of Yudhishthira to give her away. In an explicitly patriarchal response to Draupadi's arguments, Duryodhana showed his thigh to her and motioned for Draupadi to sit upon his lap. Adding more insult to the scene, Draupadi was then called a whore for marrying five men and was called to be stripped of her garments, so that she should stand naked before the all-male court. Because this scene was presented in the text with the clear purpose of offense, it shows that the epic seems to be arguing for the right of women such as Draupadi to maintain a high social standing. Or perhaps the text is intentionally adding commiseration for a historical moment in time when women, such as Draupadi, were forced to succumb to a new patriarchal order. Thus, creating a court scene where matriarchal social constructs are the true element on trial is reminiscent of the Greek play the *Eumenides* that also addressed the social elements of such a change.

Ultimately, the text shows that Draupadi was not forced to be demoralized before the court, as she prayed to the god Krishna, an avatar of the god Vishnu, to save her. Krishna answered Draupadi's pleas by bestowing her sari with endless fabric, so when Dushasana tried to unwrap her sari, so that she may face the court nude, he was unsuccessful. It is significant that a male god must intervene to save Draupadi, making it clear that when facing patriarchal forces, she was ultimately powerless. When the people of the court witnessed Krishna's intervention, they viewed the gods as angry with them, so Draupadi was pardoned. Draupadi then demanded to have herself and her husbands freed from slavery, as well as have their wealth and status returned to them. This was also agreed upon, but Duryodhana again asked the Pandavas to take part in another game of dice, where the losers would be exiled for thirteen years, and again trying to prevent war, this was agreed upon. As a result, the Pandavas lost and were forced to enter exile.

Draupadi is portrayed in the *Mahabharata* in mostly a powerful light; she "rails against a culture that values a king's duty and a brother's loyalty above a wife's honor. Her battle, moreover, is for that most ethereal of things, a woman's sacred inviolability. No self-effacing denial of life and suicide for Draupadi…. Her heroism is her fearlessness in demanding justice even though this means challenging every male figure in her life" (Mukhoty xiii). Thus, the epic gives audiences a sense of respect for Draupadi as a strong woman, perhaps as a remnant of a goddess representative or a woman living in pre–Aryan society, but it also shows Draupadi as someone fighting an impossible battle against patriarchal systems that are striving to eliminate any existing reverence or social rights for women. Therefore, Draupadi in the *Mahabharata* appears as someone who is already a product of the past; she maintains high social allowances, especially in marrying five men, but her trial scene shows that her era is coming to an end, and the new era will be ruled by patriarchal systems such as those run by the Kauravas. This glimpse of a bleak future is supported by the end of the epic, which shows the Pandavas and Kauravas taking part in a great war that sparks the Kali Yuga, the final cycle of existence, where humanity dissolves into immorality, vice, and destruction. Given that the text was recorded centuries after the events it is supposed to relate, in a time when mostly patriarchal goddesses were worshipped and Indian women were expected to be fully docile and follow the leadership of the men in their lives, one can see that history indeed marked the position of women like Draupadi as a thing of the past, as moving into India's pre-Classical period (600 BCE–250 CE) only lowered the role of women in India.

The pre-Classical period in India produced significant patriarchal changes that further affected the social positioning of women, showing in some ways that the repeated portrayal of increasingly less powerful goddesses, serving often as patriarchal constructs like Saraswati and Lakshmi, led to the wide social acceptance of female denigration. For example, women in pre-Classical India became increasingly viewed as the legal property of the male members of their households: fathers, husbands, sons, etc. (Kidwai 7). Around 100 BCE, the supplementary text to the Vedas, the Laws of Manu, defined the expectations for the social positioning of women, and it, among other social regulations, led the way for a clear degradation of the rights of women in India. Keller states that in the Laws of Manu, "Women's status was reduced to the equivalent of the lowest class," as the Laws of Manu declared that "'in childhood a woman must be subject to her father; in youth to her husband; when her husband is dead, to her sons. A woman must never be free of subjugation' (Laws of Manu V.148).... Such subjugation is to be unconditional: 'Though [he be] destitute of virtue, or seeking pleasure [elsewhere], or devoid of good qualities, [yet] a husband must be constantly worshipped as a god by a faithful wife'" (qtd. in Keller 228–9). The Laws of Manu also stated that "'Day and night must women be held by their protectors in a status of subjection'" because women were identified in the text as possessing inferior traits, such as having "'loose desires,'" "'bad temper[s],'" and were in general "'frail, irresolute, and never straight'" (qtd. in Kidwai 7). In addition, the Laws of Manu proclaimed that husbands were "explicitly given the right to beat their wives" (Keller 229). The marriageable age for girls was also lowered from twelve to eight, and in some cases, girls at about the age of four or five were promised in marriage (Keller 229). The Laws of Manu proclaimed that women were "chattel" or commodities "for a man's enjoyment" (Pal). Also, the rights that women once held to take part in religious rituals with their husbands were "abolished, and religious education was denied" (Keller 228). Pal concurs, stating that "Women's right to education was fully withdrawn with Manu's codification of the laws governing society" (Pal). Pal states that "Manu's codification of social norms considered women to be impure as well as second class citizens. Following from this, a strict prohibition and oppression of women offering prayers, sacrifices, and undertaking pilgrimages, was declared" (Pal). Brahmin priests also aided in diminishing the rights of Indian women; "Both in ritual literature and in the legal texts one can find priests creating an idealized portrait of submissive housebound women" (Lang 36). Brahmin priests considered the concept of female chastity to be of paramount importance; the "Brahmanical society stressed its power over women's sexuality," stating that "a woman's submission to male control in any sexual relationship was the principal duty of her life" (Pal). Also, during this time, the practice of purdah, requiring married women to be veiled, became widespread (Pal). Pal additionally states that in this period "Women became completely deprived of inheriting any share of their husband's property," and widows could not remarry, but only secure protection from their children (Pal). In addition, the practice of sati, discussed earlier, "increased markedly" during this period (Pal). Also, "a preference for sons was at its apex during this period" (Pal). Therefore, it is clear that the position of women drastically declined in the Indian pre–Classical period. Srivastava concurs, stating that in pre–Classical India, "Patriarchal social order backed with religious sanctions nurtured gender discrimination in all aspects of the economic, political and social life" (Srivastava). This discrimination would affect the rights of Indian women for centuries to come.

In about the sixth century CE, the sacred texts of the Tantras and the Puranas began to redefine conceptions of Hindu goddesses beyond those that were presented in Vedic and pre–Classical times. The Tantras and Puranas began to describe more dynamic and powerful roles for many of the existing Hindu goddesses. In fact, some scholars believe the revision of Hindu goddesses in the Tantras and the Puranas may reflect back to more accurate representations of what Indian goddesses looked like prior to Indo-Aryan arrival (Stone 213). It is especially in the Puranas that the possible indigenous Indus Valley reverence for a Mother Goddess is embraced once more under the concept first articulated in the Rig Veda as Devi or Mahadevi (Gupto 39). In the Puranas, Devi is conceived of as the unified concept of all of the separate goddesses in Hinduism (Gupto 39), similar to what was seen in Neolithic Slavic, Baltic, Greek, etc., regions. Phillips,

Kerrigan, and Gould explain that in the Hinduism of the Puranas, "all the goddesses are considered aspects of one great female deity" (Phillips, Kerrigan, & Gould 93). Kinsley supports this, stating that in this period "there is a tendency in many texts, myths, and rituals concerning goddesses to subsume them all under one great female being. This goddess has many names, but her most common designation is simply Devi (goddess) and Mahadevi (great goddess)" (Kinsley 132). This united concept of Devi allows the myriad representations of other Hindu goddesses thus discussed to represent aspects of one unified Goddess. This Mother Goddess principal became referred to as Shakti. Shakti was considered an embodiment of nature and all-pervading energy, as well as an abstract concept of absolute consciousness.

Frankel states that the Tantras "promulgated the idea of Shakti" (Frankel 112). According to Tantric tradition, one myth assigns the birth of the Hindu divine trinity of male gods, Brahma, Vishnu, and Shiva, as coming from Shakti/Devi (or sometimes Adya) as the Mother Goddess. Other Hindu stories of the birth of the trinity of gods attribute their creation as either coming from each other in some way, or as just happening from no female source. However, this Tantric version of creation places the Mother Goddess Devi as the creator of the gods when she takes on the form of a bird who lays three eggs, which thus produces the three primary gods of the Hindu pantheon. To appease the god Shiva, who immediately attempts to supersede Devi's authority, Devi gives Shiva her third eye and marries him. After marrying Devi, Shiva uses her third eye to burn her to ashes. From the ashes of Devi, the three goddess consorts were created: Saraswati, Lakshmi, and Parvati/Kali. Also, from the ashes of Devi came the devis/goddesses of various local settlements. Therefore, Lubell states that the concept of Shakti/Devi, as this myth illustrates, is still "the unity of all the goddess aspects" (Lubell 156–7), as the story makes clear that though Shiva tried to kill Shakti, she, as a Mother Goddess, cannot be eliminated but only transformed. In addition, this myth shows Shiva and the other Hindu gods as incomplete without their respective goddess consorts, as they, and all divine elements, are shown to come from Shakti/Devi.

Many scholars believe that the conception of the unification of all deities into Shakti emerged as a form of resistance against primarily patriarchal conceptions of Hindu divinities. The new Hindu sect of Shaktism allowed male gods and female goddesses to be better explained as compliments of one another, not as superior or inferior figures to one another. Therefore, religious narratives often began to grant more power to the sacred feminine as part of a united whole with male sacrality. For example, in Shaktism, the god Shiva became paired with Shakti, and the myths of this pairing show what appears to be an explicit attempt to reassign power and importance back to Shakti, so that followers could accept the authority of both the male and female divine forms as equal. One Hindu story discusses how a sage named Bhringi wanted to show his devotion to Shiva by circling the god, but Shiva told Bhringi that he must also encircle Shakti, because as Shiva stated "'each of us is incomplete without the other'" (qtd. in Pattanaik 27). However, Bhringi refused to pay homage to Shakti, so Shakti positioned herself on the lap of Shiva, making it impossible for Bhringi to bypass her while encircling Shiva. To try and evade Shakti, Bhringi metamorphosed into a bee and tried to fly between Shiva and Shakti. In retaliation, Shakti fused her body with that of Shiva's. Again, Bhringi metamorphosed himself into a worm to try and dig a hole between the divinities. Shakti finally declared "'If you only want him then may you be deprived of every tissue that a human gets from a woman'" (qtd. in Pattanaik 27), and with that Bhringi was transformed into a skeleton with no flesh or blood. Finally, Bhringi understood "the complimentary relationship between the god and the goddess" (Pattanaik 27). It is evident that this myth is sending a message to audiences that the goddess Shakti and all Hindu goddesses are just as powerful and necessary as the Hindu gods. The lengths this story goes to teach the resistant Bhringi this vital lesson arguably presents this myth as being used to teach followers to move past their preconceived patriarchal perceptions in order to adopt a revised faith of equality, that again might in actuality be similar to the faith of some pre–Indo-Aryan cultures.

Shaktism also allowed the powerful goddesses of Hinduism, like Durga and Kali, to better merge with seemingly patriarchal goddesses like Saraswati, Lakshmi, and Parvati, as all goddesses were now envisioned as necessary aspects of a united, all-powerful Shakti. A succinct example of Shakti's supreme role can be found in the Devi-Bhagavata Purana, believed to be composed between the ninth and fourteenth centuries, which states of the conception of Shakti: "'I am Manifest Divinity, Unmanifest Divinity, and Transcendent Divinity. I am Brahma, Vishnu and Shiva, as well as Saraswati, Lakshmi and Parvati. I am the Sun and I am the Stars, and I am also the Moon. I am all animals and birds, and I am the outcaste [sic] as well, and the thief. I am the low person of dreadful deeds, and the great person of excellent deeds. I am Female, I am Male'" (Devi-Bhagavata). This uniting of separate goddesses in the Tantras and Puranas is historically interesting, as in many other cultures, such as Greece, once goddesses were separated from the conception of a supreme Mother Goddess, they only continued to lose their position of strength once patriarchal cultural structures dominated. However, in India, the resurgence of the indigenous concept that all goddesses were connected to one central Mother Goddess, is extraordinary. It would seem that this unification of the power of Hindu goddesses would thus positively affect the position of women socially. And, this appears somewhat true, as the position of women did become slightly more elevated in India's medieval period (sixth to sixteenth centuries CE), as more and more people embraced Shaktism, and it became one of the major sects of Hinduism.

The medieval period in India did allow for some royal women to hold elevated social positions, though these historical women were certainly the exceptions to the rule. For instance, during 736–945 CE in the state of Odisha, formerly Orissa, six widowed queens and one unmarried princess served as sovereign rulers for a time (Priyabadini). In addition, Queen Didda (958–1003 CE) ruled the region of Kashmir as regent for her son. Also, in the medieval period of India, some women were able to gain considerable power through the position of regent. Most often, these women passed on the right to rule when their son/relative came of age, but some Indian women held onto their power when their son/relative died, or in some cases, even past the coming of age of the heir. For example, Queen Didda's son died, but she was able to maintain her power by, as some say, having her own grandsons killed to maintain her rule. However, it should be stated that this accusation of murder might be false, as women rulers often get credited as taking part in abhorrent acts because they are accused of being overly ambitious or even evil, just because they are women who defy the social order. What is definitively known is that during Queen Didda's rule, her kingdom remained prosperous and powerful; "Didda was an administrative genius, who propagated beneficial measures for her subjects, and her kingdom was one of peace and prosperity" (Datta). Queen Didda also attributed much of her power to her connection to the goddess Arodoxsho, a version of the goddess Lakshmi. This connection to a goddess as strengthening her right to rule is evidenced on coins that were minted during her rule that show the goddess Arodoxsho in connection to herself (Datta). Queen Didda's proclaimed connection to divinity may reveal in part why she was able to hold a position of power during patriarchal times; as was seen in many European cultures, when queens connected themselves to conceptions of female divinity, they often gained a favorable following from their subjects. In addition, Rudrama Devi in the thirteenth century was the monarch of the Kakatiya dynasty. Rudrama Devi's father, King Ganapathideva, had no sons to inherit his kingdom, so he appointed Rudrama Devi as co-regent alongside himself, until his death when Rudrama Devi was officially crowned Queen of the Empire (Hazra). Queen Rudrama Devi became a revered monarch. She ruled her kingdom with fortitude, taking part in important battles with neighboring parties, wining territories, and gaining the favor of her people by introducing "a new policy of recruiting people from non-aristocratic background as commanders in the army as well as the administration" (Hazra). Queen Rudrama Devi's new policy of inclusion was a radical step to take at that time, but ultimately the policy gained "the trust of the commoners and ... [won] new loyalists" (Hazra). Thus, many commend Rudrama Devi as an outstanding ruler within Indian history (Hazra). However, scholars believe that in order to maintain the favor of her people, Rudrama Devi purposefully donned a masculine appearance to appear more like a king rather than a queen (Hazra).

Another example of the slight elevation in the social status of some women in medieval India may be evidenced with the female Bhakti poets who were embraced during the era. Bhakti poetry was love poetry directed at divine concepts. The Bhakti movement gained many followers from all sects of society, especially women. One famous Bhakti women poet was Akka Mahadevi. Akka Mahadevi expressed her devotion to the god Shiva and criticized the relationships women were forced to hold with mortal men, famously stating in one of her poems about her own husband: "Take these husbands who die, decay—and feed them to your kitchen fires" (Akka Mahadevi). Another famous Bhakti women poet was Mirabai, who was raised within a royal household and was likewise married into royalty at a young age. However, she, worshipping the divine Krishna, chose to leave her husband and royal lifestyle behind in order to wander the countryside as an ascetic. In contemporary times, Akka Mahadevi, Mirabai, and other Bhakti women poets were recognized as among the first feminists in India; for example, Bhattacharjee states that the Bhakti movement in many ways "challenged upper-caste patriarchy and empowered women to bypass gender rigidities through numerous strategies—refusing marriage to a human being, walking out of marriage or refusing motherhood. [Because of this,] the roots of contemporary Indian feminism are often traced back to the Bhakti Movement" (Bhattacharjee). However, Jacobsh cautions that "While it is tempting to see women's participation within the Bhakti movement as a revolt against the patriarchal norms of the time, there is little evidence to support this perspective. Injustices and the patriarchal order itself were not a major focus of these poets" (Jacobsh). Instead, the Bhakti women poets "were simply individuals attempting to lead lives of devotion. Staying largely within the ... present patriarchal culture that upheld the chaste and dutiful wife as ideal, these women transferred the object of their devotion and their duties as the 'lovers' or 'wives to their Divine Lover or Husband" (Jacobsh) instead of human men. Therefore, in actuality, the Bhakti women poets of India's medieval period served to show that despite the widespread adoption of Shaktism, the new Hindu sect did little to improve the rights of most Indian women, as it appeared that patriarchal definitions of divinity, and the role of women, had become too ingrained within Indian society.

Thus, after India's medieval period, the rights of women in India only continued to decline as invasions by the patriarchal societies of the Muslims, and later the British Empire, further legitimized the existing patriarchy that had long been in place in India. In the seventh century CE the religion of Islam entered India through trade, and later through Syrian and Persian invasions. With the arrival of the monotheistic religion of Islam, that was adopted in time by many people in India, the outright exclusion of goddess worship by Muslim practitioners caused a greater devaluing of women in general. Under Muslim rule in the Mughal Era (1526–1761 CE), women remained dependent upon their fathers, husbands, sons, and male relatives, as they had in Hindu societies. Srivastava states that "Islam made the husband the head of the family and insisted that a wife should obey all his commands and should serve him with utmost loyalty" (Srivastava). Under Islamic rule, the home was still believed to be the ideal place for women to spend their lives. Furthermore, under Islamic rule, women "were prohibited to attend public functions and were not free to participate as men's equals in religious functions"; they were also "excluded from all important decision-making processes" (Srivastava). Under Muslim rule, polygamy became more commonplace among the upper classes; men often held many wives, and Muslim rulers held large harems. However, with the introduction of Islam, female adherents of the religion did gain some social allowances from those they previously held under Hindu rule; for example, Muslim widows could remarry after a specified lapse of time following her husband's death (Srivastava). Muslim women also did not practice sati.

Once European Colonialism entered India, bringing monotheistic Christian concepts to the subcontinent, goddess reverence became further removed, as Christian colonizers often criticized those who still practiced Hinduism and thus worshipped the Hindu goddesses. The goddess Kali, for example, was identified by Europeans as evil for her mythic displays of violence that were misunderstood by colonizers. Pattanaik states that "when the Europeans came to India in the sixteenth century, they could not appreciate Kali's image, especially her nakedness and violence, so far removed from the docile, virginal Mary.... In fact, Kali terrified them, and endorsed their presumptions about the natives being savages. They became convinced Hindus were worshippers of the Devil" (Pattanaik 73). In turn, colonization further disrupted the overall view of Indian women by assigning increased patriarchal roles upon women according to Western cultural norms.

Given the long history in India regarding goddess worship, there appears to be a conundrum in contemporary India, as, unlike many places on earth today, goddesses are still revered in India, but many contemporary women in India are often treated as inferior in Indian society. Though the status of women has improved in India in contemporary times, it is far from equal to the social status of men. Arranged marriages still continue, and "from age one to four, a female child's death rate is fifty percent higher than that of a male child," showing that there are still biases regarding females within Indian society (Keller 229). Indian women are not considered equal within political, social, or religious pursuits. Also, acts of violence against women are a common occurrence within contemporary India. It is thus important for the purposes of this book to address the question as to why the social role of women in India has remained so low despite the continuation of the worship of goddesses within Hinduism.

As discussed throughout this chapter, the centuries of invading cultures of myriad Indo-Aryan groups, Muslims, Europeans, etc., introduced and systematically maintained patriarchal religious concepts and social structures, which resulted in the rights of women in India becoming increasingly lower with each invasion. Though the reverence of goddesses continued for many people in India, despite the incorporation of invading patriarchal values, the Hindu goddesses that are presented for worship, as discussed, are often still portrayed as acceptable goddesses under patriarchy. Many Hindu goddesses remain portrayals of male expectations of female behavior. Saraswati, Lakshmi, and Parvati, for example, still often appear in many Hindu stories in a one-dimensional light that is only cast to represent a male designated virtue of femininity, such as fidelity to a husband, the need to sacrifice selfhood for family or state, etc. Many other goddesses, like Kali and Durga, seem supremely powerful, but when their power is examined more closely, it is often revealed that their power is subject to the demands of a male god, as was discussed. These portrayals of divine goddesses who exist to serve male gods, or at least obey their decrees, perpetuate patriarchy, and may explain, at least in part, why women often remain viewed as socially inferior in India today.

Hedman conducted research asking contemporary Indian women to comment upon the question: "Are Hindu goddesses role models for Hindu women" (Hedman)? Many contemporary Indian women who were asked this question commented that Hinduism often presented expectations for how women should act socially based on the representation of various goddesses. The women who were interviewed cited the fact that many Hindu goddesses are presented within tales to teach audiences primarily one thing—"Women should sacrifice for their husbands and be devoted to them" (Hedman). The women who were interviewed stated that Hindu women are often taught that the goddesses who are portrayed in Hindu stories as possessing the "'right' qualities" for Hindu women are Lakshmi and Parvati, as these docile and faithful goddesses are most often promoted as "role models" for Hindu women (Hedman). Therefore, Hedman believes, based on the responses of contemporary Hindu women, that goddess worship does not always "translate into better life opportunities for women" (Hedman). In fact, Hedman believes that the contemporary portrayal of goddesses in India is often "a token representation" that seems to present admirable goddesses as role models for women, but in actuality portrays patriarchal representations of goddesses who only perpetuate concepts about the inferiority of women (Hedman). This presentation of goddesses who support patriarchal agendas, such as occurred with Athena in Greek mythology, allows Hindu officials to be "absolved ... from the patriarchy ... that it is [in fact] deeply rooted in" (Hedman).

Though Hinduism largely reveres patriarchal representations of goddesses, its long history of goddess worship also includes an element that arguably can continue to elevate the social role of women—its reverence for the Mother Goddess. Though some goddesses in India were indeed degraded into separate, less powerful patriarchal examples of acceptable female behavior and roles, the reverence for the possible pre–Aryan Mother Goddess has always remained in India. The "veneration of the Divine Mother with monuments and worship dates back to 8000 BCE and is practiced still" (Phillips, Kerrigan, & Gould 112). Phillips, Kerrigan, and Gould state that "Away from large city-based temples, the Great Goddess is worshipped in a seemingly endless number of forms at folk shrines across India. Every area and village has its own deity and deities, most of whom are female" (Phillips, Kerrigan, & Gould 112). Pattanaik explains that "Grama-devis or village-goddesses are perhaps the oldest forms of religion known in India" (Pattanaik 121). These village goddesses are worshipped in Yogini Temples, temples devoted to goddesses, and many scholars believe that, at one time, these temples were all over India. Yogini temples were "usually circular and open to the sky. Alcoves in the walls held various forms of the goddess. These temples also often contained a yoni stone," which was representative of the female sexual organs and signaled goddess reverence (Pattanaik 121). The goddesses of these temples were, and still often are, worshipped independent of male gods. In addition, "An important aspect of the reverence for the divine feminine in the Hindu tradition is an awe for the sacrality of the land itself and for the Indian subcontinent as a whole" (Kinsley 178). With this view "An underlying implication of perceiving the earth as a great and powerful goddess is that the world as a whole, the cosmos itself, is to be understood as a great, living being, a cosmic organism" (Kinsley 178). Many elements of the Indian landscape thus hold divine identification, such as the river Ganges, which is worshipped as a goddess. And again, as discussed, the popular Hindu denomination of Shaktism still perpetuates a view that all of existence is embodied in the concept of a Mother Goddess. The continuity of this aspect of perhaps indigenous belief makes India a truly remarkable place, as there are few cultures today that have maintained reverence for goddesses at all, and fewer still that embrace the concept of what appears close to a Neolithic understanding of a unified Mother Goddess. It is therefore, arguably, the reverence of this type of Mother Goddess, the supremely powerful representation of the natural earth itself and embodiment of all realms of existence, that has, and will continue to, raise the social position of contemporary women in India.

Again, Hedman states that when she asked contemporary Indian women what goddess they felt was a true role model for their hopes and dreams of a better future, they overwhelmingly chose Durga and/or Kali, who are, as discussed earlier in this chapter, the Hindu goddesses many conceive of as being the most similar to the pre–Aryan Mother Goddess (Hedman). Hedman explains that for many contemporary women in India, Durga "is not like the other goddesses" because she is a warrior goddess, and "is not an ideal for being a good wife" (Hedman). Hedman feels that the draw that many contemporary Indian women feel towards Durga may stem from her being an "expression for dealing with new challenges when the society is changing. Durga does not give up; she is a fighter" (Hedman). Hedman also states that many Hindu women have "iconized Kali as the flagbearer of ... [Indian] feminism" (Hedman). Thus, by envisioning their own connections with India's most ancient Mother Goddess, in all of her forms: Durga, Kali, Devi, Shakti, the land of India itself, etc., contemporary Indian women will undoubtedly continue their fight for equality.

CHAPTER 5

# Asia

## China

In China, the Neolithic period (c. 5000–2000 BCE) provides some of the earliest examples of artifacts that may suggest the worship of female deities throughout Asia. The Hongshan culture lived in the western Laio River and Daling River regions in northern China between 4500 to 3000 BCE (Jiao 58). Jiao explains that two sites in this region included important archeological finds that suggest that the worship of primarily goddesses existed at these locations. In one of these sites, Dongshanzui, stone altars were found that "were associated with clay female figurines and fragments of life-sized female icons" (Jiao 58). In the other Hongshan site, Niuheliang, "more than ten ritual sites and tombs" were uncovered, where "the most astonishing discovery was the so-called 'Goddess Temple'" (Jiao 58). In the "Goddess Temple," "a number of fragments of human statues as well as animal figurines were uncovered," with the human figurines decidedly female (Jiao 59). In addition, "many scholars have observed that the main deity in the temple was [also] female" (Jiao 59). Jiao further states that "if we can associate these figures with deities, then the Goddess Temple in Niuheliang was actually quite a complex pantheon, [as] there is a group of goddesses instead of one, and they all seem to have different statuses or roles" (Jiao 59).

There is also evidence within myriad Chinese myths of powerful goddesses, and many scholars agree that the representations of these goddesses might display aspects of the reverence once held for Neolithic goddesses. For instance, references to Nu Wä, "the Changing Woman," might be conceptualized as a descendent from, or at least similar to, Neolithic conceptions of a Mother Goddess (Nelson 159). Stone states that remnants discussing Nu Wä exist in Zhou period mythology from about 1000 BCE, but Chinese tradition states that the story of Nu Wä repairing the universe might date as far back as 2500 BCE (Stone 27). Nu Wä, as a Mother Goddess, was envisioned as nature itself. She was also believed to have ordered the structure of all existence. In addition, Nu Wä was able to change her shape at will into many natural forms; for example, she was depicted in her myths and images in many guises, such as a beautiful goddess, a child, or a human-headed serpent (Allan & Phillips 38). Nu Wä was also described as the Mother of the Chinese people, serving as their creator. Kinney supports this, stating that in "early Chinese texts there are a few fragmentary references to a goddess who is said to have created all of humanity—Nu Wä" (Kinney 19). Some scholars believe that myths of Nu Wä may offer evidence of the communal structures of some of the cultures within Neolithic China; for instance, Junsheng states that Nu Wä is "an archetype of the great feminine spirit of the matriarchal age that once prevailed across the central plains" (Junsheng 112). The third century BCE text, the *Chuang Tzu*, supports Junsheng's assertion, as the text states that Nu Wä comes from a previous historical period known as the Great Purity, when "people knew their mothers but not their fathers" (Stone 23). During this period, which again might be a reference to China's Neolithic era, the people were said to have lived in harmony with nature under the guidance of a central female principle. In addition, Nelson states that many Chinese myths show during this period, that again might reference China's Neolithic era, that "Only queens are said to descend from a supernatural parent.... These myths suggest a time when access to the sacred was the most important element in accessing power and that the access belonged mostly or even exclusively to women" (Nelson 83).

In alignment with the reverence of a central female divinity, such as Nu Wä, there is also much evidence to suggest that Neolithic women in China held high social positions. Archeological evidence reveals that indeed many Chinese Neolithic communities were matrilineal and matriarchal (Junsheng 112). Zhang Zhongpei states that Yuanjunmiao cemetery in Shaanxi Province from the Neolithic Yangshao (c. 5000–3000 BCE) culture, provides evidence to show that Yangshao culture was matrilineal, and "that the 'social position of females was generally higher than that of males'" (qtd. in Jiao 53). Also, as discussed, the Neolithic Hongshan culture was widely believed to have revered powerful goddesses, and presumably, because of this, they also allowed women to hold roles of high authority (Nelson 160). For example, "a significant number of female skeletons have been found buried with objects such as beads, jade, bracelets, pots, ivory combs, and spindle whorls," suggesting that women held some of the highest roles within Hongshan culture (Kinney 6). Furthermore, Junsheng cites the "matriarchal system of the Naxi nationality" in the Yongning region of China's Yunnan Province as providing a modern example of a matriarchal clan that might shed light on its Neolithic counterparts within China (Junsheng 115). This community believes that they migrated to their current location from northern China as six original matriarchal clans; most within the community still connect their lineage to one of these original clans (Junsheng 116). Because of the maintenance of these communities, "many social customs of the matriarchal clan period, including the marriage form, were retained" (Junsheng 117). For instance, "genealogy is calculated on the maternal side.... Property is publicly owned ... [, and] the principle of making one's own choice" in marriage is valued (Junsheng 118–9). The modern Mosuo (or Na) culture of southern China also is matriarchal, and thus may also provide evidence of what Neolithic matriarchal clans might have looked like. For instance, the Mosuo culture does not practice marriage; "there is no such thing as a 'husband' and no particular office of 'father' ... and no word in the language to name it" (Noble 192). Because of this, there "is no such thing as a single mother or an illegitimate child. The mother is the head of the household (the grandmother the head of the whole clan) and sons stay in the household into which they were born and apply the fruits of their labor to their mother's economy.... Traditionally, men and women enjoy complete equality" (Noble 192). Similarly, during the Neolithic period in China, it is believed that "women were the mainstay of farm production," so males and females in Neolithic China also enjoyed what appears to have been a sense of equality, as they worked and lived together to achieve a fruitful lifestyle (Junsheng 112). Shlain concurs, stating that archeological evidence reveals that Neolithic China was likely egalitarian (Shlain 180).

However, a transition in belief systems occurred in many regions of China when pastoralist clans, who were often patriarchal, increasingly intermingled with sedentary and matriarchal agriculturalists. This merging of cultures resulted in an adoption of belief systems that ultimately led to many clans in Neolithic China gradually becoming predominantly patriarchal (Junsheng 115). There is evidence that during this period of the late Neolithic era in China, there was a noted decline in the rights of women, as this period is said to have succumbed to "pandemic warfare and [an elevation of] known male rulers" (Nelson 159). Kinney concurs, stating that there is archeological evidence that by late Neolithic times, "women's status in China may have declined. The greater number of graves and grave goods for males than for females suggests that social structures were becoming increasingly male dominated" (Kinney 6).

Still, in the Bronze Age Shang dynasty (1600–1046 BCE), despite the influx of patriarchal social systems, there appears a record of women among the social elite who were able to maintain positions of power. Nelson states that many women in Bronze Age China were still "important players in the power game.... Talented women could expect to take on considerable responsibility in the military, the economy, and the spirit world" (Nelson

101). One example of a powerful female ruler in this period is Fu Hao, who ruled from 1200 to 1181 BCE. Fu Hao's "tomb, which held unrivaled wealth for the period, shows how beloved she was to her people" (Kinney 7). Fu Hao was also "a leader of military campaigns" (Kinney 7); her tomb held numerous weapons that had her name inscribed on them, suggesting her participation in warfare (Kinney 7). In addition, "oracle bones suggest that ... [Fu Hao] was both a general who led armies and a lord over extensive land holdings in her own right" (Nelson 159–60). Fu Hao also held a high-ranking religious position, as she "took charge of specific rituals" (Kinney 7). Fu Hao's tomb also revealed skeletons of many women who had served as "the priestesses and perhaps the secular rulers" of their communities (Bacus 45). Therefore, the Bronze Age example of Fu Hao, and the women entombed with her, suggests that some upper-class Shang women were able to maintain autonomy and power (Bacus 44–5). Though, it is important to note that evidence suggests that this type of position for women was limited to the elite in the Shang dynasty.

Evidence has also survived that shows that female shamans, known as shamankas (*wu*), who held the ability to communicate with divinities and spirits, were an important part of Chinese Neolithic and Bronze Age communities. Shafer states that "Linguistic facts reveal the intimate interrelationships between the word *wu* (\**myu*) 'shamanka' and such words as 'mother,' 'dance,' 'fertility,' 'egg,' and 'receptacle.' The ancient shamanka then was closely related to the fecund mother, to the fertile soil, to the receptive earth" (Shafer 13). There are mythic examples that capture the role of shamankas as religious authorities in Neolithic China. For example, Young states that a myth depicting Emperor Yao, who was said to have ruled in the late Neolithic period, portrays powerful female mythic figures who are portrayed as shamankas because of their ability to fly; "The legendary Emperor Yao had two daughters, Nü Ying and O Huang, both of whom knew how to fly. At their father's request, they instructed the future emperor Shun (traditionally 2258–2208 BCE) in the art of flying, which he used not only to escape from an immediate danger but also as an expression of his divine nature and therefore of his right to rule" (Young 2–3). Young states that in this very old myth, and others like it, "flying women ... bestow blessings, such as sovereignty and supernatural gifts, on male" mythic characters (Young 3), suggesting that once powerful female shamans granted authority to male rulers, as was seen in other global cultures.

Later in the Chinese Bronze Age, the shamanka continued to play "a highly important spiritual role," as women in the Bronze Age were seen as the ones who were able to conduct "divination themselves and to have interpreted the results of divination to others" (Nelson 95). It was believed that many Chinese women in the Bronze Age maintained the spiritual authority they likely held in Neolithic times, allowing them to be revered in their Bronze Age communities as the ones who held "the power to appeal directly to the ancestors in divination by asking questions about various concerns for the future" (Nelson 95). During the Shang dynasty and into the Zhou dynasty (1046–256 BCE), "shamankas were regularly employed in the interests of human and natural fertility, above all in bringing rain to parched farmlands—a responsibility they shared with ancient kings" (Shafer 13). Though evidence suggests that shamankas in the Shang and Zhou dynasties were subject to the authority of male rulers, still the allowance for, and need of, shamankas within the communities of these periods shows the continuation of traditional beliefs that held women as possessing the ability to control the environment and communicate with spiritual beings, thus providing some women with positions of authority even when patriarchal leadership was becoming dominant in Bronze Age China.

Powerful goddesses were still revered in Bronze Age China as well, which arguably permitted the continued societal power that some women, like Fu Hao or the village shamanka, held. In one of the oldest Chinese myths, "Ten Suns" (c. 1500 BCE), a dominant Earth Mother is shown to be the mother of the earth's initial ten suns and twelve moons that were believed to once exist in the early stages of creation. The suns were said to live in the "Valley of the Light, where they were cared for by their gentle mother" (Allan & Phillips 35). Each day this heavenly mother would caringly wash each sun, preparing it for its duty in the day. It was said that this mother would then ride a chariot across the heavens, controlling the powerful dragons that pulled it, with one of the suns in tow (Allan & Phillips 35).

Also in the Shang dynasty, the divine Queen Mother of the West, Xiwangmu, was first mentioned on oracle bone inscriptions from the fifteenth century BCE. These oracle bone inscriptions revealed an "eastern" and a "western" mother, who were believed to be powerful goddesses ("Queen Mother"). Within later Zhou dynasty texts from the fourth century BCE, the Queen Mother of the West appears similar to depictions of Nu Wä, and in fact the two goddesses were later merged in conception during the Han dynasty (202 BCE–220 CE). Like Nu Wä, early portrayals of the Queen Mother of the West show her as possessing the ability to transform shape, often appearing with animalistic characteristics, such as a human with a panther's tail and tiger's fangs (Kinney 19). Some early depictions of the Queen Mother of the West show her as a ferocious earth goddess who roars like a tiger and delivers disease and punishments to humankind. In this guise, she was thought to be the "official in charge of vile plagues sent from heaven and the five dread evils" (Kinney 19–20).

However, in the later Zhou dynasty, during the Warring States period (475 BCE–221 BCE) and into the Han dynasty, likely because of the growing popularity of Confucianism and patriarchal values, the Queen Mother of the West evolved into a more acceptable form of goddess worship, according to the patriarchal social structures of the period. In was during this period that the Queen Mother of the West became presented in human form and was mostly portrayed mythically as a one-dimensional motherly, benevolent goddess who no longer brought plagues to humankind, but instead protected people from them (Kinney 19). The philosophy of Confucianism was developed during the Zhou dynasty in the sixth century BCE, and though it would not become the state ideology until the Han dynasty, Confucian values began to revise or replace images of formidable goddesses, as they did with the Queen Mother of the West. Susan Mann states that with the rise of the "'Confucian moral agenda that dominate[d] the written record' ... powerful ancient goddesses underwent a 'civilizing process in which archaic myth was overwritten by history, literature, and the arts of popular culture' becoming 'logically constituted elements' in China's patriarchal society" (qtd. in Rothschild 23–4). With this lessening of the importance of Chinese goddesses with the introduction of Confucianism, the social position of women also declined.

Confucian ideals rested on a "hierarchal ordering of the world. Its foundation was the family ... but Confucius's idea of family values depended on a wife's obedience" (Shlain 188). Confucius himself was said to declare that "'Women and people of low birth are very hard to deal with. If you are friendly with them, they get out of hand, and if you keep your distance, they resent it'" (qtd. in Keller 227). Therefore, Confucian teachings maintained that "Women were to be obedient; their primary function was for procreation, and a double standard regarding sex was imposed against women" (Keller 227). In the Confucian *Book of Rites*, it states that "'a girl at the age of ten" should cease "to go out [from the women's apartments]. Her governess [should teach] ... her pleasing speech and manners, to be docile and obedient ... to learn woman's work,' and a wife 'once mated with her husband ... will not change her feeling of duty to him, and hence when the husband dies, she will not marry again'" (qtd. in Keller 227–8). As Confucianism spread, "a long-established system of patriarchal authority" became dominant (Kinney 31). Confucian beliefs propagated the idea that "social hierarchy rather than equality produce[d] social harmony; this led to a form of female subordination in which the male head of family ... was free to assume almost unlimited control over the female and younger family members" (Kinney 31). Therefore, the later Zhou dynasty became strictly patriarchal, which directly carried over into the Qin (221–206 BCE) and Han dynasties. Befitting Confucian values, women's social roles were strictly defined in these periods, designating them to primarily work within the home at skillsets such as weaving. Women were expected to maintain Confucian values, such as obeying first their father, then their husband, and then their son. Upon marriage, women were also expected to move into the household of their husbands. In addition, in this period male children became overwhelmingly desirable.

Another clear indication of the decline of the rights of women both in myth and within Chinese culture came about in the Qin dynasty. It is said that China's first Emperor, Qin Shi Huang, attempted to manipulate history by ordaining all books revealing the history of China to be burned. Qin Shi Huang did this so that his own version of history, which followed his patriarchal agenda of becoming the sole religious and social leader of his people, would be the only written history that survived. Because of this planned manipulation of history, "the written record of the Chinese past was greatly impoverished" (Nelson 159), especially any record of past female-oriented religious beliefs, as well as evidence of previous women leaders. After this manipulation of history, Nelson explains that "Official Chinese histories since that time have tended to praise women who knew their place, and to denigrate women rulers" (Nelson 159).

As patriarchal and Confucian values continued to spread in ancient China, the position of prominent goddesses, like Nu Wä and the Queen Mother of the West, became further diminished. Nelson states that "A past complex society in which the ideology was centered on femaleness became increasingly embarrassing to the official Chinese line, and was increasingly suppressed" in the Zhou, Qin, and Han dynasties (Nelson 160). Nu Wä, the Queen Mother of the West, and other goddesses like them, became presented as lesser divinities, so they could serve as examples of what proper women should behave like within patriarchal communities. For example, a Han dynasty account lessens Nu Wä's role in creation by giving the act of creating the land and heavens to the mythic male god Pan Gu. However, Nu Wä is still cited within the myth as the creator and protector of humankind. Many other Han dynasty, and later, myths of Nu Wä were further modified to suit increasingly patriarchal social structures, making male deities also assist her in creating humankind in order to lessen her once supreme role (Allan & Phillips 42).

The once formidable and animalistic Queen Mother of the West also become modified to suit patriarchal standards during this period. In an effort to quell the Queen Mother of the West's power, she became mythically married off to the Jade Emperor. However, the Queen Mother of the West, like Nu Wä, did maintain elements of her former reverence, though again, these elements were scaled down versions of the power she once possessed. For example, showing the lasting reverence of the Queen

Mother of the West in Han dynasty mythology and beyond, she was often mythically portrayed as living on Mt. Kunlun, which was considered sacred, as it was thought to be the "axis mundi ('axis of the world') situated between heaven and earth where gods and humans commingle[d]" (Kinney 19). Additionally, the Queen Mother of the West was mythically said to live in a palace of pure gold, with five Jade Fairy Maids, and whenever "she left her paradise, she travelled on a white crane and used a flock of bluebirds as her messengers" (Allan & Phillips 78). The gardens that surrounded her palace were said to grow "the Peaches of Immortality" (Allan & Phillips 78). Such natural and mystical elements surrounding the Queen Mother of the West's palace continues to show her portrayal as a Mother Goddess who is in command of the elements of nature. However, as early as the Zhou dynasty, the Queen Mother of the West's most famous myth, the "Cowherd and the Weaving Maid," recorded in the *Shi Jing* (770–476 BCE), presents her and her granddaughter, the divine Weaving Maid, who was said to be responsible for weaving "the clouds that adorn the heavens" (Allan & Phillips 65), as secondary characters in myths that mostly focus on men.

The "Cowherd and the Weaving Maid" does not display the Queen Mother of the West or the Weaving Maid as formidable goddesses who teach the life and death lessons that Mother Goddesses impart. Instead, the myth focuses mostly on the lonely male cowherd who lives along the banks of a river, longing for a wife. The myth shows that the cowherd's longing is answered when his ox speaks to him and tells him to seek a maiden who bathes each night in the river near his home. The cowherd goes to the river and hides, and when he spots the divine Weaving Maid taking a bath with her six sisters, he instantly falls in love with her. In a common archetype of such tales, the man grabs the clothing of the goddess and only agrees to return them if she marries him. The Weaving Maid is forced to agree, so she is left by her divine sisters to live out a mortal's life on earth. As a housewife now, the Weaving Maid soon gives birth to a son. Thus, this mythic format clearly presents power being held by the mortal male character of the cowherd, as the Weaving Maid, though she is a goddess, is forced to succumb to him and symbolically lose her divinity.

The Queen Mother of the West later appears in the myth and intervenes when she learns about her granddaughter's fate. In a display of power befitting what one expects of a goddess, the Queen Mother of the West forces the Weaving Maid to return to the divine heavens with her child by lifting the whole river the cowherd and the Weaving Maid live by into the sky. The cowherd tries to follow his wife and son, but soon realizes that his efforts are useless. The cowherd then returns home, and again his ox helps him by telling him that it is going to die soon, and it wants the cowherd to take his skin after his death and use it to climb to the heavens, so he may retrieve his wife and son. The next day the cowherd does as instructed by the ox and is indeed able to reach the heavens, where he sees his wife in the distance. However, again the Queen Mother of the West intervenes and again makes the river, that is now in the heavens, a raging torrent of rapids, dividing the cowherd and the Weaving Maid once more. To retaliate, the cowherd takes out a ladle and works for days trying, scoop by scoop, to drain the river. Seeing this devotion, the Queen Mother of the West announces that "on one night each year—the seventh day of the seventh month—a flock of magpies would form a bridge across the Milky Way, permitting the two lovers to meet" (Allan & Phillips 65).

This myth shows the Queen Mother of the West, unlike her granddaughter the Weaving Maid, as holding some power; for example, she is able to lift a whole river into the heavens. However, her power is short-lived. Instead of the Queen Mother of the West serving as a goddess who forbids the cowherd from aiming for divine women, perhaps even roaring her ancient tiger's roar at him, she simply allows the male cowherd to get exactly what he wants when he displays a willingness to work for it. The cowherd's display of "love" for the Weaving Maid makes this myth often interpreted as a love story, but when examined more closely, one sees that the tale mentions nothing of the Weaving Maid's love for her husband. It also does not portray the divine Weaving Maid as carrying any attributes that present her as a powerful goddess, as the myth presents her as merely abducted by a mortal man and forced to be his housewife, with no resistance on her part, showing a clear denigration of her divine status. Additionally, the Queen Mother of the West is mostly portrayed as a product of patriarchal culture; she is mythically described as angry at first by a mortal devaluing her divine granddaughter, but in the end, she allows the mortal man to teach her a lesson about love. Thus, the format of the "Weaving Maid and the Cowherd" shows that in the Zhou dynasty, perceptions of a formidable Mother Goddess who teaches the mysteries of life and death to her subjects, has been greatly revised by patriarchal systems.

A myth of the Ba people, who thrived during the Shang and Zhou dynasties, but were ultimately eradicated in the Qin dynasty, portrays a tale that seems to depict the contention of in-coming patriarchal beliefs set against the Ba people's own traditional worship of earth goddesses (Allan & Phillips 44–5). This myth shows the character of Lin Jun, the first leader of the Ba people, falling in love with a river goddess. The myth begins with Lin Jun setting out to find his people a new place to live, as their resources in their present home were depleted. After traveling for a long time, the people encamped by the Yangyang River. That night Lin Jun took a solitary walk and spotted a beautiful woman by the bank of the river. The woman, who was dripping with water, told Lin Jun that though the land around them looked harsh, it would provide great resources for his people. The woman then left Lin Jun, but that night back in his tent, Lin Jun could think of little else besides the woman. Just as Lin Jun realized that his longing for the mysterious woman would not allow him to sleep that night, he saw that his tent flap opened, and the woman he was thinking about came inside. The pair had sex, but when Lin Jun awakened in the morning, he saw that the woman transformed before his eyes into an insect and flew away. Lin Jun knew then that the woman was a river goddess. The couple met each night after that, and every night the goddess tried to convince Lin Jun to settle his people at her location, which she said could provide enough resources for his people. However, Lin Jun proved that he couldn't trust what the goddess told him about the land providing abundant resources for his people, as he only continued to see barren land around him, so Lin Jun made up his mind that he must move his people to a new site. When the goddess learned of this, she unleashed a swarm of thick insects that plagued Lin Jun's people. Lin Jun tried demanding that the goddess stop mistreating his people this way, but she did not relent. Lin Jun then came up with a plan. He had a messenger take a green, silken thread to the riverbank and lay it on the ground, stating that Lin Jun had changed his mind, and would indeed have his people stay in the goddess's land if the goddess picked up the green thread and came to Lin Jun wearing it as "a symbol of his undying love for her" (Allan & Phillips 45). The next day, the insects increased, but when Lin Jun peered into the center of their mass, he saw one green thread hanging down from the center of the swarm. When he saw this, Lin Jun took out his bow and shot an arrow at the thread. With that, "there was a brilliant flash and a shrill whistle—and the goddess became visible, with the arrow through her heart" (Allan & Phillips 45). The goddess's body fell into the river and began to float silently away. Lin Jun's people rejoiced, as the insects dissipated and then disappeared. But Lin Jun "threw away his bow and arrows, frightened by what he had done" (Allan & Phillips 45). The people left the place immediately, but they only could find sites that were even more barren than where they had come from. As the days passed, Lin Jun found that he could not get the goddess out of his mind, no matter how hard he tried. As he was once again pondering all the events of their interactions, he saw in his mind the riverbank he fled from, and then he visualized it opening up before him to produce a staircase. When his people climbed the stairs in his mind, they were overjoyed to see a verdant and vast stretch of land. Still visualizing the scene, Lin Jun threw down some pieces of bamboo upon a rock before him, and he saw that impossibly they began to grow. Thus, Lin Jun knew that he must return to the goddess's river, so that his people could thrive.

This myth can be interpreted to show the river goddess as either benevolent or malevolent, much like the portrayal of many goddesses from other cultures who underwent a political and religious process of denigration to strip them of their former stature. The river goddess in this myth is portrayed as initially negative, as she seems to possess qualities similar to a succubus, who might be tricking Lin Jun into sleeping with her, so that she can strip him of his senses and jeopardize the wellbeing of his people. Lin Jun's denial of the river goddess shows that he does not trust the workings of the goddess, and like Gilgamesh's distrust of Ishtar, this distrust may be a signal of the shifting views regarding goddess reverence within Ba culture. The subsequent portrayal of the river goddess in this myth as vengeful, as she unleashes an unrelenting plague of insects upon the people, just as Ishtar unleashed the Bull of Heaven upon the people of Uruk, sends a message to the audience of the myth that traditional goddesses are not to be trusted. According to the plot outlined in the majority of the myth, it therefore appears right that Lin Jun killed the river goddess in order to save his people from her ability to plague them. However, the contradictory ending of the myth, when Lin Jun realizes his error in killing the goddess, reveals the lasting reverence on the part of the Ba people towards their traditional goddesses. The myth ultimately shows that when Lin Jun allowed himself to strip his fear of the goddess away, he was able to tap into a trust of the traditional beliefs of the people, where the river goddess was not evil, but a beneficent teacher capable of instructing Lin Jun on how to trust the land and the resources it would provide for his people. Thus, when Lin Jun was able to dispel his fear and distrust of the goddess, he and his people were able to receive the bounty that was hidden in the land all along—a message that seems intended for those among the Ba people who may have questioned the superiority of goddesses within their community.

As the authority of goddesses declined in the Zhou, Qin, and Han dynasties, many myths and folktales also revealed the declining rights of Chinese women since Neolithic and earlier Bronze Age periods. Written records in the *Chunqiu Zuo zhuan* (*Zuo Commentary on the Spring and Autumn Annals*) portray women in divided roles that would become the stereotypes of later Chinese folktales, such as "the earliest example of the femme fatale" (Kinney 13). One such example of a femme fatale within Chinese folklore is the historical Bao Si, who was the "concubine of the Western Zhou King You (c. 781–771 BCE)" (Kinney 26). Legends arose that portrayed Bao Si in a highly negative light. For instance, Bao Si was said to have tricked King You into replacing the position of his wife as queen with herself. Another legend of Bao Si states that she had King You so under her spell that she made him go to tremendous lengths to amuse her. For example, just for her amusement, Bao Si was said to make King You light off the village's emergency fires, that signaled the imperial guards, so often that the guards stopped believing the signal. This act caused rebel invaders to successfully attack the village and kill King You and his son. Horrific folktales like this warned audiences that women should never hold too much power over a man. Needing to create and embrace such stories that show femme fatales as responsible for the downfall of the Bronze Age dynasties in China, when some women were still permitted to hold limited social power, suggests that the folktales were invented to influence the people against accepting women in such political roles. This assertion is supported by the fact that many folktales in early Chinese literature repeatedly portray the "image of the femme fatale [to] serve as a catalyst for political decline. The fall of the legendary Xia dynasty ... as well as the downfall of the Shang and the Western Zhou are all traditionally ascribed to the pernicious influence of unscrupulous women" (Kinney 27).

In a contrasting role to the femme fatale, early Chinese folktales often presented the stereotype of the chaste widow who refused "to remarry after the death of her first husband" (Kinney 27). This type of woman was portrayed as highly devoted and sacrificial, as she was often portrayed as even committing suicide to show her devotion to her husband (Kinney 28), similar to how women within India's myths and folktales began to be displayed. Another popular one-dimensional female character of Chinese folklore was the exemplar mother. Kinney identifies the Confucian philosopher Mencius's mother as one such example (Kinney 28). Mencius's mother was said to be a widow who sacrificed everything for her son's success. When her husband died, she moved Mencius and herself to live near a graveyard, but found that Mencius imitated the grave diggers, so she moved to a market, but found that he imitated the merchants; finally she moved next to a school, which made Mencius imitate a scholar, thus leading to his lifelong success (Kinney 28). These unrealistic depictions of women, similar to the unrealistic portrayal of goddesses who became portrayed as male representations of acceptable positions of female divinity under patriarchal rule, were meant to send a message to audiences that women must sacrifice themselves to perpetuate the success of the males within their lives, thus stripping them of their own power and autonomy.

As patriarchy and Confucian ideals progressed in China, folktales also captured the condemnation of the once revered role of the shamanka by displaying the sacred practices of the shamankas as harsh and outdated in an effort to devalue the communal importance of this high societal role for women. For example, a Chinese folktale entitled the "River God's Wife," recorded in the Northern Wei dynasty (386–534 CE) but said to have originated from the Warring States period, portrays shamankas as wicked for their customs (Chu 61–8). The tale begins by showing villagers who believe that they must sacrifice a young girl to the river god by marrying her to the river, which in actuality meant taking the young girl to the river and drowning her (Chu 3). The folktale shows how the shamankas, defined in the story as "witches" often "wrested large sums of money from the people" each time they declared that a girl had to be sacrificed, which in time wiped "out many a household's savings" (Chu 63). With the people in this forlorn position, "the tale presents a savior in the form of Ximen Bao, a 'reformist' who was appointed head of Yexian County" (Chu 63). Ximen Bao arrived at the community, and when he learned of the practice of "marrying" girls to the river god, he stopped the practice by showing the people the falsehood of their beliefs. He convinced the people to dispel their old beliefs by violently killing the head shamanka, whom Ximen Bao identified as a witch. Ximen Bao threw the "old witch in her seventies with a gaudily painted face" into the river moments before the young bride was to be sacrificed to the river god. Ximen Bao then proceeded to have all the shamankas of the community thrown in the river to drown. The people of the community were at first shocked and quite fearful of the vengeance that might come to them from the river god and the shamankas, but when they saw that nothing happened, the villagers were presented as learning the error of their old beliefs from the reformer Ximen Bao. Again, the use of myths and folktales to sway popular belief against former religious concepts is a long-practiced tradition. Like this folktale, there are many similar folktales around the world that portray traditional religious beliefs as evil and in need of reform, such as the folktales of Irish saints who drove serpents or water monsters, symbolic of pagan religious beliefs, out of the land to prepare it for Christianity. The violence done by Ximen Bao in this folktale to the women who were once identified as spiritual leaders of the community suggests that the story was recorded during a period of transition, when male power was attempting to eradicate powerful religious and social roles for women. The women in the story are labeled as witches, not shamankas, to give them a derogatory title; they are also presented as greedy, as they kill the young women of the community at an astonishing rate, so they can profit from their dowries. Furthermore, the shamankas are presented as old, ugly, and outlandish in dress, a trait used in European folktales of witches, in an attempt to define them as wicked, and thus deserving of the punishment given to them by the "savior" Ximen Bao. However, as with many other similar attempts of presenting powerful women in degraded representations, such as European midwives in the role of witch, there is evidence that the common people still revered the shamankas of their communities (Shafer 14), as many Chinese people were believed to still seek the aid of their shamankas in times of need (Shafer 15).

In fact, shamankas were still an important part of the community even in the Han dynasty, as Han documents show that in the families of the "present-day province of Shangdong, the eldest daughter typically remained at home unmarried to serve as a shaman" (Kinney 22). *The Rites of Zhou* discusses the role of Han dynasty shamankas: "'The Female Shaman supervises the expiations and herbal lustrations of the calendrical year. In the events of droughts, she dances the rain sacrifice.... If a great calamity should befall the state, she chants and cries in supplication'" (qtd. in Kinney 22). The text, "Nine Songs," also discusses female shamans interacting with male deities through sexual encounters (Kinney 22). However, later in the Han dynasty, texts "condemn women who neglect their household duties and take up shamanism" (Kinney 22). In fact, Shafer states that from the Han dynasty on, "when 'Confucian' orthodoxy in cult matters was becoming increasingly important, it was generally considered an act of public morality to demolish the little unorthodox shrines and fanes of the shamanesses.... Sometimes zealous magistrates destroyed them by the thousands ... in rural towns" (Shafer 14).

The introduction of Taoism in the fourth century BCE, and its continued spread and eventual dominance in the Tang dynasty (618–907 CE) as an official state religion, allowed for the views of goddesses, and subsequently the rights of women, to become somewhat improved once more in China. This improvement for the rights of Chinese women in part had to do with Taoism's renewed reverence for goddesses over solely accepting the strict patriarchy of Confucianism; "Taoism promoted Mother *nature* as the guiding force, while Confucianism touted Father *culture*" (Shlain 187). Whereas Confucianism held women as "generally subordinate to their fathers, husbands, and sons" (Jackson 6), Lao-tzu, the legendary founder of Taoism, "transformed the mystery of the feminine spirit into his enigmatic rendering of the Tao," and this philosophy "supported egalitarian concepts," thus somewhat elevating the rights of women (Shlain 187). Taoist concepts merged nicely with tenets of traditional folk religion in China. In fact, many scholars believe that Taoism had its roots in Neolithic and early Bronze Age conceptions of Mother Goddess worship, as "All of the images of the Universal Mother are described in the *Tao Te Ching*" (Johnson 285). Johnson contends that the Taoist "reverence for life" and the "submission to the cycles of change as seen in the feminine qualities of nature" reflect upon religious beliefs found in China's Neolithic and early Bronze Age worship of earth goddesses. The Taoist concept of the yin might also be connected to traditional beliefs in Neolithic and early Bronze Age earth goddess worship (Stone 27). For example, one Taoist myth of creation, presents the concept of yin and yang as divinities who created the earth out of chaos (Rosenburg 324–5). Yang represented the male essence of life, and his body became the heavens. Yin represented the female essence of life, and her body became the earth. And from these two divinities, all the "ten thousand things in nature that populate the earth" were created (Rosenberg 326). This conception of creation, as well as the yin/yang symbol, portray a philosophy that embraces harmony and equality between both male and female concepts (Shlain 179); therefore, embracing Taoism allowed adherents to revere conceptions of divinity that represented both sexes as equal.

For example, the Taoist folktale, "Seeking Her Husband at the Great Wall" from the Tang dynasty (618–907 CE), displays renewed reverence paid to an earth goddess (Allan & Phillips 67). The tale presents a woman named Meng Jiang, who was raised by two families, the Mengs and the Jiangs, because Meng Jiang was born from a pumpkin that grew up a wall that separated the land of the two families, so both families shared the pleasure of raising Meng Jiang. Meng Jiang grew into a beautiful maiden who one day went out to bathe in a nearby pond, and as she was floating in the water, she murmured to herself that if a man should see her at this moment, she would instantly marry him. Indeed, a man named Wan was hiding in the brush and did see her, so he called to her at once and told her he was there. Meng Jiang kept her word and married Wan. Wan was hiding because he was trying to escape the cruel emperor who was involved in the task of building the Great Wall of China. A village Wise Man told the emperor that in order to finish the Great Wall, ten thousand men would have to be buried beneath it. Another Wise Man added that if the emperor just buried one man with the name Wan, meaning ten thousand, then the same desired result would ensue. Thus, shortly after Wan and Meng Jiang were married, the emperor indeed found Wan and had him buried alive at the Great Wall of China. When the emperor saw the stunning beauty of the now widowed Meng Jiang, he demanded that she marry him. Having to obey her emperor, Meng Jiang agreed, but she did "place certain conditions on her acceptance," asking for a long funeral feast and the construction of a grand altar for Wan (Allan & Phillips 67). The emperor agreed, but during the funeral ceremony, he and all of his guests were shocked to see that Meng Jiang climbed on top of her husband's funeral altar and yelled out all the insults the people wanted to say to their cruel emperor but did not dare express. When she was done, Meng Jiang threw herself off the altar and into the river where she drowned. Greatly enraged, the emperor "ordered his men to chop up her body and smash her bones" (Allan & Phillips 67). However, when the men tried to retrieve Meng Jiang's corpse, they found that it had metamorphosed into a shoal of "tiny silver fish that swam away" (Allan & Phillips 67). Taoist elements are apparent in the folktale in the portrayal of Men Jiang being birthed directly from the natural element of a pumpkin, which suggests her connection to the environment, even as a possible representation of an earth goddess. Meng Jiang's transformation upon death into dozens of fish also solidifies this connection. In addition, it is significant that this folktale displays a woman being the one who voices contempt for the unjust emperor who no one could defy because of his elevated patriarchal position. Therefore, given its construction during the Tang dynasty, this folktale may be an attempt to portray women, especially goddesses, as holding a more prominent role in Chinese culture—one that could even hold authority over a political figure such as an emperor.

Again, given the renewed reverence of feminine divinity found in Taoism, women's roles increased socially from the patriarchal restrictions of former eras. Leading up to the Tang dynasty, folktales featuring strong female protagonists from the Jin dynasty (266–420 CE) and the Wei dynasty show that Taoist elements had influenced the culture even before Taoism dominated China in the Tang dynasty. For example, in the Jin dynasty, records exist of warrior women, such as Xun Guan, Mao, and Lady Mongchi, who in times of need helped defend their cities from attack (Mayor 420). Also, folktales recount warrior women in the Wei dynasty, who may have been based on real figures, such as Hua Mulan and Hung-hsien, who were said to openly defy their era's social regulations by becoming warriors. This folkloric reverence towards defiant, strong women shows both the influence of more open-minded Taoist principles regarding women, as well as a lasting embrace by the people to revere roles held by women in previous eras of Chinese culture. In addition, the renewed reverence of feminine divinity in these eras led to some women in the Tang dynasty being permitted to once again receive a formal education. Also, Tang dynasty artistic images show women enjoying newfound freedoms such as fighting, riding horses, and even drinking and singing in taverns. In addition, upper class women in the Tang dynasty enjoyed the freedom to move about fairly independently, which was a right denied to them under Confucian rule.

The culmination of the expanded societal freedoms some women enjoyed in the Tang dynasty can perhaps best be viewed in the power Empress Wu Zetain was able to secure and maintain during her lifetime. Like other regions, Chinese society did selectively allow for the rule of a woman under rare instances when a regent was needed. Beginning as the concubine of Emperor Taizong, Wu Zetain was able to secure the affection of the emperor's son, Emperor Gaozong. Once she achieved this, it was said that Wu Zetain had Emperor Gaozong's wife and consort killed, so that she could become Empress Consort. After the death of Emperor Gaozong, Wu Zetain became regent, and then proclaimed her two sons, first Zhongzong and then Ruizong, as emperor. In quick succession, though, Wu Zetain took the power away from each of her sons, so that she could become the only female emperor in Chinese history, in a country where "women were explicitly forbidden to hold power" (Cross & Miles 59). Empress Wu Zetain is regarded as "one of China's strongest and most successful leaders," as during her reign the Chinese Empire underwent widespread expansion. Empress Wu Zetain "reduced the army's size and stopped the influence of aristocratic military men ... by replacing them with scholars" who "had to compete for government positions by taking exams, thus setting the practice of [a] government run by scholars" ("Empress"). Empress Wu Zetain also lowered "oppressive taxes, rais[ed] agricultural production, and strengthen[ed] public works" ("Empress"). She also initiated the building of many of China's renowned temples and sculptures, such as the Longman Grottos.

Rothschild states that Empress Wu Zetain was able to secure and maintain her position of authority in large part because she was able to draw upon the long history of powerful goddesses portrayed in Chinese religion. Empress Wu Zetain "could not simply invent an entirely new paradigm of political authority, divorced from precedent; [so] she ... creatively ... [drew] on a vast cultural repertoire of existing mythologies. She amassed prophecies and obscure myths connected to female deities, initially to protect her position as empress and grand dowager, and later to legitimize her new dynasty and validate her unique rule as a female emperor" (Rothschild 23). Empress Wu Zetain "was fortunate to have a large storehouse of goddess myths to draw upon" (Rothschild 24), even though this mythic storehouse had undergone great revisions due to Confucian and other patriarchal efforts. Empress Wu Zetain "attempted to reverse this process of many centuries, to unwrite the texts that tamed once-powerful divinities and un-make the 'civilizing process' that had harnessed them" (Rothschild 24). Thus, Empress Wu Zetain was able to revive "cults of ancient goddesses long fallen into disuse" (Rothschild 24). Empress Wu Zetain became an extension of the traditional goddesses that the people once, and in some cases within Chinese folk religion still, revered by declaring goddesses as her divine ancestresses (Rothschild 24). For example, Empress Wu Zetain "availed herself of the numinous remnants of the powerful mother divinity" of Neolithic and early Bronze Age belief systems (Rothschild 28). Furthermore, because Empress Wu Zetain portrayed herself as connected to divinity, the literary authors of the day "vied to draw ... associations between the goddess of antiquity and the female ruler" (Rothschild 28). Rothschild states that the "cultural resonance, maternal potency, ... divine splendor, and traditional weight" of China's traditional goddesses supported Empress Wu Zetain's "political ascent and authority, and helped to generate her inimitable power" (Rothschild 235). Empress Wu Zetain was not alone in connecting her position of political authority to the people's memories of powerful goddesses who once reigned over religious ideology, as European and Indian queens, as discussed, also at times secured and maintained the right to rule in part by promoting their own divine connections. Thus, Empress Wu Zetain, and the queens of many other cultures, show the need for people to have examples of feminine concepts of divinity/spirituality in their religious and/or spiritual beliefs in order to more readily envision women in roles of supreme authority. Because of her resurrection and promotion of China's traditional goddesses, Empress Wu Zetain went on to challenge "Confucian beliefs against ... women ... [and] began a campaign to elevate the position of women. She had scholars write biographies of famous women, and ... moved her court away from the seat of traditional male power and tried to establish a new dynasty. She said that the ideal ruler was one who ruled like a mother does over her children" ("Empress"). Though, Empress Wu Zetain "held total power for over 50 years" (Cross & Miles 56) in a prosperous and successful reign, she has often been portrayed in history as bloodthirsty and evil, as women rulers often are when patriarchal institutions take over dominance.

The somewhat liberated movements of the Tang dynasty regarding the rights of women would again sharply decline in China's Song dynasty (960–1279 CE). In the Song dynasty, Confucian values once more became dominant with the embrace of Neo-Confucianism. Thus, the embrace of powerful goddesses, such as the ones promoted by Empress Wu Zetain, again lessened, and the mythic and folkloric representations of goddesses once more became mere renditions of patriarchal standards of acceptable female roles. In fact, many scholars declare that Chinese patriarchy was "at its worse" in the Song dynasty, most evidenced by the practice of foot binding, which kept women physically dependent upon males (Shlain 196). The practice of foot binding was a method used to fetter a woman to the household of her husband's family. Song dynasty social restrictions kept women within the home, restricting them from taking part in social or political affairs. Jackson concurs, stating that in the Song dynasty, many "women became little more than playthings. Secondary wives were forbidden to talk in public, and widows were not allowed to remarry, [and]... binding the feet of women—breaking the arches and turning the toes under—became a status symbol among upper class men" (Jackson 7). Even Taoism during the Song dynasty experienced a downshift in its views towards women (Shlain 197). The sharp decline in the treatment of women in the Song dynasty would only continue within China in the dynasties to come.

The arrival of Buddhism into China also played a role in denigrating the status of Chinese women. The philosophy of Buddhism has a history of discriminating against women. According to the Indian legend of Siddhartha Gautama, in order to seek enlightenment, he found it necessary to leave behind his wife. He also believed that contact "between the two sexes could only be the result of lust and passion, so every effort should be made by pious men to not even look at a woman" (Kidwai 11). Early Buddhism encouraged "monasticism, and celibacy was extolled as the greatest of all virtues" (Kidwai 12). Also, legend states that in India the Buddha's aunt, Mahaprajapati, who raised the Buddha, was said to have asked him if she and her female companions could become nuns (Gross 9). Mahaprajapati was at first denied her request, but finally it was decreed that she, and other women, could be permitted to become Buddhist nuns; however, "the comment was made that since women had been permitted to join the order, the *dharma* (Buddhist teachings) would last only 500 years instead of 1,000 years" (Gross 9). Gross explains that as the centuries passed, the role of women within Buddhism became increasingly questioned, and "the belief that women could not attain enlightenment grew popular" (Gross 10). Mahayana and Vajrayana Buddhism eventually gained favor throughout India and Tibet, and these forms of Buddhism did favor the concept that women could attain enlightenment just as a man. However, when Buddhism entered Southeast Asia, the people there "received the older, Theravada form of Buddhism, often considered to be the most conservative towards women" (Gross 11). Thus, Buddhism in China and Japan became "institutionally male-dominated" (Gross 11). Shlain explains that when Buddhism came to China, it had experienced a shift away from defining the Buddha as only a man to promoting him as a god; in addition, the Buddha's disciples were also no longer defined as men but as Chinese saints, called Lohars (Shlain 197). In response to these concepts in 1016 CE, Taoists created their own revised sacred literature that promoted a "male hierarchy organized ... along Buddhist lines," leading to women being "more and more marginalized" (Shlain 197). It was during this time that the Taoist Lao-tzu, like the Buddha, was also elevated past a mere man to the status of a god, and Taoist priests were expected to practice celibacy (Shlain 197). Even today in China and Japan, "women's options" within Buddhism "are quite limited"; "contemporary attempts to revive nuns' ordination linages are extremely controversial and are often met with extreme skepticism, or even hostility.... The most common role for women is that of a pious, but largely invisible, lay donor. Furthermore, low evaluations of women's potential for Buddhist practice and realization are common" (Gross 11). Keller contends that "male monastic orders of Buddhism have generally relegated women to inferior and subordinate status, citing 'The

Eight Chief Rules' attributed to the Buddha, which insisted that nuns treat monks as seniors and superiors, and that nuns' formal ceremonies be conducted only under the supervision of monks" (Keller 230).

One myth from Tibet, which was absorbed by China in the Yuan dynasty (1271–1368 CE), shows how the divine women from the indigenous shamanic and animistic Bön faith of Tibet were often demonized with the coming of Buddhism. The legend discusses the Indian male mystic hero Padmasambhava "who was invited to Tibet in 762 [CE] by King Trisong Detsen to overthrown demons and spread the Buddhist faith" (Kerrigan, Bishop, & Chambers 38). Padmasambhava was said to have learned secret rites that allowed him to come to Tibet and rid it of its "demons," many of whom were female. The first "demon" Padmasambhava encountered was the goddess Mutsame, who was the guardian of the mountain pass he strove to cross; "She turned herself into two steep rock faces and tried to crush Padmasambhava between them. But Padmasambhava paralyzed [Mutsame and thus defeated her] by sticking a dagger in the ground" (Kerrigan, Bishop, & Chambers 38). Next, Padmasambhava encountered the goddess Naman, who threw thunderbolts at him, but Padmasambhava defeated her by imagining the lake she hid in as a cauldron full of boiling water, which caused her to back down before the gruesome retaliation became a reality. Padmasambhava then "struck out one of her eyes, so that she should only see truth and not illusion, and made her submit to him" (Kerrigan, Bishop, & Chambers 38). In showing the male Padmasambhava defeating revered Bön goddesses, the persuasive goal of the myth, which is the justification of Buddhism replacing the traditional goddess-oriented ideologies of Tibet, is made clear.

Furthering the calculated effort to revise the mythological beliefs of the Bön people, another myth was created that showed the Princess Kongjo as coming from China to also aid in bringing Buddhism to Tibet. When Princess Kongjo arrived, it is said that she too noticed the many "demons" that haunted the landscape of Tibet; many of whom were again female. However, Princess Kongjo stated that the bigger problem was that the whole of central Tibet was really the body of a massive demoness; "The mountains of Monpori and Chakpori were her breasts. The mountain of Bonri was her lower belly and genitalia. The lake in the Plain of Milk was the blood from her heart, and beneath the lake, in the heart itself, was a palace of black, serpent-like *klu* demons" (Kerrigan, Bishop, & Chambers 46). Princess Kongju told the people of Tibet that they must hold the demoness down, which was done by building male-oriented structures on top of her, such as the king's castle, a monastery, and many shrines to Buddha "to fasten the demoness's hands and limbs" (Kerrigan, Bishop, & Chambers 43). This visual provides yet another clear demonstration of how mythology was often created to politically sway people's traditional belief systems towards adopting patriarchal concepts. The Tibetan goddess of this myth, who is perhaps Klugyalmo Sripé Tanla Phapa, was intentionally misidentified in this myth as a demoness, though she couldn't be more clearly depicted as an earth goddess, as she is literally the land itself. Many of the people of Tibet worshipped the earth goddess Klugyalmo Sripé Tanla Phapa, known as the klu Queen Who Set the Universe in Order, before the coming of Buddhism. It was believed that the "top of her head turned into the sky and four of her teeth became the great planets Mars, Venus, Jupiter, and Saturn.... Her left eye was the sun and her right the moon. When she woke, the day began, and night fell when she went back to sleep.... Her breath created the clouds, while the winds came from her nostrils. The oceans were formed from her blood, the Earth from her flesh and the rivers from her veins" (Kerrigan, Bishop, & Chambers 68). Mythically portraying a powerful earth goddess, such as what seems to be a representation of Klugyalmo Sripé Tanla Phapa, as pinned down by placing structures that put the new incoming male-dominated faith literally on top of her, symbolically shows the audience of the myth that their earth goddess's power has been restricted by the new faith of Buddhism. It is also important to note that it is a female character, the Princess Kongju, who initiates this act, because mythically presenting a female as the one ordering acts against a goddess, such as often occurred with the Greek Athena, is again a common, persuasive tool used in order to make the actions against the original goddess appear less sacrilegious.

In time, the people of Tibet did adopt Buddhism, but they also chose to maintain goddess worship with the embrace of a Buddhist representation of a goddess—Bhrikuti and Tara, usually "regarded as two aspects of the same goddess, who appears ... [with] 108 different names" (Kerrigan, Bishop, & Chambers 43). This goddess, most often referred to as Tara, appears in the form of a compassionate Mother Goddess. In Tibet, Tara is identified as coming from the tears of the Buddhist Lord of Compassion, the male bodhisattva Avalokitesvara. However, Kerrigan, Bishop, and Chambers state that Tara predates Avalokitesvara and is more likely a representation of an earth goddess who was traditionally worshipped in Tibet, who also merged with Indian conceptions of Tara as a Shakti Mother Goddess that came into Tibet via diffusion (Kerrigan, Bishop, & Chambers 43). Female Buddhist goddesses are often mythically explained as being bodhisattvas, most often meaning that they are incarnations of the male Buddha; identifying goddesses as incarnations of the Buddha portrays these goddesses under male authority instead of as autonomous divine beings. However, Tara somewhat defies this restriction, especially in her origin story from India, which shows her as originally a human princess, who upon almost becoming a bodhisattva was told by male Buddhist monks that she would need to be first reborn as a male to finally reach enlightenment. However, the legend of Tara states that she retorted to the monks, "'Those who wish to attain supreme enlightenment in a man's body are many, but those who wish to serve the aims of beings in a woman's body are few indeed; therefore may I, until this world is emptied out, work for the benefit of all humans in a woman's body'" (Hodges 176). With this proclamation, Tara was said to be reborn as a female who went on "to meditate for 10,100, 000 years," releasing "the same number of beings from the bondage of their worldly minds," which enabled her to become a goddess (Hodges 176). In Tibet, Tara is "more than a sidekick to a male Buddha"; she is often portrayed as a forest deity, suggesting her traditional Tibetan origins, who helps anyone in need; "she dives straight in to help, no questions asked, with no discrimination, caring for all humankind fiercely, as if each were her child" (Hodges 176). In their reverence of Tara, many Tibetans also believe in tantric Buddhism, known as Vajrayana, the Diamond Path (Kerrigan, Bishop, & Chambers 77). Vajrayana Buddhism proclaims that "enlightenment is achieved by the realization that opposites are in fact one. For example, the passive must be resolved with the active. The union and resolution of opposing principles is often symbolized by the act of copulation ... when the opposing principles of male and female unite" (Kerrigan, Bishop, & Chamber 77). This idea that enlightenment only comes when unification of both male and female occurs also signals the maintenance of goddess reverence in Tibet, though it was certainly revised from traditional concepts to fit Buddhist concepts. Thus, with the perseverance of some goddess reverence in Tibet, Tibetan women often held, and still hold, social roles that were quite elevated from those of Chinese women.

In time, Buddhism in greater China did eventually "bring new options to women." In China, the goddess, sometimes defined as a bodhisattva, Guan Yin, like the Tibetan reverence for Tara, again showed a lasting reverence on the part of the Chinese people for their goddesses. In fact, some scholars state that the Buddhist Guan Yin may be connected to the Mother Goddess Nu Wä (Stone 17). The most famous Chinese myth of Guan Yin presents the goddess first as a young maiden who refused to get married, despite her powerful father's orders, because she wanted instead to become a Buddhist nun (Allan & Phillips 124–5). Guan Yin's father, Miao Zhuang, at first allowed her to become a nun, but he tried to have her killed by ordering her nunnery to be burned to the ground with Guan Yin inside. However, a rainstorm came and extinguished the flames, saving Guan Yin's life. Miao Zhuang, still intent on murdering his daughter, ordered that her head be cut off, but magically when a servant attempted this, his sword shattered. Guan Yin's father then realized that if Guan Yin was to die, he had to murder her himself, so he tracked her down and strangled her with his own hands. When Guan Yin died, "a huge tiger appeared from nowhere and carried off the corpse to a nearby pine forest" (Allan & Phillips 125). The essence of Guan Yin then journeyed to the underworld, where she transformed the land of the dead into "a veritable Paradise" (Allan & Phillips 125). With Guan Yin proving that she could supersede the power of death, she thus was permitted to leave the underworld and enter back into her body. Upon resurrecting, Guan Yin left the pine forest and made her way to a secluded island, where she was said to practice "meditation and self-discipline until she attained perfection as a bodhisattva" (Allan & Phillips 125). Guan Yin's father eventually learned that his daughter had come back to life, and though he had grown close to death due to illness, he still wished to murder his daughter once and for all. So, Miao Zhuang ordered another servant to find Guan Yin and maim her by cutting off her hands and gouging out her eyes. However, when the servant found Guan Yin, he immediately recognized her as sacred, so he refused to carry out the order. Guan Yin, though, instructed the man to follow through on her father's order. The servant did as he was told by Guan Yin and found, miraculously, that instead of Guan Yin bleeding to death, she merely took the dismembered parts of her body and turned them into a potion that would cure her father of his illness. The servant took the potion back to Miao Zhuang, and he was immediately cured. With this, Miao Zhuang renounced his kingdom and went to live with his sacred daughter on her island, which became "a place of solitude and peace where she could chant for both the living and the dead and bring to those who prayed for her ... comfort in the continuing cycle of troubles that afflict all beings in the gyre of time" (Leeming & Page, *Goddess*, 128).

The myth of Guan Yin presents her with both aspects of Buddhist values and what appears to be traditional Chinese folk reverence for earth goddesses. Guan Yin in her myth inhabits environments that are secluded and wholly natural; she also commands the environment at will while both alive and dead; these aspects certainly recall more traditional myths of earth goddesses in China. Furthermore, Guan Yin ultimately teaches her father, and thus the audience of the myth, the most profound lesson earth goddesses offer—that life and death operate within a ceaseless natural cycle. Guan Yin supersedes death twice, showing life and death to be an illusion befitting Buddhist values, but, when she dies and is resurrected after her experience in the underworld, which she shows to be a place not of death but of verdant growth, she also teaches that life and death are illusory in the system of nature as well. Furthermore, Guan Yin's myth holds a strong message for the people of China who may align themselves with beliefs similar to what her father is portrayed as holding throughout most of the myth. When Miao Zhuang believes that he should control all aspects of his daughter's life, to the extent that he feels it is his right to murder his own daughter if she breaks the current societal expectation that daughters must adhere to their father's wishes, he is representing a patriarchal set of values that is making society ill, just as he himself is portrayed as sick. However, the myth presents Guan Yin systematically teaching her father that her abilities outweigh the patriarchal notions he holds; thus, in teaching her father about the potential of women in spiritual pursuits and/or the role of the goddess, she is teaching audiences to let go of current patriarchal attitudes and societal practices that might be making them symbolically ill. Even today, Guan Yin is revered as one of the most venerated deities in China, showing again that the long-held reverence for goddesses in China underwent many changes, but to a degree, it is often still maintained for many Chinese people.

Because the portrayal of Chinese goddesses was both maintained in some circles, especially within Chinese folk religion, and heavily revised in others, due to centuries of patriarchal modification, China, similar to India, has become a place that faces complexity in their reverence for goddesses and their envisioning of social roles for women. Throughout China's long history, the rights of women have mostly shown evidence of demotion with periods of modified elevation. Women have long held subordinate positions in China, with evidence of foot-binding, female infanticide, etc., as part of Chinese history. In the twentieth century, the People's Republic of China maintained that women should hold a social position of equality, but instances of female inferiority still remained within China. From the nineteenth century into the middle of the twentieth century, traditional religious concepts were often squelched, and temples were destroyed with the growth of Nationalism and Communism, and along with this destruction, the reverence of many goddesses, who had been maintained in Chinese folk beliefs, became further erased. Today, however, the Chinese Communist Party has had to embrace the people's need to worship their traditional deities, both male and female. So, perhaps the Chinese people will do what they have always done—hold onto the female deities their ancestors worshipped until the goddesses become remembered with the power they once held, allowing the women of China to again step fully into the heightened role they once possessed.

## Japan

In Japan, women were thought to have held equal or even superior social, religious, and political power for much longer than in many other regions around the world. In fact, there is evidence that women from the Paleolithic period to the Neolithic period in Japan (13,000–400 BCE) "occupied center stage in their communities, commanding respect as the agents of reproductive power" (Aoki 64). Specifically in the Jomon period (10,000–400 BCE) women "enjoyed freedom and high position in their communities. A socially elevated woman was selected to serve as a community's matriarch. The members of the community listened to and obeyed the word of the matriarch" (Aoki 69–70). Property was also inherited matrilineally during this period. In fact, a patrilineal family was not known in Japan until Chinese customs were introduced in the late seventh and early eighth centuries CE (Aoki 70). Jackson states that "in the Chinese *Wei* accounts, Japan ... [was] described as 'queen country'" (Jackson 7), providing evidence of the extremely high social position afforded to women in Japan.

With such strong roles for women within early Japan, the maintenance of goddess worship was also very strong, a reverence that has lasted into contemporary times. The Japanese adherence to Shinto, the indigenous religion of Japan, has, since prerecorded history, maintained that the natural elements of the earth: plants, animals, landscapes, and people contain a sacred essence known as kami. Therefore, Japanese Shinto goddesses are often identified as being directly connected to the natural environment. For instance, the Ainu, the indigenous inhabitants of Japan, revere Mount Fuji as the Goddess of Fire. In addition, the principal goddess of Shinto is Amaterasu, the sun goddess. Amaterasu appears in some of Japan's earliest recorded texts in the eighth century CE, but evidence shows that her worship certainly predates her written record. As the sun goddess, Amaterasu is identified as the Queen of Heaven and the leader of the divine kami.

The reverence by the people for a principal deity in the form of a goddess allowed Japanese women to hold heightened social, political, and religious positions for centuries. As with Neolithic China, the worship of powerful goddesses in Japan allowed Japanese communities to envision females as conduits of spiritual insight and ability. Shamanesses/priestesses, later called miko, held an important position in Japanese culture. In fact, miko "still exist in Japan.... Women were and remain both ritual and secular leaders.... The system of women ritual leaders has continued in spite of invaders, trade, and other religious systems" (Nelson 132). Japanese miko were considered "clairvoyant.... Hence, they often functioned as protectors of their people. When the men in their community were to go to sea, these priestesses would predict the weather conditions and catches, and when the community went to war, they supplicated the deities for protection. As healers, these priestesses were sought to cure injuries, illnesses, and even children's tantrums by their magic and prayers" (Aoki 68). Shamanesses were an important part of Japanese communities since the Jomon period and extended to the Yayoi period (400 BCE–250 CE). In fact, in the Jomon and Yayoi periods, it was common for women to hold the position of leader as well as spiritual center of the community, such as the legendary Shamaness-Queen Himiko/Pimiko (189–248 CE).

Shamaness-Queen Himiko, who ruled Yamato, became legendary in Japan. It is said that Queen Himiko commissioned the most sacred Shinto shrine, the Great Shrine of Ise, to be built (Jackson 136). Queen Himiko chose to remain unmarried, so as to especially maintain her power and autonomy. The influence of Queen Himiko was evident in the vast area of her rulership, as well as the honor paid to her upon her death, as "over 100 of her servants [were] buried ... around her tomb" (Jackson 136). Chinese sources viewed Queen Himiko with disdain and fear, as the Chinese *Wei chih* claimed that Queen Himiko was able to "bewitch ... her subjects with magic and sorcery" (Jackson 136). This negative, and even sinister, portrayal of Himiko by the Chinese should come as no surprise given the prejudices of Chinese patriarchal culture during her reign. Like other female rulers before her, Queen Himiko was able to attain and maintain her position as ruler because her culture envisioned positions of authority as already being held by formidable goddesses. Queen Himiko especially associated herself with the Japanese sun goddess Amaterasu who, it was said, gave Queen Himiko her divine sacred mirror, which was Amaterasu's most well-known symbol, so that her rulership could be secured. If fact, Himiko in archaic Japanese "meant 'sun daughter'" (Jackson 136), showing again that when queens, or other political, social, and religious female leaders aligned themselves with goddesses, their right to lead was accepted by the people because they were used to envisioning power in the hands of a female.

During the Yamato period, which encompassed the Kofun period (c. 250–538 CE) and the Asuka period (c. 538–710 CE), the influence of Chinese culture began to manifest itself in Japan. By the late fourth century CE, Yamato rulers had begun direct communication with China. In part because of the introduction of Chinese patriarchal social and political structures, Yamato rulers began to conquer tribes throughout Japan, and based on social and political structures carried over from China, they created a centralized system of government made up of subordinate clans. During this time, clan organization became patriarchal instead of matriarchal, as patriarchs became clan leaders who were the ones now responsible for maintaining religious standards. Buddhism, with its own form of patriarchy, was also introduced to Japan in the sixth century CE.

However, even with the spread of patriarchy in the Yamato period, many Japanese "women apparently did not lose their importance in society once the Kofun chieftains imposed control over their territories" (Aoki 68–9), as many women continued to serve in powerful roles, such as that of priestess. In fact, in some regions, matriarchy still endured, such as in the Nara region in the third century CE, which was "still under the firm control of a female chieftain" (Aoki 69).

Many of Japan's most famous myths began to be recorded during this period, starting in about the eighth century CE, though as is the case with most cultures, the myths predate their first written form. Because these Japanese myths were recorded in the eighth century CE, they reveal the cultural strife between traditional belief systems, that highly revered superior goddesses along with elevated societal roles for women, and in-coming patriarchal beliefs. The Japanese creation myth provides a perfect example of this time of strife.

Japan's creation myth showcases how the divine creator beings, the goddess Izanami and the god Izanagi, created all existence. The myth states that Izanami and Izanagi created earth by stirring the vast primordial sea with a heavenly spear. They then ventured to the new earth and through a series of copulations, they produced everything in existence, including all of the earth's natural elements. Though many versions of this myth exist, in the earliest recorded version from the *Kojiki* (712 CE), before the couple had sex for the first time, they performed a ritual where they walked around a pillar in the ground, and as they met, Izanami "exclaim[ed], 'What a beautiful male you are!' and Izanagi respond[ed], 'What a beautiful female you are!'" (Aoki 66). However, because of the structure of this ritual event, after the pair had sex, Izanami gave birth to the earth's first element—a leech. The myth states that this birth was a mistake that needed to be corrected. To correct this event, the myth proclaimed that it was not proper for Izanami to have spoken first in the ritual, so it was decreed that Izanami and Izanagi must walk around the pillar once more to correct the error of their first attempt. This revision to the ritual included Izanagi as speaking first, instead of Izanami. This scene most certainly shows a symbolic representation of the shifting patriarchal power that began to take place in Japan, as it explicitly places the role of power out of the hands of the female and into the hands of the male. The over-abundant stress the myth places on correcting the error of Izanagi's and Izanami's ritual makes it likely that this scene was a later patriarchal addition to the myth. Stone concurs, stating that this odd scene places "specific emphasis on the female acceptance of secondary status. This emphasis raises the question of the possibility that this aspect of the account ... was added to justify a role reversal from the customs of earlier periods" (Stone 320). Therefore, this myth serves to show what many other patriarchal myths attempted to justify—that female power should be replaced with male power. Thus, the "changing narrative [of this myth] reflects changing social conditions, where women's roles are beginning to erode under increasingly male-centered, patriarchal institutions" (Aoki 66).

However, conflict exists in this creation myth between the traditional and new ideologies presented, as is often the case when new beliefs attempt to wipe out existing beliefs. Despite the awkward scene of ritual revision to try to secure dominance in the hands of the male, the myth continues on to show Izanami as equal, if not superior, to her husband. The myth states that once Izanami and Izanagi copulate again, they created all of the elements of earth, and of course it is Izanami who gave birth directly to these elements, giving her a more substantive role in creation. Nearing the end of creation, Izanami gave birth to fire, which brought about her death. It is the mythic portrayal of Izanami's role within the underworld that connects her to what appears to be older ideology showing her as an earth goddess with considerable power.

In the creation myth, Izanagi, lamenting his wife's death, journeyed to the underworld to try and retrieve Izanami. His role is one that is repeated in many myths from around the world where usually a male mythic character believes he can halt the natural events of life by retrieving a lost loved one from death, similar to the Greek myth of Orpheus and Eurydice or many American Indian myths with similar plot structures. However, in these underworld myths that show a male attempting to supersede nature, it is most often the female character in the myth who solidifies the fact that death is unavoidable, which in turn teaches the male mythic character about his proper role in the cycles of nature. In this Japanese creation myth, Izanagi too must realize, through the instruction of Izanami, that he cannot reverse natural law. Once in the underworld, the myth states that Izanagi saw his wife, but instead of embracing her, he acted out of fear when he saw that she had begun to decay, proving his lack of understanding about death. Struck with horror, Izanagi fled from his wife and left the underworld. Izanami in retaliation for this slight, unleashed female spirits of the dead to try and bring Izanagi back to her. As the spirits approached Izanagi, he threw a variety of elements such as peaches, grapes, or bamboo shoots, depending on the version of the myth, at the spirits. This ripe food succeeded at stopping the spirits, as they were forced to flee back to the underworld. Izanami, still enraged, cried out to Izanagi from her underworld home and told him that because of his inability to face the reality of decay when he saw her, symbolic of his inability to accept the natural necessity of death, she would forevermore unleash death to the new world they created by killing one thousand beings every day. Finally, at the end of the myth, Izanagi promised the only measure that could balance out death—the assurance of one thousand, five hundred new births every day—showing that he had finally learned the necessity of earth's cycles because of Izanami's instruction.

The myth continues to narrate the birth of the most prominent divinity in Japan—the sun goddess Amaterasu, as well as the gods Tsukuyomi and Susanoo. While Izanagi cleansed himself of his traumatic underworld experience in a river, Amaterasu and Tsukuyomi came from the tears of his eyes and rose to the sky as the sun and moon. Susanoo then came from the matter that Izanagi blew out of his nose, and he became the guardian of the seas, and in some accounts the earth.

Mythic narratives continue to state that Amaterasu was the sun and her divine brother, Tsukuyomi, was the moon, and for a time both reigned together in the heavens. However, in time Tsukuyomi killed the food goddess Ogetsuno. Mythic accounts state that Tsukuyomi went to visit Ogetsuno, who had prepared a great feast for him. But, when Tsukuyomi saw how the goddess produced food, which was done by shooting it out of her bodily orifices, he was disgusted. He therefore drew his sword and killed the goddess on the spot. When Amaterasu learned of what Tsukuyomi had done, she became so enraged that she resolved to never be seen with Tsukuyomi again; thus, this is why the sun and moon rarely appear together. Amaterasu then sent another god, Amekumabito, to make sure that Ogetsuno was indeed dead, and he found that "from her body, like a fertile field supporting crops, came a wondrous harvest of good things. On her forehead grew millet; on her stomach, rice; in her genitals, wheat and beans; in her eyebrows were silkworms; while circling her head were the ancestors of those hardy animals of the field, the ox and the horse" (Allan, Kerrigan, & Phillips 41). The mythic presentation of a male god, who co-reigns with Amaterasu, not understanding the natural functioning of the environment shows a similar theme to the Japanese creation myth that shows Izanagi's lack of understanding about nature's cycles. Amaterasu, as an earth goddess, is shown to understand these processes, just as Izanami understood them. Therefore, by Amaterasu mythically shunning Tsukuyomi for his inability to understand that the resources of the earth are all provided by way of powerful goddesses, she sends a message to audiences that demands respect for such goddesses. This myth lacks political and social attempts to supersede the power of a goddess, and instead makes it clear that the goddesses within this myth reign supreme and thus deserve the utmost respect.

Another Japanese myth of Amaterasu shows her maintaining her supreme authority, though it is challenged by a male deity. Amaterasu's brother Susanoo is shown mythically to become angry at being forced to reside on earth instead of the heavens or instead of the underworld with

Izanami. Susanoo constantly voiced his anger to his father Izanagi, who finally relented and allowed Susanoo to go to the underworld. However, before Susanoo left for the underworld, he caused the "seas to boil" and a tremendous earthquake to start (Allan, Kerrigan, & Phillips 39). Amaterasu looked down and saw that her brother was creating a storm that would cause him to rise up to the heavens, and knowing her brother's cross nature, she prepared for battle; "Her face grew dark.... She tied up her hair and her skirts.... Then picking up her great quivers, her bow of war and her sword that glimmered with the light of Heaven, she stepped forth as a warrior" (Allan, Kerrigan, & Phillips 39). When Susanoo arrived in the heavens before his sister, he swore that he only had come to say goodbye before living with the dead in the underworld, but Amaterasu did not trust him, so she gave him a challenge to test him. She stated that they should have a contest over who could bring forth children. First Amaterasu created females by breaking Susanoo's sword into pieces and breathing life into the pieces, and then Susanoo created males from Amaterasu's necklace. Susanoo was outraged to find that Amaterasu claimed that she was responsible for creating both males and females, since it was her necklace that aided Susanoo in creating males. Thus, Susanoo wished to take revenge upon his sister's power by creating destruction in the heavens as he had on earth. So, Susanoo proceeded to destroy all the celestial rice fields. His greatest offense came when he burst into Amaterasu's hall, "where the inhabitants of the celestial plain gathered each autumn to celebrate the harvest, [and] defecated and smeared his foul-smelling excrement" everywhere (Allan, Kerrigan, & Phillips 40). In another account Susanoo further offended Amaterasu by creating havoc in Amaterasu's sacred weaving hall, where it was said that the divine weavers wove the cloth for the priestesses of the sacred sun cult (Allan, Kerrigan, & Phillips 40). Enraged at her brother's offenses, Amaterasu fled to a cave and refused to come out, a mythic plot structure that is similar to the Greek Demeter's refusal to leave her cave when her daughter Persephone was abducted. With this action that deprived the earth of sunlight, the living elements on earth began to die. In a panic, the gods and goddesses finally convened and decided to send the goddess of the dawn, Ame-no-Uzume, to the mouth of the cave to try and entice Amaterasu out by doing a lewd dance, again similar to the Greek Baubo raising her skirts to entice Demeter out of her cave. The dance caused the divine beings to laugh out in delight, and Amaterasu's curiosity at the deities' laughter got the best of her, so she finally emerged from the cave, and "Light flooded from Amaterasu and, under her warm caress, fertility returned to the ... heavenly and earthly domains" (Allan, Kerrigan, & Phillips 44). Amaterasu then punished Susanoo by forcing him out of the heavens and finally into the domain of the underworld.

However, the myth continues to show that during Susanoo's descent to the underworld, he again halted his journey and spent more time on earth to complete adventures that finally taught him to respect Amaterasu's authority (Allan, Kerrigan, & Phillips 54–5). It is said that on one of his adventures, Susanoo encountered an elderly couple who were distraught because they once had eight daughters, but only the youngest remained, as each year a massive serpent, named Yamata no Orochi, ate one of their daughters. Hearing this, Susanoo volunteered to kill the serpent if he could marry the remaining daughter. The parents readily agreed, and Susanoo planned his attack by devising a plan to get the serpent drunk on rice wine. The plan worked, and Susanoo succeeded in killing the beast; he then chopped its body up into eighty pieces (Allan, Kerrigan, & Phillips 55). Susanoo found, though, that when he was cutting up the serpent's corpse, there was a sword within its body; "it was a weapon fit for a goddess," so Susanoo had the sword delivered to Amaterasu as a gift (Allan, Kerrigan, & Phillips 55). This task shows that Susanoo, though an unruly god at the start of his mythic narratives, finally learned to submit to the superior authority of his sister. This is certainly a rare mythic episode, as it shows a male deity painstakingly having to learn that superior control must lie in the hands of a female. This struggle between the authority of Amaterasu and Susanoo certainly does not end like the mating ritual of Izanami and Izanagi that is intended to ensure male authority over female authority; instead, Susanoo is portrayed as needing to accept the authority of his formidable sister. Therefore, perhaps this myth was created to counter patriarchal challengers who were vying for authority in ancient Japan.

The conflict presented in these myths show a power struggle for male and female authority in the divine realm, and as discussed, this struggle certainly mimicked what was happening in Japan during the Yamato period. The insistence on viewing the head of the pantheon as Amaterasu, despite consistent mythic male pressure to steal her position, might be a representation on the part of the people to show their hesitancy to surrender female leadership positions to male leaders, as many Japanese women still maintained "considerable influence" within many communities in the Yamato period (Aoki 64). Aoki states that "During the late sixth through mid-eighth centuries CE, Japanese women often ruled the state. This indicates that female leaders still commanded considerable influence over the island population. Altogether six women came to the throne as full-fledged sovereigns (*tenno*) of Japan" (Aiko 77). Therefore, Japan's "long-held respect for female leadership did not easily die out" (Aiko 77). With this strong allegiance of the Japanese people towards powerful goddesses, and thus powerful women, female positions of authority lasted until 1100 CE in Japan (Aiko 77).

However, between 1100 and 1600 CE, a striking shift occurred in the roles available to Japanese women. Aoki explains that "belligerent male dominance characterizes" the Kamakura (1185–1333 CE) and Muromachi (1336–1573 CE) periods (Aoki 64). Political instability and incessant warfare dominated these periods, and the might of a warrior became the deciding factor of the leaders of this era, resulting in the dominance of mostly patriarchal values. Jackson states of this period that "a strictly military society existed" where women were "excluded from any inheritance and relegated to the socially inferior status in which they remained" for centuries (Jackson 7).

As it had done in China, the introduction and eventual widespread adoption of Buddhism throughout Japan brought with it patriarchal concepts regarding the spiritual position of women. These Buddhist concepts would create a deficiency in the rights of Japanese women as well, as when women are no longer conceived of in connection to religious and spiritual positions, their social worth often plummets. Yusa states that Japanese women within Buddhist ideology were treated "as less than fit vessels for attaining enlightenment" (Yusa 83). Aoki concurs, stating that "there has been a long history of discrimination against women in the Japanese Buddhist world" (Aoki, "Women," 19). Although "women played a vital role in patronizing Buddhism" in its early years in Japan, "misogynistic" Buddhist values particularly "became prevalent around the fourteenth century, with the changes in socio-economic environments" (Yusa 83). Beginning especially in the Muromachi period, "women were strictly barred from entering the sacred precincts of Buddhist temples. Moreover, the sexist teachings of many famous and respected Buddhist gurus led religious women to accept obedience to men and a male-dominated society" (Aoki 19).

Between the twelfth and fourteenth centuries CE, Pure Land Buddhism became prevalent. This sect held the belief that for any woman to reach enlightenment, she must "despise" her female form and shed it in the Pure Land for a male form (Aiko 19). Aiko states in "the period that Pure Land Buddhism [dominated]…women were severely discriminated against in the patriarchal society of the day and had no other option but to accept an androcentric religion" (Aiko 19). However, throughout these periods, women were still highly regarded in Shinto as goddesses, but with the new influx of Buddhism, this was in many ways hard to combat.

The Edo period (1603–1868 CE) in Japan also saw further discrimination against women. In the Edo period, Confucian values that were carried over from China became heavily embraced and were once again responsible for deteriorating the rights of Japanese women. Confucian ideals, that "stressed hierarchy [and] male dominance," in large part led to the social stratification of Japanese culture into "the ruling class, townsman class, and the peasant class" (Kincaid). In addition, according to Confucian customs, "women became subservient" to male heads of households (Kincaid). In the Edo period of Japan, women also changed their names to that of their husbands; "Before ... [this] system, women were able to keep their names and own property" (Kincaid). Confucian values also were "reflected in the laws of the period," in which often proclaimed that Japanese "women did not legally exist" (Kincaid).

The low social value of women in Japan was still maintained in the Meiji period (1868–1912 CE). The effects of Imperialism with its introduction of Western and Christian values, that centered on a monotheistic male God, also played a major role in defining Japanese women as subservient. Once more in Japan, the introduction of religious and philosophical belief systems, such as Buddhism, Confucianism, and Christianity, systematically made efforts to devalue the authority of formidable Japanese goddesses, thus leading to the deterioration of the rights of Japanese women.

However, despite the many patriarchal systems that strove to devalue the spiritual and social significance of Japanese women, there still were some women who were able to defy the social systems of their era, arguably because, again, many Japanese maintained reverence for powerful Shinto goddesses such as Amaterasu, whose worship, though diminished with the introduction of Buddhist, Confucian, and Western values, still was, and is today, embraced by many. For example, Aoki states that some women within the Kamakura and Muromachi periods still "made their mark in various ways, by fighting with their male counterparts in the battlefields, by defending their inheritance rights, and by taking charge of the destiny of their clans" (Aoki 64). Also, extending as far back as the twelfth century, and continuing into today, the Noro "shrine priestesses of Okinawa have maintained their position in society, in spite of foreign influences of many kinds" (Nelson 135). Also, in the Ryūkyū Islands of Japan, of which Okinawa is the main island, women have managed to maintain dominance in religious spheres since ancient times even after Buddhism entered into Japan. Sered states that on the Ryūkyūan Islands, "Only women can officially mediate between the supernatural and human beings; women are expected to be much more knowledgeable about religious matters than men are, and men are required to participate in religious rituals led by women.... All public and almost all private religious rituals and festivals are conducted by women. In addition, personal problems are often solved by shamans, most of whom are women" (Sered 14). Perhaps, then, Japan's contemporary culture, which has drastically increased its regard for the rights of women as equal citizens, is indebted in some part to the survival of Shinto's reverence for its goddesses, whose worship has helped countless women hold places of power within Japan.

## Korea, Vietnam, and Thailand

Though the history of goddess worship and the social roles of women is powerful throughout Asian regions outside of just China and Japan, such as in Korea, Vietnam, and Thailand, given the constraints of this book serving as a survey of the topic, only brief mention of key elements regarding goddess worship within these cultures will be discussed.

Like Neolithic China, in the kingdom of Silla in ancient Korea, there is evidence that women held similar social rules as men, owned property, and also were quite mobile, suggesting the "absence of a gender hierarchy" (Bacus 55). In addition, Bacus points to the work of Sarah Nelson by stating that ruling queens in Silla were said to be descended from supernatural parentage, suggesting that this might refer to a "'time when access to the sacred was the most important element in accessing power, and that the access belonged mostly or even exclusively to women'" (qtd. in Bacus 56). Thus, "it was through women 'that males could establish their claim to the throne'" in ancient Korea (Bacus 55), as was seen in many civilizations thus far discussed in this book. In addition, Hays-Gilpin states that "in Korea more women than men served their communities as shamans" (Hays-Gilpin 89). Again, the high social status of women in ancient Korea can be arguably connected to the Korean people's reverence of powerful goddesses, such as the goddess Magohalmi, Grandmother Mago, who is often referenced as the goddess responsible for creating the natural environment, and the goddess Yeongdeung Halmang, who is the goddess of the winds and ocean, particularly of Jeju Island off the southern coast of South Korea.

Just as was seen in China and Japan, revered social roles for women in connection to goddess worship declined in Korea with the introduction of Confucianism, Buddhism, and Christianity. For instance, the reverence of the goddess Magohalmi as a creator declined as creation within new mythological systems began to be attributed to male creator deities like Mireuk or Cheonjiwang (Heavenly King); "This separation of responsibilities in the creation of the universe ... is related to the shift in the status of Korean goddesses towards marginal [male] deities" ("Grandmother Mago"). Thus, the role of the supreme creator goddess Magohalmi became reduced to "a caricature-like folk" character in Korean folklore ("Grandmother Mago"). Again, this deterioration of the role of goddesses by newer patriarchal mythological narratives was an intentional technique that was used around the world in many civilizations to denigrate more traditional representations of feminine power.

However, despite the introduction of Confucianism, Buddhism, and other religious and philosophical traditions in Korea, the reverence of powerful Korean goddesses, though diminished, still lasted in some regard, which arguably allowed women shamanesses to maintain prominent spiritual positions in Korean society, that continues even today. Female shamanism is still prevalent in Korea, and it often encapsulates all spiritual elements that are "not Confucian, Buddhist, or Christian" (Sered 17). Contemporary Korean women gain positions of social prominence by their roles in shamanistic affairs; their roles include "seek[ing] out the gods, engag[ing] them in conversation, lur[ing] them into houses, and bargain[ing] with them.... Among the reasons for consulting shamans are to communicate with and placate ancestral spirits, to pick auspicious days for weddings and funerals, and to divine causes of illness, misfortune, and family discord" (Sered 17).

In Vietnam, there is some evidence to suggest that Mother Goddess worship, and matriarchal and matrilineal social concepts, were prominent. Myriad goddesses were, and still are, worshipped in Vietnam, such as Mau Thuong Ngan, the goddess of the forest, and Mau Thoai, the goddess of water. However, again once Chinese Confucian concepts were introduced, Vietnamese culture changed over the centuries regarding its goddess reverence and its view on the rights of Vietnamese women. Despite this, many historical Vietnamese women chose to maintain concepts that were a part of their ancient traditions in order to strengthen their positions in society and combat Chinese Confucian patriarchy. For example, the historical and legendary Tru'ung sisters, Tru'ung Trac and Tru'ung Nhi, led a rebellion against the Han dynasty of China in 12–42 CE (Cross & Miles 40). Tru'ung Trac's husband was executed by Chinese overlords, and in retaliation, Tru'ung Trac and her sister Tru'ung Nhi gathered forces to stage a massive rebellion against the Chinese, where they were said to have captured over sixty-five cities occupied by the Chinese (Cross & Miles 40). When their influence finally ran out, and they were defeated, the sisters committed suicide rather than allowing the Chinese to take them captive. Cross and Miles state that "the Tru'ung sisters earned their place in Vietnamese history as the leaders of the first resistance movement after nearly 250 years of [Chinese] subjugation. [Thus] many temples are dedicated to them" in Vietnam (Cross & Miles 42). Another figure of semi-mythical account in Vietnam is the warrior woman, Trieu Au. Trieu Au was also said to have led revolts against the Chinese. Her strength and formidable nature made her become the stuff of legends, allowing her stature to become exaggerated. She was said to refuse to adopt the docile role of women in Chinese society, and instead chose to live the lifestyle of a revolutionary fighter, reminiscent of the power traditional Vietnamese goddesses once held. After her eventual defeat, it was said that Triệu Ẩu also chose suicide instead of being captured by the Chinese. It is legends such as these that show that in Vietnam, at least for a time, women held onto the belief that similar to their ancient goddesses, they held formidable strength as women. Also, the lasting reverence for the worship of Vietnamese Mother Goddesses inspired women in Vietnam in the sixteenth century CE to embrace many traditional folk elements of goddess worship into a unifying concept of the Mother Goddess Đạo Mẫu in retaliation to Confucian patriarchy.

In Thailand, traditional goddess worship was also a prominent part of the culture. Some scholars contend that the matrilineal spirit cults still in existence in northern Thailand today might represent indigenous aspects of Thai culture in regard to goddess worship. For example, in the matrilineal spirit cults of northern Thailand, it is believed that every woman holds within her a spirit, phii, that is passed down matrilineally from a mother to her daughters (Sered 18). These spirit cults state that "one woman per family [should] reside in her household until the end of her life to take care of her domestic ancestral spirits" (Sered 20). These women then act as the ritual officiants on any matters concerning the ancestral spirit of the household (Sered 20). Because of this belief that women provide this necessary connection with the family's ancestral, protective spirits, a "matrifocal kinship system was legitimized," as through "this custom, kinship lineages evolved around the female members of related families," who often made, and continue to make, important decisions within the community because of the respectability they held as religious leaders (Sered 20).

However, as with China and Japan, the arrival of Buddhism into Thailand in the third century BCE, and its continued spread, eventually led to the discrimination of women in religious positions throughout Thailand. Like elsewhere, Thai women were not allowed to become Buddhist monks, because it was believed that women would cause men to stray from their religious paths. It was believed within Buddhism in Thailand, that one could only receive spiritual and moral merit through male acts, which meant that women could only receive merit through their sons. Women were also not allowed to become literate in much of Thailand until the twentieth century, as literacy was obtained for Thai people within Buddhist monasteries. Thus, often women's "lack of literacy meant lack of knowledge of medicine, arts, and lack of social mobility and political participation" (Sered 21). Therefore, Tantiwiramanond and Pandey state that "'Buddhism became a legitimating agent for the Thai patriarchy to affirm and sanction the role of women'" (qtd. in Sered 21).

Throughout Asia, a pattern emerges that is similar to patterns witnessed around the world. In China, Japan, Korea, Vietnam, Thailand, etc., there existed many examples of reverence for powerful female deities, and befitting this, many early cultures throughout Asia were matriarchal and matrilineal. In all Asian cultures discussed, new patriarchal ideologies, such as Confucianism and Buddhism, slowly made their way into existing cultures and caused long-held beliefs surrounding goddess worship and heightened social roles for women to undergo a lengthy process of demotion. New myths were created by patriarchal social, political, and religious agents to strip goddesses from traditionally prominent roles. New patriarchal goddesses were thus often created within these new myths to become symbols for how women should act in newly created patriarchal communities. Subsequently, these new ideologies played a role in convincing populations that women should adopt subservient roles in society. However, in all Asian cultures mentioned in this chapter, reverence for goddesses in some degree has been maintained, and though many Asian countries continue to deal with patriarchal agendas and discrimination against women, it is arguably the maintained reverence of ancestral goddesses that has elevated, and will continue to elevate, the positions of women throughout Asia to the heightened status they once held.

CHAPTER 6

# Africa

Africa is the birthplace of humanity, as it is the place where hominis first emerged as early as seven million years ago. Because of this, the mythology of Africa may hold some of the most ancient concepts of goddess worship. Stone argues that if any region "of the world was to be regarded as the true home of the Goddess as the Mother of people, the extreme antiquity of human development on the continent of Africa must give highest priority to this area" (Stone 131). Upper Paleolithic rock art depicts images of women who many scholars feel might be representations of goddesses. For instance, the rock art image of what has been coined "Running Horned Woman" from Tassili N'Ajjer, Algeria is believed to be an image of a goddess from about 10,000–4000 BCE. In fact, the site of Tassili N'Ajjer in the Sahara Desert holds thousands of paintings from the Bovidian or Pastoral era (c. 4000–1800 BCE) and post–Bovidian era (1570–1432 BCE) that show "goddesses, rainmaking priestesses, or sacred female ancestors, dancing, hunting, or conversing together" (Razak 135). Furthermore, there are paintings and incised drawings, that extend over thousands of years, of what appears to be representations of goddesses found in caves all over the African continent, from Southern Africa, Zimbabwe, parts of Morocco and Libya, and around the Sahara (Stone 132).

Since there are many diverse cultures in Africa, the representations of goddesses within these myriad cultures are equally as diverse. Concepts of goddesses throughout Africa "vary from the exalted position of the Goddess Mawu as Creator of the world ... among the Dahomey, to the Goddess as the Moon in the accounts of the Mashona ... people of Zimbabwe, while the Zulu of Natal and the Woyo of Zaire both regard the Goddess as She who sends the rain" (Stone 133). Though, as stated, evidence of goddess worship exists all throughout the continent of Africa, for the purposes of this book, primarily Egypt and the sub–Saharan cultures of Africa will be examined in this chapter, as these regions provide some of the best information regarding the evolution of goddess reverence in Africa.

## Egypt

Portrayals of goddesses in Egypt can provide a great deal of information about what the goddesses of Africa may have once looked like, since most of African mythology was not written down until after the colonialization of Africa, thus obscuring its original intent. The mythology of ancient Egypt holds some of the best examples of Neolithic goddess reverence found anywhere on earth. Leeming and Page support this, stating that the "greatest and most powerful of the matrilineal cultures of the Neolithic Near East was that of Egypt, where the goddess had first reigned supreme, probably in the predynastic period (before 3000 BCE), as Nut, as the great snake Ua Zit, as the more abstract Maat, and as Hathor" (Leeming & Page, *Goddess,* 43).

The first farmers arrived in the Nile region around 6000 to 5000 BCE because of drought throughout the Sahara (Hassan 106). Hassan states "the deep religious beliefs developed in the Sahara were not forgotten" as mythological structures involving "the regenerative power of Nile water and vegetation," as connected to conceptions of earth goddesses, were brought into the Nile Valley (Hassan 106). Hassan suggests "that the images of goddesses and their iconography were deeply embedded in the early phases of cattle herding in the Sahara, in the desert west of the Nile Valley, where the concepts of the female as the source of life were depicted" (Hassan 101). Around 4500 BCE, "village agrarian chiefdoms" began to emerge, developing into the predynastic cultures of Upper and Lower Egypt (Hassan 101). As in many other regions of the world thus discussed, clay statuettes displaying what appears to be powerful earth goddesses have been discovered in the Badarian, Tasian, Gerzean, and Amratian cultures of pre-dynastic Egypt (Stone 257). By about 3000 BCE, evidence shows that supreme goddess reverence was high in these regions, as Upper Egypt was known as the land of Nekhebt, the Vulture Goddess, and Lower Egypt was known as the land of Ua zit, the Cobra Goddess (Stone 257). However, the "subsequent unification of Egypt into a single nation state" by the Pharaoh Menes in about 3200 BCE, "brought about a dramatic change in ideology, legitimating the role of a national king who incorporated and assimilated earlier deities within a cosmogonic myth that placed him as the descendent and legitimate inheritor of the throne. This change signaled a shift in the role of female deities to a supporting character" (Hassan 101). This tenet of a female deity being demoted from a position of what appears to be superior authority to that of one who supports the right of rulership to a male leader has been, as discussed, seen in many Neolithic cultures around the world. Though somewhat demoted, goddesses throughout the long three-thousand-year reign of the Egyptian Empire, maintained a central position in religious, political, and social issues.

Egyptian mythology provides a rich array of respected goddesses. Like many other cultures, the Egyptians envisioned the earth as a living goddess identified as Maat. Creation for the Egyptians also featured other prominent goddesses. In creation, Atum was the male deity who was believed to create the earth by dividing himself into male and female beings, the god Shu and the goddess Tefnut. Shu and Tefnut then produced the god Geb and the goddess Nut, who represented the earth and sky. Atum was regarded as the sun god, who each day grew from infancy to old age, until at dusk, he was swallowed by Nut, the sky goddess, "an act that the ancient texts show was considered equivalent to impregnation" (Robins 159). Each morning, Atum was born again; "Thus, the sky goddess was both the consort and the mother of the sun god and played a vital role in his cyclical renewal that was essential for the continued existence of the created universe" (Robins 159).

Another prominent goddess was the cobra goddess Ua Zit, who "was known as the third eye, the all-seeing eye" (Leeming & Page, *Goddess*, 45). Ua Zit's image was worshipped for three thousand years as "The Eye, ever present on the foreheads of ... Egyptian deities and royalty" (Stone 260). Ua Zit was viewed as a central source of knowledge. Scholars, such as Stone, state that perhaps the serpent imagery of Ua Zit may have influenced the portrayal of the goddesses or serpent priestesses of Crete, given the fairly close proximity of Crete to Egypt (Stone 261). Egypt remained largely contained throughout its rule, but the Egyptian Empire did have connections through trade and war with regions such as Sumer, Canaan, Anatolia, and Crete, so it is plausible that "certain images and theological concepts of Egypt," such as images of the goddess being connected to serpents, cows, bulls, the lotus, etc., were passed to other regional cultures (Stone 258). Indeed, it is well documented in Greek sources, such as from Herodotus, that the Greeks greatly admired the Egyptians and incorporated their religious beliefs into Greek concepts.

The goddess Hathor was one of the most beloved Egyptian goddesses, as she was the goddess with the most temples attributed to her. Thus, Hathor "stands out as the most important and most complex goddess of the New Kingdom" period in Egypt, which extended from the sixteenth through eleventh centuries BCE (Robins 160). Hathor was depicted with cow imagery, and though her name "literally means House of Horus," showing that she was assigned her name by worshippers of the god Horus, her cow association precedes her name and points to Hathor as being an extremely ancient goddess who may have once been a supreme goddess in Egypt (Stone 270). Goddesses associated with cows were portrayed in artistic imagery from Egypt as early as 4000 BCE, and it is believed that Hathor developed out of these early conceptions. Hathor was also envisioned as a sky deity. She was the daughter of the sun god Re, and as such, she was linked to the sun and its power. In addition, Hathor was often envisioned as a Mother Goddess, as she was "associated with everything that constituted fertility in ancient Egyptian thought: sexuality, childbirth, and the rearing of children" (Robins 160). Hathor was also defined as a funerary goddess, "who protected the dead and facilitated their rebirth into the afterlife" (Robins 160). Additionally showing her role as a Mother Goddess, Hathor often appeared in two forms: as the benevolent goddess Hathor, and as Sekhmet, who was depicted in the form of a ferocious lioness. One famous myth portraying Sekhmet shows her defending Re from people who strove to supersede his power. As a lioness, Sekhmet slaughtered the insolent people and enjoyed the brutal task; in fact, Sekhmet enjoyed the slaughter so much, that Re had to force her to stop by transforming her back into the other aspect of her dual role—the giver of life, Hathor. The conception of Hathor as both the giver and taker of life directly aligns her to the role of a Mother Goddess as presented in many cultures already discussed. Perhaps this is why Hathor is often credited as being the mother of the pharaohs, who served as divine representatives on earth.

The goddess Isis is the most well-known Egyptian goddess. Isis held such revered titles as "Mistress of the Cosmos.... Sovereign of all that is Miraculous, Almighty Lady of Wisdom, [and] Mother from Whom All Life Arose" (Stone 276). Isis was understood as the one who taught the people the laws of the harvest, as well as the art of healing; she also protected women in childbirth and was embraced for her superior wisdom. Isis was openly worshipped as a Mother Goddess, and in this role, she was often connected to Hathor, suggesting that the two goddesses may have at one time been conceived of as a united, supreme goddess. The "worship of Isis as a universal mother figure spread outside Egypt into the Greco-Roman world of the Mediterranean" (Robins 160). Lerner states that the cult of the Egyptian Isis offers a prime example of the power of the "diffusion and synthesizing aspect of the Great Goddess worship" (Lerner 159) in ancient times, as nearby Mediterranean cultures, such as Greece and Rome, often merged their conception of a Mother Goddess with that of Isis. Hassan concurs, stating that the "popularity of Isis was such that she assimilated the religious and cultic functions of many other goddesses" in regions throughout the Mediterranean; thus, "Isis was variously named Demeter, Thesmophorus, Selene, and Hera" (Hassah 99).

Mythically, Isis is shown to hold more power than the principle Egyptian god, the sun god Re, as she is depicted in one myth as tricking Re into divulging his sacred name, which held all of his power. The myth presents Isis as possessing most of the universe's wisdom, except the myth indicates that she reached the limit of her knowledge, so she decided to take the last remaining wisdom of the universe from the god Re, who in the myth was depicted as an old and depleted man. Isis approached the elderly Re and stole some of the drool that was seeping out of his mouth as he slept. This saliva enabled Isis to create a serpent, which she placed in the path of Re, so that he was bitten and forced to endure horrible pain. Following through on her plan, Isis drew close to Re in his painful state and declared that she was the only one who could heal him, but first he had to reveal his true name to her, which would result in him losing the power he possessed as holder of the secrets of the universe. Given no other choice, Re conceded to Isis's wish, and thus lost his power to her, mythically making Isis the most powerful divinity in the Egyptian pantheon.

The myth of Isis and her brother/husband Osiris reveals Isis's true role as a Mother Goddess. This most treasured and famous of Egyptian myths presents Osiris as the god of fertility, as wherever Osiris walked, fecundity resulted. Osiris's brother, Set, was depicted as the opposite of Osiris, as he only produced barrenness. Set was shown to be perpetually jealous of Osiris, so he killed him by trickery and secured Osiris's corpse within a box that he sent down the Nile River. While Osiris was dead, the earth entered a stage of drought, as Set was now dominant. However, when Isis, after a year's time, found the body of Osiris, she in the role of a Mother Goddess, showed her control of the forces of nature by breathing life back into the body of Osiris, which also revitalized the fertility of the earth. Osiris and Isis then hid away within the reeds of the Nile, but in time, Set found the pair and killed Osiris once more, this time cutting his corpse up into many pieces, which he spread throughout the land of Egypt.

The myth continues to show Isis as finding each piece of Osiris's corpse and putting them back together again. Missing only Osiris's penis, she constructed a new member for him out of clay. In a wonderful depiction of the role of a Mother Goddess, Isis copulated both with her husband and with the earth, given that his phallus was made of clay, and produced a son—Horus. Isis then went on to fashion "seed-like models of Osiris's missing part ... planting them in the earth, and in every spot she so blessed, the river pulsed and flooded, bringing rich silt in which maize, wheat, and other crops came to life and grew" (Leeming & Page, *Goddess*, 81). This mythic presentation of Osiris and Isis provides one of the best examples of a Neolithic myth that showcases a male consort and a Mother Goddess taking part in the necessary activities associated with death and fertility in order to assure the success of the harvest, as discussed in Chapters 2 and 3 of this book, as the copulation between Osiris and the Mother Goddess Isis, along with his death, directly initiate the renewal of the harvest. Thus, Isis, as a Mother Goddess, like many others, sends the most important of messages to audiences—that life must result in death, but that from death, new life will always emerge renewed and revitalized.

Though ancient Egypt was mostly patriarchal, there were "areas within [Egyptian] society in which women held authority or shared it with men" (Robins 157). And, as repeatedly presented in this book, the reverence for the myriad powerful goddesses of ancient Egypt directly led to the heightened social position of women in ancient Egyptian society. Robins explains that the "life-giving and regenerative aspects of female deities provided a model role of female sexuality and fertility in the human world. Women were thus regarded as having a capacity for renewal (1) through their potential for child-bearing that renewed the family, and (2) through their ability to stimulate the male to play his part in sexual interaction" (Robins 161). In addition, women in ancient Egypt were viewed as the head of the household, and thus deserved respect from their male partners. The Greek historian Diodorus Siculus noted in his *Bibliotheca Historica* that "'Among private citizens, the husband by the terms of the marriage agreement, appertains to the wife, and it is stipulated between them that the man shall obey the woman in all things'" (qtd. in Jackson 1). Also, Egyptian "women enjoyed remarkable legal equality with men throughout much of Egypt's history" (Teubal xxxiv). Egyptian women often held high religious positions as well, serving as priestesses of the myriad gods and goddesses of Egypt.

Teubal also explains that ancient Egypt was originally matrilineal, and even into dynastic times "the female line was of equal account with the male in certain respects—notably in tracing descent, inheritance, and drawing up a will" (Teubal xxxiv). Women in ancient Egypt

> enjoyed a particular position in that all landed property descended through the female line, from mother to daughter. The entail in the female line seems to have been fairly strictly adhered to, particularly in the case of the royal family. The practical result of this was that the husband enjoyed the property as long as his wife was alive, but on her death, her daughter and her daughter's husband came into possession. To avoid this loss of power on the death of the main royal heiress, the king then married anyone who could be considered the next royal heiress, in order to assume his own position. This was done irrespective of the age of the royal heiress, and is why sometimes kings married their own daughters [Seton-Williams 37].

In addition, the role of queen in ancient Egypt was often directly connected to Egypt's worship of goddesses. For example, in the Old Kingdom a vulture headdress was worn to associate the Egyptian queen with the vulture goddess Nekhbet (Robins 170). Jackson also states that "in ancient Egypt, full-blooded consanguineous marriage among royalty ... reflected the belief in divine rule. The queen bore the title of God's Wife of Amun," so in order for the "in-coming pharaoh ... to secure his right to the throne, [he] generally married the God's Wife" (Jackson 1). This arrangement meant that the queen held both her royal title, but also possessed a leadership role in religious affairs, as the God's Wife of Amun was the only one who could officiate principal religious rituals. In addition, Egyptian princesses at birth held the title of divine queen, but a man had to acquire his title of rulership only "at his coronation and could do so only by becoming the consort of a royal princess" (Jackson 2).

In fact, in Egypt "not only did descent pass through the female line, but women had the right to inherit the throne if there was no male heir" (Seton-Williams 38). Cooney states that in Egypt "female power was made possible ... in times of crisis.... As a rule, women in ancient Egypt were only allowed to rule as a regent on behalf of a man ... or as the last living member of a ruling family. [However,] given more latitude than in most other places in the ancient world, women in Egypt ... every so often popped up on the political landscape as king of all Egypt" (Cooney 227–8). For example, in Egypt's First Dynasty (3100–2900 BCE), "one woman at least, Mer-Neith, ruled as king" (Seton-Williams 38). Also, in the Third Dynasty (2686–2613 BCE), Queen Nyma'athap ruled and was "highly regarded ... [as] her cult at Saqqara was carried on for some time after her death" (Seton-Williams 38). In addition, "Nitocris of Dynasty 6 [(2345–2181 BCE)] (if Herodotus is to be believed), Sobeknefru of Dynasty 12 [(1991–1802 BCE)], Hapshetsut of Dynasty 18 [(1550–1292 BCE)], Nefertari of Dynasty 18, Tawosret of Dynasty 19 [(1292–1189 BCE)], and Cleopatra VII of the Ptolemaic Dynasty [(305–30 BCE)]" all maintained the highest position of pharaoh of Egypt (Cooney 228).

One of the most remarkable Egyptian women who served in the role of pharaoh was Hatshepsut. Hatshepsut was "only twenty years old when she methodically consolidated power and catapulted herself into the highest office in the land. She stepped into the position of king during the Eighteenth Dynasty, when the Egyptian Empire was experiencing a renaissance—imperialism made everyone rich, and new building projects were under way, including the sprawling temples of Karnak and Luxor" (Cooney 230). Thus, Hatshepsut "claimed absolute authority on a firm foundation when her civilization was at its most robust" (Cooney 230). Hatshepsut was queen regent of Thutmose III, though the boy was not her own. To secure this power, Hatshepsut superseded the authority of the boy's true mother, who would have been the one typically to hold the position of regent until her own son was old enough. In time, Hatshepsut "relinquished the titles and insignia of a queen and assumed the traditional titles of a king" (Robins 174). Hatshepsut served in the role of king long after Thutmose III came of age. Cooney states that "For more than twenty years ... [Hatshepsut] was the most powerful person in the ancient world.... She transcended patriarchal systems of authority, took on onerous responsibilities for her family, suffered great personal losses, and shaped an amazing journey" (Cooney 3). Cross and Miles state that in Hatshepsut's long reign, she "led her armies in a number of military campaigns, fighting at the head of her troops in Nubia and elsewhere. She also recognized the importance of sea power, building a great navy, which she later used for both commerce and war" (Cross & Miles 31). Cooney explains that Hatshepsut also "left behind more stone temples and monuments than any previous Egyptian king" (Cooney 230). Hatshepsut also was revered for her work towards peace, creating vast networks of trade with neighboring civilizations. Hatshepsut, therefore, was an extremely successful female pharaoh of Egypt.

To reach and then maintain the most heightened social, political, and religious role within ancient Egypt, Hatshepsut, like other global queens, aligned herself with connections to divinity. As wife of Thutmose II, Hatshepsut served as the head priestess, the God's wife of Amun, which allowed her to be viewed as the consort of the god, and thus the only one who could convene with his earthly manifestation. Because of Egyptian religious beliefs such as this that allowed women to serve as authority figures on religious matters, Hatshepsut was viewed as directly connected with the divine Amun; it was this religious authority that certainly led to her securing the position of pharaoh. In addition, to strengthen her position, Hatshepsut also claimed divine birth (Cross & Miles 31). Hatshepsut "recorded a step-by-step account of her divine origins from Amun-Re and how the god's statue revealed that she was chosen to rule all Egypt" (Cooney 231). Likewise, in religious iconography, Hatshepsut, like Cleopatra would later do, portrayed herself in a similar way to images of the most sacred Egyptian goddess—Isis, so that she would appear as a Mother Goddess to her people. Hatshepsut also would often show images of other Egyptian goddesses protecting her right to rule, such as a portrayal on a New Kingdom statue of Hatshepsut, now housed at the Metropolitan Museum of Art, that shows Hatshepsut seated with images of two goddesses on the back of her throne. Hatshepsut also ordered the construction of the Temple of Pakhet for the lioness goddesses of war Bast and Sekhmet as protectors of her rule. Despite the fact that Hatshepsut lived in a patriarchal society, the Egyptian people's reverence for powerful goddesses allowed them to accept Hatshepsut's rule. By directly aligning herself with Egyptian goddesses, and also by proclaiming herself divine, Hatshepsut was able to hold the most coveted role of power in all of ancient Egypt for over twenty prosperous years. However, after Hatshepsut's death, her reign was purposefully overshadowed by her successor, Thutmose III, to whom Hatshepsut served as regent until he was twenty-two. Thutmose III purposefully removed all artifacts that indicated that Hatshepsut had ever served as pharaoh, even to the extent of chiseling off artistic images of Hatshepsut in order to make it appear that she never existed.

The renowned Cleopatra VII (69–30 BCE) was also able to secure and maintain, for a time, the position of pharaoh within Egypt. Cleopatra was "an extremely able and ambitious woman" (Seton-Williams 44). Seton-Williams states that Cleopatra, who often gets labeled as merely a seductress whose lust for power caused her downfall, was in actuality "one of the greatest" queens of Egypt, and it is "fitting that the history of independent Egypt as such should end with a queen" (Seton-Williams 44). When Egypt was but a "puppet of Rome," the eighteen-year-old Cleopatra, along with her twelve-year-old brother Ptolemy XIII held the Egyptian throne (Cross & Miles 28). In time, Cleopatra was said to have rejected co-rule with Ptolemy XIII and attempted to govern alone, "but political courtiers staged a rebellion against her" (Cross & Miles 28). In retaliation, Cleopatra allied herself with Julius Caesar to secure Roman favor, which led to the death of Ptolemy XIII. Cleopatra thus secured rulership for herself, along with her twelve-year-old brother Ptolemy XIV, whom she later had killed by poisoning. Cleopatra then appointed her own son with Julius Caesar, Caesarion, as her co-ruler, thus securing herself as the dominant ruler. After the death of Julius Caesar, Cleopatra then aligned with Mark Antony, whom she felt was the most advanced Roman politician/general of the era, and birthed three of his children. Antony "planned to found a new imperial dynasty whose power base was to be Alexandria rather than Rome. Cleopatra would be Isis to Antony's Osiris" (Cross & Miles 30). But, in 32 BCE, the Roman Senate declared war on Cleopatra for the apparent threat her power brought to Rome. Cleopatra was said to have been present at the Battle of Actium where she inspired her men to fight on (Cross & Miles 30); however, as Octavian's army was about to capture Alexandria, Cleopatra and Mark Antony both committed suicide.

It is well known that Cleopatra, like Hatshepsut and other global female leaders, often intentionally connected herself to powerful goddesses in order to secure and maintain her rule. Like Hatshepsut, Cleopatra purposely aligned herself to the Mother Goddess Isis, often portraying herself connected to this most beloved Egyptian goddess in promotional renditions of herself. In fact, Cleopatra was well known for holding elaborate affairs that would display her in the light of being a living goddess. Cleopatra also intentionally connected herself with the Roman goddess Venus, and proclaimed her son Caesarion as the son of Venus, in an unsuccessful attempt to win over the Roman people. Cleopatra was the last true pharaoh of Egypt after the Romans made Egypt a province of the Roman

Empire, which brought new levels of Roman patriarchy to Egypt and vastly restricted the rights of Egyptian women.

Extreme patriarchy would come to dominate Egyptian women even more with the introduction of the monotheistic faith of Christianity, which stripped away any last vestiges of the positions that the mighty goddesses of Egypt once held. In addition, by 639–646 CE, Egypt fell to Muslim conquest, which further solidified clear social and religious patriarchal systems that demoted, into contemporary times, the rights of Egyptian women.

## Sub-Saharan Africa

The Sahara Desert divides the continent of Africa into two main regions. The northern region was vastly affected by Egyptian concepts, as well as elements from Mediterranean and Middle Eastern cultures that entered North Africa via diffusion; therefore, this chapter focused on Egyptian mythology as the best representation of North Africa. The African cultures south of the Sahara Desert, however, were largely unaffected by cultural diffusion from other regions around the world for centuries. For example, the faith of Islam reached sub-Saharan cultures slowly, compared to its spread in North Africa, thus preserving many of the traditional belief systems of the region.

The mythology of sub-Saharan Africa developed over thousands of years and was passed down through the oral tradition. Each culture had its own diverse belief systems, including intricate creation stories, vibrant pantheons of divine beings, and profound narratives that imparted vital life lessons. Because of widespread migrations and intercultural contact between sub-Saharan cultures, many sub-Saharan myths show some similarity between them. For example, the mythology of many sub-Saharan African cultures mostly includes a polytheistic pantheon of divine beings who hold various degrees of power, along with a reverence for spirits and ancestors. In addition, many sub-Saharan African cultures revere a central creator god or goddess. However, in the fifteenth century CE, the European slave trade entered West and Central Africa, producing a devastating impact on the cultures it affected, as fear, intercultural violence, and economic hardship plagued the regions involved. These horrific encounters, as well as European colonialism which began in the late nineteenth century, vastly disrupted, and in many cases eradicated, long-held cultural, social, and religious traditions throughout sub-Saharan Africa; therefore, a great deal of African mythology was lost to history. Some surviving sub-Saharan African myths were recorded by Europeans in the nineteenth century; however, as seen with other cultures already discussed, when an invading culture captures in written form the mythology of another culture, it often projects its own values and ideology onto the myths, often creating a mythology that is a blended form of traditional and revised content. Therefore, many sub–Saharan African myths project Western values; thus, myths that traditionally may have revered goddesses in positions of superiority were often revised to portray a male divine figure as dominant. In addition, myths that portrayed women holding central roles were likewise revised to place women in roles viewed as acceptable according to European standards of the time. Still, in some sections of sub–Saharan Africa, like predominantly West Africa, myths recording powerful goddesses were saved when transmitted into written language. Ogunleye explains that "although little is known about female deities in the ancient civilizations of Ghana, Mali, Songhai, and Kanem-Bornu, a significant amount of information is known about the role of female deities in the ancient civilizations of the Yoruba, Asante, Igbo, Dahomey, Mossi, and others. In fact, veneration for many goddesses of these ancient empires persists today throughout Africa" (Ogunleye 196).

Many of the goddesses of West Africa "were regarded as ultimate supreme beings, and as mother and earth deities of creation, fertility, and agriculture" (Ogunleye 196). For example, the Mossi revere the earth goddess Tenga; the Asante revere Asase Ya; and the Igbo of Nigeria worship Ala, who is "the dearest of all their deities, [and] is believed to have presided over the ancestors and the numinous (supernatural) owners of the soil since 3000 BCE" (Ogunleye 197). Ala is also attributed as guiding over one's moral duties, and many Igbo villages follow a custom of keeping a "life-size image of Ala … in the village, visible to all who pass by" (Stone 141).

Furthermore, many West African goddesses are associated as being creator deities. Ample evidence shows that many West African goddesses are revered as creators or co-creators of the earth and are often regarded in the role of a Great Mother (Ogunleye 196). For example, the Fon of Dahomey revere a creator goddess, Nana Buluku, who is thought to be a female supreme being who gave birth to the universe. After creation, Nana Buluku was said to give birth to the Fon creator goddess Mawu, who finished creating the landscape of earth.

A Fon myth presents the creator goddess Mawu as riding within the mouth of a massive snake, Aido-Hwedo, that "was so old … it existed even before the earth was made" (Allan, Fleming, & Phillips 48–9). Mawu created the landscape of earth riding Aido-Hwedo, which gave the landscape a serpentine shape and filled it with topographical variation. After finishing the landscape of earth, Mawu created all of the earth's botanical and animal inhabitants; however, Mawu soon realized that the earth "was too heavy," as it "was filled with an abundance of mountains, forests, herds of elephants, and beasts of prey. [So,] she knew that it needed something to support it" (Allan, Fleming, & Phillips 48). Thus, the creator Mawu instructed Aido-Hwedo "to lay himself down on the wide waters in a perfect circle with his tail in his mouth (subsequently an African symbol of eternity). On top she set the earth and the serpent prevent[ed] its sinking" (Allan, Fleming, & Phillips 48). This Fon portrayal of the serpent as an aid of the creator goddess Mawu is similar to the Greek myth of the creator goddess Eurynome with the serpent Ophion, as well as Australian Aboriginal myths of the Rainbow Serpent as creator, which will be discussed in the next chapter, showing that the symbol of the serpent as connected to goddesses may have very ancient origins.

Another myth of the goddess Mawu shows her divine daughter Gbadu noticing that the earth, long after its creation, had fallen into a deplorable state, as the people of earth had begun fighting vehemently against one another (Stone 137–40). The myth states that the goddess Gbadu sent forth her own children to teach the people of earth about the lessons of Mawu. Gbadu's children taught the people about Mawu's law of Sekpoli, which states that all people are imbued with a part of Mawu, so fighting with another is sacrilege against the Great Mother. The children of Gbadu also taught the people the gift of prophecy. All people then embraced Mawu's lessons, except a man named Awe, who thought that he was as good as Mawu. To try and prove his fully divine status, the myth states that Awe raised himself to the heavens and tried to complete a small task of creation by carving a figure of a human from wood. However, when Awe tried to breathe life into the wooden form, as Mawu had done with all living beings, the person did not come to life. Accepting his defeat and showing his reverence to Mawu, Awe ate a bowl of cereal that Mawu grew from a seed into cereal before his eyes to teach him of her superior might. Then the goddess Mawu told Awe that she had fed him the seed of death, and she instructed Awe to climb back down to earth with it, thus unleashing death to the people of earth. Mawu's portrayal in this myth as both a goddess who can create life, but also conversely take life away in death, solidifies her as a Great Mother of supreme ability.

Another West African myth from the Yoruba describes creation as occurring because of the sky god, Olorun, and the primordial water Goddess, Olokun. It is said in the myth that the creator god, Obatala, creates the earth and its inhabitants, but the goddess Olokun is presented as growing angry at Obatala for creating the inhabitants of earth, because she believes that this act will lessen worshippers' reverence for her own mighty power. So, in retaliation, Olokun unleashes a massive flood upon the newly created earth. Obatala's brother, Orunmila, wishes to help the new human beings of earth, so he goes to them, and aids them in controlling the flood. Orunmila's divine assistance unleashes outrage from Olokun. Understanding that Olokun possesses the power to create a catastrophe that could threaten all life on earth, the gods band together to come up with a plan to appease Olokun. Having solidified their plan, the gods invite Olokun to compete in a contest of her choosing, stating that the winner may decide the fate of earth's inhabitants. Olokun readily accepts the contest by challenging Olorun, the sky god, to a weaving contest. However, Olorun interestingly states that "'Olokun is a far better weaver than I am. However, I cannot give her the satisfaction of knowing that she is superior to me in anything. If I do, she will exert her powers in other ways as well, and that will disrupt the order that now exists throughout the universe. Somehow I must appear to accept her challenge and yet avoid participating in her contest'" (Rosenberg 514). So, Olorun set up a scheme to cheat at the contest, which thus secured his win in the myth. This myth transmits a message about how the more traditional goddess, Olokun, was superseded by the sky god Olorun only through treachery, because, as the myth openly states, everyone truly knows that the goddess Olokun is superior. Usually myths meant to undermine a goddess's authority at the hands of a male god clearly depict the male god as superior, but this myth makes it clear to audiences that the superior goddess Olokun was only brought down through Olorun's deception. This transparency in how Olokun lost her status suggests that the Yoruba maintained a degree of reverence for the superiority of their goddess Olokun after the recording of the myth.

The Yoruba also possess another creation myth that portrays the goddess, or orisha, Oshun, who is conceived of as the goddess of rivers, fresh water, fertility, and love. The Yoruba, as well as the Edo and Fon, revere orishas, who are often envisioned as African deities who aided in the creation of the earth and its resources, and who continue to guide and protect its inhabitants. The Yoruba myth of Oshun states that there were originally seventeen orishas, sixteen males, and one female—Oshun, who were tasked with preparing the earth for its inhabitants. The male orishas believed they did not need the aid of Oshun to complete their task. However, they soon realized that without the fresh water that Oshun provided, the earth, which soon became barren, was utterly inhospitable. It took some time, but finally the sixteen male orishas realized that their oversight of Oshun caused their task of creation to fail. So, the male orishas sought out Oshun and asked for her help in creation, which she instantly provided, thus unleashing life on planet earth. This myth, like the creation myth of Olokun, shows a unique perspective surrounding the reverence of women among the Yoruba, as Oshun is initially portrayed in what appears to be a patriarchal perception about her value as minimal alongside her sixteen male peers. However, the myth, like the one with Olokun, shows an acknowledgment that patriarchal beliefs diminish essential elements of existence, as without the essential Oshun, all humanity is portrayed in the myth as being jeopardized.

In another creation myth outside of West Africa from the Alur people of the Congo, an old woman and her granddaughter are portrayed as the divine, primeval ancestors of the people (Allan, Fleming, & Phillips 55–60). The myth shows that the grandmother and granddaughter lived together in the forest, where the grandmother held the ability to "renew herself by shedding her skin, but on pain of death had to do so in private" (Allan, Fleming, & Phillips 56). However, one day her granddaughter happened to see her grandmother without her skin on, so the grandmother died. With this, death was introduced to humankind, as the grandmother was thwarted from being able to pass on her wisdom of renewal to her granddaughter, and to the generations to come. It is significant that this myth states that death was introduced to the people because the wisdom of the divine grandmother could not be carried forward to her granddaughter. This mythic element speaks towards the Alur belief that women within the community were often viewed as the possessors of sacred knowledge regarding the cycles of life. The lost transmission of knowledge in the myth from grandmother to granddaughter might also express the Alur's belief that if their sacred knowledge could not be passed down from generation to generation, as was being threatened during colonization, then it would only lead to their culture's demise.

Similar to the grandmother goddess of the Alur people, many African goddesses were conceived of as being representations of nature's cycles, and as such, they too were connected to the processes of life, death, and rebirth. For example, many West African societies believed that people both came from an earth goddess, but also would one day be called to return to her womb within the earth. For example, the Akan people worship the Mother Goddess Atoapoma, who is revered as both the "Giver of Life" and the "Taker of Life" (Ogunleye 198). And again, the goddess Ala for the Igbo is thought to be "both the provider of life and the Mother who receives again in death" (Stone 140). Ala's womb, as with the goddess Atoapoma, is believed to be the interior of the earth itself.

Another example of a goddess both giving and taking away life comes outside of West Africa from the Ronga people of Mozambique (Allan, Fleming, & Phillips 56–7). In this myth, death is shown to be introduced to humanity through the aid of a kindly old goddess. The myth states that when the earth was new, people did not have to die unless they wanted to. If they chose death, the people would climb a rope or chain that hung down from the sky and cross into the sky realm. One day, a young woman who had no child decided that she wanted to die, so she climbed to the sky. Once there, she found an old woman who "directed her further on, telling her that if she felt an ant in her ear, she should take care not to kill it but instead listen to the advice it gave her" (Allan, Fleming, & Phillips 56). So, the young woman journeyed on, aided by an ant that indeed did climb into her ear. The ant showed the woman where she could get an infant to relieve her of the pain of not having a baby. The young woman followed the exact instructions the ant gave her, and soon she was astonished to find that she had resurrected back in the land of the living with a baby of her own. The myth concludes showing the young woman's sister also wanting to attain favor from the old goddess of the sky, so she too climbed to the sky realm; only this time, the sister treated the old woman rudely, and did not take the old woman's advice to listen to the ant. So, the old goddess killed the sister on the spot, unleashing death to all humankind forever.

Again, this myth, like many other sub-Saharan African myths, presents a goddess who is connected to both the environment and the cycles of life. The tale shows that the old goddess's environmental wisdom, portrayed mythically as listening to even the smallest elements of nature—the ants, is passed on to a young female protagonist, thus suggesting that among the Ronga, women possessed sacred wisdom in accordance with nature. Additionally, this environmental wisdom is also directly linked to spiritual concepts about life, death, and rebirth, as the young woman in this myth is taught by the old goddess that from death, new life emerges, as when she leaves the realm of death in the sky, she is resurrected along with the new life of a child. This transition of showing environmental wisdom to be spiritual wisdom, that is possessed by primarily women, as portrayed in the myth, again reveals an elevated religious role given to women by the Ronga.

As seen with the Alur and Ronga myths just discussed, there was often a link in the reverence various sub-Saharan African communities held for their goddesses and the social roles that were available to women. Again, in West Africa, the high reverence for goddesses within many West African cultures directly carried over into high positions afforded to many West African women; "The reverence in which female deities were held was manifested in the leadership roles African women played in their country's religious and political institutions" (Ogunleye 198). Ogunleye explains that "the expertise, creativity, and industriousness of the women, highborn and common alike, were indispensable to West Africa's growth and development. West African women were greatly esteemed for the important roles they played as state founders, progenitors, mothers, creators, consorts, defenders, rulers, and motivating forces in the development and advancement of their nations" (Ogunleye 193). In addition,

West African women were often regarded as a source of "life, wisdom, and inspiration, and they played leading roles in West Africa's agricultural, architectural, and scientific advancement; in the establishment and operation of governmental, educational, cultural, and religious institutions; and in business operations" (Ogunleye 193). Perhaps most enlightening on the role of women as vital to their communities, or as even sacred, can be found in the names given to African women that "indicate [the] profound regard in which they were held in ancient West African civilizations: Giver of Life, Queen Mother, Queen Sister, [and] Rainmaker" (Ogunleye 193).

There is evidence throughout sub–Saharan Africa that women served in the respected religious roles of shaman and priestess for thousands of years. Hays-Gilpin states that prehistoric rock art found in Southern Africa provides evidence of shamanistic practices involving women (Hays-Gilpin 89). In addition, ethnography suggests that in Southern Africa, "about 30 percent of women become shamans, including curers, game shamans, and rain shamans" (Hays-Gilpin 172). In West Africa, the heightened "spiritual role of Yoruba women as senior priestesses enabled them to function in complementary relationships with ruling kings or chiefs" (Razak 134). Hays-Gilpin also points out that even into modern times among the Kalahari of Southern Africa, about "a third of the women were shamans" (Hays-Gilpin 89). In general, throughout sub–Saharan African, many cultures regarded women as especially tied to their revered goddesses; thus, these sacred women were often afforded access to vital spiritual roles in their communities. For example, in Ethiopia, "women often played a pre-eminent role in spirit beliefs ... interpreting personal fortune and misfortune, and major events, in terms of spirit intervention" (T. Fernyhough & A. Fernyhough 200). T. Fernyhough and A. Fernyhough state that "such beliefs represented a cultural arena in which women were not merely devotees, but acted as intermediaries for one or more spirits. For many women this presented an 'opportunity for expression' ... [and a] 'sphere of power'" (T. Fernyhough & A. Fernyhough 200).

A myth from the Mashona people of Zimbabwe shows how women served the honored religious role of priestess within their community (Stone 142–5). The myth presents a woman, named Notambu, who served in the prestigious role of High Priestess to the goddess Jezanna, who was believed to be the provider of life, and was seen by the Mashona in the form of the moon. Notambu, in the myth, led the rituals associated with the holiest of Mashona festivals to honor Jezanna. One part of the ritual involved the Nganga, a chosen male of the village, sacrificing a child. However, the myth states that Notambu thought about how the goddess Jezanna would never want a child to be sacrificed in her honor, though it had been happening as a ritualistic act for years. Notambu, feeling sure of

Jezanna's wishes, refused to allow the child to be sacrificed. So, she swept up the child in her arms and carried her away. However, in the myth, the people misunderstood what was happening, so they followed the lead of the male Nganga, who was yelling in anger at the insult towards the sacrificial practice. Notambu ran as fast as she could with the child in her arms, and upon reaching Jezanna's sacred Lake Davisa, she appealed aloud to the goddess Jezanna. When the Nganga and the people found Notambu, they were shocked to see that Jezanna had answered Notambu's pleas, because the moonlight began to greatly intensify upon the lake. At this sight, Notambu declared to her people that the goddess Jezanna no longer wished them to sacrifice any more children. The people, hearing this, trusted the sacred role of Notambu as their High Priestess, and they rejoiced to see the grace of Jezanna in saving their future children from sacrifice. The reverence of the Mashona people to the goddess Jezanna in this myth is evidenced in their initial willing to sacrifice their children to her, but the myth also shows the elevated role of Mashona priestesses, as it is Notambu who convinces the people that they should revise their religious rites. In addition, it is significant that the wisdom of the High Priestess is presented in this myth as superior to the leading male portrayed in the myth, the Nganga. Thus, this myth shows further evidence that when communities openly worshipped goddesses, the allowance for powerful social and religious positions for women was more readily accepted.

In addition, it appears that many African communities were designed around matrilineal and matriarchal concepts. For example, "For many sedentary and nomadic peoples living in and around the ancient West African empires of Ghana, Mali, Asante, and Igbo, matters pertaining to governance and structure of their nations and families were based on matrilineal concepts. Matrilineal descent was important for succession to the throne, appointment of various ministers and functionaries, family and community rights, inheritances, and citizenship" (Ogunleye 201). The Asante, who were matriarchal, revered "queen mothers," who were "female monarchs in a hierarchical social system with a central authority that is lineage based" (Razak 134). Jackson also states that much of "Central and Eastern Africa was matrilineal"; for example, "the original inhabitants of Angola and the Kongo kingdom ... were matrilineal," and in "Buganda, among the Babito people, the Babito kings perpetuated the long-held custom of adopting the clan of their mothers" (Jackson 2).

In addition, again because powerful goddesses were widely revered in many regions of sub–Saharan Africa, many African women were conceived of by their communities as being capable of serving as valuable warriors for their people. Many sub–Saharan African women took part in the defense of their nations, becoming soldiers and militarists who led large armies into battle. Many Fon and Yoruba women, for example, were often involved in military campaigns. In the fourteenth or fifteenth centuries CE, legends recount the figure of Yennenga, a Mossi princess who commanded her own battalion (Hodges 77). In the eighteenth century, Dahomey/Fon women warriors so impressed the ruler Agaja that "he made them a regular unit of the army, called the Amazons" (Jackson 3). There are also nineteenth-century accounts that show women warriors among the Lunda and Gager tribes of Zaire (Stone 134).

Ancient West Africa also had a long history of being ruled by queens. Tenth-century BCE legends surrounding the Queen of Sheba (present day Ethiopia or Yemen) state that she descended from her father Menelik I, who was said to have come into the land and killed a massive serpent that plagued the people in order to become the king of Sheba. He then passed on the rulership to his daughter, Makeda. It is said that Makeda's "realm prospered as a centre of trade" (Allan, Fleming, & Phillips 127). Hearing of the wealth of King Solomon in Jerusalem, Makeda went there to see for herself. In time, she became pregnant by King Solomon and had a son, whom she named Menelik, after her father. Makeda prepped Menelik to be her successor. Upon coming of age, Menelik went to Jerusalem to gain his father's acknowledgment that he was indeed his son, but King Solomon tested him. Legend states that during Menelik's journey to Jerusalem, he came upon an old woman who gave him advice that easily enabled him to pass the tests placed upon him by his father, and thus King Solomon recognized Menelik as his son. However, in time, the "people grew discontented with the foreigner's exalted status," so Menelik had to return to Sheba. However, upon leaving, legend states that Menelik stole the Ark of the Covenant, which gained him a "hero's welcome" upon arriving back in Sheba, where his mother crowned him on the spot (Allan, Fleming, & Phillips 129).

Historical queens and female political leaders in sub–Saharan Africa are also well documented, such as during the first dynasty of the Benin Empire (1200 CE) (Ogunleye 203). Ogunleye states that "Before the separate Hausa states were established, the people ... were ruled by a dynasty of seventeen queens" (Ogunleye 203). Jackson states that in Bornu "the queen mother and the queen held important posts in the court. For example, the Bornu queen mother, *Maguira,* acquired great prestige and power, including veto power over the acts of the emperor" (Jackson 2). In addition, the Bornu empress, "*Gousma,* also had a role of authority" (Jackson 2). Also, the Ashanti queen mother "acted as head of state in the absence of the ruler; at his death, she nominated the next ruler. In addition, the queen mother was usually the instigator of all diplomatic exchange with other governments" (Jackson 2). In addition, among the Mossi, queens held joint rule with kings (Jackson 2). And, in West Africa, some "nations only had women rulers" (Jackson 2).

West Africa also had many examples of warrior queens, such as Queen Dahia-al Kahina, who fought against Arab invaders in the eighth century CE, and Queen Macario of the Mane people, who battled against the Portuguese at Fort Mina (Ogunleye 202). Queen Candace of Ethiopia was said to have taken "command of her army" against Roman soldiers; she was viewed as so formidable that "the loss of an eye in battle only had the effect of increasing her bravery" (Diop 48–9). Thus, it is clear that while African nations maintained their worship of goddesses, the position of women remained high in many regions of sub-Saharan Africa.

However, the role of women throughout Africa would greatly change with the introduction of monotheistic religion, as was the case in many regions around the world. Muslim concepts entered sub-Saharan Africa, primarily East and West Africa, as early as the eighth century CE, through trade, but their impact was negligible for centuries, as the spread of Islam was a gradual process in sub-Saharan Africa. In the eleventh century, the Almoravid movement increased effort of Islamic conversion throughout Northwest and West Africa, as far south as Ghana. Muslim conversion, which again mostly happened as a gradual process in East and West Africa, as Islamic forces in Africa were mostly intent on trade not conversion, with the exception of the Almoravid movement, would still, over centuries lead to "a withering away of [goddess reverence and] matrilineal and matriarchal systems" throughout East and West Africa (Ogunleye 194). As happened in other regions, the monotheistic beliefs of the Muslims eradicated concepts of female divinity for the new followers of the faith. Thus, during this period, African women "lost much of their power and influence, while the rulers of the large city-states used Islam to maintain and rationalize their power" (Ogunleye 201). With the introduction of Islam, many African women were restricted from participating in religious rituals, which resulted in their sacrality being lessened in the views of the people. In many cases, African women were also delegated to low-standing social positions that primarily focused on maintaining the home and rearing children. Also, a heightened focus on containing the sexuality of women became paramount in attempts to solidify patrilineal succession and gain dominance over pursuits traditionally held by women; therefore, much effort was put into promoting marriage for women at increasingly young ages.

A Fulani myth from Senegal provides a good example of what appears to be Islamic influence upon traditional Fulani goddess reverence and its impact on the rights of women. The myth presents a monstrous woman named Ndjeddo Dewal, who is described as a great sorceress, but elements of the myth suggest that she once was perhaps conceived of as a goddess. Ndjeddo Dewal is described in the myth as requiring blood to survive, which immediately signals her as carrying connotations of former divinity. Ndjeddo Dewal's birth also signals her as a former goddess figure, as the myth states that she was created by the Fulani central god Guéno, but some versions of the tale simply refer to the creator as "God" suggesting a Muslim influence, to serve as a "weapon" against "men [who] are easily fooled by women's beauty and the temptation of sexuality" (I. Diop 29). To portray her as evil, the myth states that Ndjeddo Dewal drinks the blood of men her seven daughters have sex with. She is said to wait in the shadows while her daughters have sex, and when they signal her, Ndjeddo Dewal appears and sucks the men's blood "through a system of tubes they accept to connect to their neck" (I. Diop, 30). However, Ndjeddo Dewal "always takes too much of ... [the mens'] blood and they die during ... intercourse" (I. Diop, 30). Ndjeddo Dewal, serving again as a possible traditional goddess figure, is able to mystically restore her daughters' hymens each time they have sex, preventing them from becoming "women, ... [wives], or mother[s]" (I. Diop, 29). Thus, Ndjeddo Dewal is shown as "opposing the generational order" by not allowing her daughters to mature (I. Diop 29). In the myth, Ndjeddo Dewal is eventually killed by the young male hero Bâgoumawel when she is fooled by him into killing her seven daughters, which in turn causes her to starve to death with the loss of her consistent source of blood (I. Diop, 30).

It is clear that this myth intentionally projects negative qualities upon the characters of Ndjeddo Dewal and her seven daughters. Ndjeddo Dewal is easily portrayed as a monster because of her thirst for human blood and her capability to control her daughters in clearly sinister behavior. However, as stated, Ndjeddo Dewal's portrayal as a mother who was both birthed by divine means and who requires human blood to survive, seems connected to portrayals of Mother Goddesses, like the Yoruba Olokun, who were capable of unleashing severe punishments when not properly revered. Many Mother Goddesses in myriad cultures, as discussed, were portrayed as both givers and takers of life; therefore, many myths from around the world often vilified these Mother Goddesses for their harsh aspects when patriarchal systems strove to gain control. When the male hero Bâgoumawel kills Ndjeddo Dewal, it certainly sends a common message about eradicating the old generation of goddesses to suit new patriarchal, and in this case Muslim, ideology. Ndjeddo Dewal's daughters are also portrayed as agents of evil for their willingness to sacrifice men to feed their mother, but their promiscuity in willingly having sex with multiple partners, while not conceiving children and remaining perpetually unmarried, becomes an element of heightened focus within the myth regarding the role of women according to Muslim standards. Thus, the mythic killing of Ndjeddo Dewal's seven daughters sends a cautionary message to audiences that if they do not stop taking part in sexual promiscuity that was seemingly connected to traditional belief systems, now deemed immoral by the new Muslim ideology, then the next generation would be thwarted just as the monstrous Ndjeddo Dewal thwarted the lives of her daughters.

With the revision of beliefs regarding powerful goddesses and high-standing roles for sub-Saharan African women, such as evidenced in this myth, it is clear that Muslim concepts in primarily East and West Africa, as well as of course North Africa, certainly played a role in demoting African goddesses and women. However, again Islam still spread slowly throughout most areas of sub-Saharan Africa, not arriving, into the regions of Central and South Africa until the seventeenth century, leading Islam to have little impact on the belief systems of the majority of sub-Saharan Africans for centuries.

Christian concepts, however, brought by Europeans as early as the fifteenth century but not extensively until colonial efforts in the nineteenth century, was an agent of widespread change regarding goddess worship and the rights of women throughout the entire continent of Africa (Diop xiv–xv). Christian colonizers rejected traditional African goddesses as pagan. As a result, as happened in many other regions which encountered Christian colonization, the worship of goddesses was often deemed evil; therefore, their reverence was abandoned by many. If it could not entirely wipe out goddess reverence, Christian influence often revised existing portrayals of African goddesses, so that once revered goddesses became replaced in ideology with gods or a central and superior god to better merge with Christian divine concepts, or became relegated to inferior roles. For example, the degradation of the goddess Mami Wata, who was revered in West, Central, and Southern Africa, is a prime example of the role European culture had upon many African goddesses. Mami Wata was originally believed to be an ancient goddess connected to life-sustaining water, and thus worshipped in high regard (Hodges 140). However, after the introduction of European religious and social concepts, conceptions of Mami Wata morphed into a mermaid creature, whose tales mostly center upon her ability to grant wealth to sailors. Hodges explains that European influence "codif[ied] Mami's appearance and ... reputation" until she became associated with materialism, so that in time, her worship took place at altars "groaning with European goods" (Hodges 142). In contemporary times, Mami Wata is still revered in Africa, and around the world, but not as the once powerful goddess that she was; instead, she has become a symbol of popular culture who embodies shallow messages about the importance of wealth and beauty, and her altars throughout Africa are still "laden with objects more associated with Western capitalist society—designer sunglasses, ... handbags, and expensive make-up" (Hodges 143).

In addition, European colonialism, that brought with it Christian views of divinity and Western patriarchal values, discriminated against many of the high-standing societal roles held by African women. Many European colonizers saw African women, and many other women of non-Western cultures, "as oppressed and servile creatures, beasts of burden, chattels who could be bought and sold"; thus, colonizers wrongly assumed that these women needed "to be liberated by 'civilization' or 'progress,' thus attaining the 'enviable' position of women in Western society" (Etienne & Leacock 1). However, what really happened was that precisely because of colonial "controls and influences, African women's social, religious, constitutional, and political rights disappeared" (Ogunleye 214). European colonizers attacked traditional "African customs, morals, and religious institutions," specifically Africa's myriad matriarchal communities (Ogunleye 214). Men, instead of women, became sought after by colonial administrations. Male chiefs, for example, were given preferential treatment as opposed to female chiefs in trade agreements. Males were also educated according to European standards. Soon patrilineal lines, in regions not already Muslim, became dominant. Male children became prized over female children. In addition, colonial expectations for the proper role of women greatly affected views of women's sexuality in many regions of Africa. European colonizers severely condemned the sexual morality of African women; for instance, issues of adultery, chastity, and divorce were held to European standards, and often identified African women as not meeting those standards (Omer). Thus, European colonizers often strove to address "African marriage and sex practices ... to give men more control over women's sexuality" (Omer). For example, "as a measure of control over women's sexuality," colonial courts "did not acknowledge any case brought without 'evidence of legal marriage' according to Christian rules" (Omer). Also, domesticity was heavily "promoted as a method of 'civilizing' women"; for instance, "missionaries were funded by the colonial state to train women on the 'modernizing' concepts of domesticity" (Omer). Thus, Allan, Fleming, and Phillips succinctly explain that throughout Africa, once colonialism and "Western influence had established itself, there was no turning back the clock. Divided into unfamiliar states, saddled with a dependent economic system and sometimes totally dispossessed—as under South Africa's apartheid system—Africans struggled to make sense of the new order" (Allan, Fleming, & Phillips 23). Therefore, women, who once held dominant social and religious roles, were often pushed into menial societal positions, and the worship of many once powerful goddesses was in time forgotten.

However, as stated in every chapter of this book, historically when new religious concepts are introduced to a region via trade, conquest, etc., the people of the region often continue to embrace elements of their traditional beliefs in various forms, whether it is through long-held festivals or customs that maintain old ways, or through the merging of traditional mythic tenets into folklore. African folktales often emerged from traditional, sacred myths as a way to maintain the reverence of traditional goddesses, though the presentation of a goddess in a folktale is often obscured. Former goddesses may appear in African folktales as an old wise woman, a mysterious maiden, or an evil witch. The complexity of the presentation of a former mythic goddess as a folkloric figure often shows the lingering conflicted feelings of the people who wrestled with modifying their ancestors' most sacred beliefs.

A good example of the complexity in presenting what might be a folkloric account of a traditional goddess can be found in the Yoruba folktale "The Hunter and his Magic Flute" (Cole 638–42). The folktale presents a monstrous female who holds the name Mother of the Forest. The folktale begins with a hunter named Ojo being warned by his people not to go too far into the wilderness alone, as this was where the Mother of the Forest resided. However, Ojo did venture deep into the wilderness one day to hunt, ignoring the wisdom of his people. Sure enough, when Ojo set up his camp for the night, he found that he was face to face with the Mother of the Forest. The monstrous woman, instead of destroying Ojo, merely spoke to him, stating "'Have no fear, hunter. I know why you come to my domain and I will not devour you if you do me no harm'" (Cole 639). With these words, the Mother of the Forest disappeared. The next morning Ojo hunted the unchartered land around him and found, that quite unlike the land he was used to, this land produced a bounty of prey. Ojo killed many animals and brought them back to his camp to prepare them for his journey home. However, in the night, the Mother of the Forest came into his camp and took his bounty. Refusing to come home empty-handed, Ojo repeated the same pattern for six days—he successfully hunted all day, only to have his product stolen by the Mother of the Forest each night. Finally, after seven days of failure, Ojo screamed out to the Mother of the Forest, "'Why have you eaten all of my meat, you old hag? Do you steal from every poor hunter who enters your forest'" (Cole 640)? Immediately, Ojo was horrified to see that the Mother of the Forest came before him in a wrath of anger. Ojo tried to flee from her, but to no avail. In final desperation, Ojo climbed a tree to evade her, but the Mother of the Forest simply used her monstrous jaws to tear the tree to shreds. This part of the folktale certainly presents the Mother of the Forest as a formidable guardian of the wilderness. Her strength, mystical abilities, monstrous appearance, as well as her title of Mother, all signal her as a remnant of what is likely a traditional nature goddess. However, the folktale takes a turn that marks it as a story that is full of societal complexity when viewing the demotion of once powerful goddesses.

As the folktale continues, Ojo is shown to be in possession of a magic flute. At the moment he is almost destroyed by the Mother of the Forest, Ojo pulls out his magic flute and proceeds to play it, which calls his hunting dogs to him. His dogs, named Cut to Pieces, Swallow Up, and Clear the Remains, signal that this myth will not revere the traditional goddess representation of the Mother of the Forest; instead, it will be like the Mesopotamian tale of Marduk slaying Tiamet or the Greek tale of Apollo slaying Gaia's serpent. Ojo's dogs arrive and succeed in destroying the Mother of the Forest by tearing her apart and consuming every bit of her (Cole 641). The folktale ends with Ojo journeying home, where he finds a beautiful maiden who tells him that when the Mother of the Forest died, she was released from a spell that kept her captive. Ojo proclaims that the maiden should become his second wife. This ending of the folktale proclaims a decidedly patriarchal message—that the old goddesses must make way for the new patriarchal order, and that once powerful women, must now be relegated to subservient positions.

However, this particular folktale takes yet another twist that shows the complexity involved in the Yoruba's true reverence for their goddesses. When Ojo takes the beautiful maiden home with him, she transforms in the night into a monstrous figure that resembles the Mother of the Forest and proceeds to consume Ojo with her many mouths. This surprise ending sends a cautionary message to audience members who might think that the power of the old goddesses is gone, as the power in this folktale is firmly placed with the goddess figures who guard the forest. This complex folktale speaks as a representation of Yoruba culture, which encountered many colonial efforts to fully convert traditional beliefs, but as this folktale shows, some traditional beliefs remain strong.

A folktale by the Shilluk people of Southern Africa also shows the complexity of transforming belief systems; only this time, this folktale captures the shifting role of women that occurred in their community (Liyong 5). This folktale presents the early days of humankind's existence, stating that in these days, there was a Kingdom of Men and a separate Kingdom of Women. Both lived apart from one another, and both were ruled by capable rulers of each sex. Each year on the anniversary of the creation of each kingdom, each kingdom would separately celebrate with great festivities. However, one year the majority of women decided that they wanted to invite the men to their kingdom for the celebration. Since this had never been done before, the ruler of the Kingdom of Women did not want this, as she believed men and women should always be separated. The women were upset to hear their ruler reject their wishes, stating "'This woman king ... did we not elect her ourselves? She is not really above us; just one head among equals. Last year she turned down another of our requests. Once is enough but twice is intolerable'" (Liyong 5). The women then decided that they were going to kill their ruler, so in the night, they snuck into her chamber and strangled her. The folktale states that God witnessed the act, which certainly seems to be a later monotheistic interjection into the story, and seeing the act, God decided to punish the women for killing their ruler. As punishment, God stated in the folktale that the women must go to the Kingdom of Men and must be forever "'subservient to men'" (Liyong 5). This news caused the women to enter "a wild frenzy ... [and] they stampeded towards the Men's Kingdom" (Liyong 5). The men saw this frenzied assault coming towards them and immediately thought that the women were declaring war on them. In retaliation, the men prepared for battle; however, as the women approached, the men saw that they did not carry any weapons, so they waited. The men were pleased to find that when the women ran into their kingdom, each woman chose a man and took him into his home. The folktale ends declaring that this is how the first marriages began for the Shilluk.

Again, this complex folktale portrays competing views on what appears to be traditional beliefs alongside new patriarchal values. The women in this folktale are presented in both a positive and a negative light. The folktale shows that the women in the tale held equal power to that of the men. Perhaps, this folktale, then, relates a semi-historical glimpse into once matriarchal social organizations among the Shilluk, similar to the myths of China that seem to capture a remnant of what matriarchy was like in Neolithic times. However, when the folktale shifts to show a monotheistic God stripping power from all the women of the tale, the folktale ultimately sends a patriarchal message to audiences about how women, though they might have once held greater power in the past, destroyed their own autonomy, and are thus, as a sex, unfit to rule.

However, like the Yoruba folktale of the Mother of Forest, the end of this folktale interjects a surprise element that calls into question the seemingly patriarchal message of the tale. This Shilluk tale ends with a declaration that states that because of the events outlined in the story, women within the Shilluk tribe are forever given the authority to ritually strangle a chief who becomes "afflicted with a severe ailment" (Liyong 5). This ritual authority given to women, which sources are in conflict over if this action actually ever took place, shows that the spiritual health of the tribe, at least as articulated in the tale, was largely in the hands of the women of the tribe. The fact that this social and religious role of great importance, as it maintains the health or demise of the tribe, is presented to women in the folktale suggests that the influx of Christian values, as the Shilluk also endured British colonial administration, did not entirely eradicate the Shilluk's reverence for the sacrality of women. With the high-standing social and religious role of the women in the tale preserved, perhaps the folktale shows the women as rightfully killing their close-minded female ruler, so that the health of the tribe could continue, as merging with the men allowed the tribe to survive through procreation. Thus, this folktale actually may present the women in the folktale as holding superior wisdom about the natural processes of life and death, which is often presented as the wisdom of goddesses within many African myths.

In contemporary Africa, gender inequality is one of the dominant issues that plagues much of the continent. In many regions throughout Africa, women today are still restricted from gaining an education or beneficial employment. Autonomy for women is hard won in many areas of Africa, as the brunt of household duties often falls to them. Violence against women is also rampant in much of Africa. Thus, the legacy of colonial rule is still heavily felt throughout many regions of Africa, as Western ideals clash with traditional African beliefs.

However, African people still maintain traditional belief systems that hold goddesses in high esteem. Diop states that in many regions of Africa "structures which favored the rule of goddesses, matriarchy, queens, etc. are indeed still present with us today" (Diop xvii). For example, in portions of West Africa, there exist secret societies of women, such as the Sande, that still lead the sacred practices for their people (Sered 30). Sande initiation rites ask that women join together in the bush to pass on "secret knowledge" between members. Sered states that these Sande women "provide sanctions for nearly every sphere of secular life. They embody and control supernatural power, lay down rules of conduct, and provide the major source of propitiation for transgressions of sacred and of secular law" (Sered 31). In addition, the Diga of south Kenya and the Bori cult of the Hausa still openly maintain religious practices that feature women in prominent positions. Sered states that these religious practices, led by women officiants, more than likely were carried over from pre–Islamic times (Sered 30). However, many traditional goddess-oriented belief systems and high-standing religious positions for women throughout Africa are still "facing erosion" (Diop xvii).

Diop states that the "monotheistic and abstract religions of Islam and Christianity ruling Africa today continue to attack" traditional goddess-focused religions (Dopi xvii). So, arguably, for African women to achieve and maintain the high social, political, and religious positions they once held, the traditional goddess-focused religions that still exist in Africa must be nurtured. As Razak states, "Since all of humanity is said to descend from a First Mother in Africa ... [reverence] of the Sacred African Feminine ... [is] important to everyone. As people in a deeply diverse and multicultural world, we all need to know that our foremothers were powerful spiritual women, and that their cultures loved and embraced them" (Razak 143), and will continue to do so in the generations to come.

Chapter 7

# The Americas and Oceania

## The Americas

It is generally believed that humans first appeared in the Americas about 15,000 to 20,000 years ago, though some believe it was far earlier. The first inhabitants of the Americas were hunter-gatherers who in time spread throughout all regions of North and South America. The diverse Amerindian tribes of the Americas, similar to the indigenous people of sub–Saharan Africa, possessed a rich mythology that extended back thousands of years through the oral tradition. However, as with a great deal of sub–Saharan African mythology, Amerindian myths were not recorded until after European contact, so once again, many myths were lost to history, and the content of those myths that survived was often compromised by European authors who added their own Western values to the narratives. Despite these issues, many Amerindian myths were preserved, and they present religious/spiritual values that are as varied as the many tribes that inhabited the Americas. In addition, often Amerindian mythology presents consistent examples of strong goddess reverence throughout all regions of the Americas.

## North America

Many North American Indian groups embraced, and continue to embrace, the concept that the earth is Mother. For example, the Athapascan people of western Canada regard the earth as a Great Mother (Stone 295). They believe that the first woman to exist was Asintmah, who was said to have created the "Great Blanket of Earth" in which she spread upon the body of her mother, the earth, so that the Great Mother could give birth to all life (Stone 295). Similarly, many Ojibwe of the Great Lakes region believe that the earth itself is a woman, Great Mother, whose honor and worship will allow the living beings of earth to prosper (Fox 349). The

Cree of Western Canada revere Messak Kummik Okwi, the primal grandmother, who ordains over all of the food of earth (Stone 288). In addition, there are many archeological sites throughout North America that present "womb, vulva, and sun symbols" as being connected to myths of American Indian Great Mothers. For example, in the Council Rocks of southern California both regional myths and rock art show "the Lone Woman of the Cave ... [as being] impregnated by the sun and giv[ing] birth to twins. Astronomical phenomena observed from the site include the sun's rays entering a cave called Womb Rock on the spring equinox sunrise" (Hays-Gilpin 76). Furthermore, an archeological site in Joshua Tree National Park in southern California "embodies the same story: the equinox sun's rays fall on a red painting of a woman in a niche. At noon on that day, a sun dagger plunges into a bedrock mortar above her" (Hays-Gilpin 76-7). Also, images portraying a Great Mother are found in Southwest rock art, particularly at a site in Hovenweep National Monument, Utah, that shows the Great Mother being impregnated by the sun and water and producing the "birth of the Puebloan Hero Twins" (Hays-Gilpin 77).

With the belief that the earth itself is a Great Mother, many North American Indian myths discuss the creation of human beings by means of emerging from the earth itself, such as the myths coming from the Hopi, Kiowa, and Navajo. The symbolism in such myths shows the earth in feminine form; therefore, it is believed that all life emerges from, and upon death will return to, the Great Mother's natural womb. Many North American Indian myths that explain life being born from a Great Mother also often display female mythic characters who are associated with aiding in creation through birthing imagery. These female characters often serve as symbolic midwives to newly created creatures as they guide them towards their emergence from the earth womb. The Hopi of Arizona embrace a myth of Grandmother Spider, for instance, that shows Grandmother Spider guiding insect-like beings through a series of layers within the earth, until they finally emerge into the current layer of existence, fully formed as human beings. One episode of this creation myth identifies Grandmother Spider as teaching the newly birthed beings about the meaning of life and death in association with the earth womb of the Great Mother. In the myth, the newly created people are horrified when they first witness death, which comes in the demise of a child. However, Grandmother Spider shows the people that the child is not dead at all, but alive and well in the third layer within the earth. Grandmother Spider thus teaches the new beings of earth a common message in Great Mother myths—that death in the womb of the Great Mother is not the end, but the means towards rebirth.

Many North American Indian creation stories also involve divine women as the creators of life. For example, the Huron or Wyandot of the region surrounding Lake Ontario and Lake Huron portray Sky Woman or Aataentsic, Ancient Woman, as aiding in creation (Hewitt 8–10). Mythically, Aataentsic was said to initially live in Sky Land, but she fell to earth one day. The earth at this time was covered in water, so an enormous turtle provided a place for Aataentsic to reside. The animals who dwelt in the water helped retrieve dirt for Aataentsic, which in turn caused the earth to become a habitable place for all living beings, including Aataentsic. Aataentsic then gave birth to her daughter, Earth Woman, who helped create the beings that would inhabit the new earth.

Many North American Indian tribes also embrace mythic females who served as culture heroes because they provided the needed resources that ensured the survival of the people of earth. For example, White Buffalo Calf Woman of the Lakota of the Great Plains shows the people that if they respect the earth, then it will provide for them, as it was she who brought the buffalo to the Lakota, providing them "meat for their food, skins for their clothes and tipis, [and] bones for their many tools" (Bastain & Mitchell 219). The Iroquois of the northern shores of Lake Ontario revere the Three Sisters as culture heroes. The most common myth of the Three Sisters shows an elderly woman discovering withered corn, bean, and squash plants crying in a field. When the woman asked why the plants were crying, they stated that they wept because the people did not care properly for them (Bastian & Mitchell 73). The old woman then relayed the wisdom of the Three Sisters to her people, and they resolved to take heed of the Three Sisters' message and nurture their corn, bean, and squash plants. In time, the people had bountiful harvests because they had learned the beneficial, long-lasting aspects of growing corn, beans, and squash together, as the Three Sisters taught them.

In addition, many North American Indians revere the Corn Mother as a cultural hero, such as the Creek, Abenaki, Cherokee, etc. The Cherokee of the southeastern United States embrace Selu as their Corn Mother. Selu's myth recounts her as a primordial mother who feeds her children by mystically being able to produce corn simply by dancing a secret dance (Humphrey 63–6). However, when her children defy her wishes and sneak to watch her sacred dance, she reveals to them that nature now requires her to be sacrificed, so that corn may continue to be produced. Selu tells her children that they must be the ones to kill her, drag her corpse over the dirt by her hair, and then watch the ground for botanical growth. Though the children are horrified by this news, they do as their mother instructed and learn that when Selu's body is received by the earth, corn indeed does grow, which assures that the generations to come will always be able to rely on corn as their staple crop.

## Chapter 7—The Americas and Oceania

The Creek of Georgia and Alabama tell a similar myth about their Corn Mother. In this myth, a grandmother instructs her grandson to sacrifice her when he accidentally spies her collecting corn and beans by scratching her thighs, which makes corn and beans pour from her body into her basket, similar to the way the Japanese food goddess, Ogetsuno, produced food. When her grandson sees this, he is disgusted and can no longer eat the food she brings back home. Because of his refusal to eat, the grandmother knows that her secret was revealed, so she tells her grandson to set her house on fire with her inside of it. Reluctantly, the boy does as he is told, and like the Cherokee tale, the grandson in this myth also learns the lesson that death is necessary for all life to continue.

The Abenaki of New York also tell a myth of a Corn Mother (Lankford 156–7). In this myth, a lonely man met a beautiful woman in the wilderness, who had long-flowing hair. The man begged the woman to stay with him, and the mystical woman agreed on the condition that the man would always do as she instructed. When the man agreed, the woman immediately told the man to set the land before them on fire, which he did. The sacred woman then instructed the man to kill her, and when the sun set, she told him to "take ... [her] by the hair and drag ... [her] over the burned ground'" (Lankford 156). The man refused to kill the woman, but the mystical woman reminded him of his promise, so the man, like the family members of the Corn Mothers in other myths, did as he was told. After, the act was done, the man saw that the first corn, that appeared to have hair just like the woman, had started to grow in the exact spot where the sacred woman's body was left. Thus, again the man in this Abenaki myth learned that from death, the survival of future generations was secured. Therefore, myths of North American Indian Corn Mothers, similar to many myths of earth goddesses discussed throughout this book, narrate lessons that help eliminate the fear of death by showing that in nature's cycles, death is only a process of transformation.

Similar to the sacrifice of the Corn Mothers, the Arctic Inuit revere the goddess Sedna for her mythic sacrifice that provided them with the food they needed to survive. Sedna's myth shows her entering into a marriage with a deceptive fulmar who forced her to live in poverty among his bird kin (Torrance 64–5). However, when Sedna's father came to rescue her from the fulmars, taking her with him in his boat, her fulmar husband chased after them with his kin, and their anger caused the sea to churn. Sedna's father threw Sedna into the sea in an attempt to save his own life, but Sedna grabbed hold of his boat. Seeing that Sedna's effort to survive would cause his boat to overturn, Sedna's father repeatedly cut off portions of her fingers, joint by joint, as she clung to his boat. However, the pieces of Sedna's severed fingers miraculously produced the first sea mammals, which went on to sustain the people forever. It is thus Sedna's tale of sacrifice, like that of the Corn Mothers, that taught the Inuit that they must remember the sacrifice of the goddess Sedna, who is said to still reside beneath the sea, when they take the life of the animals she provided.

The widespread reverence of powerful goddesses throughout North America correlates with cases of high social and religious positioning of women in many North American Indian societies prior to the arrival of the Europeans. Bastian and Mitchell state that because there are so many divine women portrayed in the most sacred of North American Indian myths, one can see this as "an indication of a society's view towards women" (Bastain & Mitchell 219). However, much of what is recorded about the role of many North American Indian women prior to the mid-eighteenth century came from recordings of European colonizers who held Western biases. For example, "European males, whose only exposure to women who did physical labor was associated with the lower class in Europe, misinterpreted the labor-intensive conditions they found in native societies [and, were thus] unable to appreciate that these were the workings of a highly complementary relationship between the genders in a tribal community" (Fox 340). Despite the inaccuracies of European recordings of the role of North American Indian women, the archeological and ethnohistoric record shows evidence that reveals that many North American Indian societies did highly value the role of women within their communities. Many American Indian tribal groups overwhelmingly recognized "the importance of women as mothers and keepers of culture, acknowledging their dependence on women for the continuity of their people" (Fox 341). Fox states that "Native women are and were mothers and creators, political figures, medicinal experts, peace keepers, and revenge seekers" (Fox 340).

The roles afforded American Indian women often "varied depending on whether they were members of matrilineal or patrilineal tribes. These differences are especially evident in terms of women's influence on decision making or ownership of property" (Fox 343). For example, the patrilineal, semi-nomadic Ojibwe often portrayed women in a role that maintained the functioning of the home, but Ojibwe women still participated in leadership roles within highly sacred ceremonial functions, such as naming ceremonies, celebrations of womanhood at puberty, marriage rites, "thanksgiving activities," and "participation in many dances—including war and victory dances" (Fox 349). Also, Ojibwe women served, and continue to serve, as leaders of their communities as members of the "Grand Medicine Society, or Midewiwin" (Fox 350). Matrilineal tribes often offered even more leadership roles to women. Bruhns and Stothert state that there "were many cases of matrilineal and matrifocal [North

American Indian] societies" where "women held key leadership roles, such as [among] the Hopi ... in which women exerted considerable influence within and beyond the family" (Bruhns & Stothert 215). The Iroquois also organized their communities according to maternal lineage, as a "person was born into the family and clan of their mother" (Fox 354). In addition, Iroquois women played a key role in social affairs, as "Clan mothers were the matrilineal heads of the families, and the female head was often the eldest woman—a woman who had proven she could handle many responsibilities" (Fox 354). Fox also contends that Iroquois women had a "significant impact on the economy of the tribe" (Fox 355), as "property use passed though the matrilineal line ... [and] women owned the house and their stores" (Fox 356). Rothenberg explains that among the Iroquois, it was believed that the "land 'belonged' to the women.... In addition to the land itself, women owned the tools of agricultural production and food preparation ... [and] controlled the distribution of cooked food. Women also determined the distribution of surpluses.... To the extent that war parties were dependent on provisions supplied by women, they could make significant determinations for or against military action by refusing provisions" (Rothenberg 69). Therefore, Iroquois women had profound leadership obligations. It was the women who chose the clan chief, and women could also "depose ... a chief if he did not do the will of the people" (Fox 356). Iroquois women were also part of medicine societies and performed important religious roles in their communities. In addition, many Pueblo communities also had matriarchies and traced lineage through matrilineal lines. Pueblo burials (1350–1500 CE) near Zuni, New Mexico, revealed that "three female leaders" were buried with rich and varied offerings, such as "grave offerings of corn, squash, utilitarian vessels, decorated bowls, grinding equipment, baskets, shaped wood, paint-grinding stones, antler tools, gourds, decorated jars, feathers, human hair, and prayer sticks" (Bruhns & Stothert 220), suggesting the high status of these females within the community.

In addition, as with many other cultures that revered powerful divine women, many North American Indian tribes also venerated female shamans, as women were believed to be especially adept at connecting with their divine female representatives. In Coastal Algonkian societies, for example, "women shamans were regarded as particularly powerful by virtue of their sex" (Grumet 54). A mythic example from the Yuchi of Tennessee portrays the divine Grandmother Sun as the instructor of all shamans. Her myth shows a group of women, who are portrayed as shamans, telling their husbands that they must kill them and then go to the cave of Grandmother Sun, so that the husbands may also become shamans. Trusting their powerful wives, the men do as they are told, by first killing their wives, and then going on to find Grandmother Sun within the recesses of the earth. Once in her presence, Grandmother Sun shows the men her ability to grow gourds from seeds right before their eyes. She then instructs the men to smash open the gourds, and when they do this, they are shocked to find that their wives emerge from the gourds, wholly resurrected. With this knowledge of the cycles of life, the men and their resurrected wives go on to serve as extraordinary shamans for their communities. A Tlingit myth of the Pacific Northwest shows another female shaman who also teaches a young man how to become a shaman. In this myth, the young man ventures upon a journey into the wilderness to seek a way to help his people who are starving. Once in the woods, he encounters the old shaman woman, Lūwat-uwadjīgĭ-cānak. Lūwat-uwadjīgĭ-cānak systematically teaches the young man the secrets of the shamans, so that when he finally ventures home, and finds that all of his people died of starvation in his absence, he knows precisely how to resurrect them all and ensure that they will never go hungry again (McCoppin, *Ecological*, 311). These myths that show women in the elevated social and religious role of shaman speaks to the high regard many North American Indian tribes held for the spiritual capacity of women, again presumably connected to the high regard they held for their wise and powerful goddesses.

Furthermore, many North American Indian myths show women in active roles upon quests to become shamans or spiritual advisors for their people, something that is rare in many mythological narratives from around the world, since many global myths often primarily focus on the heroic quests of males. Often these North American Indian mythic women venture into wilderness environments where they encounter mystical agents, most often appearing in the form of an animal, who teach them sacred knowledge that can rejuvenate their tribes. Many of these North American Indian myths showcase women marrying and having children with these mystical, often animal, teachers, signaling that they have attained the sacred knowledge held by their mystical husbands. For example, the Chiricahua Apache of Arizona and New Mexico tell a myth of a woman who saved her people from drought by being brave enough to go near a lake presided over by the sacred Water-Monster-Snake-Man. The myth states that though the woman was warned by her people to stay away from the lake, she approached it with respect and was thus able to bring its water back to her people. Because of the woman's bravery, and wisdom in knowing that she must respect nature, she soon became the wife of the sacred Water-Monster-Snake-Man, becoming sacred herself; thus, her actions forevermore allowed her people to retrieve water from the needed water source that was now protected by one of their own. The Mashpee Wampanoag of Massachusetts also tell a myth of a young girl named

Awashanks who married a trout and thus ensured that trout would always be a reliable source of sustenance for her people. In addition, the Haida of the Pacific Northwest embrace a myth of Rhipsunt, the Bear Mother, who married a bear and had his children, thus creating a lasting, spiritual bond among her people and the bears. The Blackfeet of Montana revere a woman who married a buffalo, and from him learned how to resurrect life from death. Because this woman attained this spiritual ability from her animal husband, she went on to become a great shaman for her people, teaching them the sacred Buffalo Dance (McCoppin, *Ecological*, 330). Conversely, often divine or mystical female figures appear to male characters within North American Indian myths to instruct the men towards spiritual transformation, such as is seen in a Hopi myth that shows a man named White Corn marrying a snake woman and thus becoming a powerful shaman to his people, teaching them how to become members of the Snake Clan. In addition, a Pawnee myth from the Great Plains recounts how a man named Waupee married a Star Maiden and likewise attained sacred wisdom that allowed him to rejuvenate the spiritual health of his people. Again, consistently showing sacred women or women who have been permitted to attain spiritual apotheosis within North American Indian mythic narratives reveals the high regard many tribes held for their women before European arrival.

Also, some North American Indian women served in the prestigious social role of warrior, which again was permitted because of the presentation of powerful divine women within their respective cultures. For example, the Pawnee embraced women who served as warriors, and even believed that supernatural abilities often accompanied warrior women (Holliman 182). The Hidatsa of North Dakota tell of the "exploits of Wolf Woman, who ... would join war parties of her choice, and was well respected by the community" (Holliman 183). The Oneida of the northern woodlands revere Aliquipiso as a warrior woman who saved her people from the Mingoes, the Iroquois who moved to Pennsylvania and Ohio (Monaghan 314). Furthermore, one of the roles open to Blackfeet women "was called ... 'manly hearted woman.' This was a woman who excelled in every important aspect of tribal life, including [warfare,] property acquisition and management, domestic life, and ceremonials" (Bruhns & Stothert 250–1). These "manly hearted women" were encouraged from a young age "in dominant behavior, and they led in games, played boys' sports, and took names of famous warriors for themselves. Unlike their sisters, they also were sexually aggressive and active from an early age, and this aggressive behavior and high self-esteem led them to excel in female and male tasks alike. These ... women ... gain[ed] high status through their dominant behavior" (Bruhns & Stothert 251).

European invaders, though, decimated the American Indian cultures of North America in innumerable ways. First and foremost, the conquest of the Americas resulted in the genocide of the indigenous people of the Americas, as it is estimated that ninety to ninety-five percent of American Indians were killed due to the arrival of Europeans in instances of warfare, disease, displacement, etc. Countless instances of cultural practices, social values, and political structures were lost to history with such widespread annihilation. Religious beliefs, which often involved reverence of divine women, were often eradicated with European efforts to convert American Indians to Christianity. As stated, the myths of North American Indians were only recorded after European contact; this meant that countless sacred stories had already been lost and forgotten as many North American Indians struggled to survive. Of the myths that were recorded, many of them left out portrayals of sacred women, or revised the myths to include Christian ideology, which often replaced all-powerful female creators with a male creator who resembled a Christian God. Thus, the loss of goddesses from many religious beliefs systems, as Christian ideologies gained dominance, led to many North American Indian women losing their roles as powerful religious figures within their communities. In addition, with the impact of European colonization, the high social positioning of many North American Indian women was greatly reduced and transformed. In North America, "officials who attempted to enforce European gender roles as part of a process of 'civilizing' indigenous peoples generally directed their efforts toward making native women conform to European ideals" (Hunt 7). As Brintnall explains "In indigenous communities ... men were forced into patriarchal roles in societies where gender equality and cooperation remained a strong principle.... The church encouraged native women to submit to their husbands' authority ... further undermining traditional complementary roles" (Brintnall 402). Eventually, European models of social and political systems took away the "rights and privileges" of many North American Indian women (Rothenberg 80). For example, the matriarchal societies of the Iroquois and Pueblo experienced a loss of their traditional religious values and matriarchal and matrilineal social structures. European "economic and social customs" often eradicated matrilineal rights that once gave property ownership to American Indian women (Hunt 8). For instance, "Canadian governments encouraged patriarchy by giving land to men who conformed to English customs" (Hunt 12). Furthermore, colonizers often forced women who lived in a household without a man to live in servitude (Hunt 7).

In contemporary times, American Indian women still face extreme challenges and discrimination. For instance, American Indian women are paid significantly less than "white ... men working comparable hours....

This wage gap forces too many Native American women and families into poverty" (Pathak). Furthermore, "violence against indigenous women has reached unprecedented levels on tribal lands" ("Ending Violence"). However, despite the extreme upheaval of beliefs during the American Indian holocaust, and in the centuries that followed, many North American Indians maintained their reverence for goddesses and women as connected to female sources of divinity and spiritual power. Because of this, many contemporary American Indian women continue to serve as religious and social leaders for their communities. Hopefully, this perseverance to maintain their traditional sacred belief systems will allow the North American Indian women of today to one day rise above the inequities and atrocities that are happening to them, so that they may carry on in the formidable footsteps of their ancestors.

## Mesoamerica

Mesoamerica extends from northern Mexico to Guatemala and Honduras. Archeologists believe that humans were in Mesoamerica as early as 20,000 BCE, and became agriculturalists during the period of 7000–1500 BCE, forming the first civilizations in the Early Formative period (1500–900 BCE). Some of the primary cultures of Mesoamerica included the: Olmec (c. 1200–400 BCE), Teotihuacan (c. 400 BCE–400 CE), Maya (c. 250–900 CE), Toltec (c. 800–1000 CE), and the Aztec (c. 1345–1521 CE). There is ample evidence that goddess worship throughout Mesoamerica was quite prevalent. Goddesses were worshipped as central members of Mesoamerican pantheons and had numerous male and female followers. Goddesses who were connected to the elements of the earth, such as the moon and water, as well as goddesses associated with fertility and childbirth, seem to have been "universal in Mesoamerican religion" (Stone 302). Artistic representations of goddesses, as well as women in high-standing positions, are plentiful in Mesoamerica, ranging from "abundant small ceramic and stone figurines to rare colossal statuary," such as the Coatlinchan Idol found at Teotihuacán, Mexico (Stone 295).

From about 100–750 CE, at Teotihuacán, "the center of one of the earliest and most powerful cities of prehispanic Mexico," the residents of the city were believed to embrace an earth goddess as their primary deity (Bruhns & Stothert 181). Bruhns and Stothert explain that "the preeminent deity in Teotihuacán ... [was] the goddess. She ... [was] intimately connected with the local landscape and the sacred geography of Teotihuacán.... The goddess ... [was] responsible for the fertility of the land and the general well-being of the city and its inhabitants" (Bruhns & Stothert

181). In addition to being a beneficent divinity, the goddess of Teotihuacán, like other earth goddesses, was "also a lady with destructive capabilities, as indicated by representations of her fangs, claws, and military paraphernalia. These may indicate that she also had sacrificial aspects or that blood sacrifices were made to her" (Bruhns & Stothert 181).

In addition, the Maya moon goddess, Ix Chel, was often attributed as being the "Mother of all deities" among the Maya (Stone, *Ancient*, 92). The Maya worshipped Ix Chel as the first woman of the world, who "was the shining moon, up in the heavens … the goddess of tides, and the one who provided the people with the 'knowledge of healing'" (Frankel 63). Ix Chel was also "associated with weaving, childbirth, creation, sexual 'promiscuity,' and disease" (Sigal 96). A myth involving Ix Chel shows her as the moon, which at the beginning of time was as bright and hot as the sun. The sun fell in love with Ix Chel, but this union angered Ix Chel's grandfather, who killed her by thrusting a lightning bolt at her. The myth states that as Ix Chel lay dead, "dragonflies gathered" around her corpse, "mourning with their soft buzzing. They blanketed her with their vibrating bodies as they prepared for her 13 hollow logs. On the 13th night, the logs cracked open. From 12 crawled the awesome great snakes of heaven, and from the 13th, Ix Chel herself, well and whole" (Frankel 63). As with many myths of earth goddesses, Ix Chel in this myth is portrayed as easily resurrecting because she, as the moon, is a natural element. With Ix Chel's resurrection, the sun instantly married her, and the two remained happy for a time, until the sun's brother, Chc Noh Ek, grew jealous of them and accused Ix Chel of cheating on her husband. In a flash of anger, her husband, the sun, flung Ix Chel from heaven into the Land of Volcanoes. Ix Chel was homeless, until the King of the Vultures came and offered her a place to stay if she would become his lover, and since Ix Chel felt she had no other option, she relented. In time, the sun sought out his wife and apologized to her. Ix Chel thus forgave her husband and returned home to the heavens. However, her husband began to grow angry again at Ix Chel, as he was jealous of her shining brilliance that equaled his own, so he began to beat her. Ix Chel's husband "rained down blows on her face, determined to scar her so badly no one would ever want her again" (Frankel 64). However, as Ix Chel's "brilliance dimmed, her will grew stronger," so she fled to the night sky to live alone, rejecting all male advances; "From then on, Ix Chel came and went as she willed, sometimes disappearing for days, ever solitary, ever one-in-herself" (Frankel 64). Because of her myth, Ix Chel was revered by the Maya as a powerful protector of women from about 600–1500 CE (Frankel 64).

In addition, there were dozens of Aztec goddesses in Mesoamerica as well, such as: Tlazolteotl, Fifth Goddess; Chalchiuhtlicue, the Goddess of the Jade Skirt; Cihuacoatl, Woman Serpent; and Coatlicue, Serpent Skirt (Stone 303). The Aztecs embraced "an immense pantheon of goddesses [who were] charged with a multitude of specific roles. These goddesses governed everything from childbirth and drunkenness to the confession of sins and the guarding of sweat baths" (Bruhns & Stothert 167).

The goddess Chicomecoatl was the Aztec Great Corn Mother (Stone 85). Aztec maidens would annually become representations of Chicomecoatl by partaking in a ceremony where they would embody the Corn Maidens who showed the growth process of the Corn Goddess to the people. Stone states that Chicomecoatl may have been the First Mother of the people of Mexico, as some accounts speak towards Chicomecoatl as being worshipped before the Aztecs arrived (Stone 86).

In addition, the goddess Coatlicue was revered as the Mother of all Aztec Deities (Frankel 127). Coatlicue "had many great temples built in her honor" (Frankel 127). She "gave all in life and reclaimed all in death. Her necklace of skulls reminded the Aztecs that each must return to her in their time" (Frankel 127). She was often artistically rendered with powerful imagery; Coatlicue's "hands were depicted as fanged serpents' heads, her feet as large claws. Her head ... [as] two coiled snakes' heads or her head may have been severed, the snakes thus possibly spurts of blood ... her breasts were clearly visible under a necklace consisting of human hands and hearts and a pendant made of a human skull, while her skirt [was a] ... mass of serpents" (Rostas 371). Coatlicue was also capable of "transforming herself into a snake at will" (Rostas 371). Coatlicue's myth states that she had four hundred sons and one daughter, Coyolxanliqui. One day Coatlicue found that she became impregnated when a tuft of feathers fell on her. When her daughter discovered her mother's pregnancy, she became outraged, believing that her mother had broken a moral code by having an affair at her age. So, Coatlicue's daughter convinced her brothers to kill their mother. All the brothers plotted to commit the dark task of killing Coatlicue. While Coatlicue was giving birth to her four hundredth son, her three hundred and ninety-nine sons attacked her, but the son she had just birthed, Huitzilopochtli, was born a warrior, and he immediately slaughtered all of his three hundred and ninety-nine brothers and his sister Coyolxanliqui, "thus saving his mother" (Frankel 128).

Also, the principal Aztec goddess, Cihuacoatl, "was the most feared and effective of the goddesses" (Rostas 370). Cihuacoatl was originally thought to be the goddess of wild vegetation, but Cihuacoatl's role eventually turned away from fertility and moved towards demanding sacrifice as the civilization of the Aztecs grew (Rostas 371). Cihuacoatl became a figure who was "used by the state in maintaining its apparatus of government" (Rostas 371). To the Aztecs, Cihuacoatl "personified the collective hunger for human victims of all of the deities. There were more festivals for her than any other deity in the annual calendar" (Rostas 371). Cihuacoatl's "lower face was made only of bone"; she had "wide open [jaws that were] waiting for victims. Her hair was long and stringy and a pair of knives formed a diadem on her forehead. She was related to evil omens, was savage and brought misery to 'men'.... She was a night walker, screaming and weeping copiously, but she was also a warrior; on her back she carried the knife of sacrifice swaddled like a child" (Rostas 370).

The Aztec goddess Mayuel was the goddess of the "intoxicating liquid of the *maguey (metl)* plant"; she was said to have four hundred breasts and to have birthed four hundred stars (Stone 91). The goddess Mayuel was believed to offer women in childbirth the means to ease the pain through her maguey plant, which was said to nourish the first people to exist according to Aztec belief (Stone 91).

The Cuna people of Panama revered the divine Mu Olokukurtilisop, Giant Blue Butterfly Lady, as the one who gave birth to the sun. Her myth states that she also took the sun as her lover, and then gave birth to the moon. Once she gave birth to the moon, Mu Olokukurtilisop made her son/grandson her lover and gave birth to the stars. Next, Mu Olokukurtilisop mated with the many stars that filled the sky, and from this, she created all the animals and plants of the earth (Stone 78). To honor Mu Olokukurtilisop, the Cuna brought the remains of their dead to the caves that were believed to be the womb of Mu Olokukurtilisop, from which all life on earth was birthed (Stone 78). Fertility rites of young women also incorporated the goddess Mu Olokukurtilisop. Young girls entering womanhood were instructed to lie upon the ground while old women threw soil upon them, to invoke Mu Olokukurtilisop; next the young women would have "the red juice of the saptur [tree], the menstrual blood of Mu" painted upon their faces, as they performed a dance to honor the rite of passage (Stone 79).

Once again, the high regard for goddesses within the many cultures of Mesoamerica's history was also tied to centuries of women holding high social and religious roles within their communities. Many archeological artifacts portraying women suggest that they held prominent positions within early Mesoamerican societies (Stone 295). In Oaxaca, "women as well as men occup[ied] ruling positions" (Bruhns & Stothert 230). In Maya culture, women held high positions as well; one such example shows the highest class of women dressing in costumes that were "virtually identical to that of a male god of corn" (Stone 295). In addition, many Maya women were buried in "high-status tombs"; the numbers of "such burials equals that of men" (Stone 305). Maya women were also depicted as ruling cities, such as in the Maya city of Palenque. Records at Palenque indicate that two

Chapter 7—The Americas and Oceania           225

of the city's rulers were in fact women: Kanal-ikal, who began her rule in 583 CE, and Zak K'uk,' who started her rule in 612 CE (Stone 309).

In addition, there is evidence that the widespread belief in myriad powerful goddesses throughout Mesoamerica directly led to women being associated with respected religious positions. For example, women held the position of shaman within some communities within Mesoamerica (Bruhns & Stothert 169). Bruhns and Stothert state that "In the Late Preclassic [(400 BCE–250 CE)] ceramic figures from western Mexico, female personages carry out activities ... identified as shamanistic" (Bruhns & Stothert 171). Also, in Mixtec culture, women held the roles of priestesses and sacred oracles (Stone 295). There were also "priestesses among the Aztecs during their initial migration into the Valley of Mexico, and priestesses and other women played important roles" in the annual honoring of Aztec deities (Bruhns & Stothert 182). Aztec girls were able to join either a secular school or a religious school where they could become priestesses who served Aztec goddesses (Stone 300). Furthermore, it is clear that Aztec women's "professional participation was essential in [religious] ceremonies, as well as in the everyday functioning of temples and their business" (Bruhns & Stothert 182). Aztec women also participated in many public religious rituals where they often impersonated goddesses.

In addition, many Mesoamerican cultures believed that the earth and all the elements of existence should always be in a state of balance; this was reflected most especially in the necessary role of both male and female in Mesoamerican ideology (Stone 297). Within Mesoamerican cultures, concepts of femininity were viewed as complementary to masculine elements; therefore, Mesoamerican women in general were recognized as being just as essential as men within religious and social spheres (Stone 298). Thus, Gimeno asserts, that because of this embrace of the necessity of both sexes in creating a balanced civilization, many Mesoamerican societies "gave women a far more important status and role than in Western civilization" (qtd. in Ramos-Escandon 121).

However, European invasions that introduced Christian doctrine would cause, in most cases, the outright eradication of goddess worship in Mesoamerica, which in time greatly reduced the social positioning of Mesoamerican women. Much of the indigenous autonomy of the Mesoamerican people ended abruptly in the sixteenth century CE with the arrival of the Spanish, led by Hernán Cortés. As in North America, millions of Mesoamerican people were murdered, enslaved, or died from illnesses brought over from Europe; thus, Mesoamerican culture was threatened on all fronts. Colonizers worked fast to transform existing sacred locations into sites of Catholic worship, as colonizers forced indigenous populations to adopt Christianity. Mesoamerican goddesses were identified as pagan, and their worship became banned in many regions, subsequently eliminating the revered spiritual roles for many women within Mesoamerican communities. Mesoamerican women were thus expected to emulate European social and religious roles for women, which held, and continue to hold, them in inferior positions under Western systems and expectations of patriarchy.

However, as the Irish had done when Christianity threatened Celtic beliefs systems, the Maya incorporated the new religious concepts of their colonizers with conceptions of their own divinities; "For the Maya people, the preconquest gods became a part of Catholic ritual" (Sigal 106). For instance, the Catholic Virgin Mary "was presented to the Maya as an important figure.... The Maya saw her picture, and they saw the reverence given to her by the Spaniards. Thus, they interpreted her as the central goddess in the Catholic pantheon" (Sigal 106). Many Maya texts written after the arrival of the Spanish displayed Ix Chel, the Maya "Moon Goddess and the Virgin Mary playing the same role, being seen as mother goddesses, and doing the same things in the texts" (Sigal 119–20). Sigal states that Catholicism actually "presented the Moon Goddess with the possibility of survival. She survived, vastly altered, in the figure of the Virgin Mary. She also maintained a powerful existence of her own in those parts of the Maya universe where Mary dared not tread" (Sigal 126). Therefore, even today many people in Mesoamerica, revere the Virgin Mary in a highly similar way to how many of their ancestors worshipped their ancient goddesses.

## South America

South America was inhabited at least 14,000 years ago. Agriculturalists began producing sedentary villages from about 5,000 to 2,000 years ago in primarily the central Andean region of South America, which includes Ecuador, Peru, Bolivia, and northern Chile. This Andean region held many cultures that produced lasting archeological evidence, such as: the Chavín of the Early Horizon (c. 800–200 BCE); the Huari and Tiahuanaco of the Middle Horizon (c. 600–1000 CE); and the Inca of the Late Horizon (1476–1532 CE). Similar to Mesoamerica, these Andean cultures, as well as the other cultures of South America, displayed a vast and diverse mythology that included a high reverence for female deities; however, again, this mythology was passed down through the oral tradition for centuries and was not recorded until after the arrival of the Spanish in 1532 CE, posing problems in the preservation of the mythic record.

Still, of the South American myths that survived, many portray a widespread belief in myriad powerful goddesses. Many creator goddesses exist in a vast number of regions throughout South America. For example, the Amazonian Baniwa and Wakuén worship Amáru, who was said to have "breathed ... [life] into existence at the beginning of time" (Monaghan 352). The Tariana of Brazil "worship the goddess Coadidop as the creator of the earth and its elements" (Bierhorst 55). The Chibcha of Colombia revere the goddess Bachúe, who was said to first reside in the primordial sea before coming on land and producing the earth's first inhabitants (Monaghan 353). Also, in Columbia, the people of the Sierra Nevada revere Gauteovan as the goddess who "created the sun from her menstrual blood," and then proceeded to create "the visible and the invisible worlds" (Monaghan 355). The Yaruro of Venezuela worship "the creator goddess Kuma ... [who] was the first living being on earth, for which reason the people said, 'Everybody sprang from Kuma'" (Monoghan 356). The goddess Kuma then created and gave birth to the elements of earth; after this, she found human beings living below the earth, so she pulled them up into the sunlight and cared for the people until they could prosper on their own.

In addition, the indigenous inhabitants of South America believed in myriad representations of goddesses who played a central role in their conceptions of the natural world. The Amazonian Tukano people worshipped Abé mango as a sun goddess, and the Araucanians of Chile worshipped Auchimalgen as the goddess of the moon. Auchimalgen was said to be "a seer," who could foretell "great events by changing the color of her face" (Monaghan 352). In addition, a myth of the Arawak on the Guyana coast of South America shows the power of the earth goddess Seamother (Nauwald 137-9). The myth starts with a chieftain named Arawanili who finds that his people are dying from a strange illness. Distraught, Arawanili goes to the sea to ask for help. In response, the water before Arawanili was mythically said to open up, and in front of him, and "out of the depths of the sea arose the Seamother" (Nauwald 138). The Seamother told Arawanili that she heard his pleas to save his people. She gave him a magic twig and told him to plant it on top of a nearby hill, where he should tend for it carefully. When the tree produced fruit, he should bring the fruit to her. Arawanili did as he was instructed and brought the fruit to Seamother. Seamother arose once more from the waves and showed Arawanili how to open the fruit, fill it with pebbles, and adorn it with a wooden handle decorated with feathers, so that the first shaman rattle could be created (Nauwald 138). From that day on, Arawanili became a powerful shaman to his people precisely because the divine Seamother made Arawanili "strong with her knowledge" of nature (Nauwald 139).

The Andean Inca and Quechua worshipped Mama Cocha as the

goddess of all bodies of water, including the ocean. Mama Cocha produced all the bounty the ocean and lakes held. She also controlled the weather associated with the ocean and could, if appeased by offerings from the people, calm the seas and storms. Water in Inca belief was believed to have healing properties, so Mama Cocha was also believed to be a goddess associated with healing.

Mama Ocllo was the Inca goddess of fertility, and Mama Sara was the Inca goddess of grain and corn; thus, Mama Ocllo and Mama Sara assured a successful harvest for the people. In addition, Mama Quilla, sometimes Mama Killa, was the Inca Moon Goddess. Mama Quilla was believed to be married to the Inca Sun god Inti. When lunar eclipses occurred, the Inca were said to believe that a wild animal was chasing Mother Quilla, and if the animal succeeded in catching her, the Inca believed that they would be forced to endure nights with no light from the moon. As the moon, Mama Quilla was envisioned as being connected to the menstrual cycle of women; therefore, she was revered as especially sacred to women. Mama Quilla had many temples devoted to her; the most prominent was in the Inca capital of Cuzco, where temples priestesses maintained rites connected to her.

The most revered divinity for the Inca and Quechua was the goddess Pachamama, the Earth Mother. Pachamama was, and still is for the Quechua people, believed to have created the earth itself, along with all the inhabitants of the earth. After creation, Pachamama was believed to reside within the earth, where she looked over the elements of her creation. Martín states that Pachamama "is the mother of the mountains, of life that is born and grows, of all people. It is because of her that fruit ripens, animals multiply, and women have babies. It is she who controls frosts and rains ... thunder and storms" (Martín xiv). Thus, Pachamama ensures "fertility, productivity and safety" for all her beings (Harvey 398). In addition, it is believed that when living beings die, they return to Pachamama. However, like other Earth Mothers discussed in this book, Pachamama is also sometimes connected to the destructive aspects of nature, as she is "capable of malicious attacks and voracious hunger" (Harvey 398). As in Mesoamerica, when the Spanish brought Catholicism into the region, Pachamama's "benign aspects" were "associated with the Virgin Mary," while her seemingly malign forces were labeled as pagan, and thus evil (Harvey 397). Harvey states that Catholic "shrines to the [Virgin Mary] appeared in sites that had previously been dedicated to Pachamama ... and [contemporary] Andean people often address Pachamama as if addressing a Christian saint, calling her Santa Tierra Pachamama (Saint Earth Pachamama)" (Harvey 397).

Concerning the Inca Empire, it is often stated that the male god

Viracocha, the god associated with rain and thunder, gained supremacy over the revered Pachamama during Inca rule. For example, many Inca myths state that it was in fact Viracocha who created the earth and its inhabitants. However, many scholars assert that it was not until the arrival of the Spanish, who, when writing down Inca myths for the first time, projected their own Western conceptions onto the Inca pantheon, placing the revered Pachamama below that of the male god Viracocha, when in reality the worship of Pachamama was the dominant form of reverence among the common population (Stone 76).

Because many South American societies embraced powerful goddesses, many women "served as curers, soothsayers, shamans, ... sacrificers and sacrifices, divine ancestors, and innovators of and participants in domestic and community cults ... and ritual practices" (Bruhns & Stothert 167). For example, in Brazil, Tupinamba women "enjoyed a large degree of influence and independence"; one such reflection of this is seen in Tupinamba marriage customs, which "followed a matrilocal pattern" (Fishman 71). Additionally, artistic depictions on funerary vases of the Moche of northern Peru show women holding the prominent role of priestess; these depictions suggest that "women could take an important place in rituals with supernatural and political content" in Moche society (Niles 316). In the Jama Valley of Ecuador, "the skeleton of a woman buried in an unusual, extended position with a suite of offerings ... [was] interpreted as evidence" that she may have been a shaman (Bruhns & Stothert 171). In addition, Inca women played a crucial role in maintaining Inca religious beliefs through their involvement in sacred rituals (Bruhns & Stothert 240). For example, Inca Chosen Women were held in high esteem within the Inca Cult of the Moon, which revered the moon goddess Mama Quilla (Niles 330). Also, Inca priestesses served the Corn Mother, Mama Sara, at her cult in Pimachi. Even in death, Inca "mummified women were venerated" (Niles 332). Some royal Inca women also maintained political roles, even becoming formidable queens. In addition, Inca queens, like many other queens from various cultures, "established their right to power by means of claimed descent from a goddess" (Nelson 8). Also, some Inca women were recorded as taking part in important military battles (Niles 331). Likewise, the Kamayurá of the Amazon Basin of Brazil tell a legend that showcases their acceptance of women warriors. The legend states that the Yamuricumá were women who had lost their husbands, so they "dressed as warriors and ... wandered the world, calling women away from their homes to join them as warriors" (Monaghan 360).

South American Indian mythology, like North American Indian mythology, includes a plethora of myths that showcase women as equally able to attain spiritual apotheosis upon active quests, such as is shown in a myth from the Opayé of Mato Grosso, Brazil. The myth shows a young woman who greatly worried about the difficulty her people had in securing a reliable food source, so she wished that she could learn to hunt like a jaguar. With this wish, a jaguar indeed appeared and asked the woman for her hand in marriage. Because the woman respected the jaguar, and was willing to merge with him through marriage, and later by becoming a jaguar herself, her people also learned to revere the jaguar as sacred, and thus learned techniques from the jaguars that ensured their survival. The Yanomamö of Brazil and Venezuela tell of a similar myth about a woman named Petá who married four brothers. The brothers fought often over who got to have sex with Petá, so "she tied their penises up while they slept, attaching them with strings to their waistbands. Only when she untied them could they have intercourse with her.... Petá [thus] enjoyed all four husbands" (Monaghan 358). In time, Petá gave birth to the Yanomamö people and reigned as their chief. But one night, Petá found that a jaguar had come for her and drug her through the forest to its den. Once in the cave of the jaguar, Petá saw that the den harbored two jaguar cubs that were near starvation next to their dead mother. Instead of being overcome by fear, Petá, like the wise woman of the Opayé myth, chose to respect the jaguars by treating the young jaguar cubs as her own babies. Petá lived in the cave, nursing the cubs back to health with her own milk. In time, Petá's four husbands found her and attempted to rescue her, but Petá soon showed them that she wasn't in need of saving, as she freely walked out of the cave with two fully grown jaguars by her side. At this, the dead jaguar mother was miraculously resurrected, and Petá returned to her people having secured the protection of the jaguars for all time. Again, as with the North American Indian myths that showed women attaining the highest levels of spiritual wisdom when they merged with nature, South American Indian myths that similarly present women as able to attain apotheosis and subsequently revitalize the health of their tribe, such as was shown in these myths, reveals the high regard many South American women held within their respective cultures.

In the Andes region of South America, just as in Mesoamerica, the introduction of Catholicism, with its insistence on the worship of only one male God and its strict demand of adherence to the new faith enforced during conquest, undermined years of traditional Inca goddess worship. The Spanish "destroyed the religious-political organization of the Cuzco elite," which included eradicating the position of goddesses and sacred women within Inca religion (Silverblatt 153). European social models and religious beliefs often destroyed the "social, political, and economic institutions that ... guaranteed" Inca women their social and religious rights (Etienne & Leacock 18). Silverblatt contends that Catholic priests "brought suits against several women in Pimachi," the Inca sacred cult dedicated to the Corn Mother Mama Sara, accusing the priestesses "of being 'confessors, dogmatists, witches, and mistresses of [idolatrous] ceremonies'" (Silverblatt 157). In fact, a great deal of Inca religious practices maintained by women "became linked with sorcery, which in terms of Western thought of the late Middle Ages involved a contract with the devil. As in Western Europe of the fifteenth to seventeenth centuries, which was shaken by intense witch hunts, the Catholic Church organized expeditions against 'idolatry' in the Andes" (Silverblatt 174). In fact, one hundred years after Christianity dominated the Andes, the Catholic Church spearheaded a movement to eradicate any existing legacy of "underground ... indigenous religion" (Silverblatt 174).

As with North America and Mesoamerica, because of the lasting impact of genocide and colonialization, South American indigenous people faced the downfall of countless aspects of their culture. The social, political, and religious legacies of colonialization still hold power in South America. For example, South American indigenous women face widespread racism, gender inequality, lack of education, poverty, etc., as a direct legacy of European conquest. However, as with many regions around the globe, many indigenous people throughout South America, despite European persecution, often maintained their traditional beliefs in secret or through the maintenance of folk customs, festivals, and folktales that still held remnants of sacred goddess reverence. For example, Andean women during colonialization, and into contemporary times, created an "underground female culture of resistance ... marked by a return to the ancient traditions of pre-Columbian society" (Silverblatt 179). Because of resistance efforts to preserve traditional religious concepts, many Andean men and women still revere elements associated with the traditional worship of goddesses and the sacred positioning of women. Again, hopefully these lasting concepts that envision divinity and spirituality in feminine terms might help resolve some of the contemporary injustices that still linger throughout South America.

# Oceania

## Australia

It is believed that Australia has been inhabited by humans for 65,000 years (Allan, Fleming, & Kerrigan 9). Therefore, Australian Aboriginal mythology, passed down through the oral tradition, extended over thousands of years, and was as diverse as the many cultures that inhabited

Australia. However, like much of African and Amerindian mythology, Australian Aboriginal mythology was only recorded after European colonizers entered Australia, which again means that much of the content of Australian Aboriginal mythology was lost to history, and the myths that did survive often included European elements that altered the traditional meaning of the myths. Still, from the mythology that survived, there exists a rich presence of reverence for sacred ancestral women who are often revered as the creators of the landscape that the people inhabit. Aboriginal Australian mythology most often does not include gods and goddesses but ancestral "human beings with supernatural powers ... [who] are neither worshipped nor propitiated" (White & Payne 251). These ancestral creators are believed to have existed in Dreamtime, which is the Aboriginal Australian time of creation, and after they finished aiding in creation, they often became natural elements, such as stars, rocks, trees, etc. For example, the belief in Milapukala, as the All-Mother, pervades Aboriginal Australian religion in many regions. It is said that Milapukala "commanded all manner of animal and plant life to come" into existence (Allan, Fleming, & Kerrigan 35).

Also, Kunapipi, "Old Woman" was revered as the First Mother or first ancestress throughout many regions of Australia. Kunapipi's womb was believed to be connected to the caves within the earth which housed the spirits of living beings before and after death (Stone 160). Kunapipi was thus said to give birth to all of the inhabitants of earth after emerging from the primordial sea and travelling throughout the land of Australia. It was believed that she could transform into either male or female form. Kunapipi was deeply connected to the sacred Rainbow Serpent.

Depending on the culture, the Rainbow Serpent holds many names, and is envisioned as either male or female, and in some cases both genders. When the Rainbow Serpent is presented as female in Aboriginal Australian mythology, she "represents both life and death. She brings fertility, crops, and sustenance, but, if she's angry and withholds the supply, famine and destruction stalk the red earth" (Hodges 161). The Rainbow Serpent is also sometimes presented as having created the earth and its inhabitants (Wilkinson 209); its serpentine body creating the varied landscape of Australia. The Rainbow Serpent also is often viewed as providing water and rain for the inhabitants of earth.

One myth of Dreamtime displays the sacred ancestresses, the Wawalag sisters, and their interaction with the Rainbow Serpent (Allan, Fleming, & Kerrigan 34–5). The myth presents the Wawalag sisters walking out of the primordial sea and stepping onto land for the first time. The sisters found that the animals they hunted upon this new land did not remain dead for long, as each time the girls killed an animal to consume

## Chapter 7—The Americas and Oceania 233

it, the animal would immediately resurrect. The youngest of the sisters, who was pregnant, soon gave birth in this strange new land. After giving birth, she went to the water to wash herself, but the afterbirth and her blood caused the waters to surge, and suddenly the Rainbow Serpent, presented in this myth as male, rose up from the water and swallowed the Wawalag sisters and the newborn baby. Some versions of the myth contend that the Rainbow Serpent was offended by the blood of the Wawalag sister within his watery domain. However, most versions of the myth state that the Rainbow Serpent consumed the Wawalag sisters because he wanted to possess their reproductive wisdom, as the Wawalag sisters were said to be the daughters of the Earth Mother Kunapipi (Allan, Fleming, & Kerrigan 34). Kunapipi, as stated, was often presented as being connected with the Rainbow Serpent, as both beings symbolized agents of femininity and masculinity necessary for creation and sustainability. Therefore, this myth shows that when the Rainbow Serpent, in male form, consumed the daughters and grandchild of Kunapipi, he was internalizing the feminine aspect of Kunapipi, becoming more powerful. However, the myth states that snakes in the region witnessed what the Rainbow Serpent had done in swallowing the three innocents, and they became so outraged that they caused a great storm to be unleashed. The ferocity of the storm caused the Rainbow Serpent to vomit the sisters and the baby up again, resurrecting them, just like the animals earlier within the myth. When the sisters and the baby were resurrected, they possessed part of the masculine wisdom the Rainbow Serpent held, making them, as well as their mother Kunapipi, more powerful, just as the Rainbow Serpent tried to do when he consumed the trio. The Wawalag sisters then went on to become carriers of sacred feminine and masculine wisdom, as well as holders of knowledge about the cycles of life and death, which they imparted to the people.

The Gamilaraay of New South Wales, Australia, revere Yhi as a primordial ancestress of the sun. Yhi's myth states that she lived in Dreamtime, sleeping, until one day, she awakened and provided light to the world. The myth states that as Yhi walked about the new earth, the land responded to her touch, and vegetation grew wherever she stepped. She entered the interior of the earth, and her light and warmth caused the animals and insects of the earth to be birthed. She then entered the water, and again her light and warmth caused fish to be created. Yhi then returned to her sky domain to rest, but the new beings of earth became fearful as she slept, because the earth was filled with darkness. However, as dawn emerged and Yhi reappeared, the beings of earth realized that Yhi would always be with them.

Among the Yolngu in the Northern Territory of Australia, the two Djang'kawu sisters, as well as their brother, were also believed to have aided in creation. The Djang'kawu sisters and their brother were said to have created the land, as well as the vegetation and animals needed to populate the earth. Then the Djang'kawu sisters gave birth to the first people of the clans in the region. Using their digging sticks, the sisters next created freshwater springs to sustain the beings of earth. Once their work was complete, the two sisters performed the first ceremonial rituals that would comprise the Yolngu religion.

In Queensland, Anjea was a fertility ancestress who harbored the spirits of the dead before they were reincarnated. After birth, a child's grandmother was said to take the child's placenta and bury it in the earth, placing sticks around the spot, so that Anjea would find it and carry "the spirit away ... until the person whose spirit it was" died (Earthist). Anjea was then said to place the spirit of the deceased into mud to form another infant, which she then placed within the womb of a mother, so that the spirit could be reincarnated. It was thus Anjea's ministrations that ensured that all people carried a part of the land of Australia within them.

Another ancestress associated with fertility was Dilga of the Karadjeri of Western Australia. Dilga is presented in a myth where she is said to be the mother of the famous Bagadjimbiri brothers, who aided her in the creation of the earth. However, after creating the environment, the Bagadjimbiri brothers were killed by a quoll in its den within the earth. When Dilga learned of this, she became outraged and flooded the interior of the earth with her milk. Her milk thus killed the quoll and resurrected her sons, who went on to live in the sky realm as clouds.

A myth from southeastern Australia shows the significance of the famous ancestresses, the Seven Sisters, or Karatgurk sisters, of Aboriginal Australian mythology. The Seven Sisters were said in Dreamtime to be the only ones who understood the mystery of the natural element of fire (Allan, Fleming, & Kerrigan 61). Because of this knowledge, the Seven Sisters were the only beings who could cook their food, and they were not willing to share their wisdom with anyone. However, the Seven Sisters were tricked into angering snakes beneath the ground when a crow convinced them to dig into the earth with their sticks that they always kept lit to make fire. The snakes beneath the ground, again like the myth of the Rainbow Serpent, caused the earth to shake when they were disturbed, which forced the Seven Sisters to drop their fire sticks. The crow then grabbed the fire sticks and gave fire to humankind. At this insult, the Seven Sisters retreated into the night sky to become the eternal stars of the Pleiades (Allan, Fleming, & Kerrigan 61). The Seven Sisters, like other earth goddesses discussed in this book, are thus portrayed as holders of wisdom connected to the natural environment, and they additionally became natural figures by transforming shape into the stars of the Pleiades upon their departure from human existence.

The most famous myth of the Seven Sisters, that is told widely throughout much of Australia, discusses how they were being pursued by one man, sometimes various versions of the myth states that it was many men, as they were journeying across the land. As the man kept getting closer to the Seven Sisters, they were able to continually evade him. In their final act of avoidance, they all leapt high into the sky and again, like the other myth just discussed, become the stars of the Pleiades.

Another Aboriginal Australian myth displays again sisters as ancestresses of the people who, like the myth of the Seven Sisters, were continually pursued by a male, only in this myth, it is made clear that the man intends to rape the sisters. The ancestral sisters in this myth take it upon themselves to place power into their own hands by deciding to capture their pursuer. The sisters work together to track down the man, spy on his actions, and come up with a plan to capture him. The sisters then hide at nightfall and sing a song to the man that puts him into a deep sleep. The sisters then hit the man on the head, which causes him to go unconscious. After this, the sisters "perform debilitating acts upon their captive; they dismember his body and discard the dismembered parts, so that he will never again desire or be able to pursue women" (White & Payne 182). Once this act is done, the sisters meet a group of women and unite with them, which initiates another "dreaming" or mythic cycle (White & Payne 282).

In many of these myths discussing the sacred ancestresses of the people, it is important to point out the element of solidarity among the women of the myths, as repeatedly Aboriginal Australian myths showcase women as sisters or as part of groups to send a message about the strength women possess when they are united. The ancestral women of these myths all possess secret knowledge, whether it be about how to form landscapes, resurrect life from death, create and maintain fire, or evade pursuers. This knowledge is something that is often presented in the myths as being wisdom that primarily women possess, and this idea correlates with the Aboriginal Australian cultural belief that women indeed hold separate sacred knowledge from the wisdom men possess. This concept of "women's knowledge" also is apparent in the fact that many of these myths repeatedly showcase male/female relationships, where the women are pursued or tricked into giving up parts of their knowledge; however, Payne states that often in Aboriginal Australian myth, the females assert their independence, and thus secure their right to possess their own wisdom by outwitting or successfully fleeing from male pursuers, as occurred with the Wawalag sisters and the Seven Sisters (White & Payne 280).

As stated, there existed, and continues to exist among Aboriginal Australians, the belief that some myths, ceremonies, and sacred places should only be known to women, and likewise the same was true for men's myths, ceremonies, and sacred places. In Aboriginal Australian life, the separation of the sexes was a common occurrence in both sacred and secular circumstances, but this was not done out of sexism; instead, it was done with the realization that "each sex [was] in control of its own domain," and the domains were "interdependent and complimentary" (White & Payne 267). White and Payne explain that "Aboriginal women had a flourishing ritual life including a corpus of mythology distinct from, yet complimentary to that of Aboriginal men" (White & Payne 268). For example, in Pitjantjatjara and Warlpiri cultures of Western Australia, part of the sacred knowledge women possessed included stories connected to sacred sites that were given to them by their own "mythical ancestresses" (White & Payne 258). Hays-Gilpin also states that Aboriginal Australian women held gender specific knowledge and responsibilities (Hays-Gilpin 99). One such responsibility for Aboriginal Australian women was to "maintain the health of those living around them," as this was the "expected duty of all women who ... received ... ritual training" (White & Payne 275). Certain women, who either birthed children or who were recognized as ngankari, "women whose proven curative powers set them aside as especially effective executants of curative rites" (White & Payne 275), held a responsibility to maintain the health of the community. Illness among many Aboriginal Australians was believed to be associated with supernatural forces; therefore, the mystical powers of the ngankari were believed to be vitally important. In addition, the songs the ngankari sang when a community member was giving birth were considered highly sacred and could not be sung for any other reason. Some Aboriginal Australian women were also viewed as possessing mystical abilities to control love; this power was referred to as illpintji (White & Payne 275). Women knowledgeable in illpintji had "the power to overturn others' relationships and restore social order"; therefore, illpintji knowledge was "both highly respected and highly feared amongst women and men" (White & Payne 276). Furthermore, oftentimes it was the role of the Aboriginal Australian women to arrange marriages. Therefore, it appears evident that pre-contact Aboriginal Australian "women were as powerful in their own domain as men were in theirs" (White 267).

However, as in India, Africa, and the Americas, when Europeans began to settle in Australia in the eighteenth century, women lost a considerable part of their former roles when their religious beliefs and social systems were persecuted. Many narratives of sacred ancestresses, as well as sacred ceremonies, were abandoned as populations of Aboriginal Australians were decimated with European conquest. Thus, many of Australia's sacred myths went untold, or were vastly transformed according to Christian standards. Once again, as with Africa and the Americas, the role of women was misinterpreted by European sources, as Europeans classified Aboriginal Australian women by Western standards. Early European texts identified Aboriginal Australian women "as mere chattels of the men, and since the same reports proclaimed that Australian Aborigines were without any religion, the ritual status of women did not arise" (White & Payne 266). As discussed, many Aboriginal Australian customs, such as rituals based on "dreaming affiliation" and land ties, initiation rituals, and marriage rites, provided autonomy to Aboriginal women and displayed them often as keepers of sacred wisdom, but most of these customs were rejected by colonizers (Bell 244). Bell states that the "male bias" brought with colonization "constrained and restricted Aboriginal women, limiting them to ... [a] dishonored image" (Bell 242). Furthermore, as in India, Africa, and the Americas, European colonizers set forth social agendas that fit Western terms of civilization, which "denied legitimacy to women while according limited recognition to men in the new social order" (Bell 265). European "models of marriage and male-female relationships ... emphasize[d] dominance and control" in Australia (Bell 265). Thus, Aboriginal Australian women lost the respected, and sometimes sacred, positions they once held.

As with contemporary indigenous women within the Americas, many contemporary Aboriginal Australian women are subjects of discrimination, sexism, and violence, as the destructive legacy of colonialism lingers throughout Australia. However, many Aboriginal Australian women refused to abandon the sacred positioning they held prior to European contact. For example, "In some of the communities of the Western and Central Deserts, [Aboriginal Australian] women have clung more firmly to their old ways, so that the [traditional] ceremonies are regularly performed" (White & Payne 254), just as is seen with the maintenance of traditional customs among the South American Quechua and many other Amerindian communities. Again, hopefully the maintenance of their traditional roles regarding their high social and religious rites will allow Aboriginal Australian women to once more secure what is owed to them from their ancestral mothers and grandmothers.

## *Polynesia*

As far back as 3000 years ago, Polynesians left Taiwan and began expanding across the Pacific Ocean to Melanesia, then Fiji, Samoa, Tonga, Hawaii, the Marquesas, Easter Island, and New Zealand. The rich cultural history of Polynesia produced a mythology that was as varied as the cultures of Polynesia; however, as was the case in sub–Saharan Africa, the Americas, and Australia, Polynesia myths were not recorded until after European contact, which again compromised the integrity of the myths.

Because of the broad scope of this book, the only Polynesian mythology that is examined in this chapter is that of the Māori and Hawaiian cultures because of their abundant goddess-oriented belief systems.

## New Zealand

The Māori populated New Zealand in about 1000 CE from Eastern Polynesia. Māori religion includes a pantheon of gods and goddesses that often represent natural elements. Papatuanuku (Papa) was the Māori Mother Earth, and her husband was the sky god Rangi. The Māori creation myth shows the primordial parents, Papa and Rangi, as being separated by their children because of the couple's incessant copulation, which kept their children locked within Papa's womb. One of their children, once freed by birth, Tāne, became the main creator of life on earth. Tāne created his own wife from the soil, and the couple produced a daughter named Hine-titama. Tāne insisted on marrying Hine-titama, but to evade the shame of marrying her father, she retreated to the underworld and became Hine-nui-te-pō, the goddess of death. Hine-nui-te-pō's position as the goddess of death solidified that each earthly being had to one day succumb to death and enter her domain. Presenting both the earth and the underworld as represented by goddesses certainly shows the value the Māori held for their divine women.

Polynesian societal systems often operated upon a strict set of guidelines that ranked people according to a different status. Under this system, women were often considered inferior to men. Thus, some Māori myths do present women in inferior roles. However, similar to the division of religious and societal elements based on gender that was seen in Aboriginal Australian communities, the Māori, as well as other Polynesian cultures, also believed in the necessity of balance between the sexes, as both males and females were viewed as necessary; thus, the unification of the sexes was viewed as essential towards bringing harmony to Polynesian societies. Therefore, many Māori myths often reveal the resolution of a tension surrounding male and female roles. Often male Māori heroes appear as representations of explicit masculinity; however, it is precisely their heightened masculinity that often gets them into trouble. Therefore, it is often the female characters of Māori mythology that serve to balance the men's endeavors, so that a harmonious outcome can be achieved.

The myths surrounding the famed Polynesian hero Maui, who was heavily embraced by the Māori, offers perhaps the best mythic examples within Polynesia of an explicitly male hero needing to learn lessons from divine females in order to achieve a state of harmony. In his myths, Maui is consistently shown to jump into heroic acts using tenets that are associated in Polynesian mythology with heightened masculinity, such as his enormous strength, bravery, and willingness to act with force. However, Maui repeatedly is shown that his feats of strength and bravery alone must be balanced with concepts he learns from the many Polynesian goddesses he encounters upon his adventures. For example, Maui's mythic cycle begins with Maui's birth. His mother Taranga is a goddess associated with the underworld. Upon giving birth to Maui, who is born prematurely, Taranga discards him into the sea where he is reared by natural elements. This initial mythic scene propels Maui to serve as a hero upon a lifelong quest, because his abandonment by his mother initiates a drive in Maui to connect with his lost mother, which symbolically becomes a quest for Maui to unite with the feminine aspects of existence in order to self-actualize. Maui's mythic narrative continues to show him maturing into a man and seeking out Taranga. When he finds her, he is shown as needing to prove to her that he is indeed one of her sons. It appears that Taranga, though she says she accepts Maui as her own, really sets up a test for him. The myth continues on to show that each day Taranga leaves her home to go upon a journey. Resolved to fully understand his mother, Maui follows Taranga as she leaves one day. Maui soon learns that his divine mother journeys each day to the underworld. Once within the underworld, Maui reveals himself to his mother, who, as if she planned the whole series of events as a test, grants Maui a ritual meant to give him immortality. However, Taranga's ritual, which is performed with the help of Maui's father Makeatutara, only grants Maui partial divinity, which means that Maui is only semi-divine and will one day die.

This fact of mortality for Maui sets in motion the primary feats Maui accomplishes within his heroic adventures, as he is repeatedly shown as wrestling with the factuality of death, which again for him appears in the form of goddesses associated with the underworld, just like his mother. For instance, Maui was credited as fishing up Te Ika-a-Māui, the North Island of New Zealand, using a magic fishhook he created from the jawbone he stole from his divine grandmother Muri, who is also shown as an underworld divinity. Using deception and force, Maui stole Muri's jawbone from her, which for a time gained him heroic status, but ultimately, Maui's disregard for his underworld grandmother would catch up with him. Maui also was credited as providing fire to humankind, which he obtained again from another divine female who resided in the underworld—this time his other divine grandmother Mahuika, the goddess of fire. Again, showing still that he has not fully united with what the many underworld goddesses in his life represent, Maui disrespects the fire goddess Mahuika by again using trickery and force to steal her sacred fire.

It is Maui's final mythic act that fully allows him to learn from the underworld goddesses within his myths. Maui is shown as again transgressing the underworld in order to try and kill Hine-nui-te-pō, the Polynesian goddess of death, and thus eradicate death for all living beings. The audacity of this act solidifies that Maui, throughout all of his exploits, has not learned what the many underworld goddesses he has encountered represent—the natural necessity of death. Maui, in an explicitly masculine display, enters Hine-nui-te-pō's vagina in order to try and kill her from the inside. However, what he does not know is that Hine-nui-te-pō's vagina is "edged with flints and flash[es] like lightening" (Orbell 291). Therefore, Maui, with all of his bravado and masculine effort, is no match at all for Hine-nui-te-pō, as she simply slices him in half between her legs, killing him. Heroes are not often portrayed as being ultimately killed by goddesses within global mythology. In Greek and Mesopotamian mythology, for example, the myths that strove to impart messages of the superiority of patriarchal gods often showed male heroes killing monstrous females who were once formidable goddesses. However, in this myth from Polynesia, a culture that is often defined as extremely patriarchal, it is significant that their most revered male hero Maui is clearly being instructed to finally accept the superiority of the underworld goddesses within Polynesian religion. Many global earth goddesses, as discussed often in this book, teach male mythic characters about the necessity of nature's cycles, of which death is required, so that they may spiritually evolve. Because the revered Maui is presented as being repeatedly forced to learn this lesson from the female divinities in his mythic narratives, his myths certainly present Polynesian goddesses as deserving of the utmost respect.

A myth showcasing the Māori hero Tāwhaki and his wife Tangotango presents another good example of a myth meant to teach audiences about the respect women deserve. Tāwhaki is exemplified in many myths as the ideal Māori man. In this particular myth, Tangotango, a divine woman who came from the sky, marries Tāwhaki, and before she gives birth to their child, she tells Tāwhaki that if she gives birth to a son, she will rear him, but if the child is born a girl, she wants Tāwhaki to care for her. This request demands that the social expectation of Māori culture be reversed, as Māori men usually cared for male children, and women cared for female children. In the myth, Tangotango gives birth to a daughter, so Tāwhaki agrees to care for her, but when he is washing his daughter, he is so offended by her smell that he refuses to care for her any longer. In retaliation and "deeply offended, Tangotango snatches up the child. She stands weeping on the roof of their house, then she disappears up to the sky and does not return" (Orbell 293). Some myths of Tāwhaki show him going up to the sky realm to try and retrieve Tangotango and his daughter, but once there, he is forced to contend with his powerful divine grandmother, Whaitiri, or thunder, who "is a powerful and enigmatic figure.... [who] has control over the supply of food, especially birds and fish, which she can make plentiful or scarce" (Orbell 293). The divine Whaitiri proceeds to forcibly teach her grandson Tāwhaki to give women the respect they deserve.

This mythic tradition that shows a divine wife leaving her husband to return to her celestial realm is quite common in many cultures. For instance, in an act of resistance, the once divine swan maidens of Russian mythology similarly leave their husbands behind after being forced to endure the drudgery of the life of a housewife. Swan maiden myths, such as this Russian version, were also common in the Polynesian mythology of Melanesia. One Melanesian myth shows divine women visiting earth disguised as swans. A man spied the divine women as they removed their swan wings to bathe, and desiring them, he stole the wings of one woman. Without her wings, the divine woman was forced to marry the man, become a housewife, and raise his children. After many years, the man began to beat his wife. Distraught, the divine woman cried so often that her tears eventually washed the dirt away from the floor of her home, revealing where her husband had buried her wings. With this discovery, the divine woman adorned herself once more in her magical wings and flew away from her life of drudgery forever (Allan, Fleming, and Kerrigan 85). This Melanesian myth, like the Māori myth of Tangotango, serves to educate audiences on the need to be wary of existing patriarchal systems that may exist within Polynesian culture. Both the Melanesian swan maiden and Tangotango are disrespected by their husbands, and though they are presented as divine women, like the underworld goddesses in the myths of Maui, they are portrayed in these myths as connected to the plight of real women in Polynesian culture who may be undervalued. Thus, myths such as these taught Polynesian audiences that disrespecting any woman was similar to disrespecting a goddess, again showing the high regard often afforded to women within Polynesian belief systems.

In addition, though many Polynesian myths display male protagonists, the success of their heroic journey, like Maui's, often depends upon females. As Katharine Luomala states "'Scarcely a Polynesian hero can be found who within five minutes of a narrator's time is not being helped in an adventure and saved from failure or restored to life by his faithful and magically-skilled sister, mother, or blind old grandmother'" (qtd. in Orbell 300). Orbell concludes that often Māori men socially took for granted the "supportive, nurturing capacity" of the women around them, regarding it as "so inevitable, so 'natural'" (Orbell 300), yet, it is undeniable that Māori myths repeatedly remind these men not to forget the necessary role of women, not just as helpers upon male quests, but as those who often possess mystical or spiritual knowledge that is vital to accomplish any task of note. One such example displays a mythic male, Ngātoro-i-rangi, upon his heroic quest when he almost succumbs to death from incessant cold. It is Ngātoro-i-rangi's two sisters, Te Pupu and Te Hoata, who come to him in his time of need and warm him using their mystical knowledge of the natural world, as his sisters possess a connection with the "supernatural fire located within volcanoes and hot springs" (Orbell 302). Another Māori myth shows the male hero Rata coming to a standstill in his heroic quest, until his mother, Hine-tua-hōanga comes to his aid. Hine-tua-hōanga again possesses mystical abilities that come from her connection to nature, as her back is made of sandstone, so she is able to tell her son to sharpen his adze on her back, so he can cut down a tree to make a canoe and continue on his quest (Orbell 302).

Finally, often Māori mythology showcases mythic females who undertake their own heroic quests, which is a somewhat rare element of many global mythologies. For example, one myth of Hine-te-iwaiwa, "a very early ancestor" of the Māori, shows her mythically undertaking a long and arduous journey in order to find a man she wished to marry—Tinirau, "ruler of all the fish in the ocean" (Orbell 294). To find this coveted husband, Hine-te-iwaiwa had to travel to Motu-tapu, Sacred Island. Indeed Hine-te-iwaiwa successfully arrived on Motu-tapu, and once there, she used powerful magic to get rid of Tinirau's existing wives, turning them into jade, and thus gaining the prized husband she desired. In Māori culture, there are multiple legends that show a female character setting out on a "secret, difficult journey, alone or with a single servant" (Orbell 299). It is significant that these types of myths are prized within Māori culture, as it shows a respect for women who carve their own way. Orbell concurs, stating that within Māori culture, "We can at least conclude that the idea of a woman asserting her independence and determining her own future was an attractive one: to women clearly, but also, judging from the popularity of these stories, to men as well" (Orbell 299).

Because of the reverence paid to powerful goddesses, as well as respected mythic women in Māori mythology, Māori women held important roles within their communities. Again, though Māori culture was patriarchal, there still existed social and religious positions of respect that showed a cultural veneration of Māori women. For example, women of rank within Māori culture could act as a *"ruahine ... who in religious ritual removed an excess of tapu, or sacredness.... Women, being essentially noa, or everyday/profane, had the power of removing tapu when this had become necessary, and they took part, therefore, in many rituals"* (Orball 297). In addition, because women were attributed as the ones who first introduced some staple crops to the people, such as the "highly prized kumara, or sweet potato," Māori women often held the honorable position of being responsible for maintaining the cultivation of the people's staple crops (Orbell 297).

However, like other locations that came under colonial rule, the Māori of New Zealand lost considerable reverence for their divine and human women as a result of European indoctrination. Europeans arrived in New Zealand in the eighteenth century, and as they had done elsewhere, their introduction of diseases, enforced economic, social, political, and legal restrictions, and monotheistic religion decimated the traditional belief systems of the existing populations of New Zealand. Because the traditional views of the Māori largely became compromised under European rule, esteemed social and religious roles for Māori women were mostly obliterated for a time when the Māori population decreased to alarming numbers.

Many Māori, though, were able to preserve key elements of their traditional beliefs, and though Māori women today encounter rampant discrimination and gender inequality, once more it is sincerely hoped that the high positions Māori goddesses and women once held will carry over into securing a heightened future for contemporary Māori women.

## Hawaii

It is believed that Polynesians arrived in Hawaii about 1500 years ago. Much of their religious beliefs carry similar tenets as found in greater Polynesian mythology, such as mythological concepts of the Māori. For example, Hawaiian religion also envisions that the universe is divided between male and female forces. Diab states that "The acceptance of this essential male and female duality is applied to all aspects of the universe" (Diab 308). For instance, the Hawaiian male and female creator deities, Ku and Hina, are equally matched.

In general, Polynesian mythology, and especially Hawaiian mythology, identifies the goddess Hina as central to creation. Ka'ili states that the goddess Hina "is one of the oldest ... [and] most widely known [deities] throughout Polynesia.... Hina is closely linked to the moon, ocean, sea creatures (particularly sharks, corals, and spiny creatures), tapa making, mat weaving, coconut, breadfruit, and beauty" (Ka'ili). Many goddesses are attributed as holding the name Hina in Polynesian mythology, such as: Hina, the woman of Lalo-Hana, who was said to have "left her home at the bottom of the sea and lived with chief Koni-konia" (Diab 309); Hina-a-ke-ahi, who was responsible for giving fresh spring water to the first people; Hina-puku-iʻa, the goddess of fishermen; and

Hina-hanaia-i-ka-malma, the goddess of the moon. It is not always clear which Hina is being referred to within various mythological narratives, as often separate goddesses are referred to as simply Hina; this connection in name signals the unification of these separate goddesses with the central concept of Hina as a Mother Goddess figure. Hina is often portrayed as paired with male gods to create a state of balance and harmony. In her myths, she often appears as powerful as any male deity or mythic figure.

In Hawaiian mythology, Hina is often paired with the revered Polynesian hero Maui, who was discussed in the previous section on Māori mythology. In Hawaiian mythology, Hina mythically appears as: Maui's grandmother, identified as Hina; his mother, also identified as Hina; his wife, Hina; his sister, Hina, or even as an animal, and in these roles, she is portrayed as being "the supreme source of Māui's mana, supernatural power" (Kaʻili). For instance, it is Maui's sister, Hina, who gives him her hair to help him ensnare the sun to aid humanity in lengthening the duration of the days. Maui's wife, Hina, appears in Hawaiian mythology most often in a myth that associates her with Tuna-roa, a giant eel, who tried to have sex with Hina. Hina told Maui about the eel's indiscretions, and Maui proceeded to butcher Tuna-roa when he found him, by decapitating him and cutting up the pieces of his body, which grew to become some of the staple foods of the Hawaiians. In a version of this myth from Tahiti, Tuna-roa is Te Tuna, who is initially married to Hina. To win Hina, Maui also kills Te Tuna, which produces the first coconuts. The myths that show Maui connected with Hina present them as complimentary male and female forces. Hina, as a unified goddess symbol, and Maui, as the quintessential male hero, represent the necessary unification of the sexes often displayed in Hawaiian, and greater Polynesian, mythology.

Another Hawaiian myth of Hina, portrayed as Hina-hanaia-i-ka-malma, first portrays her as a mortal woman. Her myth shows her as enjoying motherhood, but as her children grew and left home, she found herself extremely unhappy with an abusive husband who demanded that she work night and day. Hina prayed for release from her unhappy life. One day, a rainbow heard her pleas. The rainbow placed itself in front of Hina, and immediately trusting this natural element, Hina climbed up the rainbow. However, as Hina climbed, she found that the intensity of the sun's heat was too much for her, so she was forced to slide down and go back to her unhappy life. But, that night, as Hina listened to the insults of her husband, she resolved again to find a way to traverse to the heavens now that the rainbow had shown her this possibility. Hina went outside, and saw, that though it was dark, the rainbow was impossibly still there waiting for her. Hina saw that without the sun's heat, she could now climb the rainbow to the moon. Hina's husband awoke and saw his wife begin to climb the rainbow, so he ran after her and pulled hard upon her foot, trying to drag her back down to earth with him. Hina's husband pulled so hard that he broke every bone in Hina's foot. However, when he saw that Hina held fast to the rainbow, though she was in intense pain, he finally let go of her forever. Though she was in agony, Hina still trudged up the rainbow, asking for assistance from the stars. The heavens helped her, and Hina finally reached the moon, where she is said to reside to this day as the moon goddess, serving as a guide and protector of the Hawaiian people because she once learned about the hardships humans, particularly women, often face. Again, similar to the Māori myths that displayed a commiseration for undervalued women, the fact that the Hawaiian people revere a myth such as this, that displays the plight of mistreated women, also shows their commiseration for goddesses and women alike who do not receive the respect they deserve.

In addition, the Hawaiian goddess Haumea also holds a central position in Hawaiian mythology. Haumea is the "patroness of childbirth"; she is also "associated with the establishment of food supplies, and is thus regarded as a goddess of fertility" (Diab 310). Often the goddess Haumea is attributed as aiding in the creation and "continuation of the human race" (Diab 310). Furthermore, Haumea is also often referenced as an "Earth Mother figure" (Diab 310). In this role, she is able to transform from a beautiful maiden to an old woman, as she presides over the cycles of nature.

The Hawaiian goddess Pele, the goddess of the volcano, is also a central Hawaiian divinity. Portrayed mythically as a volcano, Pele is easily associated as a nature goddess. Pele is responsible for creating the islands of Hawaii, but also she is capable of destroying the islands whenever she pleases. Pele, like the goddess Haumea and other nature goddesses, is also able to easily transform into other guises besides that of just a volcano; for instance, she can appear as a young or an old woman. One Hawaiian myth of Pele shows her adopting the form of a young maiden when she spied a handsome prince named Lohiau. Upon seeing Pele, Lohiau at once fell in love with her, and the pair were married. However, Pele, once married, decided that she had to return to her position as the goddess of volcanoes, so she left Lohiau. Distraught by his wife's disappearance, Lohiau died of grief. Pele's mythic abandonment of Lohiau marks her as holding a high degree of independence and responsibility. However, the myth continues on to show that after some time had passed, Pele began to unexpectedly miss Lohiau, so she asked her divine sister, Hiiaká, to find him. Hiiaká soon discovered that Lohiau had died, so she went to the underworld to retrieve him, but when Hiiaká saw Lohiau for the first time, she too instantly fell in love with him. So, Hiiaká helped Lohiau leave the underworld, resurrecting him, and the two, now in love with each other, presented themselves to Pele. Pele, seeing her sister's and her husband's betrayal, killed Lohiau again by burning him to ashes. Showing her true love for Lohiau, Hiiaká decided to live forever within the underworld, so that she could be with Lohiau. Seeing Hiiaká's love for Lohiau, Pele resurrected both Lohiau and Hiiaká and allowed them to live together on earth. This myth certainly shows Pele in a powerful light. Her earth goddess imagery shows her as easily capable of controlling the landscape and its elements, but she also is portrayed, along with her divine sister, Hiiaká, as possessing the ability to both take and create life anew, showing the goddess Pele as holding a highly revered place in the Hawaiian pantheon.

Because of the reverence Hawaiians devoted to their goddesses, Hawaiian women were also able to hold high social and religious positions. For instance, female priestesses who worshipped the goddess Pele, known as kahunas, were considered to be of the "highest rank" (Diab 326). In addition, Hawaiian women in general were often viewed as particularly adept at being prophets or seers, identified as kaula, because of their connections to Hawaii's revered goddesses (Nelson 8). In addition, there were also "politically powerful women" in Hawaii (Diab 326), many of whom were Hawaiian queens, who held "privileged connections to the sacred" that influenced their ability to reign successfully (Nelson 8). There are also records of Hawaiian female warriors, who "expected and were accorded no consideration because of their sex" (Diab 326). In addition, ideals of female beauty for Hawaiians incorporated "size and strength" (Diab 326), as Hawaiian women were "powerful swimmers, surfers and climbers, just as the men were.... [Thus,] feats of athleticism, exhibiting strength and stamina, would present no threat to ... femininity" (Diab 326). The history of surfing in Hawaii also shows the high regard for Hawaiian women. Surfing was an integral aspect of Hawaiian life before European colonization. Hawaiian goddesses and divine women, such as Hiiaká, Pele's sister, and Mamala, a divine shapeshifter, were noted surfers, who used surfing for mystical purposes, such as healing the ill. Following in the footsteps of these adept divine surfers, Hawaiian women were held "in the highest regard for their skill, grace and poise as surfers" (Hill). Hawaiian legends abound of skilled female surfers, such as the chiefess Punahoa, whose surfing abilities were often challenged by men, but never overcome, and Princess Kelea, who in 1445 "was known as the best surfer on Maui" (Hill). However, when Europeans entered Hawaii, "notions of religiosity and ... rigid gender divisions" made surfing an "endeavor only for men" (Hill).

Once again, as occurred in so many regions around the world, the arrival of the Europeans, and their monotheistic conceptions of divinity, decimated much of the existing cultural, social, and religious beliefs of the Hawaiian people. Thousands of native Hawaiians died as a result of the introduction of disease brought by Europeans, and the economic and social upheaval of colonization destroyed long-held traditions in almost every arena of Hawaiian culture. The introduction and enforced indoctrination of Christianity assaulted beliefs surrounding the worship of goddesses. European models for the rights of women also stripped many Hawaiian women from holding their former respected religious and social roles. Therefore, Hawaiian women, like the women of many other colonized areas, often became identified as inferior citizens who were to be positioned under the guidance of male authority according to European standards.

Because of this assault on the traditional culture of Hawaii, Hawaiian women in contemporary times still struggle with the long-term effects of colonization, as many native Hawaiian women today experience widespread instances of poverty and gender inequality. However, as was seen in Australia and New Zealand, many Hawaiians today combat the inequalities they face under a European/American model of society by embracing the belief systems of their ancestors. As seen with many other cultures discussed in this book, the traditional beliefs of the Hawaiians, though almost destroyed, did indeed survive through the insistence on the part of many Hawaiian people to maintain their old ways. For instance, a cultural legend exists in Hawaii that shows an exemplary case of the maintenance of goddess worship in Hawaii among the people. When Christianity arrived to Hawaii, it discouraged, and later outlawed, the reverence for Hawaiian goddesses, such as Pele, by identifying them as pagan and even evil. However, when the volcano Mauna Loa erupted in 1880, legend states that the Princess Ruth Keelikolanin walked up to the edge of the lava flow and recited the chants that the priestesses of Pele used to recite, while offering gifts of silk and brandy to Pele (Stone 164). The legend proclaims that the volcano's eruptions ceased the next day, saving the town of Hilo (Stone 164). Because of the perseverance of traditional beliefs by people like Princess Ruth Keelikolanin, many Hawaiians still openly revere Pele, regularly leaving her offerings to ask her to spare their cities. Contemporary Hawaiians additionally maintain the reverence of their other traditional divine beings and continue to venerate the landscape of Hawaii as sacred. It is arguably the maintenance of these beliefs, that honor both males and females as spiritually vital, that will allow native Hawaiians to once more find the rich life presented to them by their ancestors.

# Conclusion

Women should be outraged that even in contemporary times female political leaders around the globe are few and far between, just as they should be equally outraged that religious officials in many of the world's most cherished religions still do not permit women to hold leadership positions. Sexism still exists in innumerable instances throughout the world; sexual harassment, domestic violence, unequal pay, inequality in leadership positions, etc., are sadly common issues global women must face in most global cultures. Of course, these gender-related issues do not stem from only the fact that divinity and/or heightened spirituality around the world is most often perceived in male forms, but as this book has argued, in order for society to more readily accept women as equals, as deserving of elevated social and religious roles, they must be able to envision the highest conceptions of spirituality as both male and female.

As shown throughout this book, the conception of a sole male God or supreme male deities "reflects and strengthens patriarchy" (Sered 172). For example, Mary Daly argues that the conception in many religions of a monotheistic God, or superior god or gods in polytheistic pantheons, as male, has often historically made "'the oppression of women appear right and fitting. If God in 'his' heaven is a father ruling 'his' people, then it is ... according to divine plan ... that society be male-dominated'" (qtd. by Sered 172). Thus, as stated repeatedly in this book, because of the creation and propagation of multiple world religions and philosophies that worship one male God, primarily male gods, and/or view spirituality as mostly attained by males, women throughout history have been pushed "into an inferior and marginal position, excluding them from full participation in the social, cultural, and religious life of the community" (Armstrong, vii).

In many global regions, the status of women both in religious and social spheres has begun to improve in contemporary times. Many women have rebelled against the restrictions placed on them by patriarchal religions. For example, women "have been ordained as rabbis, ministers, and priests. They have written theological and legal works to contest a hitherto unchallenged male supremacy" (Armstrong vii). Likewise, "feminist theologians are trying to transform monotheistic traditions that they do not want to leave by reviving, importing, and inventing goddesses, female aspects of the deity, and female imagery" (Stuckey 211). But sadly, some religious officials view this feminist revision to their religion as sacrilege and "have often tried to put women back in their old marginal place" (Armstrong x). For example, Armstrong states that in Judaism, Christianity, and Islam, "the more conservative believers have responded to the emancipation of women in modern culture by over-stressing traditional restrictions. Haredi Jews have been known to attack members of their ultra-orthodox community who allow their wives and daughters to infringe the strict dress code.... In some Muslim circles, the veiled woman has become a sign of the integrity of Islam; and in the United States, Protestant fundamentalists ... see feminism as one of the great evils of our time" (Armstrong x). Even more disturbing, Keller discusses that according to "anthropological data collected on 156 societies worldwide" a correlation exists in these societies "between exclusive male gods and violence against women" (Keller 234). In contrast to this, "in cultures ... [that] worshipped a female deity or equal female and male deities as creator gods ... physical abuse and rape were infrequent" (Keller 234). Therefore, Keller succinctly states that "when ultimate divinity is ascribed" absolutely or even predominantly "to one gender ... then this is a problem for persons of all genders" (Keller 234).

To move forward towards equality, societies must begin to imagine spiritual conceptions and/or deities that represent both sexes and are "equally accessible to all" (Gerstenberger 110). This revising of religion and/or spirituality is imperative for women to reach their spiritual potential, as a society "that chooses a gender-balanced religion would likely be one to accord equal respect and sacredness to women and men, girls and boys, both within the domestic as well as the public spheres" (Keller 235).

But in the meantime, women cannot necessarily wait for widespread change to happen regarding the social transformation of conceptions of divinity and spirituality. Instead, today, individual girls and women must choose for themselves how to envision divinity and/or sacrality. Individual reconsideration of what we have been taught as children, what is predominantly projected socially, and what is ordained in religious settings is paramount towards finding a divine and/or sacred representation within oneself that fits the nuances of what it is to be a woman.

Today, there exists many alternatives to practicing monotheism or polytheistic faiths dominated by male gods. For instance, many contemporary religions exist that are female-centered, such as within the Ryūkyūan cultures of Japan, the Sande of West Africa, and the matrilineal groups of

Northern Thailand. Sered notes that among many female-centered religions, differences appear between them and the dominant patriarchal religions embraced around the world, and it is these differences that present new spiritual options to many women when choosing their own beliefs today. For example, many female-centered religions embrace the sacred nature of motherhood; "Through ritual and theology, female-dominated religions enhance, dramatize, and strengthen women's identities as mothers" (Sered 73). In addition, many female-centered religions tend to focus on elements of healing; women as mothers are often concerned with children's health as "domestic healers"; therefore, "In women's religions, this informal role is enhanced and formalized" (Sered 103). Women's experiences often focus more on the importance of relationships; thus, this is also often incorporated into women's religions, as they "tend to have an interpersonal rather than an individualistic orientation. Women-centered religions rarely include hermits or yogis dwelling in mystical isolation…. Far more typical of female-dominated religions are rituals and belief systems well designed to strengthen bonds among people" (Sered 121). Also, Sered explains that "Women's religions, on the whole, do not emphasize compliance to one specific set of doctrines"; in fact, many of these female-centered religions are "internally eclectic, easily and consciously absorbing new ideas or deities" (Sered 243). Women-centered religions also tend to focus on present reality instead of on an afterlife; "the focus is so much on the here and now that there is almost no elaboration of creation stories or end-of-the-days scenarios" (Sered 145). In fact, in many women-centered religions around the world, "devotees learn to make profane experiences sacred, to enhance the quality of their current lives, to comprehend the supernatural already present within the natural world, and to invite the divine into their lives or even into their own bodies" (Sered 145). For example, "Northern Thai matrilineal spirit cults are entirely focused on this world" (Sered 146), and the Ryūkyūan of Japan emphasize the sacrality of the present moment rather than "metaphysical speculation" (Sered 146). In addition, within Korean shamanism, known for possessing a strong female focus, concepts such as heaven or hell are not of value; "there is no good or bad place to go after death, there is no reward or punishment for souls based on what they did in this life, and there is no notion or rebirth of the soul…. Korean shamanism is totally this-worldly in its affirmation of the importance of living and life in this world" (Sered 146). Furthermore, many women-centered religions revere the natural world, and the spirits that they often believe reside within nature, over worshipping abstract concepts of a universal deity. For example, the Ryūkyūan revere kami within the natural world; the matrilineal clans of Northern Thailand also worship the spirits of nature all around them. Finally, and very significantly, often it is women who hold positions of spiritual authority in women-centered religions.

Today, outside of organized religion, there also exists much focus on worshipping conceptions, either ancient or contemporary, of goddesses. Goddess-centered belief systems, like Feminist Goddess Worship, Wicca, etc., have expanded in contemporary times. Stuckey states that contemporary goddess worship "is very empowering to women" (Stuckey 176), as worshipping goddesses allows many women to easily conceive of themselves as tied to divinity and spirituality, as they of course share the same form. Worshipping goddesses also allows women to often connect more readily to the cycles of nature, as many goddesses throughout history, and today in modern Wicca for instance, are personified forms of the environment and its occurrences. Finally, worshipping goddesses in contemporary times can empower women to embrace the concept that women's bodies and regenerative powers are sacred (Stuckey 176), just as they are portrayed in their goddess representatives.

Also, one need not ascribe to any religion at all to still embrace a powerful sense of female spirituality. There are innumerable paths to spirituality around the world, each as individualized as each person on the planet. Many people individually choose to envision divinity in a form that holds meaning for them personally. For example, often divinity is conceived of as not encumbered by human traits, such as gender, emotion, etc. Many people instead choose to view divinity as an unfathomable force that may or may not be concerned with human affairs. Others envision divinity or spiritual concepts as concretely tied to the natural world, where again human conceptualizations and limitations are irrelevant.

Regardless of the religious or spiritual path one chooses, women today must arguably learn the truth about what their own ancestors once believed. Women today must know that in almost every region around the world, goddesses once reigned as powerful, formidable figures. Women should also know that because societies worshipped strong female divinities, they often easily accepted women in central religious and social roles. Women should readily know that their female ancestors were warriors, priestesses, healers, social leaders, and queens. When women learn about divine women who were readily worshipped and human women who led their communities, perhaps they will go on to teach their children, friends, partners, and communities about these historical women, so that the rights of women within society will once again reach the heights they were meant to reach. But more importantly, when women remember that since the beginning of human history, conceptions of divinity matched their own form, then they will reignite a very old reserve of peace and fulfillment within themselves, as they remember the sacrality that has always lied within them.

# Bibliography

Adovasio, J.M., Olga Soffer, and Jake Page. *The Invisible Sex: Uncovering the True Roles of Women in Pre-history*. New York: HarperCollins, 2007.

Aeschylus. *Eumenides* (458 BCE). Trans. by E.D.A. Morshead. Web. March 31, 2022.

Aiko, Ōgoshi. "Women and Sexism in Japanese Buddhism: A Reexamination of Shinran's View of Women." *Japan Christian Review*, 59. 1993. 19–25.

Akka Mahadevi. "I Have Fallen in Love." *Poem Hunters*. Web. Retrieved February 24, 2021.

al-Fassi, Hatoon. "Women in Pre-Islamic Arabia: Nabataea." *British Archaeological Reports International Series*, 2007.

Allan, Tony, and Charles Phillips. *Chinese Myth: Land of the Dragon*. London: Duncan Baird, 1999, 44–5.

Allan, Tony, Charles Phillips, and Michael Kerrigan. *Persian Myth: Wise Lord of the Sky*. London: Duncan Baird, 1999, 122–3.

Allan, Tony, Clifford Bishop, and Charles Phillips. *Medieval Myth: Legends of Chivalry*. London: Duncan Baird, 2000, 66–7.

Allan, Tony, Fergus Fleming, and Charles Phillips. *African Myth: Voices of the Ancestors*. London: Duncan Baird, 1999.

Allan, Tony, Fergus Fleming, and Michael Kerrigan. *Oceanian Myth: Journeys Through Dreamtime*. London: Duncan Barid, 1999.

Allan, Tony, Michael Kerrigan, and Charles Phillips. *Japanese Myth: Realm of the Rising Sun*. London: Duncan Baird, 2000.

Andersen, Johannes C. *Myths and Legends of the Polynesians* (1928). New York: Dover, 1995.

Anthony, David W. *The Horse, the Wheel, and Language: How Bronze-Age Riders from the Eurasian Steppes Shaped the Modern World*. Princeton UP, 2010.

Aoki, Michiko Y. "Women in Ancient Japan." *Women's Roles in Ancient Civilizations*. Edited by Bella Vivante. Westwood, CT: Greenwood Press, 1999, 63–84.

Apuleius. *The Golden Ass*. Trans. by E.J. Kenney. New York: Penguin, 1998.

Armstrong, Karen. "Introduction." *Daughters of Abraham: Feminist Thought in Judaism, Christianity and Islam*. Gainesville, FL: UP of Florida, 2001, vii–xiii.

Asbjørnsen, Peter Christen, and Jørgen Moe. "East of the Sun and West of the Moon." https://www.pitt.edu/~dash/norway034.html. Accessed on May 13, 2019.

Bacus, Elisabeth A. "Gender in East and Southeast Asian Archeology." *Worlds of Gender: The Archeology of Women's Lives Around the Globe*. Ed. by Sarah Milledge Nelson. Lanham, MD: Altamira Press, 2007, 39–72.

Baring, Anne, and Jules Cashford. *The Myth of the Goddess: Evolution of an Image*. London: Penguin, 1993.

Barnes, Craig S. *In Search of the Lost Feminine: Decoding the Myths That Radically Reshaped Civilization*. Golden, CO: Folcrum Publishing, 2006.

Bastian, Dawn, and Judy Mitchell. *Handbook of Native American Mythology*. Oxford: Oxford UP, 2008.

Bell, Diane. "Choices in the 'Marriage Market.'" *Women and Colonization: Anthropological Perspectives*. Edited by Mona Etienne and Eleanor Leacock. New York: Bergin & Garvey, 1980, 239–69.

*Beowulf.* Trans. by Kevin Crossley-Holland. Suffolk: Phobe Phillips Edition, 1987.
Bhattacharjee, Debanjali. "Hinduism and Women: Glimpses from a Feminist Perspective." Web. Retrieved February 21, 2021.
Bierhorst, John. *The Mythology of South America.* William Marrow and Co. Inc., 1988.
Birkhäuser-Oeri, Sibylle. *The Mother: Archetypal Image in Fairy Tales.* Edited by Marie-Louise Von Franz. Trans. by Michael Mitchell. Toronto: Inner City Books, 1988.
Borgeaud, Philippe. *Mother of the Gods: From Cybele to the Virgin Mary.* Translated by Lysa Hochroth. Baltimore: Johns Hopkins UP, 1996.
Brintnall, Kent L. "Gender and Mesoamericans Religions." *Religion: Embodied Religion.* Farmington Hills: Gale, Cengage Learning, 2016.
Bruhns, Karen Olsen and Karen E. Stothert. *Women in Ancient America.* Norman: U of Oklahoma P, 1999.
Burkert, Walter. *Greek Religion* (1977). Boston: Harvard UP, 1985.
Caldecott, Moyra. *Women in Celtic Myth: Tales of Extraordinary Women from the Ancient Celtic Tradition.* Rochester, VT: Destiny Books, 1988.
Campbell, Joseph. *Goddesses: Mysteries of the Feminine Divine.* Edited by Safron Rossi. Novato, CA: New World Library, 2013.
Carey, Nick. "Czechs in History." *Radio Prague International,* March 21, 2001. Web. Retrieved 17, 2021.
Cauvin, Jacques. *The Birth of the Gods and the Origins of Agriculture.* Trans. by Trevor Watkins. Cambridge: Cambridge UP, 2000.
Chu, Nan. "Goddess Chang E Ascends to the Moon." *Women in Chinese Folklore.* Beijing: China Publications Centre, 1983, 61–8.
Clark, Christine G. "Women's Right in Early England." *BYU Review,* Vol. 1995, Issue 1, 206–36.
Cole, Joanna, Ed. *Best Loved Folktales from Around the World.* New York: Anchor Books, 1982.
Conway, John. "The Significance of the Bull in the Minoan Religion." Synonym. Web. Retrieved March 31, 2022.
Cooney, Kara. *The Woman Who Be King.* New York: Crown Publishers, 2014.
Crawford, Jane. "Cartimandua, Boudicca, and Rebellion: British Queens and Roman Colonial Views." *Women and the Colonial Gaze.* Edited by Tamara L. Hunt and Micheline R. Lessard. New York: New York UP, 2002, 17–28.
Cross, Robin and Rosalind Miles. *Warrior Women: Years of Courage and Heroism.* New York: Metro Books, 2011.
Datta, Saurav Ranjan. "Remembering Brave Indian Queens: 10 Powerhouses History Has Forgotten." *Ancient Origins.* April 16, 2020. Web. Retrieved February 23, 2021.
Davis-Kimball, Jeannine. "Nomads and Patriarchy." *The Rule of Mars: Readings and Origins, History and Impact of Patriarchy.* Manchester, CT: Knowledge, Ideas, and Trends Publishers, 2005, 127–142.
_____. *Warrior Women: An Archeologist's Search for History's Hidden Heroines.* New York: Warner Books, 2002.
*Devi-Bhagavata Purana.* Trans. by Swami Vijñanananda 1921. *Wisdom Library.* Web. Retrieved February 25, 2022.
Diab, Elizabeth. "Hawaii." *The Feminist Companion to Mythology.* Edited by Carolyne Larrington. London: Pandora Press, 1992, 305–32.
Diop, Cheikh Anta. *The Cultural Unity of Black Africa: The Domains of Matriarchy and Patriarchy in Classical Antiquity.* London: Karnak House, 1989.
Diop, Ismahan Soukeyna. *African Mythology, Femineity, and Maternity.* Cham, Switzerland: Palgrave Macmillan, 2019.
Dixson, Alan F. and Barnaby J. Dixson. "Venus Figurines of the European Paleolithic: Symbols of Fertility or Attractiveness?" *Hindawi: Journal of Anthropology,* Jan. 3, 2012. Retrieved September 18, 2020, from Hindawi.com.
Dominguez, Diana. *Historical Residues in the Old Irish Legends of Queen Medb: An Expanded Interpretation of the Ulster Cycle.* Lewiston: Edwin Mellen Press, 2010.
Dooley, Ann. *Playing the Hero: Reading the Irish Saga Táin.* Toronto: U of Toronto P, 2006.
Earthist, Jassy Watson. "Anjea: A Prayer in Paint for the Protection of This Sacred Land." *Feminism and Religion,* June 5, 2015. Web. Retrieved April 1, 2022.

Egeler, Matthias. *Celtic Influences in Germanic Religion*. Munchen: Utz, 2013.
Eisler, Riane. *The Chalice and the Blade: Our History, Our Future*. San Francisco: Harper and Row, 1987.
Ellis-Davidson, H.R. *Gods and Myths of Northern Europe* [1964]. New York: Penguin, 1988.
"Empress Wu Zetain." *Female Heroes of Asia: China*. Web. Retrieved April 14, 2021.
"Ending Violence Against Native Women." *Indian Law Resource Center*. Web. Retrieved 4, 2021.
Esposito, John. L. "Introduction: Women, Religion, and Empowerment." *Daughters of Abraham: Feminist Thought in Judaism, Christianity, and Islam*. Gainesville: UP of Florida, 2001, vii-xiii.
Etienne, Mona and Eleanor, Leacock. *Women and Colonization: Anthropological Perspectives*. New York: Bergin & Garvey, 1980.
*European Union External Action Service 2011-2021*. Web. Retrieved March 21, 2022.
Fernyhough, Timothy, and Anna Fwernyhough. "Women, Gender History, and Imperial Ethiopia." *Women and the Colonial Gaze*. Edited by Tamara L. Hunt and Micheline R. Lessard. New York: New York UP, 2002, 188-201.
Fishman, Laura. "French Views of Native American Women in the Early Modern Era: The Tupinamba of Brazil." *Women and the Colonial Gaze*. Edited by Tamara L. Hunt and Micheline R. Lessard. New York: New York UP, 2002, 65-78.
Fox, Mary Jo Tippeconnic. "Women in Ancient North America." *Women's Roles in Ancient Civilizations*. Edited by Bella Vivante. Westwood, CT: Greenwood Press, 1999, 339-362.
Frankel, Valerie Estelle. *From Girl to Goddess: The Heroine's Journey Through Myth and Legend*. Jefferson, NC: McFarland, 2010.
Frothingham, A.L. "Medusa, Apollo, and the Great Mother." *American Journal of Archeology 15* (3) (July 1911), pp. 349-77.
Gerstenberger, Erhard S. *Yahweh the Patriarch: Ancient Images of God and Feminist Theology*. Minneapolis: Fortress Press, 1996.

Gimbutas, Marija. Dexter, Miriam Robbins; Jones-Bley, Karlene (eds.). *The Kurgan Culture and the Indo-Europeanization of Europe: Selected Articles from 1952 to 1993*. Washington, D.C.: Institute for the Study of Man, 1997.
Goodison, Lucy & Christine, Morris. "Beyond the Great Mother: The Sacred World of the Minoans." *Ancient Goddesses*. Editors Lucy Goodison & Christine Morris. Madison: U or Wisconsin P, 1998, 113-32.
Grammatikakis, Ioannis Emm. "The Woman in Minoic Crete." *National Library of Medicine*, Jul 24(7). 968-72. Web. doi: 10.3109/14767058.2010.531328. Epub 2010 Dec 1.
"Grandmother Mago." *Encyclopedias of Korean Folk Culture*. Web. Retrieved April 20, 2021.
Gräslund, Anne-Sofie. "The Position of Iron Age Scandinavian Women: Evidence from Graves and Rune Stones." *Gender and the Archeology of Death*. Edited by Bettina Arnold and Nancy L. Wicker. Lanham, MD: Altamira Press, 2001, 81-102.
Green, Miranda J. "Some Gallo-British Goddesses: Iconography and Meaning." *Ancient Goddesses*. Editors Lucy Goodison & Christine Morris. Madison: U of Wisconsin P, 1998, 180-96.
Grimm, Jacob and Wilhelm Grimm. *The Complete First Edition: The Original Folk and Fairy Tales of the Brothers Grimm*. Trans. and Ed. by Jack Zipes. Princeton: Princeton and Oxford UP, 2014.
Gross, Rita M. *Buddhism After Patriarchy: A Feminist History, Analysis, and Reconstruction of Buddhism*. New York: State University of New York Press, 1993.
Gruber, Mayer I. "Women in the Ancient Levant." *Women's Roles in Ancient Civilizations*. Edited by Bella Vivante. Westwood, CT: Greenwood Press, 1999, 115-154.
Grumet, Robert Steven. "Sunksquaws, Shamans, and Tradeswomen: Middle Atlantic Coastal Algonkian Women During the 17th and 18th Centuries." *Women and Colonization: Anthropological Perspectives*. Edited by Mona Etienne and Eleanor Leacock. New York: Bergin & Garvey, 1980, 43-62.

Gupto, Arun. *Goddesses of Kathmandu Valley: Grace, Rage, and Knowledge.* New York: Routledge, 2016.

Haarmann, Harald. "Why Did Patriarchy Supersede Egalitarianism?" *The Rule of Mars: Readings and Origins, History and Impact of Patriarchy.* Manchester, CT: Knowledge, Ideas, and Trends Publishers, 2005, 163–74.

Hallett, Judith P. "Women in the Ancient Roman World." *Women's Roles in Ancient Civilizations.* Edited by Bella Vivante. Westwood, CT: Greenwood Press, 1999, 257–292.

Harvey, Penelope. "South America: The Interpretation of Myth." *The Feminist Companion to Mythology.* Edited by Caolyne Larrington. London: Pandora Press, 1992, 388–410.

Hassan, Fekri A. "The Earliest Goddesses of Egypt: Divine Mothers and Cosmic Bodies." *Ancient Goddesses.* Editors Lucy Goodison & Christine Morris. Madison: U of Wisconsin P, 1998, 98–122.

Hay, Maciamo. "5000 Years of Migrations from the Eurasian Steppes to Europe." *Eupedia.* 2018. Web. Retrieved October 29, 2019.

Hays-Gilpin, Kelley A. *Ambiguous Images: Gender and Rock Art.* Lanham, MD: Altamira Press, 2004.

Hazra, Nivedita. "Rudrama Devi: The Queen Who Wore a King's Image." *Feminism in India.* Nov. 8, 2019. Web. Retrieved February 25, 2022.

Hedman, Hanna. "Hindu Goddesses as Role Models for Women? a Qualitative Study of Some Middle Class Women's Views on Being a Woman in the Hindu Society." *Institutionen För Humaniora Och Samhällsvetenskap.* June 2007. Web. Retrieved February 17, 2021.

Hewitt, J.N.B. *Iroquoian Cosmology.* Sacred Texts. Web; Joseph Bruchac. *Native Plant Stories.* Golden, CO: Fulcrum Publishing, 1995, 8–10.

Hill, Lauren L. "The Abundant Roots of Women Surfing: Hawaiian Medicine Women, Goddesses, & Polynesian Royalty." From: *She Surf: The Rise of Female Surfing.* New York: Gesalten, 2020. Web. Retrieved March 30, 2022.

Hodges, Kate. *Warriors, Witches, Women: Mythology's Fiercest Females.* London: White Lion Publishing, 2020.

Hollimon, Sandra E. "Warfare and Gender in the Northern Plains: Osteological Evidence of Trauma Reconsidered." *Gender and the Archeology of Death.* Edited by Bettina Arnold and Nancy L. Wicker. Lanham, MD: Altamira Press, 2001, 179–93.

Hollman, Gemma. "Royal Witches: From Joan of Navarre to Elizabeth Woodville." *The History Press.* October 2019. Retrieved September 17, 2020, from historyextra.com.

Hubbs, Joanna. *Mother Russia: The Feminine Myth in Russian Culture.* Bloomington: Indiana UP, 1988.

Humphrey, Cheryl. The Haunted Garden. New York: Self-Published, 2012, 63–6.

Hunt, Tamara L. "Introduction." *Women and the Colonial Gaze.* Edited by Tamara L. Hunt and Micheline R. Lessard. New York: New York UP, 2002, 1–14.

"Hymn CXXV. Vak." *Hymns of the Rig Veda.* Trans. By Ralp T.H. Griffith. 1896. Sanskirt Web. Web. Retrieved February 17, 2021.

"Indo-European Migrations Explained." Retrieved October 31, 2019, from Everythingexplainedtoday.com.

Jackson, Guida M. *Women Who Ruled.* Oxford, Clio Press, 1990.

Jacobsh. Deborah. "Bhakti Women and Poetry." Jan. 29, 2017. Web. Retrieved February 21, 2021.

Jastrow, Assyria, M. *The Civilization of Babylonia and Assyria* (1915). Web. Sacred Texts. Retrieved March 31, 2022.

Jeffreys, Sheila. *Man's Dominion: The Rise of Religion and the Eclipse of Women's Rights.* New York: Routledge, 2012.

Jiao, Tianlong. "Gender Studies in Chinese Neolithic Archeology." *Gender and the Archeology of Death.* Edited by Bettina Arnold and Nancy L. Wicker. Lanham, MD: Altamira Press, 2001, 51–62.

Johnson, Buffie. *Lady of the Beasts: The Goddess and Her Sacred Animals.* Rochester, VT: Inner Traditions International, 1994.

Johnson-Staver, Ruth. *A Companion to Beowulf.* Westport, CT: Greenwood Publishers, 2005.

Junsheng, Cai. "The Projection of Gender Relations in Prehistoric China." *The Rule of Mars: Readings and Origins, History and Impact of Patriarchy.* Manchester, CT: Knowledge, Ideas, and Trends Publishers, 2005, 111–26.

Kaʻili, Tēvita O. "Goddess Hina: The Missing Heroine from Disney's Moana." *Huffington Post*, Nov. 26, 2016. Web. Retrieved March 30, 2022.

Keller, Mara Lynn. "Violence Against Women and Children in Religious Scriptures and in the Home." *The Rule of Mars: Readings and Origins, History and Impact of Patriarchy*. Manchester, CT: Knowledge, Ideas, and Trends Publishers, 2005, 225–40.

Kerrigan, Michael, Alan Lothian, and Piers Vitebsky. *Middle Eastern Myths: Epics of Early Civilization*. London: Duncan Baird, 1998.

Kerrigan, Michael, Charles Bishop, and Fergus Fleming. Tibetan and Mongolian Myth: The Diamond Path. London: Duncan Baird, 1998.

Kidwai, M.H. *Woman Under Different Social and Religious Laws (Buddhism, Judaism, Christianity and Islam)*. Delhi: Seema Publications, 1976.

Kincaid, Chris. "Gender Expectations of Edo Period Japan." *Japan Powered*. April 26, 2016. Web. Retrieved April 20, 2021.

Kinney, Anne Behnke. "Women in Ancient China." *Women's Roles in Ancient Civilizations*. Edited by Bella Vivante. Westwood, CT: Greenwood Press, 1999, 3–34.

Kinsley, David. *Hindu Goddesses: Visions of the Divine Feminine in the Hindu Religious Tradition*. Berkeley: U of California P, 1988.

Lang, Karen. "Women in Ancient India." *Women's Roles in Ancient Civilizations*. Edited by Bella Vivante. Westwood, CT: Greenwood Press, 1999, 35–62.

Lankford, George E. *Native American Legends*. Atlanta: August House Publishers, 1987.

Larrington, Carolyne. *The Feminist Companion to Mythology*. London: Pandora Press, 1992, 156.

Leonard, Scott, and Michael McClure. *Myth and Knowing*. Boston: McGraw-Hill, 2004.

Lerner, Gerda. *The Creation of Patriarchy*. New York: Oxford UP, 1986.

Liyong, Taban lo. *Women in Folktales and Short Stories of Africa*. Pietersburg: Azalea Publishers, 1997.

Lubell, Winifred Milius. *The Metamorphosis of Baubo: Myths of Woman's Sexual Energy*. Nashville: Vanderbilt UP, 1994.

Luthra, Rahsmi. "Clearing Sacred Ground: Women-Centered Interpretations of the Indian Epics." *Feminist Formations*, 26.2 (Summer 2014): 135–161.

MacLeod, Sharon. *The Divine Feminine in Ancient Europe: Goddesses, Sacred Women, and the Origins of Western Culture*. Jefferson, NC: McFarland, 2014.

Mallory, J.P. (1999). *In Search of the Indo-Europeans* (2nd ed). London: Thames and Hudson, 1991.

Mark, Joshua J. "Women in Ancient Persia." *World History Encyclopedia*. Jan. 30, 2020. Web. Retrieved October 18, 2021.

Martín, Paula. *Pachamama Tales: Folklore from Argentina, Bolivia, Peru, Paraguay, and Uruguay*. Santa Barbara: CA, Libraries Unlimited, 2014.

Matthews, Caitlin. *The Celtic Tradition*. Shaftesbury, Dorset: Element Books Limited, 1995.

Mayor, Adrienne. *The Amazons: Lives and Legends of Warrior Women Across the Ancient World*. Princeton: Princeton UP, 2014.

McClure, Peter, and Robin Headlam Wells. "Elizabeth I as a Second Virgin Mary." *Renaissance Studies 4(1)*, 38–70. DOI:10.1111/j.1477-4658.1990.tb00409.x.

McCoppin, Rachel. *Ecological Heroes of Amerindian Mythology*. Dubuque, IA: Kendall Hunt, 2019.

_____. *The Hero's Quest and the Cycles of Nature: An Ecological Interpretation of World Mythology*. Jefferson, NC: McFarland, 2016.

_____. *The Lessons of Nature in Mythology*. Jefferson, NC: McFarland, 2015.

McCoy, Daniel. "Freya." *Norse Mythology for Smart People*. Retrieved November 30, 2020. Web.

Meier-Seethaler, Carola. "On the Patriarchal Transformation of Matricentric Cultures." *The Rule of Mars: Readings and Origins, History and Impact of Patriarchy*. Manchester, CT: Knowledge, Ideas, and Trends Publishers, 2005, 155–62.

Monaghan, Patricia. *Encyclopedia of Goddesses and Heroines*. Novato, CA: New World Library, 2014.

Mukhoty, Ira. *Heroines: Powerful Indian Women of Myth and History*. New Delhi: Aleph Book Company, 2017.

Mundal, Elsa. "The Double Impact of

Christianization for Women in Old Norse Culture." *Department of Archaeology, History, Cultural Studies and Religion—AHKR [840]*. 2001. Pp. 237–53.

Munn, Mark. *The Mother of the Gods, Athens, and the Tyranny of Asia*. Berkeley: U of California P, 2006.

Nauwald, Nana. *Flying with Shamans in Fairy Tales and Myths*. Havelte, Holland: Binkey Kok, 2004.

Nelson, Sarah Milledge. *Ancient Queens: Archeological Explorations*. New York: Altamira Press, 2003.

_____. *Shamans, Queen, and Figurines: The Development of Gender Archeology*. Walnut Creek, CA: Left Coast Press, 2015.

Nemet-Nejat, Karen Rhea. "Women in Ancient Mesopotamia." *Women's Roles in Ancient Civilizations*. Edited by Bella Vivante. Westwood, CT: Greenwood Press, 1999, 85–114.

Niles, Susan A. "Women in the Ancient Andes." *Women's Roles in Ancient Civilizations*. Edited by Bella Vivante. Westwood, CT: Greenwood Press, 1999, 313–338.

Noble, Vicki. "From Priestess to Bride: Marriage as a Colonizing Process in Patriarchal Conquest." *The Rule of Mars: Readings and Origins, History and Impact of Patriarchy*. Manchester, CT: Knowledge, Ideas, and Trends Publishers, 2005, 187–206.

Oelschlaeger, Max. *The Ideas of Wilderness: From Prehistory to the Age of Ecology*. New Haven: Yale UP, 1991.

Ogunleye, Tolagbe. "Women in Ancient West Africa." *Women's Roles in Ancient Civilizations*. Edited by Bella Vivante. Westwood, CT: Greenwood Press, 1999, 189–218.

Omer, Rabah. "The Modern and the Traditional: African Women and Colonial Morality." *Inquiries Journal: Social Sciences, Arts, and Humanities* 9.10, 2017. Web. Retrieved March 25, 2022.

Orbell, Margaret. "Māori Mythology." *The Feminist Companion to Mythology*. Edited by Caolyne Larrington. London: Pandora Press, 1992, 288–304.

Pal, Bhaswati. "The Saga of Women's Status in Ancient Indian Civilization." *Miscellanea Geographica*, Vol. 23, Issue 3. July 2019. Web. Retrieved February 11, 2021. DOI: https://doi.org/10.2478/mgrsd-2019-0012.

Pathak, Arohi. "How the Government Can End Poverty for Native American Women." Oct. 22, 2021. *CAP*. Web. Retrieved March 1, 2022.

Pattanaik, Devdutt. *7 Secrets of the Goddess: From the Hindu Trinity Series*. Chennai: Westland Publications, 2014.

Phillips, Charles, and Michael Kerrigan. *Forests of the Vampire: Slavic Myth*. London: Duncan Baird, 1999.

Phillips, Charles, Michael Kerrigan, & David Gould. *The Eternal Cycle: Indian Myth*. London: Duncan Baird, 1998.

Porter, Dorothy Carr. "The Social Centrality of Women in *Beowulf*: A New Context." *The Heroic Age*, Issue 5, Summer/Autumn 2001. Web.

Priyabadini, Sucheta. "Voices of Women of Odisha." *Odisha Review*. March 2012. Web. Retrieved February 25, 2022.

"Queen Mother of the West—Episode 74." *Chinese Mythology Podcast*. August 17, 2018. Web. Retrieved April 8. 2021.

Ramos-Escandon, Carmen. "The Aztecs at the End of the Nineteenth Century." *Women and the Colonial Gaze*. Edited by Tamara L. Hunt and Micheline R. Lessard. New York: New York UP, 2002, 117–22.

Razak, Arisika. "Sacred Women of Africa and the African Diaspora: A Womanist Vision of Black Women's Bodies and the African Sacred Feminine." *The International Journal of Transpersonal Studies* 35.14. 2016, 129–47.

Reaves, William P., *Odin's Wife: Mother Earth in Germanic Mythology*. Coppell, TX: William P. Reaves Publishing, 2018.

Rig Veda. Trans. by Ralph T.H. Griffith. Web. *SacredTexts*. Retrieved March 30. 2022.

Robins, Gay. "Women in Ancient Egypt." *Women's Roles in Ancient Civilizations*. Edited by Bella Vivante. Westwood, CT: Greenwood Press, 1999, 155–188.

Rosenburg, Donna. *World Mythology: An Anthology of the Great Myths and Epics*. Lincolnwood, IL: NTC Publishing Group, 1999.

Rossi, Safron. "Introduction." *Goddesses: Mysteries of the Feminine Divine*. Written by Joseph Campbell. Novato, CA: New World Library, 2013.

Rostas, Susanna. "Mexican Mythology." *The Feminist Companion to Mythology*. Edited by Caolyne Larrington. London: Pandora Press, 1992, 362–387.

Rothenberg, Diane. "The Mothers of the Nation." *Women and Colonization: Anthropological Perspectives.* Edited by Mona Etienne and Eleanor Leacock. New York: Bergin & Garvey, 1980, p. 63-87.

Rothschild, Harry N. *Emperor Wu Zhao and Her Pantheon of Devis, Divinities, and Dynastic Mothers.* New York: Columbia UP, 2015.

"Seeresses of the Viking Period." *National Museum of Denmark.* Retrieved December 3, 2020. Web.

Sered, Susan Starr. *Priestess, Mother, Sacred Sister: Religions Dominated by Women.* Oxford: Oxford UP, 1994.

Seton-Williams, M.V. "Egypt: Myth and the Reality." *The Feminist Companion to Mythology.* Edited by Caolyne Larrington. London: Pandora Press, 1992, 23-47.

Shafer, Edward H. *The Divine Woman: Dragon Ladies and Rain Maidens.* San Francisco: North Point Press, 1980.

Shlain, Leonard. *The Goddess Versus the Alphabet.* New York: Penguin, 1998.

Sigal, Pete. *From Moon Goddesses to Virgins: The Colonization of Yucatecan Maya Sexual Desire.* Austin: U of Texas P, 2000.

Silverblatt, Irene. "Andean Women Under Spanish Rule." *Women and Colonization: Anthropological Perspectives.* Edited by Mona Etienne and Eleanor Leacock. New York: Bergin & Garvey, 1980, 149-85.

Sproul, Barbara C. *Primal Myths: Creation Myths Around the World* (1971). New York: HarperCollins, 1991.

Srivastava, P. "Status of Women in India: Ancient, Medieval, and Modern." *Sociology Discussion.* Web. Retrieved Feb. 10, 2021.

Stone, Merlin. *Ancient Mirrors of Womanhood: A Treasury of Goddess and Heroine Lore from Around the World.* Boston: Beacon Press, 1990.

Stuckey, Johanna H. *Women's Spirituality: Contemporary Feminist Approaches to Judaism, Christianity, Islam and Goddess Worship.* Toronto: Inanna Publications, 2010.

"Symbolism in Portraits of Queen Elizabeth I." *Royal Museums of Greenwich.* Web. Retrieved October 12, 2021.

Tacitus. *The Agricola and Germania.* New York: Penguin, 1970.

*Tain* (1st ed). Oxford: Oxford UP, 2002.

Teubal, Savina J. *Hagar the Egyptian: The Lost Tradition of the Matriarchs.* San Francisco: Harper & Row, 1990.

Torrance, Robert M. *Encompassing Nature.* Washington, D.C.: Counterpoint, 1999, 64-5.

Tringham, Ruth & Margaret Conkey. "Rethinking Figurines: A Critical View from Archeology of Gimbutas, the 'Goddess' and Popular Culture." *Ancient Goddesses.* Editors Lucy Goodison & Christine Morris. Madison: U of Wisconsin P, 1998, 22-45.

Van der Crabben, Jan. "Migration Age." *Ancient History Encyclopedia.* July 15, 2010. Web.

Van der Toorn, Karel. "Goddesses in Early Israelite Religion." *Ancient Goddesses.* Editors Lucy Goodison & Christine Morris. Madison: U of Wisconsin P, 1998, 83-97.

Vivante, Bella. *Women's Roles in Ancient Civilizations.* Edited by Bella Vivante. Westwood, CT: Greenwood Press, 1999, xi-xvii; 219-256.

Voyatzis, Mary E. "From Athena to Zeus: An A-Z Guide to the Origins of Greek Goddesses." *Ancient Goddesses.* Editors Lucy Goodison & Christine Morris. Madison: U of Wisconsin P, 1998, 133-47.

Vycinas, Vincent. *The Great Goddess of the Aistian Mythical World.* New York: Peter Lang, 1990.

Vytkovskaya, Julia. "Celtic Goddesses: Myths and Mythology." *The Feminist Companion to Mythology.* Edited by Caolyne Larrington. London: Pandora Press, 1992, 118-36.

Wemple, Suzanne Fonay. *Women in Frankish Society: Marriage and the Cloister 500 to 900.* Philadelphia: U of Pennsylvania P, 1981.

Westervelt, W.D. *Hawaiian Legends of Old Honolulu.* Boston: G.H. Ellis Press, 1915. Web. *Sacred Texts.* Retrieved March 30, 2022.

White, Isobel, & Helen Payne. "Australian Aboriginal Myth." *The Feminist Companion to Mythology.* Edited by Caolyne Larrington. London: Pandora Press, 1992, 251-287.

Wilkinson, Philip. *Myths and Legends: An Illustrated Guide to the Origins and Meanings.* New York: Metro Books, 2009.

Wolkstein, Diane, and Samuel Noah Kramer. *Inanna, Queen of Heaven and Earth: Her Stories and Hymns from Sumer.* New York: Harper and Row, 1983.

Wood, Juliette. *The Celts: Life, Myth, and Art.* London: Watkins, 1998.

Woodard, Roger D., Ed. *To Fetch Some Golden Apples: Readings in Indo-European Myth, Religion, and Society.* Dubuque, IA: Kendall/Hunt Publishing, 2006.

Young, Serenity. *Women Who Fly: Goddesses, Witches, Mystics, and Other Airborne Females.* New York: Oxford UP, 2018, 173–8.

Yusa, Michiko. "Japanese Buddhism and Women: The Lotus, Amida, and Awakening." The Dao Companion to Japanese Buddhist Philosophy. June 2019. 83–133.

Zipes, Jack. *The Irresistible Fairy Tale.* Princeton: Princeton UP, 2012.

# Index

Aataentsic 214
Abé mango 227
Actaeon 103
Adam 80-2, 99, 128
Aditi 121
Ahura Mazda 85
Ala 195, 198
Al-Lat 85
Al-Uzza 85
Amáru 227
Amaterasu 172-3, 176-8, 180
Ame-no-Uzume 177
Anahita 85
Anat 72-3, 76-7, 89
Anatolian mythology 57-61
Andraste 27
Anjea 234
Aphrodite 46, 93, 95, 101, 112, 116, 129
Apollo 92, 105-6, 125, 208
Apsu 69
Arduinna 22
Ariadne 108-9
Arjuna 135-6
Artemis 9, 55, 60-1, 103-4, 112, 115
Artio 9, 22
Asase Ya 195
Asherah 71-2, 76-7
Asintmah 212
Astarte 72, 77, 116
Athena 55, 99, 104-9, 112, 116, 124, 128, 146, 168
Atoapoma 198
Attis 59-60, 63, 113-7
Atum 187
Auchimalgen 227
Australian Aboriginal mythology 231-7

Awashanks 219
Azar 85

Baal 72-3, 77
Baba Yaga 52
Bachúe 227
Baduhenna 38
Baldur 44-6
Baltic mythology 15-20, 45
Bao Si 158-9
Bast 192
Baubo 102, 177
Belobog 16
Beowulf 38-42
Berchta 51-2
Beycesultan 58
Bhakti poets 143
Bhūmi 132
Boann 22
Boudica 27
Brahma 126, 128-9, 140-1
Brigid 33, 51
Bronze Age 15, 33, 69, 71, 73, 78, 93, 111, 116, 150-2, 158-9, 161, 164
Buddha 166-8
Buddhism 5, 166-71, 173, 179-84

Callisto 9
Calypso 108
Çatal Hüyük 57-8, 60
Celtic mythology 20-33
Chalchiuhtlicue 222
Chicomecoatl 223
Chinese mythology 148-71
Christianity 5, 19, 28, 30-3, 36-8, 41-2, 45-6, 49-53, 71, 74, 78-9, 83-4, 111, 114-9, 144, 160, 180-2, 194, 205-6, 210, 220, 225-6, 228, 230-1, 236-7, 247, 249
Cihuacoatl 223-4
Circe 107-8
Cleopatra 192-4
Coadidop 227
Coatlicue 223
Colonialism 144, 186, 194, 198, 205-6, 208, 210, 220, 225, 229, 231, 236-7, 243, 246-7
Confucianism 5, 153-4, 159-61, 164-6, 179-82, 184
Corn Mother 214-5
Cronus 94-6, 104
Cybele 59-61, 112-7
Czernobog 16

Danu 21-2
Đạo Mẫu 183
Dazhbog 16
Demeter 45, 100-3, 114, 177, 188
Devi 121, 123, 132, 139-40, 147
Didda 142
Dilga 234
Dionysus 100, 114-5
Disir 47
Divoká Šárka 18
Djang'kawu sisters 233-4
Dodola 16
Draupadi 135-8
Dumuzi 62-4, 67, 73, 116
Durga 123-7, 141, 145, 147

Echidna 96
Egyptian mythology 186-94

# Index

Eira 44
El 71–2
Eleusinian Mysteries 102, 114
Eliade, Mircea 4
Elizabeth I 55–6
Enkidu 67
Enlil 65
Eōstrev 51
Ephesus 58, 60–1
Epona 22, 31–2
Ereshkigal 63–4, 72
Erinyes 105–7
Ertha 35
Estan 58
Europa 100, 109
Eurynome 97, 100, 196
Eve 80–1, 99–101, 118, 128

Freya 35
Freyja 44, 46–9, 51
Frigg 35, 44–7, 51, 63
Frija 35, 40
Fu Hao 151

Gaia 94, 96–8, 105, 125, 208
Gauteovan 227
Gayatri 128
Gbadu 196
Geb 187
Gefjon 44
Germanic mythology 33–43
Gilgamesh 66–8, 104, 107, 158
Gimbutas, Marija 4, 11–3
Grandmother Spider 213
Grandmother Sun 217–8
Great Mother 3–4, 9–10, 15–6, 75, 80, 98, 102, 110, 112–3, 116–7, 195–6, 212–3
Greek mythology 89–111
Guan Yin 169–71

Hades 101–2, 107, 109, 112
Hanna 58
Hathor 116, 186–8
Hatshepsut 191–3
Haumea 245
Hel 45–7, 63
Hera 65, 93–4, 96–9, 101, 103, 112, 126, 129, 188
Hiiaká 245–6
Himiko 173

Hina 243–4
Hinduism 5, 123–47
Hine-nui-te-pō 238, 240
Hine-te-iwaiwa 242
Hlin 44
Holla 45
Horus 116, 187, 189
Hua Mulan 163
Hygd 38–40

Idun 47
Imperialism 180
Inanna 62–4, 66, 73, 89, 116
Indian mythology 120–47
Indo-European 11–8, 20–3, 25, 33–5, 43, 58–60, 74, 85, 91–3, 95–6, 100, 110–2, 121–2
Indra 121, 135
Io 100
Iron Age 14–5, 22–3, 26, 36, 60, 69, 73, 78
Ishtar 63–4, 66–8, 72–3, 76–7, 104, 107, 116, 158
Isis 45, 112, 114, 116, 188–9, 192–3
Islam 5, 71, 74, 78–9, 83–8, 144, 194, 203–5, 210, 249
Israelite religion 73–84
Istustaya 58
Ix Chel 222, 226
Izanagi 174–7
Izanami 174–7

Japanese mythology 171–81
Jesus Christ 61, 114–7
Jezanna 200–1
Jezebel 77–8
Judaism 5, 71, 74, 77, 82–4, 114–5, 249
Juno 112–3
Jupiter 111–2

Kali 123–7, 130–1, 140–1, 144–5, 147
Kamrusepa 58
Klugyalmo Sripé Tanla Phapa 168
Korean mythology 181–2
Kostroma 19–20
Krishna 137, 143
Ku 243
Kuma 227

Kunapipi 232–3
Kunti 135–6
Kupala 16

Lada 16
Lady of the Lake 52
Lakshmi 126, 129–32, 138, 140–1, 145–6
Lato 100
Leda 100
Levantine mythology 71–84
Lilith 81–2
Lin Jun 156–8
Loki 45–7
Lūwat-uwadjīgī-cānak 218

Maat 186–7
Macha 23–4, 29
Magohalmi 181
Mahadevi 140
Mahuika 239
Male consort 60, 63–4, 67–8, 94, 108, 135, 189
Mama Cocha 227–8
Mama Ocllo 228
Mama Quilla 228–9
Mama Sara 228–9, 231
Mami Wata 205–6
Manat 85
Marduk 69–70, 73–4, 92, 100, 125, 208
Marzanna 16
Mati Syra Zemlya 16
Mau Thoai 182
Mau Thuong Ngan 182
Maui 238–9, 241, 244
Mawu 185, 195–6
May Queen 50
Mayuel 224
Medb 24–5, 28–31, 40–1
Medusa 99, 109–10
Melusine 54
Meng Jiang 162–3
Mesoamerican mythology 221–6
Mesopotamian mythology 61–71
Messak Kummik Okwi 213
Metis 97, 104
Milapukala 232
Minerva 112–3
Minotaur 108–9
Mithra 85

Mitra 121
Mokosh 16, 19
Morgan le Fay 52
Morrígan 23-5, 30-1, 45, 52
Mot 72
Mother Goddess 11, 15-6, 23, 35, 57-62, 64-5, 67-9, 72-3, 76, 80-1, 89-90, 93-6, 103, 105, 114, 116, 120, 123-7, 131-2, 134, 139-41, 146-8, 155, 161, 168, 170, 182-3, 188-9, 192, 198, 204, 226, 244
Mother Holle 52
Mother of the Forest 207-9
Mother Zhemyna 16-7
Mu Olokukurtilisop 224
Muri 239
Mutsame 167

Naman 167
Nammu 61, 64
Nana Buluku 195
Ndjeddo Dewal 203-4
Nehalennia 36
Nekhebt 186, 190
Neolithic period 11, 13-5, 35, 57-8, 60-2, 75, 90, 94-5, 99, 101, 104, 108, 120-1, 123-4, 126, 139, 147-52, 158, 161, 164, 172, 181, 186, 189, 209
Nerthus 35-6, 41, 43
Nidaba 62
Nina 62, 64
Ninhursag 62, 65, 67
Ninlil 62, 65
Ninmah 62
Nintu 59
Norns 47
Norse mythology 43-50
North American Indian mythology 212-21
Nu Wä 148, 152-4, 170
Nut 186-7

Obatala 196-7
Odin 43-8, 51
Odysseus 107-8
Ogetsuno 176, 215
Olokun 196-8, 204
Olorun 196-7
Ophion 97, 196
Orishas 197

Orpheus 114, 175
Orunmila 196-7
Oshun 197-8
Osiris 114, 116, 189, 193

Pachamama 228-9
Paleolithic period 3-4, 14-5, 22, 103, 172, 185
Pandora 100-1
Papatuanuku 238
Papaya 58
Parvati 126, 130-1, 140-1, 145-6
Pasiphae 109
Paul 115
Pele 245-6
Penelope 108
Perchta 51-2
Perkunas 17
Persephone 100-2, 112, 114, 116, 177
Perseus 109-10
Persian mythology 84-88
Perun 16, 121
Polynesian mythology 237-47
priestess 17, 22, 26-7, 33, 52, 57, 62-3, 65-6, 79, 89, 95, 110, 151, 172, 174, 177, 180, 185, 187, 190, 192, 200, 225, 228-9, 231, 246-7, 251
Prometheus 100
Proto-Indo-Europeans 11-2

Queen Mother of the West 152-6
Queen of Sheba 202

Rainbow Serpent 196, 232-3
Rama 132-4
Rangi 238
Ravana 132-3
Re 188-9
Rhea 94, 96-100
Rhiannon 31-2, 41
Rhipsunt 219
Rigantona 31-2
Roman mythology 111-7
Rudrama Devi 142-3
Rusalki 19-20

Sacred Marriage 22, 26, 50, 62-3, 65, 107, 113

Sandraudiga 38
Saraswati 126-31, 138, 140-1, 145
Sati 126, 130-1, 133-4
Scáthach 26
Seamother 227
Sedna 215-6
Sekhmet 188, 192
Selu 214
Semele 100, 115
serpent 80-1, 97-100, 109-10, 124-5, 149, 160, 178, 187, 189, 196, 202, 223, 232-4
Set 189
Sequana 22
Seven Sisters 234-5
Shakti 140-1, 147, 168
Shaktism 140-3, 147
Shaman 2, 7, 16, 47-8, 151-2, 159-61, 172-3, 180-2, 200, 217-9, 225, 227, 229, 250
Shapash 72
Sheilah-Na-Gig 22, 32-3
Shinto 172-3, 179-81
Shiva 126-8, 130-1, 133-4, 140-1, 143
Shu 187
Sif 47
Sita 129, 132-5
Skaði 47
Slavic mythology 15-20, 45
Snow White 52
South American Indian mythology 226-31
Stribog 16
Sub-Saharan African mythology 194-211
Susanoo 176-8
Syn 44

Tammuz 63-4, 67, 73, 116
Tangotango 240-1
Taoism 5, 161-3, 165
Tara 168-9
Taranga 239
Taru 59
Tāwhaki 240-1
Tefnut 187
Telepinu 59
Tenga 195
Thai mythology 183
Themis 97
Theseus 108-9

Thor  43, 121
Three Sisters  214
Tiamet  69, 73–4, 92, 100, 125, 208
Tlazolteotl  222
Trieu Au  182–3
Tru'ung sisters  182
Tsukuyomi  176
Typhon  96–7

Ua Zit  186–7
Uranus  94–5, 97

Valkyries  47–8
Var  44
Varuna  121
Vayu  85, 135
Vedic religion  121–2, 126, 128, 131, 136
Veles  16

Venus  193
Venus figurines  10
Vesta  112
Vestal Virgins  113
Vietnamese mythology  182–3
Viracocha  229
Virgin Mary  19, 37, 55–6, 61, 114–7, 144, 226, 229
Vishnu  126, 129, 132, 137, 140–1
Völva  48–9

warrior women  2, 7, 12–4, 18, 22–3, 26–7, 29, 38, 43, 47–9, 73, 163, 182, 201–3, 219, 229, 246, 251
Wawalag sisters  232–3
Wealhtheow  38–40
Weaving Maid  155–6

Whaitiri  240
White Buffalo Calf Woman  214
Wild Hunt  51
witch  53, 55, 119, 160, 231
Woden  37, 40, 43, 51
Woodville, Elizabeth  54–5
Wu Zetain  163–5

Yahweh  70, 73–81, 104, 115
Yama  135
Yeongdeung Halmang  181
Yhi  233

Zeus  65, 92–106, 109, 112, 115, 121, 125–6, 128
Zoroastrianism  85–6
Zorvan  85

www.ingramcontent.com/pod-product-compliance
Lightning Source LLC
Chambersburg PA
CBHW032034300426
44117CB00009B/1060